ANNUAL EDITIONS

American Government 09/10

Thirty-Ninth Edition

EDITOR

Bruce Stinebrickner
DePauw University

Bruce Stinebrickner is professor of political science at DePauw University in Greencastle, Indiana, and has taught American politics at DePauw since 1987. He has also taught at Lehman College of the City University of New York (1974–1976), at the University of Queensland in Brisbane, Australia (1976–1987), and in DePauw programs in Argentina (1990) and Germany (1993). He served fourteen years as chair of his department at DePauw after heading his department at the University of Queensland for two years. He earned his BA *magna cum laude* from Georgetown University in 1968, his MPhil from Yale University in 1972, and his PhD from Yale in 1974.

Professor Stinebrickner is the coauthor (with Robert A. Dahl) of *Modern Political Analysis,* sixth edition (Prentice Hall, 2003), and has published articles on the American presidential selection process, American local governments, the career patterns of Australian politicians, and freedom of the press. He has served as editor of thirty-one earlier editions of this book as well as fourteen editions of its *State and Local Government* counterpart in the McGraw-Hill Contemporary Learning Series. His current research interests focus on government policies involving children (e.g., schooling, child custody, adoption, and foster care). In both his teaching and his writing, Professor Stinebrickner applies insights on politics gained from living, teaching, and lecturing abroad.

 **Higher Education**

Boston   Burr Ridge, IL   Dubuque, IA   New York   San Francisco   St. Louis
Bangkok   Bogotá   Caracas   Kuala Lumpur   Lisbon   London   Madrid   Mexico City
Milan   Montreal   New Delhi   Santiago   Seoul   Singapore   Sydney   Taipei   Toronto

The McGraw-Hill Companies

Mc Graw Hill **Higher Education**

ANNUAL EDITIONS: AMERICAN GOVERNMENT, THIRTY-NINTH EDITION

Published by McGraw-Hill, a business unit of The McGraw-Hill Companies, Inc., 1221 Avenue of the Americas, New York, NY 10020. Copyright © 2010 by The McGraw-Hill Companies, Inc. All rights reserved. Previous edition(s) 2004, 2008, 2009. No part of this publication may be reproduced or distributed in any form or by any means, or stored in a database or retrieval system, without the prior written consent of The McGraw-Hill Companies, Inc., including, but not limited to, in any network or other electronic storage or transmission, or broadcast for distance learning.

Some ancillaries, including electronic and print components, may not be available to customers outside the United States.

Annual Editions® is a registered trademark of The McGraw-Hill Companies, Inc.
Annual Editions is published by the **Contemporary Learning Series** group within the McGraw-Hill Higher Education division.

1 2 3 4 5 6 7 8 9 0 QPD/QPD 0 9

ISBN 978–0–07–812769–4
MHID 0–07–812769–6
ISSN 0891–3390

Managing Editor: *Larry Loeppke*
Senior Managing Editor: *Faye Schilling*
Developmental Editor: *Debra A. Henricks*
Editorial Coordinator: *Mary Foust*
Editorial Assistant: *Nancy Meissner*
Production Service Assistant: *Rita Hingtgen*
Permissions Coordinator: *Lenny J. Behnke*
Senior Marketing Manager: *Julie Keck*
Marketing Communications Specialist: *Mary Klein*
Marketing Coordinator: *Alice Link*
Project Manager: *Joyce Watters*
Design Specialist: *Tara McDermott*
Senior Production Supervisor: *Laura Fuller*
Cover Graphics: *Kristine Jubeck*

Compositor: Laserwords Private Limited
Cover Image: The McGraw-Hill Companies (inset); National Archives and Records Administration (background)

Library in Congress Cataloging-in-Publication Data
Main entry under title: Annual Editions: American Government 2009/2010.
1. American Government—Periodicals.
I. Stinebrickner, Bruce, *comp.* II. Title: American Government.
658'.05

www.mhhe.com

Editors/Advisory Board

Members of the Advisory Board are instrumental in the final selection of articles for each edition of ANNUAL EDITIONS. Their review of articles for content, level, currentness, and appropriateness provides critical direction to the editor and staff. We think that you will find their careful consideration well reflected in this volume.

Preface

In publishing ANNUAL EDITIONS we recognize the enormous role played by the magazines, newspapers, and journals of the public press in providing current, first-rate educational information in a broad spectrum of interest areas. Many of these articles are appropriate for students, researchers, and professionals seeking accurate, current material to help bridge the gap between principles and theories and the real world. These articles, however, become more useful for study when those of lasting value are carefully collected, organized, indexed, and reproduced in a low-cost format, which provides easy and permanent access when the material is needed. That is the role played by ANNUAL EDITIONS.

*A*merican Government 09/10 is the thirty-ninth edition in an *Annual Editions* series that has become a mainstay in many introductory courses on the American political system. The educational goal is to provide a readable collection of up-to-date articles that are informative, interesting, and stimulating to students beginning their study of the American political system.

As everyone reading this book knows, 2008 was an election year. The entire U.S. House of Representatives, approximately one-third of the U.S. Senate, and, of course, the presidency and vice-presidency were at stake. As 2008 began, Senator Hillary Clinton of New York was the clear front-runner to become the Democratic nominee, with former North Carolina Senator John Edwards and Illinois Senator Barack Obama rounding out the top tier of the Democratic field. Former New York mayor Rudy Giuliani and former Massachusetts governor Mitt Romney seemed to be the two leading Republican candidates, with Senator John McCain of Arizona, former Tennessee Senator Fred Thompson, and former Arkansas governor Mike Huckabee also being seen as contenders for the Republican nomination.

Neither parties' nomination process turned out as expected. By late March, Republican John McCain had clinched his party's nomination, while, on the Democratic side, the two surviving Democratic candidates, early front-runner Clinton and surprisingly strong challenger Obama, continued battling for their party's nomination. Clinton's withdrawal in June ended her dream, at least for 2008, of becoming the first woman president of the United States. The stage was set for a general election campaign pitting the first African American major party presidential nominee, Democrat Obama, against a candidate, Republican McCain, who, if elected, would be the oldest person to take the presidential oath of office for the first time.

Obama entered the general election campaign with formidable advantages. He had vanquished a strong, well-known, well-financed opponent in his party's nomination contest, and raised and spent a record amount of money in doing so. He had a well-oiled campaign organization operating in a favorable year for Democrats because of widespread disenchantment with incumbent Republican president George W. Bush, who had the lowest presidential public approval ratings ever recorded. Obama was young, photogenic, energetic, and an eloquent speaker to boot. He had seized the mantle of "change" during his nomination campaign, and continued to advocate that cause against McCain. By declining public financing for his general election campaign—the only presidential candidate to do so since the system began in 1976—Obama gained at least a three-to-one spending advantage over his opponent, an asset that he put to good use in blanketing much of the country with television advertising that McCain's more limited budget could not match.

Polls showed McCain only slightly behind Obama in late August when vice-presidential selections were announced. Obama chose Senator Joe Biden of Delaware, a veteran senator with considerable foreign policy expertise who had himself competed for the 2008 Democratic presidential nomination before withdrawing the day after Obama won the Iowa caucuses. To most Americans, Biden seemed well suited to serve as first in the line of presidential succession. In a surprise move, McCain chose Governor Sarah Palin, a relative unknown who had served two years as governor of Alaska. While the selection of a spirited female candidate in her forties brought much media attention to the McCain campaign, Palin's nomination worked to undercut McCain's repeated assertion that Obama was too inexperienced to serve as president. Despite the initial energizing effect of Palin's selection, questions about her suitability to serve the proverbial one heartbeat away from the presidency grew. The McCain campaign limited journalists' access to her, and she performed unimpressively in the few interviews in which she participated. By Election Day, Americans' doubts about whether Governor Palin was ready to be vice-president lessened support for the McCain-Palin ticket. In the end, Obama won a comfortable 7% victory over McCain in the popular vote and a 365 to 173 margin in the Electoral College. The Democratic party gained seven senate seats, bringing the number of senators expected to caucus with the Democrats to fifty-eight, with the outcome of one senate race undecided as of this writing. In House of Representatives elections, Democrats gained twenty-two seats, bringing their total in the 435-member house to 257, with one contest undecided.

All in all, the November 2008 elections resulted in solid Democratic victories, even if not quite the huge landslide for which the most optimistic of Democrats had hoped. President-elect Obama turned quickly to assembling the team that would become the public face of the Obama administration in January 2009.

In yet another unexpected twist that worked to Democratic candidate Obama's advantage during the general election campaign, a financial crisis shook the foundations of Wall Street, the banking and credit industries, and the underpinnings of today's global economy. By the time voters went to the polls on 4 November 2008, it was the economy—and *not* the Iraq war, the war on terror, health care, or global warming— that was foremost on their minds. For most American voters, Obama seemed better equipped to handle the financial mess than his Republican opponent.

In his remarkable presidential election victory in 2008, candidate Obama had prominently and convincingly worn the mantle of "change." But his announcements of top-level aides and Cabinet nominees in the days and weeks after the election named mostly experienced and well-known individuals, most of whom had worked in the Clinton administration during the 1990s. Among Obama's headline nominations were Hillary Clinton—yes, Hillary Clinton!—to be secretary of state, and Defense Secretary Robert Gates, a Republican appointed by President Bush, to continue in his job. When asked how his announced team of experienced and well-known nominees, most of whom were veterans of the Clinton administration, was consistent with "change," president-elect Obama coolly responded that as president it was *his* responsibility to supply the vision of change and his subordinates' responsibility to carry out that vision.

As I write this preface in December 2008, there is great anticipation and interest in the coming Obama administration, and rightly so. How will President Obama and his economic team address the financial and economic troubles that seem likely to constitute the biggest downturn that the world has seen since the Great Depression? How will he prioritize economic recovery in comparison with health care reform, global warming, homeland security, and the like? How—and how soon—will he withdraw American troops from Iraq? And how will he address the growing insurgency in Afghanistan and tense relations with a key nation in that region, Pakistan, whose ties with its neighbor India have been strained by terrorist attacks in Mumbai in late November 2008?

In my preface to last year's edition of this book, I wrote "Every time I work on the preface for a new edition of this book, I am led to write that the coming year will be another interesting one for students of American politics. The year 2008 promises to be no exception." At the risk of sounding trite and self-congratulatory, I want to say "I told you so." Consider some political highlights of 2008: the vanquishing of a formidable and historic woman front-runner (Hillary Clinton) by a candidate (Obama) who will be the first African American president of the United States; the raising of a record amount of campaign funds by a presidential candidate (Obama); the unprecedented use of the Internet for raising campaign funds and political advertising (Obama); a presidential election in which one party's ticket was led by an African American (Obama) and the other party's ticket had a woman (Palin) as its vice-presidential nominee; financial/economic troubles that are already bringing back dismal memories of the dislocations of the Great Depression and which threaten the very existence of the "Big Three" U.S. automobile makers; and, last but not least, the unmistakable increase in overall voter turnout and youth involvement in the election campaign that marked Obama's remarkable run to the White House. What a year indeed!

The first year of the Obama presidency, 2009, may well prove to be every bit as interesting and consequential as 2008 was. Careful observation of American politics as it unfolds on a day-to-day basis can teach us a great deal about both the regularities and unpredictable aspects of the American political system. The selections in this book should help readers comprehend and even anticipate what will happen in the year to come and, perhaps more importantly, enhance their understanding of the characteristic functioning of the American political system.

The systems approach provides a rough organizational framework for this book. The first unit focuses on ideological and constitutional underpinnings of American politics, from both historical and contemporary perspectives. The second unit treats the major institutions of the national government. The third covers the "input" or "linkage" mechanisms of the system—political parties, elections, interest groups, and media—and also contains a special section on the 2008 elections. The fourth and concluding unit shifts the focus to policy choices that confront the government in Washington and resulting "outputs" of the political system.

Each year thousands of articles about American politics are published, and deciding which to reprint in a collection of readings such as this can be difficult. Articles are chosen with an eye toward providing viewpoints from left, right, and center. About half of the selections in this book are new to this year's edition, a reflection of continuing efforts to help keep those who read this book abreast of important contemporary developments in the American political system. Next year will bring another opportunity for change, and you, the reader, are invited to participate in the process. Please complete and return the postage-paid article rating form on the last page of the book and let us know your reactions and suggestions for improvement.

Bruce Stinebrickner
Editor

Contents

UNIT 1
Foundations of American Politics

Part A.   Basic Documents

1. The Declaration of Independence, Thomas Jefferson,
The Declaration of Independence, 1776

This document formally announces that 13 former British colonies have become the
free and independent United States of America. It eloquently identifies certain **historic
principles** on which their claim to independence rests.   **2**

2. The History of The Constitution of the United States,
The Constitution of the U.S., 1787

The Constitution provides an organizational blueprint for the national government and for
the **federal** relationship between the national government and the states. In addition, the
first 10 amendments, commonly known as the **Bill of Rights,** spell out limits on what the
government can do. A commentary accompanying the actual document provides a brief
account of the writing of the Constitution and also notes some of its significant features.   **4**

3. The Size and Variety of the Union as a Check on Faction:
Federalist No. 10, James Madison, *The Federalist Papers,* 1787

James Madison argues in support of the union of the 13 states under the new **Constitution.** According to Madison, a system of **representative democracy** governing a large
territory and many people will help control the undesirable effects of *"faction."*   **15**

4. Checks and Balances: Federalist No. 51, James Madison,
The Federalist Papers, 1787

According to James Madison, both the **separation of powers** among three branches of
government and the **division of powers** between the states and the central government
will help preserve **representative democracy** under the new **Constitution.**   **18**

Part B.   Contemporary Views and Values

5. America the Untethered, David Rieff, *The New York Times Magazine,*
July 2, 2006

David Rieff reports the ways in which Americans' attitudes differ from people's attitudes
in other countries. He also discusses the implications of **American exceptionalism** for
the role of the United States in world affairs.   **20**

6. How Big Government Got Its Groove Back, William Galston,
The American Prospect, June 2008

William Galston argues that the national government must again expand its role in the
face of economic dislocations, growing **economic inequality,** looming government
budget deficits, globalization, and the like.   **22**

**7. The Changing Face of Poverty in America: Why Are So Many
Women, Children, Racial and Cultural Minorities Still Poor?,**
William E. Spriggs, *The American Prospect,* May 2007

William Spriggs reports the extent of **poverty** among **children, women,** and **racial
minorities** in the United States, and argues that **government policies** that treat a variety of groups differently are responsible for many of the income and wealth disparities.   **26**

The concepts in bold italics are developed in the article. For further expansion, please refer to the Topic Guide.

UNIT 2
Structures of American Politics

The concepts in bold italics are developed in the article. For further expansion, please refer to the Topic Guide.

The concepts in bold italics are developed in the article. For further expansion, please refer to the Topic Guide.

UNIT 3
Process of American Politics

The concepts in bold italics are developed in the article. For further expansion, please refer to the Topic Guide.

UNIT 4
Products of American Politics

The concepts in bold italics are developed in the article. For further expansion, please refer to the Topic Guide.

The concepts in bold italics are developed in the article. For further expansion, please refer to the Topic Guide.

Correlation Guide

The *Annual Editions* series provides students with convenient, inexpensive access to current, carefully selected articles from the public press. **Annual Editions: American Government 09/10** is an easy-to-use reader that presents articles on important topics in the study of American government. For more information on *Annual Editions* and other *McGraw-Hill Contemporary Learning Series* titles, visit www.mhcls.com.

This convenient guide matches the units in **Annual Editions: American Government 09/10** with the corresponding chapters in three of our best-selling McGraw-Hill American Government textbooks by Harrison et al., Patterson, and Losco/Baker.

Annual Editions: American Government 09/10	American Democracy Now by Harrison et al.	We the People, 8/e by Patterson	AM GOV 2009 by Losco/Baker
Unit 1: Foundations of American Politics	**Chapter 1:** American Democracy: People, Politics, and Participation **Chapter 2:** The Constitution **Chapter 3:** Federalism **Chapter 4:** Civil Liberties **Chapter 5:** Civil Rights	**Chapter 1:** American Political Culture: Seeking a More Perfect Union **Chapter 2:** Constitutional Democracy: Promoting Liberty and Self-Government **Chapter 3:** Federalism: Forging a Nation **Chapter 4:** Civil Liberties: Protecting Individual Rights **Chapter 5:** Equal Rights: Struggling Toward Fairness	**Chapter 1:** Citizenship in Our Changing Democracy **Chapter 2:** The Constitution: The Foundation of Citizens' Rights **Chapter 3:** Federalism: Citizenship and the Dispersal of Power **Chapter 4:** Civil Liberties: Expanding Citizens' Rights **Chapter 5:** Civil Rights: toward a More Equal Citizenry
Unit 2: Structures of American Politics	**Chapter 11:** Congress **Chapter 12:** The Presidency **Chapter 13:** The Bureaucracy **Chapter 14:** The Judiciary	**Chapter 11:** Congress: Balancing National Goals and Local Interests **Chapter 12:** The Presidency: Leading the Nation **Chapter 13:** The Federal Bureaucracy: Administering the Government **Chapter 14:** The Judiciary: Applying the Law	**Chapter 11:** Congress: Doing the People's Business **Chapter 12:** The Presidency: Power and Paradox **Chapter 13:** Bureaucracy: Citizens As Owners and Consumers **Chapter 14:** The Courts: Judicial Power in a Democratic Setting
Unit 3: Process of American Politics	**Chapter 6:** Political Socialization and Public Opinion **Chapter 7:** Interest Groups **Chapter 8:** Political Parties **Chapter 9:** Elections, Campaigns, and Voting **Chapter 10:** The Media	**Chapter 6:** Public Opinion and Political Socialization: Shaping the People's Voice **Chapter 7:** Political Participation and Voting: Expressing the Popular Will **Chapter 8:** Political Parties, Candidates, and Campaigns: Defining the Voters' Choice **Chapter 9:** Interest Groups: Organizing for Influence **Chapter 10:** The News Media: Communicating Political Images	**Chapter 6:** Public Opinion: Listening to Citizens **Chapter 7:** Political Participation: Equal Opportunities and Unequal Voices **Chapter 8:** Interest Groups in America **Chapter 9:** Parties and Political Campaigns: Citizens and the Electoral Process **Chapter 10:** Media: Tuning In or Turning Out
Unit 4: Products of American Politics	**Chapter 15:** Economic Policy **Chapter 16:** Domestic Policy **Chapter 17:** Foreign Policy and National Security	**Chapter 15:** Economic and Environmental Policy: Contributing to Prosperity **Chapter 16:** Welfare and Education Policy: Providing for Personal Security and Need **Chapter 17:** Foreign and Defense Policy: Protecting the American Way	**Chapter 15:** Public Policy: Responding to Citizens **Chapter 16:** Foreign and Defense Policy: Protecting American Interests in the World

Topic Guide

This topic guide suggests how the selections in this book relate to the subjects covered in your course. You may want to use the topics listed on these pages to search the Web more easily.

On the following pages a number of Web sites have been gathered specifically for this book. They are arranged to reflect the units of this Annual Editions reader. You can link to these sites by going to *http://www.mhcls.com*.

All the articles that relate to each topic are listed below the bold-faced term.

Internet References

The following Internet sites have been selected to support the articles found in this reader. These sites were available at the time of publication. However, because Web sites often change their structure and content, the information listed may no longer be available. We invite you to visit http://www.mhcls.com for easy access to these sites.

Annual Editions: American Government 09/10

General Sources

John F. Kennedy School of Government
http://www.ksg.harvard.edu

Starting from Harvard University's KSG page, you will be able to click on a huge variety of links to information about American politics and government, ranging from political party and campaign data to debates of enduring issues.

Library of Congress
http://www.loc.gov

Examine this Web site to learn about the extensive resource tools, library services/resources, exhibitions, and databases available through the Library of Congress in many different subfields of government studies.

National Center for Policy Analysis
http://www.ncpa.org

Through this site, access discussions on an array of topics that are of major interest in the study of American government, from regulatory policy and privatization to economy and income. The Daily Policy Digest is also available.

UNIT 1: Foundations of American Politics

National Archives and Records Administration (NARA)
http://www.archives.gov

This official site, which oversees the management of all federal records, offers easy access to background information for students interested in the policy-making process, including a search of federal documents and speeches, and much more.

Opinion, Inc.: The Site for Conservative Opinion on the Web
http://www.opinioninc.com

Open this site for access to political, cultural, and Web commentary on a number of issues from a conservative political viewpoint. The site is updated frequently.

Smithsonian Institution
http://www.si.edu

This site provides access to the enormous resources of the Smithsonian, which holds some 140 million artifacts and specimens in its trust for "the increase and diffusion of knowledge." Here you can learn about American social, cultural, economic, and political history from a variety of viewpoints.

UNIT 2: Structures of American Politics

Department of State
http://www.state.gov

View this site for understanding into the workings of a major U.S. executive branch department. Links explain exactly what the department does, what services it provides, and what it says about U.S. interests around the world, along with much more information.

Federal Reserve System
http://www.federalreserve.gov

Consult this page to learn the answers to FAQs about the Fed, the structure of the Federal Reserve System, monetary policy, and more. It provides links to speeches and interviews as well as essays and articles presenting different views on the Fed.

Supreme Court/Legal Information Institute
http://supct.law.cornell.edu/supct/index.html

Open this site for current and historical information about the Supreme Court. The LII archive contains many opinions issued since May 1990 as well as a collection of nearly 600 of the most influential decisions of the Court.

United States House of Representatives
http://www.house.gov

This Web page of the House of Representatives will lead you to information about current and past House members and agendas, the legislative process, and more. You can learn about events on the House floor as they happen.

United States Senate
http://www.senate.gov

This U.S. Senate Web page will lead to information about current and past Senate members and agendas, legislative activities, and committees.

UNIT 3: Process of American Politics

The Gallup Organization
http://www.gallup.com

Open this Gallup Organization home page for links to an extensive archive of public opinion poll results and special reports on a variety of topics related to American society, politics, and government.

The Henry L. Stimson Center
http://www.stimson.org

The Stimson Center, a nonprofit and self-described nonpartisan organization, focuses on issues where policy, technology, and politics intersect. Use this site to find assessments of U.S. foreign and domestic policy and other topics.

Influence at Work
http://www.influenceatwork.com

This commercial site focuses on the nature of persuasion, compliance, and propaganda, with many practical examples and applications. Students of such topics as the roles of public opinion and media influence in policy making should find these discussions of interest. The approach is based on the research and methods of influence expert Dr. Robert Cialdini.

LSU Department of Political Science Resources
http://www.lsu.edu/politicalscience

This extensive site will point you to a number of resources for domestic and international political and governmental news, including LSU's Political Science WWW Server, which is maintained by a dedicated group of professionals.

Internet References

NationalJournal.com
http://nationaljournal.com

This is a major site for information on American government and politics. There is discussion of campaigns, the congressional calendar, a news archive, and more for politicians and policymakers. Membership is required, however, to access much of the information.

Poynter Online
http://www.poynter.org

This research site of the Poynter Institute for Media Studies provides extensive links to information and resources about the media, including media ethics and reportage techniques. Many bibliographies and Web sites are included.

RAND
http://www.rand.org

RAND is a nonprofit institution that works to improve public policy through research and analysis. Links offered on this home page provide for keyword searches of certain topics and descriptions of RAND activities and major research areas.

Real Clear Politics
http://www.realclearpolitics.com

This site presents in a timely and easily accessible manner almost all the latest published poll results on a variety of political topics, including, of course, how candidates are faring during election campaigns. There are also commentaries from a range of sources about campaigns and American politics more generally. It is a popular and authoritative source for so-called political junkies.

UNIT 4: Products of American Politics

American Diplomacy
http://www.unc.edu/depts/diplomat/

American Diplomacy is an online journal of commentary, analysis, and research on U.S. foreign policy and its results around the world.

Cato Institute
http://www.cato.org/research/ss_prjct.html

The Cato Institute presents this page to discuss its Project on Social Security Privatization. The site and its links begin from the belief that privatization of the U.S. Social Security system is a positive goal that will empower workers.

Foreign Affairs
http://www.foreignaffairs.org

This home page of the well-respected foreign policy journal is a valuable research tool. It allows users to search the journal's archives and provides indexed access to the field's leading publications, documents, online resources, and more. Links to dozens of other related Web sites are possible from here.

International Information Programs
http://usinfo.state.gov

This wide-ranging page offered by the State Department provides definitions, related documentation, and a discussion of topics of concern to students of American government. It addresses today's hot topics as well as ongoing issues that form the foundation of the field. Many Web links are provided.

STAT-USA
http://www.stat-usa.gov/stat-usa.html

This essential site, a service of the Department of Commerce, contains daily economic news, frequently requested statistical releases, information on export and international trade, domestic economic news and statistical series, and databases.

Tax Foundation
http://www.taxfoundation.org/index.html

Ever wonder where your taxes go? Consult the site of this self-described "nonprofit, nonpartisan policy research organization" to learn the history of "Tax Freedom Day," tax burdens around the United States, and other information about your tax bill or taxes in general.

UNIT 1

Foundations of American Politics

Unit Selections

1. **The Declaration of Independence,** Thomas Jefferson
2. **The History of The Constitution of the United States,** *The Constitution of the U.S.,* 1787
3. **The Size and Variety of the Union as a Check on Faction: Federalist No. 10,** James Madison
4. **Checks and Balances: Federalist No. 51,** James Madison
5. **America the Untethered,** David Rieff
6. **How Big Government Got Its Groove Back,** William Galston
7. **The Changing Face of Poverty in America: Why Are So Many Women, Children, Racial and Cultural Minorities Still Poor?,** William E. Spriggs
8. **The Climate for Change,** Al Gore
9. **Beyond Hillary: Strength in Numbers,** Ann Friedman
10. **It Is Time to Repair the Constitution's Flaws,** Sanford Levinson
11. **If Washington Blows Up,** Bruce Ackerman
12. **Pursuit of Habeas,** Jack Hitt
13. **Is Judicial Review Obsolete?,** Stuart Taylor Jr.
14. **Two Takes: Pulpit Politics Is Free Speech/Campaigns Can Split Churches,** Ron Johnson Jr. and Barry W. Lynn

Key Points to Consider

- What do you think would surprise the Founders most about the values and ideals held by Americans today?

- Which ideals, ideas, and values seem likely to remain central to American politics, and which seem likely to erode and gradually disappear?

- To what "rights" do you think all Americans are entitled? How, if at all, has September 11 affected Americans' thinking on this matter?

- What makes constitutional interpretation and reinterpretation necessary in the American political system?

- Do you consider yourself a conservative, a liberal, a socialist, a reactionary, or what? Why?

Student Web Site
www.mhcls.com

Internet References

National Archives and Records Administration (NARA)
http://www.archives.gov
Opinion, Inc.: The Site for Conservative Opinion on the Web
http://www.opinioninc.com
Smithsonian Institution
http://www.si.edu

This unit treats some of the less concrete aspects of the American political system—historic ideals, contemporary ideas and values, and constitutional and legal issues. These dimensions of the system are not immune to change. Instead, they interact with the wider political environment in which they exist, and they are modified accordingly. Usually this interaction is a gradual process, but sometimes events foster more rapid change.

Human beings can be distinguished from other species by their ability to think and reason at relatively high levels of abstraction. In turn, ideas, ideals, values, and principles can and do play important roles in politics. Most Americans value ideals such as democracy, freedom, equal opportunity, and justice. Yet, the precise meanings of these terms and the best ways of implementing them are the subject of much dispute in the political arena. Such ideas and ideals, as well as disputes about their "real" meanings, are important elements in the practice of American politics.

Although the selections in this unit span more than 200 years, they are clearly related to one another. Understanding contemporary political viewpoints is easier if the ideals and principles of the past are also taken into account. In addition, we can better appreciate the significance of historic documents such as the Declaration of Independence and the Constitution if we are familiar with contemporary ideas and perspectives.

The interaction of different ideas and values plays an important part in the continuing development of the "foundations" of the American political system.

The first section of this unit includes several historic documents from the eighteenth century. The first is the Declaration of Independence. Written in 1776, it proclaims the Founders' views of why independence from England was justified and, in so doing, identifies certain "unalienable" rights that "all men" are said to possess. The second document, the Constitution of 1787, remains in effect to this day. It provides an organizational blueprint for the structure of American national government, outlines the federal relationship between the national government and the states, and expresses limitations on what government can do. Twenty-seven amendments have been added to the original Constitution in two centuries. In addition to the Declaration of Independence and the Constitution, the first section includes two selections from *The Federalist Papers,* a series of newspaper articles written in support of the proposed new Constitution. Appearing in 1787 and 1788, *The Federalist Papers* treated various provisions of the new Constitution and argued that putting the Constitution into effect would bring about good government.

The second section treats contemporary political ideas and viewpoints. As selections in this section illustrate, efforts to apply or act on political beliefs in the context of concrete circumstances often lead to interesting commentary and debate. "Liberal" and

© Comstock/PunchStock

"conservative" are two labels often used in American political discussions, but political views and values have far more complexity than can be captured by those two terms.

Selections in the third section show that constitutional and legal issues and interpretations are tied to historic principles as well as to contemporary ideas and values. It has been suggested that throughout American history almost every important political question has at one time or another appeared as a constitutional or legal issue.

The historic documents and the other selections in this unit might be more difficult to understand than the articles in other units. Some of them may have to be read and reread carefully to be fully appreciated. But to grapple with the important material treated here is to come to grips with a variety of conceptual blueprints for the American political system. To ignore the theoretical issues raised would be to bypass an important element of American politics today.

The Declaration of Independence

THOMAS JEFFERSON

When in the Course of human events, it becomes necessary for one people to dissolve the political bands which have connected them with another, and to assume among the powers of the earth, the separate and equal station to which the Laws of Nature and of Nature's God entitle them, a decent respect to the opinions of mankind requires that they should declare the causes which impel them to the separation.—We hold these truths to be self-evident, that all men are created equal, that they are endowed by their Creator with certain unalienable Rights, that among these are Life, Liberty and the pursuit of Happiness.—That to secure these rights, Governments are instituted among Men, deriving their just powers from the consent of the governed.—That whenever any Form of Government becomes destructive of these ends, it is the Right of the People to alter or to abolish it, and to institute new Government, laying its foundation on such principles and organizing its powers in such form, as to them shall seem most likely to effect their Safety and Happiness. Prudence, indeed, will dictate that Governments long established should not be changed for light and transient causes; and accordingly all experience hath shewn, that mankind are more disposed to suffer, while evils are sufferable, than to right themselves by abolishing the forms to which they are accustomed. But when a long train of abuses and usurpations, pursuing invariably the same Object evinces a design to reduce them under absolute Despotism, it is their right, it is their duty, to throw off such Government, and to provide new Guards for their future security.—Such has been the patient sufferance of these Colonies; and such is now the necessity which constrains them to alter their former Systems of Government. The history of the present King of Great Britain is a history of repeated injuries and usurpations, all having in direct object the establishment of an absolute Tyranny over these States. To prove this, let Facts be submitted to a candid world.—He has refused his Assent to Laws, the most wholesome and necessary for the public good.—He has forbidden his Governors to pass Laws of immediate and pressing importance, unless suspended in their operation till his Assent should be obtained; and when so suspended, he has utterly neglected to attend to them.—He has refused to pass other Laws for the accommodation of large districts of people, unless those people would relinquish the right of Representation in the Legislature, a right inestimable to them and formidable to tyrants only.—He has called together legislative bodies at places unusual, uncomfortable, and distant from the depository of their public Records, for the sole purpose of fatiguing them into compliance with his measures.—He has dissolved Representative Houses repeatedly, for opposing with manly firmness his invasions on the rights of the people.—He has refused for a long time, after such dissolutions, to cause others to be elected; whereby the Legislative powers, incapable of Annihilation, have returned to the People at large for their exercise; the State remaining in the meantime exposed to all the dangers of invasion from without, and convulsions within.—He has endeavoured to prevent the population of these States; for that purpose obstructing the Laws for Naturalization of Foreigners; refusing to pass others to encourage their migrations hither, and raising the conditions of new Appropriations of Lands.—He has obstructed the Administration of Justice, by refusing his Assent to Laws for establishing Judiciary powers.—He has made Judges dependent on his Will alone, for the tenure of their offices, and the amount and payment of their salaries.—He has erected a multitude of New Offices, and sent hither swarms of Officers to harass our people, and eat out their substance. He has kept among us, in times of peace, Standing Armies without the Consent of our legislatures.—He has affected to render the Military independent of and superior to the Civil power.—He has combined with others to subject us to a jurisdiction foreign to our constitution, and unacknowledged by our laws; giving his Assent to their Acts of pretended Legislation:—For quartering large bodies of armed troops among us:—For protecting them, by a mock Trial, from punishment for any Murders which they should commit on the Inhabitants of these States:—For cutting off our Trade with all parts of the world:—For imposing Taxes on us without our Consent:—For depriving us in many cases, of the benefits of Trial by Jury:—For transporting us beyond Seas to be tried for pretended offences:—For abolishing the free System of English Laws in a neighboring Province, establishing therein an Arbitrary government, and enlarging its Boundaries so as to render it at once an example and fit instrument for introducing the same absolute rule into these Colonies:—For taking away our Charters, abolishing our most valuable Laws and altering fundamentally the Forms of our Governments:—For suspending our own Legislatures, and declaring themselves invested with power to legislate for us in all cases whatsoever.—He has abdicated Government here, by declaring us out of his Protection and waging War against us.—He has plundered our seas, ravaged our Coasts, burnt our towns, and destroyed the lives of our people.—He is at this time transporting large Armies of foreign Mercenaries to compleat the works of death, desolation and tyranny, already begun with circumstances of Cruelty & perfidy scarcely paralled in the most barbarous ages, and totally unworthy the Head of a civilized nation.—He has constrained our fellow Citizens taken Captive on the high Seas to bear Arms against their Country, to become the executioners of their friends and Brethren, or to fall themselves by their Hands.—He has excited domestic insurrections amongst us, and has endeavoured to bring on the inhabitants of our frontiers, the merciless Indian Savages, whose known rule of warfare, is an undistinguished destruction of all ages, sexes and conditions. In every stage of these Oppressions We have Petitioned for Redress in the most humble terms: Our repeated Petitions have been answered only by repeated injury. A Prince, whose character is thus marked by every act which may define a Tyrant, is unfit to be the ruler of a free people. Nor have We been wanting in attentions to our British brethren. We have warned them from time to time of attempts by their legislature to extend an unwarrantable jurisdiction over us. We have reminded them of the circumstances of our emigration and settlement here. We have appealed to their native justice and magnanimity, and we have conjured them by the ties of our common kindred to disavow these usurpations, which would inevitably interrupt our connections and correspondence. They too have been deaf to the voice of justice and of consanguinity. We must, therefore, acquiesce in the necessity, which denounces our Separation, and hold them, as we hold the rest of mankind, Enemies in War, in Peace Friends.—

WE, THEREFORE, the Representatives of the UNITED STATES OF AMERICA, in General Congress, Assembled, appealing to the Supreme Judge of the world for the rectitude of our intentions, do, in the Name, and by Authority of the good People of these Colonies, solemnly publish and declare, That these United Colonies are, and of Right ought to be FREE AND INDEPENDENT STATES; that they are Absolved from all Allegiance to the British Crown, and that all political connection between them and the State of Great Britain, is and ought to be totally dissolved; and that as Free and Independent States, they have full Power to levy War, conclude Peace, contract Alliances, establish Commerce, and to do all other Acts and Things which Independent States may of right do.—And for the support of this Declaration, with a firm reliance on the protection of divine Providence, we mutually pledge to each other our Lives, our Fortunes and our sacred Honor.

The History of The Constitution of the United States

CONSTITUTION OF THE UNITED STATES. The Articles of Confederation did not provide the centralizing force necessary for unity among the new states and were soon found to be so fundamentally weak that a different political structure was vital. Conflicts about money and credit, trade, and suspicions about regional domination were among the concerns when Congress on February 21, 1787, authorized a Constitutional Convention to revise the Articles. The delegates were selected and assembled in Philadelphia about three months after the call. They concluded their work by September.

The delegates agreed and abided to secrecy. Years afterward James Madison supported the secrecy decision writing that "no man felt himself obliged to retain his opinions any longer than he was satisfied of their propriety and truth, and was open to the force of argument." Secrecy was not for all time. Madison, a delegate from Virginia, was a self-appointed but recognized recorder and took notes in the clear view of the members. Published long afterward, Madison's Journal gives a good record of the convention.

The delegates began to assemble on May 14, 1787, but a majority did not arrive until May 25. George Washington was elected President of the Convention without opposition. The lag of those few days gave some of the early arrivals, especially Madison, time to make preparations on substantive matters, and Gov. Edmund Jennings Randolph presented a plan early in the proceedings that formed the basis for much of the convention deliberations. The essentials were that there should be a government adequate to prevent foreign invasion, prevent dissension among the states, and provide for general national development, and give the national government power enough to make it superior in its realm. The decision was made not merely to revise the articles but to create a new government and a new constitution.

One of the most crucial decisions was the arrangement for representation, a compromise providing that one house would represent the states equally, the other house to be based on popular representation (with some modification due to the slavery question). This arrangement recognized political facts and concessions among men with both theoretical and practical political knowledge.

Basic Features. Oliver Wendell Holmes, Jr., once wrote that the provisions of the Constitution were not mathematical formulas, but "organic living institutions *[sic]* and its origins and

growth were vital to understanding it." The constitution's basic features provide for a supreme law—notwithstanding any other legal document or practice, the Constitution is supreme, as are the laws made in pursuance of it and treaties made under the authority of the United States.

The organizational plan for government is widely known. Foremost is the separation of powers. If the new government were to be limited in its powers, one way to keep it limited would have been executive, legislative, and judicial power [given] to three distinct and non-overlapping branches. A government could not actually function, however, if the separation meant the independence of one branch from the others. The answer was a design to insure cooperation and the sharing of some functions. Among these are the executive veto and the power of Congress to have its way if it musters a super-majority to override that veto. The direction of foreign affairs and the war power are both dispersed and shared. The appointing power is shared by the Senate and the president; impeaching of officers and financial controls are powers shared by the Senate and the House.

A second major contribution by the convention is the provision for the judiciary, which gave rise to the doctrine of judicial review. There is some doubt that the delegates comprehended this prospect but Alexander Hamilton considered it in *Federalist* No. 78: "The interpretation of the laws is a proper and peculiar province of the Courts. . . . Wherever a particular statute contravenes the Constitution, it will be the duty of the judicial tribunals to adhere to the latter and disregard the former."

Another contribution is the federal system, an evolution from colonial practice and the relations between the colonies and the mother country. This division of authority between the new national government and the states recognized the doctrine of delegated and reserved powers. Only certain authority was to go to the new government; the states were not to be done away with and much of the Constitution is devoted to insuring that they were to be maintained even with the stripping of some of their powers.

It is not surprising, therefore, that the convention has been called a great political reform caucus composed of both revolutionaries and men dedicated to democracy. By eighteenth-century standards the Constitution was a democratic document, but standards change and the Constitution has changed since its adoption.

Change and Adaptation. The authors of the Constitution knew that provision for change was essential and provided for it in Article V, insuring that a majority could amend, but being restrictive enough that changes were not likely for the "light and transient" causes Jefferson warned about in the Declaration of Independence.

During the period immediately following the presentation of the Constitution for ratification, requiring assent of nine states to be effective, some alarm was expressed that there was a major defect: there was no bill of rights. So, many leaders committed themselves to the presentation of constitutional amendments for the purpose. Hamilton argued that the absence of a bill of rights was not a defect; indeed, a bill was not necessary. "Why," he wrote, in the last of *The Federalist Papers,* "declare things that shall not be done which there is no power to do?" Nonetheless, the Bill of Rights was presented in the form of amendments and adopted by the states in 1791.

Since 1791 many proposals have been suggested to amend the Constitution. By 1972 sixteen additional amendments had been adopted. Only one, the Twenty-first, which repealed the Eighteenth, was ratified by state conventions. All the others were ratified by state legislatures.

Even a cursory reading of the later amendments shows they do not alter the fundamentals of limited government, the separation of powers, the federal system, or the political process set in motion originally. The Thirteenth, Fourteenth, Fifteenth, and Nineteenth amendments attempt to insure equality to all and are an extension of the Bill of Rights. The others reaffirm some existing constitutional arrangements, alter some procedures, and at least one, the Sixteenth, states national policy.

Substantial change and adaptation of the Constitution beyond the formal amendments have come from national experience, growth, and development. It has been from the Supreme Court that much of the gradual significant shaping of the Constitution has been done.

Government has remained neither static nor tranquil. Some conflict prevails continually. It may be about the activities of some phase of government or the extent of operations, and whether the arrangement for government can be made responsive to current and prospective needs of society. Conflict is inevitable in a democratic society. Sometimes the conflict is spirited and rises to challenge the continuation of the system. Questions arise whether a fair trial may be possible here or there; legislators are alleged to be indifferent to human problems and pursue distorted public priorities. Presidents are charged with secret actions designed for self-aggrandizement or actions based on half-truths. Voices are heard urging revolution again as the only means of righting alleged wrongs.

The responses continue to demonstrate, however, that the constitutional arrangement for government, the allocation of powers, and the restraints on government all provide the needed flexibility. The Constitution endures.

Adam C. Breckenridge, University of Nebraska-Lincoln

The Constitution of the United States

We the People of the United States, in Order to form a more perfect Union, establish Justice, insure domestic Tranquility, provide for the common defence, promote the general Welfare, and secure the Blessings of Liberty to ourselves and our Posterity, do ordain and establish this Constitution for the United States of America.

Article. I.

SECTION. 1. All legislative Powers herein granted shall be vested in a Congress of the United States, which shall consist of a Senate and House of Representatives.

SECTION. 2. The House of Representatives shall be composed of Members chosen every second Year by the People of the several States, and the Electors in each State shall have the Qualifications requisite for Electors of the most numerous Branch of the State Legislature.

No Person shall be a Representative who shall not have attained to the age of twenty five Years, and been seven Years a Citizen of the United States, and who shall not, when elected, be an Inhabitant of that State in which he shall be chosen.

Representatives and direct Taxes shall be apportioned among the several States which may be included within this Union, according to their respective Numbers, which shall be determined by adding to the whole Number of free Persons, including those bound to Service for a Term of Years, and excluding Indians not taxed, three fifths of all other Persons. The actual Enumeration shall be made within three Years after the first Meeting of the Congress of the United States, and within every subsequent Term of ten Years, in such Manner as they shall by Law direct. The Number of Representatives shall not exceed one for every thirty Thousand, but each State shall have at Least one Representative; and until such enumeration shall be made, the State of New Hampshire shall be entitled to chuse three, Massachusetts eight, Rhode-Island and Providence Plantations one, Connecticut five, New York six, New Jersey four, Pennsylvania eight, Delaware one, Maryland six, Virginia ten, North Carolina five, South Carolina five, and Georgia three.

When vacancies happen in the Representation from any State, the Executive Authority thereof shall issue Writs of Election to fill such Vacancies.

The House of Representatives shall chuse their Speaker and other Officers; and shall have the sole Power of Impeachment.

SECTION. 3. The Senate of the United States shall be composed of two Senators from each State, chosen by the Legislature thereof, for six years; and each Senator shall have one Vote.

Immediately after they shall be assembled in Consequence of the first Election, they shall be divided as equally as may be into three Classes. The Seats of the Senators of the first Class shall be vacated at the Expiration of the second Year, of the second Class at the Expiration of the fourth Year, and of the third Class at the Expiration of the sixth Year, so that one third may be chosen every second year; and if Vacancies happen by Resignation, or otherwise, during the Recess of the Legislature of any State, the Executive thereof may make temporary Appointments until the next Meeting of the Legislature, which shall then fill such Vacancies.

No Person shall be a Senator who shall not have attained to the Age of thirty Years, and been nine Years a Citizen of the United States, and who shall not, when elected, be an Inhabitant of that State for which he shall be chosen.

The Vice President of the United States shall be President of the Senate, but shall have no Vote, unless they be equally divided.

The Senate shall chuse their other Officers, and also a President pro tempore, in the Absence of the Vice President, or when he shall exercise the Office of President of the United States.

The Senate shall have the sole Power to try all Impeachments. When sitting for that Purpose, they shall be on Oath or Affirmation. When the President of the United States is tried the Chief Justice shall preside: And no Person shall be convicted without the Concurrence of two thirds of the Members present.

Judgment in Cases of Impeachment shall not extend further than to removal from Office, and disqualification to hold and enjoy any Office of honor, Trust or Profit under the United States: but the Party convicted shall nevertheless be liable and subject to Indictment, Trial, Judgment and Punishment, according to Law.

SECTION. 4. The Times, Places and Manner of holding Elections for Senators and Representatives, shall be prescribed in each State by the Legislature thereof; but the Congress may at any time by Law make or alter such Regulations, except as to the Places of chusing Senators.

The Congress shall assemble at least once in every Year, and such Meeting shall be on the first Monday in December, unless they shall by Law appoint a different Day.

SECTION. 5. Each House shall be the Judge of the Elections, Returns and Qualifications of its own Members, and a Majority of each shall constitute a Quorum to do Business; but a smaller Number may adjourn from day to day, and may be authorized to compel the Attendance of absent Members, in such Manner, and under such Penalties as each House may provide.

Each House may determine the Rules of its Proceedings, punish its Members for disorderly Behaviour, and, with the Concurrence of two thirds, expel a Member.

Each House shall keep a Journal of its Proceedings, and from time to time publish the same, excepting such Parts as may in their Judgment require Secrecy; and the Yeas and Nays of the Members of either House on any question shall, at the Desire of one fifth of those Present, be entered on the Journal.

Neither House, during the Session of Congress, shall, without the Consent of the other, adjourn for more than three days, nor to any other Place than that in which the two Houses shall be sitting.

SECTION. 6. The Senators and Representatives shall receive a Compensation for their Services, to be ascertained by Law, and paid out of the Treasury of the United States. They shall in all Cases, except Treason, Felony and Breach of the Peace, be privileged from Arrest during their Attendance at the Session of their respective Houses, and in going to and returning from the same; and for any Speech or Debate in either House, they shall not be questioned in any other Place.

No Senator or Representative shall, during the Time for which he was elected, be appointed to any civil Office under the Authority of the United States, which shall have been created, or the Emoluments whereof shall have been encreased during such time; and no Person holding any Office under the United States, shall be a Member of either House during his Continuance in Office.

SECTION. 7. All Bills for raising Revenue shall originate in the House of Representatives; but the Senate may propose or concur with amendments as on other Bills.

Every Bill which shall have passed the House of Representatives and the Senate, shall, before it become a Law, be presented to the President of the United States; If he approve he shall sign it, but if not he shall return it, with his Objections to that House in which it shall have originated, who shall enter the Objections at large on their Journal, and proceed to reconsider it. If after such Reconsideration two thirds of that House shall agree to pass the Bill, it shall be sent, together with the Objections, to the other House, by which it shall likewise be reconsidered, and if approved by two thirds of that House, it shall become a Law. But in all such Cases the Votes of both Houses shall be determined by Yeas and Nays, and the Names of the Persons voting for and against the Bill shall be entered on the Journal of each House respectively. If any Bill shall not be returned by the President within ten Days (Sundays excepted) after it shall have been presented to him, the Same shall be a Law, in like Manner as if he had signed it, unless the Congress by their Adjournment prevent its Return, in which Case it shall not be a Law.

Every Order, Resolution, or Vote to which the Concurrence of the Senate and House of Representatives may be necessary (except on a question of Adjournment) shall be presented to the President of the United States; and before the Same shall take Effect, shall be approved by him, or being disapproved by him, shall be repassed by two thirds of the Senate and House of Representatives, according to the Rules and Limitations prescribed in the Case of a Bill.

SECTION. 8. The Congress shall have Power To lay and collect Taxes, Duties, Imposts and Excises, to pay the Debts and provide for the common Defence and general Welfare of the United States; but all Duties, Imposts and Excises shall be uniform throughout the United States;

To borrow Money on the credit of the United States;

To regulate Commerce with foreign Nations, and among the several States, and with the Indian Tribes;

To establish an uniform Rule of Naturalization, and uniform Laws on the subject of Bankruptcies throughout the United States;

To coin Money, regulate the Value thereof, and of foreign Coin, and fix the Standard of Weights and Measures;

To provide for the Punishment of counterfeiting the Securities and current Coin of the United States;

To establish Post Offices and post Roads;

To promote the Progress of Science and useful Arts, by securing for limited Times to Authors and Inventors the exclusive Right to their respective Writings and Discoveries;

To constitute Tribunals inferior to the supreme Court;

To define and punish Piracies and Felonies committed on the high Seas, and Offences against the Law of Nations;

To declare War, grant Letters of Marque and Reprisal, and make Rules concerning Captures on Land and Water;

To raise and support Armies, but no Appropriation of Money to that Use shall be for a longer Term than two Years;

To provide and maintain a Navy;

To make Rules for the Government and Regulation of the land and naval Forces;

To provide for calling forth the Militia to execute the Laws of the Union, suppress Insurrections and repel Invasions;

To provide for organizing, arming, and disciplining, the Militia, and for governing such Part of them as may be employed in the Service of the United States, reserving to the States respectively, the Appointment of the Officers, and the Authority of training the Militia according to the discipline prescribed by Congress;

To exercise exclusive Legislation in all Cases whatsoever, over such District (not exceeding ten Miles square) as may, by Cession of Particular States, and the Acceptance of Congress, become the Seat of the Government of the United States, and to exercise like Authority over all Places purchased by the Consent of the Legislature of the State in which the Same shall be, for the Erection of Forts, Magazines, Arsenals, dock-Yards, and other needful Buildings;—And

To make all Laws which shall be necessary and proper for carrying into Execution the foregoing Powers, and all other Powers vested by this Constitution in the Government of the United States, or in any Department or Officer thereof.

SECTION. 9. The Migration or Importation of such Persons as any of the States now existing shall think proper to admit, shall not be prohibited by the Congress prior to the Year one thousand eight hundred and eight, but a Tax or duty may be imposed on such Importation, not exceeding ten dollars for each Person.

The Privilege of the Writ of Habeas Corpus shall not be suspended, unless when in Cases of Rebellion or Invasion the public Safety may require it.

No Bill of Attainder or ex post facto Law shall be passed.

No Capitation, or other direct, Tax shall be laid, unless in Proportion to the Census or Enumeration herein before directed to be taken.

No Tax or Duty shall be laid on Articles exported from any State.

No Preference shall be given by any Regulation or Commerce or Revenue to the Ports of one State over those of another; nor shall Vessels bound to, or from, one State, be obliged to enter, clear or pay Duties in another.

No Money shall be drawn from the Treasury, but in Consequence of Appropriations made by Law; and a regular Statement and Account of the Receipts and Expenditures of all public Money shall be published from time to time.

No Title of Nobility shall be granted by the United States: And no Person holding any Office of Profit or Trust under them, shall, without the Consent of the Congress, accept of any present Emolument, Office, or Title, of any kind whatever, from any King, Prince, or foreign State.

SECTION. 10. No State shall enter into any Treaty, Alliance, or Confederation; grant Letters of Marque and Reprisal; coin Money; emit Bills of Credit; make any Thing but gold and silver Coin a Tender in Payment of Debts; pass any Bill of Attainder, ex post facto Law, or Law impairing the Obligation of Contracts, or grant any Title of Nobility.

No State shall, without the Consent of the Congress, lay any Imposts or Duties on Imports or Exports, except what may be absolutely necessary for executing its inspection Laws: and the net Produce of all Duties and Imposts, laid by any State on Imports or Exports, shall be for the Use of the Treasury of the United States; and all such Laws shall be subject to the Revision and Controul of the Congress.

No state shall, without the Consent of Congress, lay any Duty of Tonnage, keep Troops, or Ships of War in time of Peace, enter into any Agreement or Compact with another State, or with a foreign Power, or engage in War, unless actually invaded, or in such imminent Danger as will not admit of delay.

Article. II.

SECTION. 1. The executive Power shall be vested in a President of the United States of America. He shall hold his Office during the Term of four Years, and, together with the Vice President, chosen for the same Term, be elected as follows.

Each State shall appoint, in such Manner as the Legislature thereof may direct, a Number of Electors, equal to the whole Number of Senators and Representatives to which the State may be entitled in the Congress: but no Senator or Representative, or Person holding an Office of Trust or Profit under the United States, shall be appointed an Elector.

The Electors shall meet in their respective States, and vote by Ballot for two Persons, of whom one at least shall not be an Inhabitant of the same State with themselves. And they shall make a List of all the persons voted for, and of the Number of Votes for each; which List they shall sign and certify, and transmit sealed to the Seat of Government of the United States, directed to the President of the Senate. The President of the Senate shall, in the Presence of the Senate and House of Representatives, open all the Certificates, and the Votes shall then be counted. The Person having the greatest Number of Votes shall be the President, if such Number be a Majority of the whole Number of Electors appointed; and if there be more than one who have such Majority, and have an equal Number of Votes, then the House of Representatives shall immediately chuse by Ballot one of them for President; and if no Person have a Majority, then from the five highest on the List the said House shall in like Manner chuse the President. But in chusing the President,

the Votes shall be taken by States, the Representation from each State having one Vote; a quorum for this Purpose shall consist of a Member or Members from two thirds of the States, and a Majority of all the States shall be necessary to a Choice. In every Case, after the Choice of the President, the Person having the greatest Number of Votes of the Electors shall be the Vice President. But if there should remain two or more who have equal Votes, the Senate shall chuse from them by Ballot the Vice President.

The Congress may determine the Time of chusing the Electors, and the Day on which they shall give their Votes; which Day shall be the same throughout the United States.

No Person except a natural born Citizen, or a Citizen of the United States, at the time of the Adoption of this Constitution, shall be eligible to the Office of President; neither shall any person be eligible to that Office who shall not have attained to the Age of thirty five Years, and been fourteen Years a Resident within the United States.

In Case of the Removal of the President from Office, or of his Death, Resignation, or Inability to discharge the Powers and Duties of the said Office, the Same shall devolve on the Vice President, and the Congress may by Law provide for the Case of Removal, Death, Resignation or Inability, both of the President and Vice President, declaring what Officer shall then act as President, and such Officer shall act accordingly, until the Disability be removed, or a President shall be elected.

The President shall, at stated Times, receive for his Services, a Compensation, which shall neither be encreased nor diminished during the Period for which he shall have been elected, and he shall not receive within that period any other Emolument from the United States, or any of them.

Before he enter on the Execution of his Office, he shall take the following Oath or Affirmation:—"I do solemnly swear (or affirm) that I will faithfully execute the Office of President of the United States, and will to the best of my Ability, preserve, protect and defend the Constitution of the United States."

SECTION. 2. The President shall be Commander in Chief of the Army and Navy of the United States, and of the Militia of the several States, when called into the actual Service of the United States; he may require the Opinion, in writing, of the principal Officer in each of the executive Departments, upon any Subject relating to the Duties of their respective Offices, and he shall have Power to grant Reprieves and Pardons for Offences against the United States, except in Cases of Impeachment.

He shall have Power, by and with the Advice and Consent of the Senate, to make Treaties, provided two thirds of the Senators present concur; and he shall nominate, and by and with the Advice and Consent of the Senate, shall appoint Ambassadors, other public Ministers and Consuls, Judges of the supreme Court, and all other Officers of the United States, whose Appointments are not herein otherwise provided for, and which shall be established by Law: but the Congress may by Law vest the Appointment of such inferior Officers, as they think proper, in the President alone, in the Courts of Law, or in the Heads of Departments.

The President shall have Power to fill up all Vacancies that may happen during the Recess of the Senate, by granting

Commissions which shall expire at the End of their next Session.

SECTION. 3. He shall from time to time give to the Congress Information of the State of the Union, and recommend to their Consideration such Measures as he shall judge necessary and expedient; he may, on extraordinary Occasions, convene both Houses, or either of them, and in Case of Disagreement between them, with Respect to the Time of Adjournment, he may adjourn them to such Time as he shall think proper; he shall receive Ambassadors and other public Ministers; he shall take Care that the Laws be faithfully executed, and shall Commission all the Officers of the United States.

SECTION. 4. The President, Vice President and all civil Officers of the United States, shall be removed from Office on Impeachment for, and Conviction of, Treason, Bribery, or other high Crimes and Misdemeanors.

Article. III.

SECTION. 1. The judicial Power of the United States, shall be vested in one supreme Court, and in such inferior Courts as the Congress may from time to time ordain and establish. The Judges, both of the supreme and inferior Courts, shall hold their Offices during good Behaviour, and shall, at stated Times, receive for their Services, a Compensation, which shall not be diminished during their Continuance in Office.

SECTION. 2. The judicial Power shall extend to all Cases, in Law and Equity, arising under this Constitution, the Laws of the United States, and Treaties made, or which shall be made, under their Authority;—to all Cases affecting Ambassadors, other public Ministers and Consuls;—to all Cases of admiralty and maritime Jurisdiction;—to Controversies to which the United States shall be a Party;—to Controversies between two or more States;—between a State and Citizens of another State;—between Citizens of different States;—between Citizens of the same State claiming Lands under Grants of different States, and between a State, or the Citizens thereof, and foreign States, Citizens or Subjects.

In all Cases affecting Ambassadors, other public Ministers and Consuls, and those in which a State shall be Party, the supreme Court shall have original Jurisdiction. In all the other Cases before mentioned, the supreme Court shall have appellate Jurisdiction, both as to Law and Fact, with such Exceptions, and under such Regulations as the Congress shall make.

The Trial of all Crimes, except in Cases of Impeachment, shall be by Jury; and such Trial shall be held in the State where the said Crimes shall have been committed; but when not committed within any State, the Trial shall be at such Place or Places as the Congress may by Law have directed.

SECTION. 3. Treason against the United States, shall consist only in levying War against them, or in adhering to their Enemies, giving them Aid and Comfort. No Person shall be convicted of Treason unless on the Testimony of two Witnesses to the same overt Act, or on Confession in open Court.

The Congress shall have Power to declare the Punishment of Treason, but no Attainder of Treason shall work Corruption of Blood, or Forfeiture except during the Life of the Person attained.

Article. IV.

SECTION. 1. Full Faith and Credit shall be given in each State to the public Acts, Records, and judicial Proceedings of every other State. And the Congress may by general Laws prescribe the Manner in which such Acts, Record and Proceedings shall be proved, and the Effect thereof.

SECTION. 2. The Citizens of each State shall be entitled to all Privileges and Immunities of Citizens in the several States.

A Person charged in any State with Treason, Felony, or other Crime, who shall flee from Justice, and be found in another State, shall on Demand of the executive Authority of the State from which he fled, be delivered up, to be removed to the State having Jurisdiction of the Crime.

No Person held to Service or Labour in one State, under the Laws thereof, escaping into another, shall, in Consequence of any Law or Regulation therein, be discharged from such Service or Labour, but shall be delivered up on Claim of the Party to whom such Service or Labour may be due.

SECTION. 3. New States may be admitted by the Congress into this Union; but no new State shall be formed or erected within the Jurisdiction of any other State; nor any State be formed by the Junction of two or more States, or Parts of States, without the Consent of the Legislatures of the States concerned as well as of the Congress.

The Congress shall have Power to dispose of and make all needful Rules and Regulations respecting the Territory or other Property belonging to the United States; and nothing in this Constitution shall be so construed as to Prejudice any Claims of the United States, or of any particular State.

SECTION. 4. The United States shall guarantee to every State in this Union a Republican Form of Government, and shall protect each of them against Invasion; and on Application of the Legislature, or of the Executive (when the Legislature cannot be convened) against domestic Violence.

Article. V.

The Congress, whenever two thirds of both Houses shall deem it necessary, shall propose Amendments to this Constitution, or, on the Application of the Legislature of two thirds of the several States, shall call a Convention for proposing Amendments, which, in either Case, shall be valid to all Intents and Purposes, as Part of this Constitution, when ratified by the Legislatures of three fourths of the several States, or by Conventions in three fourths thereof, as the one or the other Mode of Ratification may be proposed by the Congress; Provided that no Amendment which may be made prior to the Year One thousand eight hundred and eight shall in any Manner affect the first and fourth Clauses in the Ninth Section of the first Article; and that no State, without its Consent, shall be deprived of its equal Suffrage in the Senate.

Article. VI.

All Debts contracted and Engagements entered into, before the Adoption of this Constitution, shall be as valid against the United States under this Constitution, as under the Confederation.

This Constitution, and the Laws of the United States which shall be made in Pursuance thereof; and all Treaties made, or which shall be made, under the Authority of the United States, shall be the supreme Law of the Land; and the Judges in every State shall be bound thereby, any Thing in the Constitution or Laws of any State to the Contrary notwithstanding.

The Senators and Representatives before mentioned, and the Members of the several State Legislatures, and all executive and judicial Officers, both of the United States and of the several States, shall be bound by Oath or Affirmation, to support this Constitution; but no religious Test shall ever be required as a Qualification to any Office or public Trust under the United States.

New Hampshire	JOHN LANGDON
	NICHOLAS GILMAN
Massachusetts	NATHANIEL GORHAM
	RUFUS KING
Connecticut	Wm. SAML JOHNSON
	ROGER SHERMAN
New York . . .	ALEXANDER HAMILTON
New Jersey	WIL: LIVINGSTON
	DAVID BREARLEY
	Wm. PATERSON
	JONA: DAYTON
Pennsylvania	B FRANKLIN
	THOMAS MIFFLIN
	ROBt MORRIS
	GEO. CLYMER
	THOs. FITZSIMONS
	JARED INGERSOLL
	JAMES WILSON
	GOUV MORRIS
Delaware	GEO: READ
	GUNNING BEDFORD jun
	JOHN DICKINSON
	RICHARD BASSETT
	JACO: BROOM
Maryland	JAMES McHENRY
	DAN OF St THOs. JENIFER
	DANL CARROLL
Virginia	JOHN BLAIR
	JAMES MADISON Jr.
North Carolina	Wm. BLOUNT
	RICHd. DOBBS SPAIGHT
	HU WILLIAMSON
South Carolina	J. RUTLEDGE
	CHARLES COTESWORTH PINCKNEY
	CHARLES PINCKNEY
	PIERCE BUTLER
Georgia	WILLIAM FEW
	ABR BALDWIN

Article. VII.

The Ratification of the Conventions of nine States, shall be sufficient for the Establishment of this Constitution between the States so ratifying the Same.

Done in Convention by the Unanimous Consent of the States present the Seventeenth Day of September in the Year of our Lord one thousand seven hundred and Eighty seven and of the Independence of the United States of America the Twelfth In witness whereof We have hereunto subscribed our Names,

Go. WASHINGTON—Presidt. and deputy from Virginia
In Convention Monday, September 17th 1787.

Present The States of

New Hampshire, Massachusetts, Connecticut, Mr. Hamilton from New York, New Jersey, Pennsylvania, Delaware, Maryland, Virginia, North Carolina and Georgia.

Resolved,

That the preceeding Constitution be laid before the United States in Congress assembled, and that it is the Opinion of this Convention, that it should afterwards be submitted to a Convention of Delegates, chosen in each State by the People thereof, under the Recommendation of its Legislature, for their Assent and Ratification; and that each Convention assenting to, and ratifying the Same, should give Notice thereof to the United States in Congress assembled. Resolved, That it is the Opinion of this Convention, that as soon as the Conventions of nine States shall have ratified this Constitution, the United States in Congress assembled should fix a Day on which Electors should be appointed by the States which shall have ratified the same, and a Day on which the Electors should assemble to vote for the President, and the Time and Place for commencing Proceedings under this Constitution. That after such Publication the Electors should be appointed, and the Senators and Representatives elected: That the Electors should meet on the Day fixed for the Election of the President, and should transmit their Votes certified, signed, sealed and directed, as the Constitution requires, to the Secretary of the United States in Congress assembled, that

Ratification of the Constitution

State	Date of Ratification
Delaware	Dec 7, 1787
Pennsylvania	Dec 12, 1787
New Jersey	Dec 19, 1787
Georgia	Jan 2, 1788
Connecticut	Jan 9, 1788
Massachusetts	Feb 6, 1788
Maryland	Apr 28, 1788
South Carolina	May 23, 1788
New Hampshire	June 21, 1788
Virginia	Jun 25, 1788
New York	Jun 26, 1788
Rhode Island	May 29, 1790
North Carolina	Nov 21, 1789

the Senators and Representatives should convene at the Time and Place assigned; that the Senators should appoint a President of the Senate, for the sole Purpose of receiving, opening and counting the Votes for President; and, that after he shall be chosen, the Congress, together with the President, should, without Delay, proceed to execute this Constitution.

By the Unanimous Order of the Convention
Go. WASHINGTON—Presidt.
W. JACKSON Secretary.

ARTICLES IN ADDITION TO, AND AMENDMENT OF, THE CONSTITUTION OF THE UNITED STATES OF AMERICA, PROPOSED BY CONGRESS, AND RATIFIED BY THE SEVERAL STATES, PURSUANT TO THE FIFTH ARTICLE OF THE ORIGINAL CONSTITUTION.

Amendment I.

Congress shall make no law respecting an establishment of religion, or prohibiting the free exercise thereof; or abridging the freedom of speech, or of the press; or the right of the people peaceably to assemble, and to petition the Government for a redress of grievances.

Amendment II.

A well regulated Militia, being necessary to the security of a free State, the right of the people to keep and bear Arms, shall not be infringed.

Amendment III.

No Soldier shall, in time of peace be quartered in any house, without the consent of the Owner, nor in time of war, but in a manner to be prescribed by law.

Amendment IV.

The right of the people to be secure in their persons, houses, papers, and effects, against unreasonable searches and seizures, shall not be violated, and no Warrants shall issue, but upon probable cause, supported by Oath or affirmation, and particularly describing the place to be searched, and the persons or things to be seized.

Amendment V.

No person shall be held to answer for a capital, or otherwise infamous crime, unless on a presentment or indictment of a Grand Jury, except in cases arising in the land or naval forces, or in the Militia, when in actual service in time of War or public danger; nor shall any person be subject for the same offence to be twice put in jeopardy of life or limb; nor shall be compelled in any criminal case to be a witness against himself, nor

be deprived of life, liberty, or property, without due process of law; nor shall private property be taken for public use, without just compensation.

Amendment VI.

In all criminal prosecutions, the accused shall enjoy the right to a speedy and public trial, by an impartial jury of the State and district wherein the crime shall have been committed, which district shall have been previously ascertained by law, and to be informed of the nature and cause of the accusation; to be confronted with the witnesses against him; to have compulsory process for obtaining witnesses in his favor, and to have the Assistance of Counsel for his defence.

Amendment VII.

In Suits at common law, where the value in controversy shall exceed twenty dollars, the right of trial by jury shall be preserved, and no fact tried by a jury, shall be otherwise re-examined in any Court of the United States, than according to the rules of the common law.

Amendment VIII.

Excessive bail shall not be required, nor excessive fines imposed, nor cruel and unusual punishments inflicted.

Amendment IX.

The enumeration in the Constitution, of certain rights, shall not be construed to deny or disparage others retained by the people.

Amendment X.

The powers not delegated to the United States by the Constitution, nor prohibited by it to the States, are reserved to the States respectively, or to the people.

Amendment XI.
(Adopted Jan. 8, 1798)

The Judicial power of the United States shall not be construed to extend to any suit in law or equity, commenced or prosecuted against one of the United States by Citizens of another State, or by Citizens or Subjects of any Foreign State.

Amendment XII.
(Adopted Sept. 25, 1804)

The Electors shall meet in their respective states and vote by ballot for President and Vice-President, one of whom, at least, shall not be an inhabitant of the same state with themselves; they shall name in their ballots the person voted for as President, and in distinct ballots the person voted for as Vice-President, and they shall make distinct lists of all persons voted for as President, and of all persons voted for as Vice-President, and of the number of votes for each, which lists they shall sign and certify, and transmit sealed to the seat of the government of the United States, directed to the President of the Senate;—The President of the Senate shall, in the presence of the Senate and House of Representatives, open all the certificates and the votes shall then be counted;—The person having the greatest number of votes for President, shall be the President, if such number be a majority of the whole number of Electors appointed; and if no person have such majority, then from the persons having the highest numbers not exceeding three on the list of those voted for as President, the House of Representatives shall choose immediately, by ballot, the President. But in choosing the President, the votes shall be taken by states, the representation from each state having one vote; a quorum for this purpose shall consist of a member or members from two-thirds of the states, and a majority of all the states shall be necessary to a choice. And if the House of Representatives shall not choose a President whenever the right of choice shall devolve upon them, before the fourth day of March next following, then the Vice-President shall act as President, as in the case of the death or other constitutional disability of the President.—The person having the greatest number of votes as Vice-President, shall be the Vice-President, if such number be a majority of the whole number of Electors appointed, and if no person have a majority, then from the two highest numbers on the list, the Senate shall choose the Vice-President; a quorum for the purpose shall consist of two-thirds of the whole number of Senators, and a majority of the whole number shall be necessary to a choice. But no person constitutionally ineligible to the office of President shall be eligible to that of Vice-President of the United States.

Amendment XIII.

(Adopted Dec. 18, 1865)

SECTION 1. Neither slavery nor involuntary servitude, except as a punishment for crime whereof the party shall have been duly convicted, shall exist within the United States, or any place subject to their jurisdiction.

SECTION 2. Congress shall have power to enforce this article by appropriate legislation.

Amendment XIV.

(Adopted July 28, 1868)

SECTION 1. All persons born or naturalized in the United States and subject to the jurisdiction thereof, are citizens of the United States and of the State wherein they reside. No State shall make or enforce any law which shall abridge the privileges or immunities of citizens of the United States; nor shall any State deprive any person of life, liberty, or property, without due process of law; nor deny to any person within its jurisdiction the equal protection of the laws.

SECTION 2. Representatives shall be apportioned among the several States according to their respective numbers, counting the whole number of persons in each State, excluding Indians not taxed. But when the right to vote at any election for the choice of electors for President and Vice President of the United States, Representatives in Congress, the Executive and Judicial officers of a State, or the members of the Legislature thereof, is denied to any of the male inhabitants of such State, being twenty-one years of age, and citizens of the United States, or in any way abridged, except for participation in rebellion, or other crime, the basis of representation therein shall be reduced in the proportion which the number of such male citizens shall bear to the whole number of male citizens twenty-one years of age in such State.

SECTION 3. No person shall be a Senator or Representative in Congress, or elector of President and Vice President, or hold any office, civil or military, under the United States, or under any State, who, having previously taken an oath, as a member of Congress, or as an officer of the United States, or as a member of any State legislature, or as an executive or judicial officer of any State, to support the Constitution of the United States, shall have engaged in insurrection or rebellion against the same, or given aid or comfort to the enemies thereof. But Congress may by a vote of two-thirds of each House, remove such disability.

SECTION 4. The validity of the public debt of the United States, authorized by law, including debts incurred for payment of pensions and bounties for services in suppressing insurrection or rebellion, shall not be questioned. But neither the United States nor any State shall assume or pay any debt or obligation incurred in aid of insurrection or rebellion against the United States, or any claim for the loss or emancipation of any slave; but all such debts, obligations and claims shall be held illegal and void.

SECTION 5. The Congress shall have power to enforce, by appropriate legislation, the provisions of this article.

Amendment XV.

(Adopted March 30, 1870)

SECTION 1. The right of citizens of the United States to vote shall not be denied or abridged by the United States or by any State on account of race, color, or previous condition of servitude.

SECTION 2. The Congress shall have power to enforce this article by appropriate legislation.

Amendment XVI.

(Adopted Feb. 25, 1913)

The Congress shall have power to lay and collect taxes on incomes, from whatever source derived, without apportionment among the several States, and without regard to any census or enumeration.

Amendment XVII.

(Adopted May 31, 1913)

The Senate of the United States shall be composed of two Senators from each State, elected by the people thereof, for six years; and each Senator shall have one vote. The electors in each State shall have the qualifications requisite for electors of the most numerous branch of the State legislatures.

When vacancies happen in the representation of any State in the Senate, the executive authority of such State shall issue writs of election to fill such vacancies: Provided, That the legislature of any State may empower the executive thereof to make temporary appointments until the people fill the vacancies by election as the legislature may direct.

This amendment shall not be so construed as to affect the election or term of any Senator chosen before it becomes valid as part of the Constitution.

Amendment XVIII.

(Adopted Jan. 29, 1919)

SECTION 1. After one year from the ratification of this article the manufacture, sale or transportation of intoxicating liquors within, the importation thereof into, or the exportation thereof from the United States and all territory subject to the jurisdiction thereof for beverage purposes is hereby prohibited.

SECTION 2. The Congress and the several States shall have concurrent power to enforce this article by appropriate legislation.

SECTION 3. This article shall be inoperative unless it shall have been ratified as an amendment to the Constitution by the legislatures of the several States, as provided in the Constitution, within seven years from the date of the submission hereof to the States by the Congress.

Amendment XIX.

(Adopted Aug. 26, 1920)

The right of citizens of the United States to vote shall not be denied or abridged by the United States or by any State on account of sex.

Congress shall have power to enforce this article by appropriate legislation.

Amendment XX.

(Adopted Feb. 6, 1933)

SECTION 1. The terms of the President and Vice President shall end at noon on the 20th day of January, and the terms of Senators and Representatives at noon on the 3d day of January, of the years in which such terms would have ended if this article had not been ratified; and the terms of their successors shall then begin.

SECTION 2. The Congress shall assemble at least once in every year, and such meeting shall begin at noon on the 3d day of January, unless they shall by law appoint a different day.

SECTION 3. If, at the time fixed for the beginning of the term of the President, the President elect shall have died, the Vice President elect shall become President. If a President shall not have been chosen before the time fixed for the beginning of his term, or if the President elect shall have failed to qualify, then the Vice President elect shall act as President until a President shall have qualified; and the Congress may by law provide for the case wherein neither a President elect nor a Vice President elect shall have qualified, declaring who shall then act as President, or the manner in which one who is to act shall be selected, and such person shall act accordingly until a President or Vice President shall have qualified.

SECTION 4. The Congress may by law provide for the case of the death of any of the persons from whom the House of Representatives may choose a President whenever the right of choice shall have devolved upon them, and for the case of the death of any of the persons from whom the Senate may choose a Vice President whenever the right of choice shall have devolved upon them.

SECTION 5. Sections 1 and 2 shall take effect on the 15th day of October following the ratification of this article.

SECTION 6. This article shall be inoperative unless it shall have been ratified as an amendment to the Constitution by the legislatures of three-fourths of the several States within seven years from the date of its submission.

Amendment XXI.

(Adopted Dec. 5, 1933)

SECTION 1. The eighteenth article of amendment to the Constitution of the United States is hereby repealed.

SECTION 2. The transportation or importation into any State, Territory, or possession of the United States for delivery or use therein of intoxicating liquors, in violation of the laws thereof, is hereby prohibited.

SECTION 3. This article shall be inoperative unless it shall have been ratified as an amendment to the Constitution by conventions in the several States, as provided in the Constitution, within seven years from the date of the submission hereof to the States by the Congress.

Amendment XXII.

(Adopted Feb. 27, 1951)

SECTION 1. No person shall be elected to the office of the President more than twice, and no person who has held the office of President, or acted as President, for more than two years of a term to which some other person was elected President shall be elected to the office of the President more than once. But this Article shall not apply to any person holding the office of President when this Article was proposed by the Congress, and shall not prevent any person who may be holding the office of President, or acting as President, during the term within which this Article becomes operative from holding the office of President or acting as President during the remainder of such term.

SECTION 2. This Article shall be inoperative unless it shall have been ratified as an amendment to the Constitution by the legislatures of three-fourths of the several States within seven years from the date of its submission to the States by the Congress.

Amendment XXIII.

(Adopted Mar. 29, 1961)

SECTION 1. The District constituting the seat of Government of the United States shall appoint in such manner as the Congress may direct:

A number of electors of President and Vice President equal to the whole number of Senators and Representatives in Congress to which the District would be entitled if it were a State, but in no event more than the least populous State; they shall be in addition to those appointed by the States, but they shall be considered, for the purposes of the election of President and Vice President, to be electors appointed by a State; and they shall meet in the District and perform such duties as provided by the twelfth article of amendment.

SECTION 2. The Congress shall have power to enforce this article by appropriate legislation.

Amendment XXIV.

(Adopted Jan. 23, 1964)

SECTION 1. The right of citizens of the United States to vote in any primary or other election for President or Vice President, for electors for President or Vice President, or for Senator or Representative in Congress, shall not be denied or abridged by the United States or any State by reason of failure to pay any poll tax or other tax.

SECTION 2. The Congress shall have the power to enforce this article by appropriate legislation.

Amendment XXV.

(Adopted Feb. 10, 1967)

SECTION 1. In case of the removal of the President from office or of his death or resignation, the Vice President shall become President.

SECTION 2. Whenever there is a vacancy in the office of the Vice President, the President shall nominate a Vice President who shall take the office upon confirmation by a majority vote of both houses of Congress.

SECTION 3. Whenever the President transmits to the President pro tempore of the Senate and the Speaker of the House of Representatives his written declaration that he is unable to discharge the powers and duties of his office, and until he transmits to them a written declaration to the contrary, such powers and duties shall be discharged by the Vice President as Acting President.

SECTION 4. Whenever the Vice President and a majority of either the principal officers of the executive departments or of such other body as Congress may by law provide, transmit to the President pro tempore of the Senate and the Speaker of the House of Representatives their written declaration that the President is unable to discharge the powers and duties of his office, the Vice President shall immediately assume the powers and duties of the office as Acting President.

Thereafter, when the President transmits to the President pro tempore of the Senate and the Speaker of the House of Representatives his written declaration that no inability exists, he shall resume the powers and duties of his office unless the Vice President and a majority of either the principal officers of the executive department or of such other body as Congress may by law provide, transmit within four days to the President pro tempore of the Senate and the Speaker of the House of Representatives their written declaration that the President is unable to discharge the powers and duties of his office. Thereupon Congress shall decide the issue, assembling within forty-eight hours for that purpose if not in session. If the Congress within twenty-one days after receipt of the latter written declaration, or, if Congress is not in session, within twenty-one days after Congress is required to assemble, determines by two-thirds vote of both Houses that the President is unable to discharge the powers and duties of his office, the Vice President shall continue to discharge the same as Acting President; otherwise, the President shall resume the powers and duties of his office.

Amendment XXVI.

(Adopted June 30, 1971)

SECTION 1. The right of citizens of the United States, who are 18 years of age or older, to vote shall not be denied or abridged by the United States or by any state on account of age.

SECTION 2. The Congress shall have the power to enforce this article by appropriate legislation.

Amendment XXVII.

(Adopted May 7, 1992)

No law, varying the compensation for the services of the Senators and Representatives, shall take effect, until an election of Representatives shall have intervened.

The Size and Variety of the Union as a Check on Faction
Federalist No. 10

JAMES MADISON

To the People of the State of New York:

Among the numerous advantages promised by a well-constructed Union, none deserves to be more accurately developed than its tendency to break and control the violence of faction. The friend of popular governments never finds himself so much alarmed for their character and fate, as when he contemplates their propensity to this dangerous vice. He will not fail, therefore, to set a due value on any plan which, without violating the principles to which he is attached, provides a proper cure for it. The instability, injustice, and confusion introduced into the public councils, have, in truth, been the mortal diseases under which popular governments have everywhere perished; as they continue to be the favorite and fruitful topics from which the adversaries to liberty derive their most specious declamations. The valuable improvements made by the American constitutions on the popular models, both ancient and modern, cannot certainly be too much admired; but it would be an unwarrantable partiality, to contend that they have as effectually obviated the danger on this side, as was wished and expected. Complaints are everywhere heard from our most considerate and virtuous citizens, equally the friends of public and private faith, and of public and personal liberty, that our governments are too unstable, that the public good is disregarded in the conflicts of rival parties, and that measures are too often decided, not according to the rules of justice and the rights of the minor party, but by the superior force of an interested and overbearing majority. However anxiously we may wish that these complaints had no foundation, the evidence of known facts will not permit us to deny that they are in some degree true. It will be found, indeed, on a candid review of our situation, that some of the distresses under which we labor have been erroneously charged on the operation of our governments; but it will be found, at the same time, that other causes will not alone account for many of our heaviest misfortunes; and, particularly, for that prevailing and increasing distrust of public engagements, and alarm for private rights, which are echoed from one end of the continent to the other. These must be chiefly, if not wholly, effects of the unsteadiness and injustice with which a factious spirit has tainted our public administrations.

By a faction, I understand a number of citizens, whether amounting to a majority or minority of the whole, who are united and actuated by some common impulse of passion, or of interest, adverse to the rights of other citizens, or to the permanent and aggregate interests of the community.

There are two methods of curing the mischiefs of faction: the one, by removing its causes; the other, by controlling its effects.

There are again two methods of removing the causes of faction: the one, by destroying the liberty which is essential to its existence; the other, by giving to every citizen the same opinions, the same passions, and the same interests.

It could never be more truly said than of the first remedy, that it was worse than the disease. Liberty is to faction what air is to fire, an aliment without which it instantly expires. But it could not be less folly to abolish liberty, which is essential to political life, because it nourishes faction, than it would be to wish the annihilation of air, which is essential to animal life, because it imparts to fire its destructive agency.

The second expedient is as impracticable as the first would be unwise. As long as the reason of man continues fallible, and he is at liberty to exercise it, different opinions will be formed. As long as the connection subsists between his reason and his self-love, his opinions and his passions will have a reciprocal influence on each other; and the former will be objects to which the latter will attach themselves. The diversity in the faculties of men, from which the rights of property originate, is not less an insuperable obstacle to a uniformity of interests. The protection of these faculties is the first object of government. From the protection of different and unequal faculties of acquiring property, the possession of different degrees and kinds of property immediately results; and from the influence of these on the sentiments and views of the respective proprietors, ensues a division of the society into different interests and parties.

The latent causes of faction are thus sown in the nature of man; and we see them everywhere brought into different degrees of activity, according to the different circumstances of civil society. A zeal for different opinions concerning religion, concerning government, and many other points, as well of speculation as of practice; an attachment to different leaders ambitiously contending for pre-eminence and power; or to persons of other descriptions whose fortunes have been interesting to the human passions, have, in turn, divided mankind into parties, inflamed them with mutual animosity, and rendered them much more disposed to vex and oppress each other than to co-operate for their common good. So strong is this propensity of mankind to fall into mutual animosities, that where no substantial occasion presents itself, the most frivolous and fanciful distinctions have been sufficient to kindle their unfriendly passions and excite their most violent conflicts. But the most common and durable source of factions has been the various and unequal distribution of property. Those who hold and those who are without property have ever formed distinct interests in society.

Those who are creditors, and those who are debtors, fall under a like discrimination. A landed interest, a manufacturing interest, a mercantile interest, a moneyed interest, with many lesser interests, grow up of necessity in civilized nations, and divide them into different classes, actuated by different sentiments and views. The regulation of these various and interfering interests forms the principal task of modern legislation, and involves the spirit of party and faction in the necessary and ordinary operations of the government.

No man is allowed to be a judge in his own cause, because his interest would certainly bias his judgment, and, not improbably, corrupt his integrity. With equal, nay with greater reason, a body of men are unfit to be both judges and parties at the same time; yet what are many of the most important acts of legislation, but so many judicial determinations, not indeed concerning the rights of single persons, but concerning the rights of large bodies of citizens? And what are the different classes of legislators but advocates and parties to the causes which they determine? Is a law proposed concerning private debts? It is a question to which the creditors are parties on one side and the debtors on the other. Justice ought to hold the balance between them. Yet the parties are, and must be, themselves the judges; and the most numerous party, or, in other words, the most powerful faction must be expected to prevail. Shall domestic manufactures be encouraged, and in what degree, by restrictions on foreign manufactures? are questions which would be differently decided by the landed and the manufacturing classes, and probably by neither with a sole regard to justice and the public good. The apportionment of taxes on the various descriptions of property is an act which seems to require the most exact impartiality; yet there is, perhaps, no legislative act in which greater opportunity and temptation are given to a predominant party to trample on the rules of justice. Every shilling with which they overburden the inferior number, is a shilling saved to their own pockets.

It is in vain to say that enlightened statesmen will be able to adjust these clashing interests, and render them all subservient to the public good. Enlightened statesmen will not always be at the helm. Nor, in many cases, can such an adjustment

be made at all without taking into view indirect and remote considerations, which will rarely prevail over the immediate interest which one party may find in disregarding the rights of another or the good of the whole.

The inference to which we are brought is, that the *causes* of faction cannot be removed, and that relief is only to be sought in the means of controlling its *effects*.

If a faction consists of less than a majority, relief is supplied by the republican principle, which enables the majority to defeat its sinister views by regular vote. It may clog the administration, it may convulse the society; but it will be unable to execute and mask its violence under the forms of the Constitution. When a majority is included in a faction, the form of popular government, on the other hand, enables it to sacrifice to its ruling passion or interest both the public good and the rights of other citizens. To secure the public good and private rights against the danger of such a faction, and at the same time to preserve the spirit and the form of popular government, is then the great object to which our inquiries are directed. Let me add that it is the great desideratum by which this form of government can be rescued from the opprobrium under which it has so long labored, and be recommended to the esteem and adoption of mankind.

By what means is this object attainable? Evidently by one of two only. Either the existence of the same passion or interest in a majority at the same time must be prevented, or the majority, having such coexistent passion or interest, must be rendered, by their number and local situation, unable to concert and carry into effect schemes of oppression. If the impulse and the opportunity be suffered to coincide, we well know that neither moral nor religious motives can be relied on as an adequate control. They are not found to be such on the injustice and violence of individuals, and lose their efficacy in proportion to the number combined together, that is, in proportion as their efficacy becomes needful.

From this view of the subject it may be concluded that a pure democracy, by which I mean a society consisting of a small number of citizens, who assemble and administer the government in person, can admit of no cure for the mischiefs of faction. A common passion or interest will, in almost every case, be felt by a majority of the whole; a communication and concert result from the form of government itself; and there is nothing to check the inducements to sacrifice the weaker party or an obnoxious individual. Hence it is that such democracies have ever been spectacles of turbulence and contention; have ever been found incompatible with personal security or the rights of property; and have in general been as short in their lives as they have been violent in their deaths. Theoretic politicians, who have patronized this species of government, have erroneously supposed that by reducing mankind to a perfect equality in their political rights, they would, at the same time, be perfectly equalized and assimilated in their possessions, their opinions, and their passions.

A republic, by which I mean a government in which the scheme of representation takes place, opens a different prospect, and promises the cure for which we are seeking. Let us examine the points in which it varies from pure democracy, and we shall comprehend both the nature of the cure and the efficacy which it must derive from the Union.

The two great points of difference between a democracy and a republic are: first, the delegation of the government, in the latter, to a small number of citizens elected by the rest; secondly, the greater number of citizens, and greater sphere of country, over which the latter may be extended.

The effect of the first difference is, on the one hand, to refine and enlarge the public views, by passing them through the medium of a chosen body of citizens, whose wisdom may best discern the true interest of their country, and whose patriotism and love of justice will be least likely to sacrifice it to temporary or partial considerations. Under such a regulation, it may well happen that the public voice, pronounced by the representatives of the people, will be more consonant to the public good than if pronounced by the people themselves, convened for the purpose. On the other hand, the effect may be inverted. Men of factious tempers, of local prejudices, or of sinister designs, may, by intrigue, by corruption, or by other means, first obtain the suffrages, and then betray the interests, of the people. The question resulting is, whether small or extensive republics are more favorable to the election of proper guardians of the public weal; and it is clearly decided in favor of the latter by two obvious considerations.

In the first place, it is to be remarked that, however small the republic may be, the representatives must be raised to a certain number, in order to guard against the cabals of a few; and that, however large it may be, they must be limited to a certain number, in order to guard against the confusion of a multitude. Hence, the number of representatives in the two cases not being in proportion to that of the two constituents, and being proportionally greater in the small republic, it follows that, if the proportion of fit characters be not less in the large than in the small republic, the former will present a greater option, and consequently a greater probability of a fit choice.

In the next place, as each representative will be chosen by a greater number of citizens in the large than in the small republic, it will be more difficult for unworthy candidates to practise with success the vicious arts by which elections are too often carried; and the suffrages of the people being more free, will be more likely to centre in men who possess the most attractive merit and the most diffusive and established characters.

It must be confessed that in this, as in most other cases, there is a mean, on both sides of which inconveniences will be found to lie. By enlarging too much the number of electors, you render the representative too little acquainted with all their local circumstances and lesser interests; as by reducing it too much, you render him unduly attached to these, and too little fit to comprehend and pursue great and national objects. The federal Constitution forms a happy combination in this respect; the great and aggregate interests being referred to the national, the local and particular to the State legislatures.

The other point of difference is, the greater number of citizens and extent of territory which may be brought within the compass of republican than of democratic government; and it is this circumstance principally which renders factious combinations less to be dreaded in the former than in the latter. The smaller the society, the fewer probably will be the distinct parties and interests composing it; the fewer the distinct parties and interests, the more frequently will a majority be found of the same party; and the smaller the number of individuals composing a majority, and the smaller the compass within which they are placed, the more easily will they concert and execute their plans of oppression. Extend the sphere and you take in a greater variety of parties and interests; you will make it less probable that a majority of the whole will have a common motive to invade the rights of other citizens; or if such a common motive exists, it will be more difficult for all who feel it to discover their own strength, and to act in unison with each other. Besides other impediments, it may be remarked that, where there is a consciousness of unjust or dishonorable purposes, communication is always checked by distrust in proportion to the number whose concurrence is necessary.

Hence, it clearly appears, that the same advantage which a republic has over a democracy, in controlling the effects of faction, is enjoyed by a large over a small republic,—is enjoyed by the Union over the States composing it. Does the advantage consist in the substitution of representatives whose enlightened views and virtuous sentiments render them superior to local prejudices and to schemes of injustice? It will not be denied that the representation of the Union will be most likely to possess these requisite endowments. Does it consist in the greater security afforded by a greater variety of parties, against the event of any one party being able to outnumber and oppress the rest? In an equal degree does the increased variety of parties comprised within the Union, increase this security. Does it, in fine, consist in the greater obstacles opposed to the concert and accomplishment of the secret wishes of an unjust and interested majority? Here, again, the extent of the Union gives it the most palpable advantage.

The influence of factious leaders may kindle a flame within their particular States, but will be unable to spread a general conflagration through the other States. A religious sect may degenerate into a political faction in a part of the Confederacy; but the variety of sects dispersed over the entire face of it must secure the national councils against any danger from that source. A rage for paper money, for an abolition of debts, for an equal division of property, or for any other improper or wicked project, will be less apt to pervade the whole body of the Union than a particular member of it; in the same proportion as such a malady is more likely to taint a particular county or district, than an entire State.

In the extent and proper structure of the Union, therefore, we behold a republican remedy for the diseases most incident to republican government. And according to the degree of pleasure and pride we feel in being republicans, ought to be our zeal in cherishing the spirit and supporting the character of Federalists.

PUBLIUS

Federalist No. 10, from *The Federalist Papers*, 1787.

Checks and Balances
Federalist No. 51

James Madison

To the People of the State of New York:

To what expedient, then, shall we finally resort, for maintaining in practice the necessary partition of power among the several departments, as laid down in the Constitution? The only answer that can be given is, that as all these exterior provisions are found to be inadequate, the defect must be supplied, by so contriving the interior structure of the government as that its several constituent parts may, by their mutual relations, be the means of keeping each other in their proper places. Without presuming to undertake a full development of this important idea, I will hazard a few general observations, which may perhaps place it in a clearer light, and enable us to form a more correct judgment of the principles and structure of the government planned by the convention.

In order to lay a due foundation for that separate and distinct exercise of the different powers of government, which to a certain extent is admitted on all hands to be essential to the preservation of liberty, it is evident that each department should have a will of its own; and consequently should be so constituted that the members of each should have as little agency as possible in the appointment of the members of the others. Were this principle rigorously adhered to, it would require that all the appointments for the supreme executive, legislative, and judiciary magistracies should be drawn from the same fountain of authority, the people, through channels having no communication whatever with one another. Perhaps such a plan of constructing the several departments would be less difficult in practice than it may in contemplation appear. Some difficulties, however, and some additional expense would attend the execution of it. Some deviations, therefore, from the principle must be admitted. In the constitution of the judiciary department in particular, it might be inexpedient to insist rigorously on the principle: first, because peculiar qualifications being essential in the members, the primary consideration ought to be to select that mode of choice which best secures these qualifications; secondly, because the permanent tenure by which the appointments are held in that department, must soon destroy all sense of dependence on the authority conferring them.

It is equally evident, that the members of each department should be as little dependent as possible on those of the others, for the emoluments annexed to their offices. Were the executive magistrate, or the judges, not independent of the legislature in this particular, their independence in every other would be merely nominal.

But the great security against a gradual concentration of the several powers in the same department, consists in giving to those who administer each department the necessary constitutional means and personal motives to resist encroachments of the others. The provision for defence must in this, as in all other cases, be made commensurate to the danger of attack. Ambition must be made to counteract ambition. The interest of the man must be connected with the constitutional rights of the place. It may be a reflection on human nature, that such devices should be necessary to control the abuses of government. But what is government itself, but the greatest of all reflections on human nature? If men were angels, no government would be necessary. If angels were to govern men, neither external nor internal controls on government would be necessary. In framing a government which is to be administered by men over men, the great difficulty lies in this: you must first enable the government to control the governed; and in the next place oblige it to control itself. A dependence on the people is, no doubt, the primary control on the government; but experience has taught mankind the necessity of auxiliary precautions.

This policy of supplying, by opposite and rival interests, the defect of better motives, might be traced through the whole system of human affairs, private as well as public. We see it particularly displayed in all the subordinate distributions of power, where the constant aim is to divide and arrange the several offices in such a manner as that each may be a check on the other—that the private interest of every individual may be a sentinel over the public rights. These inventions of prudence cannot be less requisite in the distribution of the supreme powers of the State.

But it is not possible to give to each department an equal power of self-defence. In republican government, the legislative authority necessarily predominates. The remedy for this inconveniency is to divide the legislature into different branches; and to render them, by different modes of election and different principles of action, as little connected with each other as the nature of their common functions and their common dependence on the society will admit. It may even be necessary to guard against dangerous encroachments by still further precautions. As the weight of the legislative authority requires that it should be thus divided, the weakness of the executive may require, on the other hand, that it should be fortified. An absolute negative on the legislature appears, at first view, to be the natural defence with which the executive magistrate should be armed. But perhaps it would be neither altogether safe nor alone sufficient. On ordinary occasions it might not be exerted with the requisite firmness, and on extraordinary occasions it might be perfidiously abused. May not this defect of an absolute negative be supplied by some qualified connection between this weaker department and the weaker branch of the stronger department, by which the latter may be led to support the constitutional rights of the former, without being too much detached from the rights of its own department?

If the principles on which these observations are founded be just, as I persuade myself they are, and they be applied as a criterion to the several State constitutions, and to the federal Constitution, it will be found that if the latter does not perfectly correspond with them, the former are infinitely less able to bear such a test.

There are, moreover, two considerations particularly applicable to the federal system of America, which place that system in a very interesting point of view.

First. In a single republic, all the power surrendered by the people is submitted to the administration of a single government; and the usurpations are guarded against by a division of the government into distinct and separate departments. In the compound republic of America, the power surrendered by the people is first divided between two distinct governments, and then the portion allotted to each subdivided among distinct and separate departments. Hence a double security arises to the rights of the people. The different governments will control each other, at the same time that each will be controlled by itself.

Second. It is of great importance in a republic not only to guard the society against the oppression of its rulers, but to guard one part of the society against the injustice of the other part. Different interests necessarily exist in different classes of citizens. If a majority be united by a common interest, the rights of the minority will be insecure. There are but two methods of providing against this evil: the one by creating a will in the community independent of the majority—that is, of the society itself; the other, by comprehending in the society so many separate descriptions of citizens as will render an unjust combination of a majority of the whole very improbable, if not impracticable. The first method prevails in all governments possessing an hereditary or self-appointed authority. This, at best, is but a precarious security; because a power independent of the society may as well espouse the unjust views of the major, as the rightful interests of the minor party, and may possibly be turned against both parties. The second method will be exemplified in the federal republic of the United States. Whilst all authority in it will be derived

from and dependent on the society, the society itself will be broken into so many parts, interests and classes of citizens, that the rights of individuals, or of the minority, will be in little danger from interested combinations of the majority. In a free government the security for civil rights must be the same as that for religious rights. It consists in the one case in the multiplicity of interests, and in the other in the multiplicity of sects. The degree of security in both cases will depend on the number of interests and sects; and this may be presumed to depend on the extent of country and number of people comprehended under the same government. This view of the subject must particularly recommend a proper federal system to all the sincere and considerate friends of republican government, since it shows that in exact proportion as the territory of the Union may be formed into more circumscribed Confederacies, or States, oppressive combinations of a majority will be facilitated; the best security, under the republican forms, for the rights of every class of citizens, will be diminished; and consequently the stability and independence of some member of the government, the only other security, must be proportionally increased. Justice is the end of government. It is the end of civil society. It ever has been and ever will be pursued until it be obtained, or until liberty be lost in the pursuit. In a society under the forms of which the stronger faction can readily unite and oppress the weaker, anarchy may as truly be said to reign as in a state of nature, where the weaker individual is not secured against the violence of the stronger; and as, in the latter state, even the stronger individuals are prompted, by the uncertainty of their condition, to submit to a government which may protect the weak as well as themselves; so, in the former state, will the more powerful factions or parties be gradually induced, by a like motive, to wish for a government which will protect all parties, the weaker as well as the more powerful. It can be little doubted that if the State of Rhode Island was separated from the Confederacy and left to itself, the insecurity of rights under the popular form of government within such narrow limits would be displayed by such reiterated oppressions of factious majorities that some power altogether independent of the people would soon be called for by the voice of the very factions whose misrule had proved the necessity of it. In the extended republic of the United States, and among the great variety of interests, parties, and sects which it embraces, a coalition of a majority of the whole society could seldom take place on any other principles than those of justice and the general good; whilst there being thus less danger to a minor from the will of a major party, there must be less pretext, also, to provide for the security of the former, by introducing into the government a will not dependent on the latter, or, in other words, a will independent of the society itself. It is no less certain than it is important, notwithstanding the contrary opinions which have been entertained, that the larger the society, provided it lie within a particular sphere, the more duly capable it will be of self-government. And happily for the *republican cause,* the practicable sphere may be carried to a very great extent, by a judicious modification and mixture of the *federal principle.*

PUBLIUS

Federalist No. 51, from *The Federalist Papers,* 1787.

The Way We Live Now

America the Untethered

DAVID RIEFF

National holidays, like the Olympics or the World Cup, are times when national differences inevitably take center stage. It would be as unreasonable to expect a French person to care deeply about the Fourth of July celebration in the United States as it would be to expect an American to be stirred by the annual 14th of July military parade down the Champs-Élysées in Paris. Another way of putting this is to say that for all the loose talk about America's exceptional place in the world—talk that tends to be positive at home and increasingly negative abroad—every nation, not just the United States, considers itself exceptional to some extent.

"America Against the World," a recent book based on comprehensive polling data from the Pew Research Center's Global Attitudes Project, makes the point that our exceptionalism is not exceptional with particular force. While a robust 60 percent of Americans agree with the proposition that "our culture is superior to others," such self-confidence pales next to that of South Korea and Indonesia, where some 90 percent of the population assents to the idea. The book's authors, Andrew Kohut and Bruce Stokes, also note that "poll after poll finds the Japanese to be the most pessimistic of people, expressing far less satisfaction with their lot in life than might be expected given their relatively high per capita incomes. Yet, compared to other Asians, the Japanese are, like Americans, highly self-reliant and distrustful of government and, like Europeans, secular. It is the Japanese public, not the American public, that is most exceptional in the world."

And yet even if America is not more anomalous than a number of other countries, our anomalies are what make the difference in contemporary global affairs. Ever since the time of Tocqueville, observers have commented on various peculiar characteristics of the American people: their belief in the power of the will, their suspicion of government, their conviction in their own benevolence. Of course, some facets of American exceptionalism are more recent in origin. For example, our particular focus on terrorism has everything to do with the entirely warranted sense of vulnerability that we all felt after 9/11. But the Pew surveys make clear that there's much more to America's exceptionalism than that. For example, while people in most of the world look to government to solve their problems,

Americans do not. They are strongly attached to their belief in individual responsibility and unwilling to hold "outside factors" responsible for failure in life. Indeed, the American commitment to such beliefs appears to be becoming stronger with time. In this respect, at least, we are becoming more different.

Does all of this make American exceptionalism a vital national resource or a serious problem, both for the world as a whole and for the United States in particular? However appealing our individualism and positive thinking may be, such traits easily translate in the global context into hubris and a refusal to cooperate with others—in other words, into unilateralism. Americans may cherish in themselves what, in the military, is called the "hoo-ah" spirit—an optimistic mind-set that, as Kohut and Stokes put it, fosters the belief that "technology, and Americans, can fix anything." But in our soberer, less celebratory moments, we know that there are no unilateral American solutions to multilateral problems and that most of the great challenges we face in today's world are multilateral—from terrorism to global warming, and AIDS to mass migration. In the streets of Baghdad and the deserts of Al Anbar, we have learned that optimism and self-reliance are simply not enough. In fairness, recent efforts by critics to lay our hubris at the Bush administration's door fall wide of the mark. Our particular sense of national entitlement, of being specially chosen, is a bipartisan affair. After all, it was Madeleine Albright who, while serving as Bill Clinton's secretary of state, declared the United States to be "the indispensable nation."

Obviously, the United States will remain strong enough to exercise considerable power for the foreseeable future. In the medium term, however, an America that does not understand—and makes little effort to understand—why it has become so unpopular abroad is almost certain to find itself both disliked and ineffective in many parts of the world. Indeed, just last month, the Pew Global Attitudes Project issued a new survey showing that anti-Americanism, which seemed to be in decline a year ago, is again on the rise. By 41 percent to 34 percent, a plurality of Britons believe that the U.S. military presence in Iraq is a greater danger to world peace than the government of Iran—this in Tony Blair's Britain, supposedly America's staunchest ally. The Bush administration clearly realizes that such findings are not good news and has greatly toned down its earlier unilateralist swagger.

Of course, if unilateralism is a dead end, multilateralism is no panacea—as the current impasse with Iran demonstrates. But we have to start somewhere. Simply to repeat that we live in a post-9/11 world, while the Europeans have not yet heard the bad news—in other words, waiting for our allies to come around to seeing things as we do in the United States—is unlikely to do anything but aggravate the differences that already exist.

Even during the cold war, when America was a creditor nation and its allies largely accepted their subaltern status, the United States needed the assent of its global partners. Unilateralism is still less of an option today—something we should not lose sight of on even that most "unilateralist" of holidays, the Fourth of July.

DAVID RIEFF, a contributing writer, last wrote for the magazine about Mexico's presidential race.

How Big Government Got Its Groove Back

The New Democrats' intellectual architect argues that today's economy requires an expanded role for government.

WILLIAM A. GALSTON

I n 1996, President Bill Clinton proclaimed that the era of big government was over. It is now clear that the era of the end of big government is over.

The post–World War II social contract—an expanding public safety net, provision of health care and retirement benefits through a substantially unionized private sector, and robust personal savings—is under severe stress. To respond effectively to our long-term challenges, the federal government must command an increased share of gross domestic product and extend its reach in other ways as well. The public sector will be called upon to provide new forms of insurance against economic risks and volatility and to assume more responsibility for health insurance and retirement security. To the extent that markets cannot police themselves or provide reasonable returns for workers, government will have to step in. Through the public mobilization of capital and will, we must supply the public goods—investment in infrastructure, research, and post-secondary education, among others—that we have neglected at our peril. And many millions of Americans will be unable to save for the future without new forms of public encouragement and support.

As well, we will have to construct a new legal and institutional framework that counters the increasing asymmetries of bargaining power that employees in most occupations now experience. While the right to organize and bargain collectively must be aggressively enforced, the kind of union movement that dominated the field from the 1930s through the 1960s may not be adequate for the 21st century. To the extent that it is not, we will need something to supplement it, such as new legal protections for individual workers. For without effective countervailing power, employees will not be able to negotiate for a reasonable share of productivity gains, median wages and earnings will grow slowly, if at all, and the fortunate few at the top will continue to commandeer the fruits of economic growth. At the same time, the private sector will have to do its part to help finance programs for which the public sector assumes increased responsibility. And individuals will have to shoulder more responsibility, in proportion to their means, for their savings and security.

In short, we need nothing less than a new social contract that reorganizes responsibilities among government, individuals, and the private sector. It will take time, experimentation, and political contestation to hammer out its terms.

This would never have been easy, and it is especially challenging now. With large short-term and long-term deficits looming, clearing fiscal space for new initiatives will be difficult at best. And while the public is demanding change, the current administration's woeful performance since 2002 has reduced public trust and confidence in government's ability to produce change.

The alternative to a new social contract is no contract—a society in which the strong take what they can and the weak endure what they must.

But however difficult it may be, we must begin the task of reconciling basic moral commitments with stubborn new realities. The alternative to a new contract is *no* contract—a society in which the strong take what they can and the weak endure what they must.

F rom June 1982 until November 1984, I served as issues director for Walter Mondale's presidential campaign. The failure of that honorable venture—the last campaign of the New Deal era—propelled me and many others into a period of rethinking that lasted through the remainder of the 1980s and into the early 1990s. We came to believe that the Democratic Party's economic program and governance philosophy reflected an industrial era that was giving way to new modes of production and new technological sources of economic growth. We believed, as well, that the party had come to be viewed as fiscally unreliable and as fixated on redistribution at the expense of broad-based economic growth. These propositions helped shape the economic outlook of the New Democratic movement and the platform on which Bill Clinton ran successfully for president in 1992. And after a slow and controversial start, they contributed to the robust, widely shared growth of the mid- and late 1990s.

At the peak of the Clinton boom a decade ago, optimistic beliefs dominated the landscape. With a regime of more open trade, the United States could compete effectively in the post–Cold War global economy. The market would not only generate wealth but also regulate itself with declining government oversight. Government would become more market-like, substituting incentives and technology-based efficiency for obsolescent command-and-control strategies.

There was evidence to support these beliefs. As productivity surged, wages increased across the board, as did labor force participation. Unemployment fell to record lows, and manufacturing jobs held their own. Inflation remained low and actually fell in the health-care sector. Although the personal-savings rate continued its decades-long decline, the steady increase in housing prices enabled families to build their net worth. Fiscal restraint turned deficits into surpluses, shrank the federal government's share of GDP, and stabilized the value of the dollar in international markets.

From today's vantage point, however, the 1990s appear to have been the proverbial calm before the storm. Although the Bush administration's misguided fiscal and foreign policies have worsened our plight, our problems are structural and long-term, and no simple return to the status-quo ante will resolve them. Most analysts and policy-makers underestimated the impact of huge numbers of new workers in China, India, and the former Soviet Union entering the global market system. International economic forces are limiting wages for most U.S. workers, increasing income inequality, and heightening pressure on the World War II–era system of benefits provided through the private sector. In these circumstances, average families have resorted to record levels of borrowing to maintain purchasing power, driving the savings rate into negative territory for the first time on record and raising personal consumption to an unsustainable 70 percent of GDP. The Bush administration has squandered the resources it could have used to ease the reform of the large entitlement programs. And the back-loaded costs of deregulation are now clear: among them, an epidemic of corporate misconduct and crisis in credit markets, here and abroad.

I t is easy to dismiss all this as the latest iteration of the gloom-and-doom narrative that every economic down-cycle generates. But there is evidence that our difficulties are more than cyclical.

Compensation. Recent work by MIT economists Frank Levy and Peter Temin shows that a wedge has been driven between productivity gains and compensation (wages plus health care and fringe benefits) for full-time workers at peak earning age. Since 1980, productivity has increased by 71 percent while median compensation rose by only 19 percent, and 82 percent of personal income gains went to the top 1 percent of the population.

In recent years, these trends have actually worsened. Since 2000, labor productivity has grown by 16 percent, but the median weekly compensation of male high school graduates has declined slightly. To be sure, education matters more than it used to: The difference in median weekly wages of college and high school graduates has just about doubled since 1980. One reason is that the supply of highly educated workers has not kept pace with technological advances. As Claudia Goldin and Lawrence Katz, two economists at Harvard, have recently shown, gains in educational attainment for workers born in 1975 are only one quarter as great as for workers born in 1945. According to David Ellwood at the Kennedy School, if current trends continue, college graduates will constitute only a slightly higher percentage of the work force in 2025 than they do today. The share of male college graduates may actually decline.

But recently, not even a college education is allowing workers to keep up with productivity. Since 2000, compensation for college graduates without further training has grown by only 3 percent. Only men with post-graduate education have managed to keep up with productivity growth. While women have done slightly better, two thirds of them have lagged behind productivity growth, too.

Between 1950 and the early 1980s, median family income rose more rapidly than did incomes at the very top. After sharply rising inequality during the Ronald Reagan and George H.W. Bush presidencies, this trend was briefly interrupted during 1995–2000, when incomes in every quintile rose at roughly the same rate. Since then, all the gains have gone to the top 1 percent of earners. This explains why 2002–2007 is likely to prove the only economic cycle on record in which median family incomes failed to reach, let alone exceed, their peak in the previous cycle.

Below the very top, all income groups have experienced a decline in median incomes during the current economic cycle: 2 percent for the top third, 3 percent for the middle, and 5 percent for the bottom. During this period, however, real median family expenditures have risen across the board. Debt has filled the gap. After rising only slightly faster than the overall economy during the 1990s, household borrowing has soared since 2000 and now totals almost $14 trillion—about 98 percent of GDP, up from 69 percent just seven years ago. Debt service has risen from 11 percent of disposable income in 1994 to more than 14 percent today.

Mortgage debt accounts for most of this increase. While housing prices were rising rapidly, homeowners withdrew hundreds of billions of dollars in home equity to finance current consumption. As housing prices have reversed course, families can no longer use their homes as piggy banks, depressing purchasing power and boosting bankruptcy and foreclosure rates.

Analysts have long debated whether these economic trends are "hollowing out" the middle class. Evidence is accumulating that they are. Between 1970 and 2006, the share of adults living in the middle-income tier declined from 40 percent to 35 percent, while both upper- and lower-income tiers increased.

The shrinking of the middle class was especially pronounced among adults aged 18 to 29—from 45 percent to 37 percent—and among 30- to 44-year-olds—47 percent to 38 percent. Only retirees became more likely to live in the middle class.

Private-sector benefits. The private sector is struggling with two safety-net issues—pensions and health care. After World War II, defined-benefit plans ("pensions"), under which firms assumed the responsibility and risk of providing guaranteed retirement incomes to workers, spread rapidly. They reached their peak in the late 1970s, when 62 percent of workers were covered solely by such plans. Today, that figure is down to only 10 percent. In place of pensions, most workers now have defined-contribution plans in which they, rather than their firms directly, face the risks of future economic performance. Many workers withdraw funds from these plans when they change jobs, jeopardizing their retirement security.

Private-sector employers are retreating from employee health insurance as well. Of companies with more than 200 workers, 66 percent had retiree health-care plans in 1988, versus only 33 percent today. In 2000, 69 percent of employers offered coverage to their workers; in 2003, 65 percent; by 2006, that figure had fallen to only 61 percent.

Annual health-care premiums have increased by 87 percent during this decade, more than four times as fast as workers' earnings. The share of earnings consumed by premiums has risen accordingly, pricing many workers out of the market. As a result, although the economy has 4 million more jobs today than in 2000, the number of workers with company-sponsored plans has not increased, and the share covered under such plans has fallen from 64.2 percent to 59.7 percent. Although health coverage under public low-income programs rose from 10.6 percent to 12.9 percent of the population between 2000 and 2006, this was not enough to counterbalance reductions in the private sector. As a result, the number of uninsured rose from 38.4 million to 47 million—from 13.7 percent to 15.8 percent of the total. There is no precedent for such trends during periods of economic recovery and growth.

In recent years, health insurance has been recognized as an issue of economic competitiveness as well as social policy. In 2005, for example, Toyota chose to locate its newest assembly plant in Ontario, Canada, rather than in Alabama. The firm's management cited two reasons: the lower quality of the U.S. work force, and the competitive disadvantage of raising the price of every car to cover employee health care. In areas of our economy subject to international competition, our World War II–era model of employer-provided health insurance—a global outlier—is unlikely to remain viable.

Manufacturing. The past decade has been one of the worst on record for U.S. manufacturing. After three decades of relative stability, manufacturing employment began a slow decline in 1998 that accelerated into a rout in 2001. Nearly 4 million jobs have disappeared, and manufacturing's share of total employment has declined by three percentage points.

It is customary, and not entirely wrong, to point to productivity gains as the principal culprit. Manufacturing investment in research and development accounts for more than half of all U.S. research and development, and it has paid off. Over the past three decades, manufacturing productivity has risen more than 3 percent per year, compared to only 2 percent per year for the rest of the economy. This helps explain how the sector can produce more than 12 percent of the economy's total output with only 10 percent of the work force.

And this trend is accelerating. After growing by 2.7 percent per year from 1977 to 1992, manufacturing productivity grew by 4.7 percent yearly during the past 15 years. In 2002 alone, it rose by 10.6 percent, the largest year-over-year increase ever recorded, followed by two years of 6 percent growth.

The other half of the story is a slowdown in manufacturing output. During the 1991–2000 economic cycle, output just about kept pace with productivity, rising at 4.2 percent per year. In the most recent 2001–2007 cycle, however, output rose only a third as fast, 1.4 percent annually, far behind productivity gains. Massive job loss was the inevitable result. A Congressional Budget Office analysis concludes that for manufacturing, the period since 2001 is more like the severe double-dip recession of the late 1970s and early 1980s than the relatively mild recession of the early 1990s.

U.S. manufacturing is so productive that its jobs offer higher pay and better benefits. An analysis by Robert Scott at the Economic Policy Institute shows that manufacturing workers without a college degree enjoy a 9 percent wage premium over similar workers in other sectors. All other things equal, then, the recent massive job loss in manufacturing has exerted downward pressure on wages. On average, noncollege manufacturing workers who lose jobs paying $16.49 per hour will exchange them for jobs paying only $15.10, and fewer of the replacement jobs will offer affordable health insurance.

While these facts explain the tenor of the 2008 presidential campaign throughout the deindustrializing Midwest, they do not prove that outsourcing and trade are to blame for our manufacturing woes. In fact, the bulk of U.S. overseas investment is in other high-income countries, all of which have more robust regimes of worker protection than we do. And recent studies suggest that this investment generates more—not less—employment in the United States. Productivity increases are driven by technological advances and increased global competition from both high-income countries and from nations, such as China and India, whose low-wage structure exerts downward pressure on the wages of lower-skilled U.S. workers.

While it is tempting to try to insulate ourselves from these forces, that course would prove counterproductive and futile. Instead, we should use public policy to spread the gains of economic growth, create equal opportunity for all, and insure workers against wage and income losses against which they cannot protect themselves.

Rebuilding the social contract is our key domestic challenge during the next generation. While some of its elements will require trial and error, others are tolerably clear.

First, as employer-provided benefits continue to shrink, we will need to create means-tested, market-based alternatives. Some version of the Massachusetts model represents the next step in health insurance; some experts believe that it will function as a way-station on the road to a more unified system of public finance. A system matching individual contributions to savings accounts with means-tested employer and public contributions would help defined-contribution retirement plans fill the void created by the disappearance of traditional pensions. Automatically enrolling employees in such plans unless they affirmatively opt out may yield near-universal participation. If not, a mandatory savings program may well be necessary. Workers below a low-income threshold would receive employer and public matches without having to make automatic contributions from wages.

Second, whatever the relation between globalization and wage stagnation may be, it is unrealistic and unfair to expect workers to tolerate a situation in which they bear the costs of economic change while receiving none of the benefits of economic growth. At the very least, we can index the minimum wage to inflation and expand the Earned Income Tax Credit to cover single workers. And we should create an actuarially sound insurance system—financed by a modest increase in the payroll tax—that would compensate workers for abrupt downward lurches in wages.

Third, we cannot rebuild U.S. manufacturing on the basis of 20th-century industries. Steel mills and automobile plants will never again provide expanding employment opportunities. This does not mean that employment in the sector is fated to continue its decline. One piece of the answer is to focus on the bottlenecks that are harming our economy and society. This means investing much more in 21st-century infrastructure—not only roads and bridges but also airports and light rail. In addition, we should encourage the development of technologies in areas, such as alternative energy and environmental protection, for which there is growing demand, at home and abroad.

And fourth, despite clear market signals that post-secondary education and training are essential, too many young adults are not getting the message. Lower-income students from families without a history of college education are unwilling to incur debt, in part because they do not yet believe in the promised returns on education, and in part because they doubt their capacity to repay loans. This is a market failure that hurts the country as well as the individuals who underinvest in their future. The

public sector should follow the lead of a handful of elite private universities, which have begun to make higher education free for working- and middle-class students. This would require means-tested higher education grants that would allow students below a certain income threshold to attend public universities and community colleges and emerge debt-free.

There is no way to build a 21st-century social contract without increasing the size of the federal government well beyond the one-fifth share of GDP it has averaged in recent decades.

There is no way to build a 21st-century social contract without increasing the size of the federal government well beyond the roughly one-fifth share of GDP that it has averaged in recent decades. At the same time, we cannot expand government indefinitely without reducing long-term economic growth. If we make no policy changes, government will command more than 26 percent of GDP by 2030. If we simply put the programs I have recommended on top of the existing baseline, that figure would increase still more.

This leads to a controversial point, with which I conclude. To be sustainable and pro-growth, we will need a new approach toward the large entitlement programs—especially Medicare and Medicaid—that drive so much of the long-term increase in the federal budget. While universal health insurance would give us a fighting chance to restrain the rate of growth in medical costs, we will probably have to go further. One possibility would be to change our budget procedures. We could establish long-term budgets for public health-care programs and require Congress to close the gap between projections and actual results by either raising revenues or reducing benefits. But whatever we do in this area, we will have to rethink the comfortable assumption that a 21st-century social contract can simply add a new wing to the existing edifice.

WILLIAM A. GALSTON is a senior fellow in governance studies at the Brookings Institution.

The Changing Face of Poverty in America

Why Are So Many Women, Children, Racial and Cultural Minorities Still Poor?

WILLIAM E. SPRIGGS

"Water, water everywhere, nor any drop to drink."
—Samuel Taylor Coleridge,
The Rime of the Ancient Mariner

In 1960 American workers produced a gross domestic product of $13,847 (in year 2000 dollars) for every man, woman, and child in the country. By 1969, GDP per capita rose to $18,578. In that period, the poverty rate for American children dropped almost by half, from 26.5 percent to 13.8 percent. The most recent data, for 2005, show child poverty has risen again, to 17.1 percent, while the GDP per capita stood at $37,246, roughly double the value in 1969. How did the nation become twice as wealthy but its children become poorer?

In 2000, the number of poor Americans reached an 11-year low at 31.6 million, and the poverty rate stood at a 26-year low at 11.3 percent. While the nation again became richer after the post-2001 recovery, more than 5 million Americans fell into poverty, and the latest figures put the number of poor Americans at 36.9 million people.

To put a face on American poverty, it is important to first put that poverty in context—to understand not just who is poor today but to examine how poverty changes over time. With that perspective, we can appreciate that in a nation as wealthy as the United States, poverty is not intractable.

"The federal government declared war on poverty, and poverty won."
—Ronald Reagan

That line from President Reagan's 1988 State of the Union address, was used to ridicule Lyndon Johnson's efforts to fight poverty. President Johnson launched that fight in March 1964, submitting the Economic Opportunity Act to Congress and saying these words: "Because it is right, because it is wise, and because, for the first time in our history, it is possible to conquer poverty . . ."

Johnson believed that a wealthy nation produces enough for each individual citizen to live above poverty. This was a question of political and moral will, not an economic constraint. So, he differentiated between the day's global struggle to end poverty in countries like Mali and Haiti, where there was a real economic constraint to be overcome, and the situation in America, a land that was not poor in resources but that lacked moral conviction. The Johnson legacy shows a path of poverty for black children, a primary beneficiary of LBJ's programs. In 1965, almost 66 percent of black children lived below the poverty line. In four short years, that share was cut to 39.6 percent, a tremendous accomplishment. By contrast, the Reagan legacy shows a path of poverty for black children from 1981 to 1989, the era of Reagan and George Bush Senior. In 1980, 42.1 percent of black children lived below the poverty line; and by 1988 that share had risen to 42.8 percent. Yes, poverty won.

How Policy Influences Poverty

The face of poverty in America is the result of policy choices, of political will, and of moral conviction—or its absence. The incidence of poverty is heavily concentrated in the United States across the South and the Southwest. The legacy of slavery is part of that story. Forty percent of America's poor live in the South. Four of today's five poorest states were ones that existed in the old Confederacy. Of the onetime Confederate states, only two—Florida and Virginia—do not rank in the current 20 states with the highest poverty levels.

Why do some people lack the income to rise above poverty? For many, the reason is that they do not work; for others, the reason is that they work but do not earn enough money. Nonworkers include the elderly, the disabled, and children, as well as the unemployed. And public policy treats different groups differently.

The Social Security old-age program insures virtually all retired workers against the risk of outliving their savings. The old-age benefit formula is tied to the rising productivity of current workers, indexing the benefits to the average national wage. The shared risk, and the insured shared prosperity, explain why the poverty rate for those over 65 has declined from more than 28 percent in 1966 (nearly double the national poverty rate of 14.7 percent) to 10.1 percent today (below the national rate of 12.6 percent). In 1974, the poverty rate for the Census category of white non-Hispanic seniors, at 12.5 percent, was double the poverty rate for working-age (18–64) white non-Hispanics, at 5.9 percent. Today, the poverty rate for the two age groups is virtually equal, at 7.9 percent for seniors and 7.8 percent for working-age white non-Hispanics.

Another group of people who do not work, by law, are children. But their income is derived mostly from their parents. The rise in child poverty, therefore, reflects the rise in the inequality of their parents' earnings. So, while 9.8 percent of the poor are seniors, 33.5 percent of the poor are children. Children make up a much higher share of the poor among blacks (41.9 percent of poor blacks) and Hispanics (42.6 percent of poor Hispanics) than among whites (24.5 percent of poor whites). And while the poverty rate of seniors has shown a steady trend downward as national income has risen, child poverty rates are as intractable as the growing inequality in working families' earnings.

The wide divergence in how public policy treats different groups was not Congress' original intent. The Social Security Act of 1935 sought to protect the incomes of those who did not work because of age or a poor economy by establishing a federal framework for unemployment insurance, old-age benefits, and assistance to women with dependent children. In 1939, the old-age benefit structure was fully federalized to produce consistent benefits. But, Aid to Families with Dependent Children (AFDC) and the unemployment-insurance system were put in state hands. And in the 1990s, AFDC was transformed from its Social Security Act roots into a state block grant. The mostly state-run unemployment-insurance system, meanwhile, is strained by the transformation of the economy from one in which workers could expect to be laid off in recessions and then rehired into one based on the structural creation and destruction of whole industries and occupations.

Children in our antipoverty system are oddly split. Today, more children receive a check from the Old Age, Survivors and Disability Insurance (OASDI) Program than are helped by the new Temporary Assistance for Needy Families (TANF) program that replaced AFDC. Some children, therefore, enjoy their parents' protection against the loss of income from disability, untimely death, or old age, and receive benefits that are based on the same formula used for the old-age benefit. Low-income black children are especially helped by the disability benefits their parents receive, or by the survivor benefits that the child receives—because the benefit formula is national and intended to alleviate poverty.

By contrast, children receiving TANF aid are subject to the whim of their state. In 2004, a widowed mother and two children, on average, received a monthly OASDI survivors' benefit of $1,952. Those two children would live above the federal poverty line. The TANF benefit for the same family, however, could range from $170 a month in Mississippi to $215 in Alabama to $240 in Louisiana to $625 in New Hampshire, leaving children in all of those states far below the poverty line. Adjusting for inflation, the survivors' benefit has been increasing since 1970, while the average benefit under AFDC (and now TANF) has been falling. While the OASDI benefit level is set by a federal formula, policy-makers in states with higher shares of black TANF recipients choose lower benefit levels.

Like TANF recipients, unemployed workers are also at the mercy of their state; the average weekly benefit can range from $179 a week in Mississippi to $320 in New Jersey. In the 1950s, close to half of the nation's unemployed workers received benefits; today, only about 35 percent do. This varies widely by state, from 21 percent in Wyoming to 24 percent in Texas to 58 percent in Pennsylvania to 71 percent in New Jersey. And the percentage of earned income replaced by unemployment benefits has steadily fallen as well.

Diligent and Still Poor

An ongoing topic of debate is the relationship of child poverty and parents' income to the increase in single-parent households. Other things being equal, two parents in a household usually earn more than one, but they are not assured of earning their family's way out of poverty. Hispanic and black children have roughly similar levels of poverty—33.2 percent for black children, and 27.7 percent for Hispanic children. Yet 41 percent of black families with children are married, whereas 68 percent of Hispanic families with children are married. In 1974, when the poverty rate among black children was at 39.6 percent, 56 percent of black families with children were married. Two-income families today are less likely to be poor, but much is at work besides family structure.

To be poor is to lack income, so the core issue is earnings. In 1962, on the eve of the March on Washington for Jobs and Justice in 1963, the median income of black men was below the poverty threshold for a family of three, but by 1967 it was above that level (not until 1995 did it get above the poverty level for a family of four). Because of the rise in the earnings of black women, poverty among black children fell in the 1990s, just as the rise in the earnings of black men helped lower black children's poverty level in the 1960s. By 1997, the median income of black women rose above the poverty level for a family of three.

Among the poor, 11.4 percent work full time, year-round. These 2.9 million Americans are directly hurt by minimum-wage laws that have lagged behind costs of living. This problem is especially acute for Asians and Hispanics, where 18 percent of the working poor worked full time, year-round.

Recent immigrants who are not citizens have a poverty rate of 20.4 percent. Like all groups, noncitizen immigrants had falling poverty rates in the 1990s as the labor market expanded: Their poverty rate fell from 28.7 percent in 1993 to a low of 19.2 percent in 2000. Then, following the national trend, their poverty rate started to climb. During the Reagan administration, the United States suffered its highest national unemployment rates since the Great Depression. In the black community, the effects were devastating: The unemployment rate for adult (over age 20) black men peaked at more than 20 percent in December 1982; during the entire Reagan presidency, the unemployment rate for adult black men remained in double digits. The highest recorded unemployment rate for adult white men was 9 percent in November and December 1982. But for black men, the unemployment rate remained above that mark for 182 straight months (15 years), from October 1979 to November 1994. Because children do not work and need working adults to support them, it is hardly surprising that during that period, black child poverty rates remained intractable above 40 percent.

Poverty for women is disproportionately higher than for men, 14.1 percent compared to 11.1 (in 2005), primarily because of higher rates of poverty among female-headed households, gaps in poverty for the elderly (7.3 percent for men over age 65 compared to 12.3 percent for women in 2005), and for single women (24.1 percent) compared to single men (17.9 percent) living alone. The gap reflects persistent gaps in earnings between men and women, though that gap is falling. White non-Hispanic men, age 25 and over, with a high-school diploma have a median income of $35,679, while women, age 25 and over, need a college degree to have a similar median income ($36,532 in 2005). And, while the median income of white males has been above the poverty line for a family of five since 1959, the median income for women only broke above the poverty line for a family of three in 1990. The persistent gap is best reflected in differences in poverty among the elderly, where the life-long earnings of women mean they have lower assets in Social Security benefits than do men, despite the progressive structure of the benefit formula. The gap among the elderly also reflects issues of access to jobs with pensions for women.

Women who are the single head of household face the extra burden of earning enough to raise dependent children out of poverty. This risk a woman faces of helping non-working dependents is not shared by society, as would be a woman's efforts to care for her elderly parents. The result is that female-headed households, harmed by the significant earnings gap between men and women, have a poverty rate of 31.1 percent compared to male-headed households (with no wife present) of 13.6 percent, while the overall poverty rate for families is 10.8 percent.

Full Employment and Its Limits

It took the presidency of Bill Clinton, with its expansive labor market and increases in the minimum wage and the Earned Income Tax Credit, to dramatically improve the incomes of poor and minority families. As job creation reached a record pace,

the unemployment rate for black men plummeted, reaching a recorded low of 6 percent in March 1999. With work comes income, and poverty for black families fell. This history suggests something about the proper way to view responsibility and poor people as agents in their own fate: Usually they are not victims of themselves, but of bad economic policies and barriers to opportunity.

Under Reagan, who ridiculed antipoverty efforts, the number of black children living below the poverty line increased by 200,000, from 3.9 million in 1980 to 4.1 million in 1988. During the Clinton years, the black child poverty rate fell steadily, from 46.3 percent to a record-low 30 percent, lifting about 1.6 million black children out of poverty. For all children, the poverty rate fell annually during Clinton's presidency, reaching a 30-year low of 15.6 percent when he left office. But those reduced poverty rates may be the best we can achieve simply by getting jobs for parents. While lower than during the Reagan years, they do not equal the lows America has achieved for its senior citizens, or the general population. And those gains reversed course when George W. Bush became president.

Because of record job creation in the 1990s, the number of people who worked and were poor declined from 10.1 million in 1993 to 8.5 million by 2000; greatly increased working hours and higher wages meant higher incomes. But during the current expansion, a record 48 months was required to get payroll employment back to the level preceding the employment downturn that began in late 2000, a lag not matched since Herbert Hoover. So while full employment is necessary to alleviate poverty, it is far from sufficient.

In short, America knows how to address poverty. Its great success in lowering the poverty level of those over 65 has changed the face of poverty. But for those subject to the whims of state differences and the correlation of race with state policies to address poverty, there have been great intractable issues that have left the face of poverty disproportionately young, black, Hispanic, and female. Growing inequality in the labor market, moreover, has increased the share of the poor who are of working age, and stagnant federal minimum-wage laws have increased the oxymoron of full-time, year-round working poor people.

In a nation with a per capita GDP above the poverty line for a family of four, it is appalling that almost 3 million people work full time, year-round and are poor, and that more than 12 million American children are living in poverty. Lyndon Johnson proposed to fight poverty "because it is right, because it is wise." In a land of vast wealth, twice as rich as America in the 1960s, can today's leaders rise to the occasion?

WILLIAM E. SPRIGGS chairs the Department of Economics at Howard University. He is a senior fellow at the Economic Policy Institute and former executive director of the National Urban League Institute for Opportunity and Equality.

The Climate for Change

AL GORE

The inspiring and transformative choice by the American people to elect Barack Obama as our 44th president lays the foundation for another fateful choice that he—and we—must make this January to begin an emergency rescue of human civilization from the imminent and rapidly growing threat posed by the climate crisis.

The electrifying redemption of America's revolutionary declaration that all human beings are born equal sets the stage for the renewal of United States leadership in a world that desperately needs to protect its primary endowment: the integrity and livability of the planet.

The world authority on the climate crisis, the Intergovernmental Panel on Climate Change, after 20 years of detailed study and four unanimous reports, now says that the evidence is "unequivocal." To those who are still tempted to dismiss the increasingly urgent alarms from scientists around the world, ignore the melting of the north polar ice cap and all of the other apocalyptic warnings from the planet itself, and who roll their eyes at the very mention of this existential threat to the future of the human species, please wake up. Our children and grandchildren need you to hear and recognize the truth of our situation, before it is too late.

Here is the good news: the bold steps that are needed to solve the climate crisis are exactly the same steps that ought to be taken in order to solve the economic crisis and the energy security crisis.

Economists across the spectrum—including Martin Feldstein and Lawrence Summers—agree that large and rapid investments in a jobs-intensive infrastructure initiative is the best way to revive our economy in a quick and sustainable way. Many also agree that our economy will fall behind if we continue spending hundreds of billions of dollars on foreign oil every year. Moreover, national security experts in both parties agree that we face a dangerous strategic vulnerability if the world suddenly loses access to Middle Eastern oil.

As Abraham Lincoln said during America's darkest hour, "The occasion is piled high with difficulty, and we must rise with the occasion. As our case is new, so we must think anew, and act anew." In our present case, thinking anew requires discarding an outdated and fatally flawed definition of the problem we face.

Thirty-five years ago this past week, President Richard Nixon created Project Independence, which set a national goal that, within seven years, the United States would develop "the potential to meet our own energy needs without depending on any foreign energy sources." His statement came three weeks after the Arab oil embargo had sent prices skyrocketing and woke America to the dangers of dependence on foreign oil. And—not coincidentally—it came only three years after United States domestic oil production had peaked.

At the time, the United States imported less than a third of its oil from foreign countries. Yet today, after all six of the presidents succeeding Nixon repeated some version of his goal, our dependence has doubled from one-third to nearly two-thirds—and many feel that global oil production is at or near its peak.

Some still see this as a problem of domestic production. If we could only increase oil and coal production at home, they argue, then we wouldn't have to rely on imports from the Middle East. Some have come up with even dirtier and more expensive new ways to extract the same old fuels, like coal liquids, oil shale, tar sands and "clean coal" technology.

But in every case, the resources in question are much too expensive or polluting, or, in the case of "clean coal," too imaginary to make a difference in protecting either our national security or the global climate. Indeed, those who spend hundreds of millions promoting "clean coal" technology consistently omit the fact that there is little investment and not a single large-scale demonstration project in the United States for capturing and safely burying all of this pollution. If the coal industry can make good on this promise, then I'm all for it. But until that day comes, we simply cannot any longer base the strategy for human survival on a cynical and self-interested illusion.

Here's what we can do—now: we can make an immediate and large strategic investment to put people to work replacing 19th-century energy technologies that depend on dangerous and expensive carbon-based fuels with 21st-century technologies that use fuel that is free forever: the sun, the wind and the natural heat of the earth.

What follows is a five-part plan to repower America with a commitment to producing 100 percent of our electricity from carbon-free sources within 10 years. It is a plan that would simultaneously move us toward solutions to the climate crisis and the economic crisis—and create millions of new jobs that cannot be outsourced.

First, the new president and the new Congress should offer large-scale investment in incentives for the construction of concentrated solar thermal plants in the Southwestern deserts, wind farms in the corridor stretching from Texas to the Dakotas and advanced plants in geothermal hot spots that could produce large amounts of electricity.

Second, we should begin the planning and construction of a unified national smart grid for the transport of renewable electricity from the rural places where it is mostly generated to the cities where it is mostly used. New high-voltage, low-loss underground lines can be designed with "smart" features that provide consumers with sophisticated information and easy-to-use tools for conserving electricity, eliminating inefficiency and reducing their energy bills. The cost of this modern grid—$400 billion over 10 years—pales in comparison with the annual loss to American business of $120 billion due to the cascading failures that are endemic to our current balkanized and antiquated electricity lines.

Third, we should help America's automobile industry (not only the Big Three but the innovative new startup companies as well) to convert quickly to plug-in hybrids that can run on the renewable electricity that will be available as the rest of this plan matures. In combination with the unified grid, a nationwide fleet of plug-in hybrids would also help to solve the problem of electricity storage. Think about it: with this sort of grid, cars could be charged during off-peak energy-use hours; during peak hours, when fewer cars are on the road, they could contribute their electricity back into the national grid.

How we can save the economy and the earth at the same time.

Fourth, we should embark on a nationwide effort to retrofit buildings with better insulation and energy-efficient windows and lighting. Approximately 40 percent of carbon dioxide emissions in the United States come from buildings—and stopping that pollution saves money for homeowners and businesses. This initiative should be coupled with the proposal in Congress to help Americans who are burdened by mortgages that exceed the value of their homes.

Fifth, the United States should lead the way by putting a price on carbon here at home, and by leading the world's efforts to replace the Kyoto treaty next year in Copenhagen with a more effective treaty that caps global carbon dioxide emissions and encourages nations to invest together in efficient ways to reduce global warming pollution quickly, including by sharply reducing deforestation.

Of course, the best way—indeed the only way—to secure a global agreement to safeguard our future is by re-establishing the United States as the country with the moral and political authority to lead the world toward a solution.

Looking ahead, I have great hope that we will have the courage to embrace the changes necessary to save our economy, our planet and ultimately ourselves.

In an earlier transformative era in American history, President John F. Kennedy challenged our nation to land a man on the moon within 10 years. Eight years and two months later, Neil Armstrong set foot on the lunar surface. The average age of the systems engineers cheering on Apollo 11 from the Houston control room that day was 26, which means that their average age when President Kennedy announced the challenge was 18.

This year similarly saw the rise of young Americans, whose enthusiasm electrified Barack Obama's campaign. There is little doubt that this same group of energized youth will play an essential role in this project to secure our national future, once again turning seemingly impossible goals into inspiring success.

AL GORE, the vice president from 1993 to 2001, was the co-recipient of the Nobel Peace Prize in 2007. He founded the Alliance for Climate Protection and, as a businessman, invests in alternative energy companies.

Beyond Hillary

Strength in Numbers

The focus this primary season has been on the ambitions and achievements of one woman, but women won't claim their share of political power until they achieve critical mass at all levels of government.

ANN FRIEDMAN

In 1992, the much-vaunted "Year of the Woman" when 27 women were elected to Congress, Sen. Barbara Mikulski of Maryland said, "Calling 1992 the Year of the Woman makes it sound like the Year of the Caribou or the Year of the Asparagus. We're not a fad, a fancy, or a year."

To a certain degree, Mikulski was right. It wasn't just a fad; the numbers of women in Congress have slowly and steadily increased since then. But there has never since been an election like 1992, with a sizable class of incoming women legislators. And, needless to say, women have yet to achieve anything close to parity at the highest levels of government.

Hillary Clinton's historic campaign for president has inspired some important conversations about women in politics, mostly focused on how sexism has played out in her campaign, or how voters have responded to a female candidate for such a high office. But it's time for us to look down the pipeline. Progressives have a vested interest in getting more women into office—and not only because it's good to have our elected bodies better reflect the population. Nearly 30 percent of women in Congress are members of the Progressive Caucus, while only 10 percent of men in Congress are. As blogger Matt Stoller put it, "The more women in office, the more progressives in office." (For a look at some up-and-coming progressive women in politics, see the chart on page 32.)

For all the progress made in electing women over the past 16 years, however, the glass ceiling remains stubbornly in place. None of the remarkable individual women who have risen to the highest ranks of our political system—Nancy Pelosi, Hillary Clinton—has been more than a crack in the glass. To be sure, they are inspirational pioneers who give us a first glimpse of a better, more equitable future. But the glass ceiling won't truly be shattered until women have achieved a critical mass in government.

Despite the drama and excitement that have accompanied Clinton's campaign, we're not at a high point for women in politics. The high-water mark came nearly two decades ago.

The biggest shifts toward a more woman-friendly political culture all happened between 1991 and 1993. Those years saw not only the largest group of women elected to Congress but to state legislatures and as governors. That's also when Democratic women came together to form the Women's Leadership Forum to get more women involved in the party. Whether it was the Anita Hill hearings (which some women have cited as the reason they chose to run for office) or simply an unusual number of open seats, a record-breaking number of women seized the moment and, for the first time as a group, got a foothold in national politics.

Those days feel a long way away. Since the Year of the Woman, the number of women in national office has leveled off. Today, women are still less than 25 percent of senators, representatives, governors, and state legislators. The 2008 election isn't shaping up to be much different. In 1992, 11 women were candidates in Senate races. So far this year, only two women have won Senate primaries. We currently have eight women governors (including Democrat Janet Napolitano, whom Dana Goldstein profiles in this issue), and this election year will see 11 gubernatorial races. Thus far, only two women have won primaries. Compare that to the record-setting year for women governors, 1994, which saw 34 women file for races and 10 win their primaries. It's clear we aren't going anywhere fast.

Those numbers mirror the situation for women in other careers. In almost every professional field, women are stuck at the 25 percent barrier. We're less than 25 percent of corporate officers, law partners, writers for major magazines, and Wall Street execs. And I would argue it's the same set of factors (partners unwilling to shoulder their share of the child-care burden, inflexible workplace policies, straight-up sexism) that keep women from rising through the ranks of both corporations and Congress. Outliers like Pelosi and Clinton—and Fortune 500 CEOs like Xerox's Ann Mulcahy—do not in themselves amount to the shift necessary to make lasting change. When a magazine hires a female editor-in-chief, the number of women's bylines does not automatically increase. I would argue that the reason sweeping change doesn't occur is not because these remarkable women aren't doing enough. It's simply that one woman at the top cannot change an entire culture. Looking at these numbers across the board, it's clear that the real ceiling is not limiting individual women's ambitions. It's keeping women as a group from breaking the 25 percent barrier.

We need to change our political culture, not just have one woman triumph over it.

If we want to cross that threshold, we need to look at the system. We're never going to successfully implement quotas as other countries have, and it takes time to change the traditional views about a woman's proper place in society that persist in certain U.S. regions. But those who would agree with the statement, "We need more women in positions of political power"—most of the Democratic Party leadership and most readers of this magazine, I'd guess—need to take a step back in the wake of Clinton's candidacy and, rather than examine what went wrong in the Clinton example, look at how to ensure we don't have to rely on outliers like Clinton in elections for the next 30 years. The real goal should be to identify significant numbers of female candidates as future leaders and promote them through the ranks in a far more conventional manner. In other words, to change our very political culture—not just have one woman triumph over it.

That's why the Year of the Woman was actually important, despite the fact that it did not usher in a new, woman-friendly era of politics. It showed us how a group of women in politics could support each other and rise through the ranks together, rather than a single woman simply trying to play the game with the boys. The four Democratic women senators elected in 1992 held meetings as a group once they had made it to Capitol Hill (they were joined by Mikulski, who was already serving in the Senate), and discussed the problems they were facing in the boys'-club culture. At times they issued joint statements that began with, "We, the women of the Senate." The women in the House demanded equal access to the main gym and fitness facilities, because the women's gym had fallen into disrepair. The Democratic women also consistently voted together—including lending crucial support to President Bill Clinton during the 1993 budget battle. All this amounted to a subtle shift in the culture of the U.S. Congress—not a sea change but a bigger step toward breaking the 25 percent barrier (and thus the glass ceiling) than Hillary Clinton's candidacy.

Our recent political history offers many examples of women in national politics who boosted each other's careers. One key way to get more women into office is to ask them to run (as Ezra Klein points out in this issue), and women are often the ones doing the asking. Pelosi was elected to Congress in part because

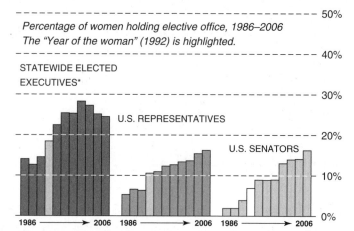

Percentage of women holding elective office, 1986–2006
The "Year of the woman" (1992) is highlighted.

*Elected executive positions vary by state, but can include governors, lieutenant governors, attorneys general, secretaries of state, treasurers, and auditors.

she was handpicked in 1987 by the dying Rep. Sala Burton to be her successor. Louisiana's Mary Landrieu was pushed to enter politics by Gov. Ann Richards of Texas—Landrieu lost her 1995 gubernatorial bid but was elected to the Senate the following year. And once they're elected, women are more likely to turn to other women for mentorship. Sen. Barbara Mikulski made how-to manuals for the Democratic women who joined the Senate in 1992, Eleanor Clift and Tom Brazaitis note in their 2003 book, *Madam President*. Mikulski's guidebook, titled "Getting Started in the Senate," contained tips on everything from responding to constituent mail to getting a good committee appointment.

Of course, women can increase their political prominence in ways besides winning electoral office. The Democratic Party has long anointed its rising stars by designating them to give speeches at the Democratic National Convention or the official response to the president's State of the Union address. There are also cabinet positions, which carry great political power. (Only 37 women have ever been cabinet members.) Using these appointments to elevate more women in politics is something we should demand of all elected progressives.

Until a critical mass is reached, this sort of concerted effort to promote women in politics is crucial. In an ideal world, such efforts would start with party apparatuses like the Democratic campaign committees taking pains to encourage women to run for office—and then supporting their campaigns. They would continue with donations from groups like EMILY's List and, after women are elected, with additional support and mentoring from their colleagues in Congress. Mikulski, for her part, was shepherded through her first year in the Senate by her Democratic colleagues Paul Sarbanes of Maryland and Ted Kennedy of Massachusetts. She called them her "Galahads."

The goal, though, is to shift the political culture enough so that newly elected women don't need Galahads. Since the 1970s, many women, in politics and business, have "broken the glass ceiling" alone. But until women are lined up behind (and next to) that one woman who busts through, it's going to be hard for us to move beyond the exceptions like Hillary Clinton.

It Is Time to Repair the Constitution's Flaws

Sanford Levinson

In 1987 I went to a marvelous exhibit in Philadelphia commemorating the bicentennial of the drafting of the U.S. Constitution. The exhibit concluded with two scrolls, each with the same two questions: First, "Will You Sign This Constitution?" And then, "If you had been in Independence Hall on September 17, 1787, would you have endorsed the Constitution?" The second question emphasized that we were being asked to assess the 1787 Constitution. That was no small matter inasmuch as the document did not include *any* of the subsequent amendments, including the Bill of Rights. Moreover, the viewer had been made aware in the course of the exhibit that the Constitution included several terrible compromises with slavery.

Even in 1987, because of those compromises I tended to regard the original Constitution as what the antislavery crusader William Lloyd Garrison so memorably called "a covenant with death and an agreement with hell." So why did I choose to sign the scroll? I was impressed that Frederick Douglass, the great black abolitionist, after an initial flirtation with Garrison's rejectionism, endorsed even the antebellum Constitution. He argued that, correctly understood, it was deeply antislavery at its core.

The language of the Constitution—including, most importantly, its magnificent preamble—allows us to mount a critique of slavery, and much else, from within. The Constitution offers us a language by which we can protect those rights that we deem important. We need not reject the Constitution in order to carry on such a conversation. If the Constitution, at the present time, is viewed as insufficiently protective of such rights, that is because of the limited imagination of those interpreters with the most political power, including members of the Supreme Court. So I added my signature to the scroll endorsing the 1787 Constitution.

On July 3, 2003, I was back in Philadelphia to participate in the grand opening of the National Constitution Center. The exhibit culminated in Signers' Hall, which featured life-size (and lifelike) statues of each of the delegates to the constitutional convention. As one walked through the hall and brushed against James Madison, Alexander Hamilton, and other giants of our history, one could almost feel the remarkable energy that must have impressed itself on those actually in Independence Hall.

As was true in 1987, the visitor was invited to join the signers by adding his or her own signature to the Constitution. Indeed, the center organized a major project during September 2003 called "I Signed the Constitution." Sites in all 50 states were available for such a signing. Both the temporary 1987 exhibit and the permanent one that remains at the National Constitution Center leave little doubt about the proper stance that a citizen should take toward our founding document.

This time, however, I rejected the invitation to re-sign the Constitution. I had not changed my mind that in many ways it offers a rich, even inspiring, language to envision and defend a desirable political order. Nor did my decision necessarily mean that I would have preferred that the Constitution go down to defeat in the ratification votes of 1787–88. Rather, I treated the center as asking me about my level of support for the Constitution *today* and, just as important, whether I wished to encourage my fellow citizens to reaffirm it in a relatively thoughtless manner. As to the first, I realized that I had, between 1987 and 2003, become far more concerned about the inadequacies of the Constitution. As to the second, I had come to think that it is vitally important to engage in a national conversation about its adequacy rather than automatically to assume its fitness for our own times.

My concern is only minimally related to the formal rights protected by the Constitution. Even if, as a practical matter, the Supreme Court reads the Constitution less protectively with regard to certain rights than I do, the proper response is not to reject the Constitution but to work within it by trying to persuade fellow Americans to share our views of constitutional possibility and by supporting presidential candidates who will appoint (and get through the Senate) judges who will be more open to better interpretations. Given that much constitutional interpretation occurs outside the courts, one also wants public officials at all levels to share one's own visions of constitutional possibility—as well, of course, as of constitutional constraints. And that is true even for readers who disagree with me on what specific rights are most important.

So what accounts for my change of views since 1987? The brief answer is that I have become ever more despondent about many structural provisions of the Constitution that place almost insurmountable barriers in the way of any acceptable contemporary notion of democracy. I put it that way to acknowledge that "democracy" is most certainly what political theorists call an "essentially contested concept." It would be tendentious to claim that there is only one understanding—such as "numerical majorities always prevail"—that is consistent with "democracy." Liberal constitutionalists, for example, would correctly place certain constraints on what majorities can do to vulnerable minorities.

That being said, I believe that it is increasingly difficult to construct a theory of democratic constitutionalism, *applying our own 21st-century norms,* that vindicates the Constitution under which we are governed today. Our 18th-century ancestors had little trouble integrating slavery and the rank subordination of women into their conception of a "republican" political order. *That* vision of politics is blessedly long behind us, but the Constitution is not. It does not deserve rote support from Americans who properly believe that majority rule, even if tempered by the recognition of minority rights, is integral to "consent of the governed."

I invite you to ask the following questions:

1. Even if you support having a Senate in addition to a House of Representatives, do you support as well giving Wyoming the same number of votes as California, which has roughly 70 times the population? To the degree that Congress is in significant ways *unrepresentative,* we have less reason to respect it. It is not a cogent response, incidentally, to say that any such inequalities are vitiated by the fact that the House of Representatives is organized on the basis of population, putting to one side issues raised by partisan gerrymandering. The very nature of our particular version of bicameralism, after all, requires that both houses assent to any legislation. By definition, that means that the *Senate can exercise the equivalent of an absolute veto power* on majoritarian legislation passed by the House that is deemed too costly to the interests of the small states that are overrepresented in the Senate, especially those clustered together in the Rocky Mountain area and the upper Midwest.

2. Are you comfortable with an Electoral College that, among other things, has since World War II placed in the White House five candidates—Truman, Kennedy, Nixon (1968), Clinton (1992 and 1996), and Bush (2000)—who did not get a majority of the popular vote? In at least two of those elections—in 1960, for which evidence exists that Nixon would have won a recount, and in 2000—the winners did not even come in first in the popular vote. The fact is that presidential candidates and their campaign managers are not necessarily trying to win the popular vote, except as an afterthought. Instead they are dedicated to putting together a coalition of states that will provide a majority of the electoral votes.

3. Are you concerned that the president might have too much power, whether to spy on Americans without any Congressional or judicial authorization or to frustrate the

will of a majority of both houses of Congress by vetoing legislation with which he disagrees on political, as distinguished from constitutional, grounds? At the very least, it should be clear from recent controversies that the present Constitution does not offer a clear understanding of the limits of presidential power, particularly during times of presidentially perceived emergencies.

4. Are you concerned about whether the country is well served by the extended hiatus between election day and the presidential inauguration some 10 weeks later, during which lame-duck presidents retain full legal authority to make often controversial decisions? Imagine if John Kerry had won the 2004 election, and President Bush had continued to make decisions about policy on Iraq, Iran, and North Korea that would have greatly affected his administration. Much of the hiatus is explicable only with regard to the need for the Electoral College to operate (which serves as an additional reason to eliminate that dysfunctional institution).

5. Are you satisfied with a Constitution that, in effect, maximizes the baleful consequences of certain kinds of terrorist attacks on the United States? If a successor to United Flight 93 were to succeed in a catastrophic attack on the House of Representatives and the Senate, we could find ourselves in a situation where neither institution could operate—because the Constitution makes it impossible to replace disabled (as distinguished from dead) senators or to fill House vacancies by any process other than an election. That would contribute to the overwhelming likelihood of a presidential dictatorship. The Constitution is written for what is termed "retail" vacancies, which occur only occasionally and are easily subject to being handled by the existing rules. Should "wholesale" vacancies occur, however, the present Constitution is nothing less than a ticking time bomb.

6. Do you really want justices on the Supreme Court to serve up to four decades and, among other things, to be able to time their resignations to mesh with their own political preferences as to their successors?

7. Finally, do you find it "democratic" that 13 legislative houses in as many states can block constitutional amendments desired by the overwhelming majority of Americans as well as, possibly, 86 out of the 99 legislative houses in the American states? No other country—nor, for that matter, any of the 50 American states—makes it so difficult to amend its constitution. Article V of our Constitution constitutes an iron cage with regard to changing some of the most important aspects of our political system. But almost as important is the way that it also constitutes an iron cage with regard to our imagination. Because it is so difficult to amend the Constitution—it seems almost utopian to suggest the possibility, with regard to anything that is truly important—citizens are encouraged to believe that change is almost never desirable, let alone necessary.

One might regard those questions as raising only theoretical, perhaps even "aesthetic," objections to our basic institutional structures *if* we feel truly satisfied by the outcomes generated by our national political institutions. But that is patently not the case. Consider the results when samples of Americans are asked whether they believe the country is headed in the right or the wrong direction. In April 2005, a full 62 percent of the respondents to a CBS poll indicated that they believed that the country was headed in "the wrong direction." A year later, a similar CBS poll found that 71 percent of the respondents said that the country was "on the wrong track," with unfavorable ratings for Congress and the president, and only a slim majority approving of the Supreme Court. Surely that comprehensive sense of dissatisfaction is related for most Americans to a belief that our political institutions are *not* adequately responding to the issues at hand. Serious liberals and conservatives increasingly share an attitude of profound disquiet about the capacity of our institutions to meet the problems confronting us as a society.

To be sure, most Americans still seem to approve of their particular members of Congress. The reason for such approval, alas, may be the representatives' success in bringing home federally financed pork, which scarcely relates to the great national and international issues that we might hope that Congress could confront effectively. In any event, we should resist the temptation simply to criticize specific inhabitants of national offices. An emphasis on the deficiencies of particular officeholders suggests that the cure for what ails us is simply to win some elections and replace those officeholders with presumptively more virtuous officials. But we are deluding ourselves if we believe that winning elections is enough to overcome the deficiencies of the American political system.

We must recognize that substantial responsibility for the defects of our polity lies in the Constitution itself. A number of wrong turns were taken at the time of the initial drafting of the Constitution, even if for the best of reasons given the political realities of 1787. Even the most skilled and admirable leaders may not be able to overcome the barriers to effective government constructed by the Constitution. In many ways, we are like the police officer in Edgar Allen Poe's classic *The Purloined Letter,* unable to comprehend the true importance of what is clearly in front of us.

If I am correct that the Constitution is both insufficiently democratic, in a country that professes to believe in democracy, and significantly dysfunctional, in terms of the quality of government that we receive, then it follows that we should no longer express our blind devotion to it. It is not, as Thomas Jefferson properly suggested, the equivalent of the Ark of the Covenant. It is a human creation open to criticism and even to rejection. You should join me in supporting the call for a new constitutional convention.

SANFORD LEVINSON is a professor of law at the University of Texas Law School. This essay is adapted from *Our Undemocratic Constitution: Where the Constitution Goes Wrong (And How We the People Can Correct It),* to be published next month by Oxford University Press. Copyright © 2006 by Oxford University Press.

As seen in *Chronicle of Higher Education,* Vol. 53, Iss. 8, October 13, 2006, pp. B10; adapted from *Our Undemocratic Constitution: Where the Constitution Goes Wrong (And How We the People Can Correct It),* by Sanford Levinson, Oxford University Press, 2006. Copyright © 2006 by Oxford University Press, Ltd. Reprinted by permission.

If Washington Blows Up

Think the unthinkable: It's 2009, and our government is decapitated in a terrorist attack. Who will become Speaker? Who'll sit on the Supreme Court? And as for the presidency . . .

BRUCE ACKERMAN

November 2009: After a hard-fought victory the year before, the new Democratic administration has come out of the starting gates in good shape. With the airwaves full of brave talk of new initiatives, there is real hope of a new beginning.

Then the unthinkable happens. A small nuclear device rips the heart out of Pennsylvania Avenue: The White House is totally obliterated; Capitol Hill looks like a war zone. Most of the nation's leaders are lost beneath the rubble. Under current constitutional provisions and law, here's what happens next: The secretary of defense, safe in the Pentagon, seems to be the next in line under the presidential succession statute. After swearing to uphold the Constitution as acting president, he immediately puts the country under martial law, suspending habeas corpus until Congress once again comes into session.

A couple of hours later, he comes before the television cameras to emphasize the need for action on another front. As his second formal decision, he is replenishing the Supreme Court by appointing nine distinguished jurists—six Democrats and three Republicans—to serve on the bench until the end of the congressional session. These recess appointments will assure the rule of law until the Senate can come back into operation and consider more permanent appointments.

Day 2. Emergency teams are hard at work searching for survivors. The secretary of state emerges from the ruins of Foggy Bottom. If the team had found her yesterday, she would have become acting president, since the succession statute places her first in line among Cabinet officers. But under the law, she lost her rights once the secretary of defense took the oath.

Day 3. The president pro tem of the Senate is in a different legal position: The statute does give him the right to bump the defense secretary out of office. The Senate was (narrowly) Republican before the blast, at which time it had selected a distinguished 86-year-old member to serve in this dignified, but powerless, position. Since the senior senator was at his suburban retreat at the time the bomb went off, he is safe and sound, and considers his options. The defense secretary, he is

convinced, is a shallow, power-hungry, left-wing fanatic with dictatorial ambitions. After thinking about it overnight, the senator reluctantly concludes that the republic needs him. Rising to the occasion, he announces that he will exercise his statutory option and serve as acting president.

Despite the senator's dark suspicions, the secretary does not resist this new transition of power. He immediately yields to the clear demands of the succession law, and accompanies the new acting president to the oath-taking ceremony: A shaken nation turns on the television to see one of its elder statesmen assume a position that will obviously overwhelm him.

Day 4. The House and Senate are beginning to revive. Acting under the 17th Amendment, governors in each state are appointing new senators to replace those found dead. In a few more days, the Senate will reconvene with a large complement of members.

The House is another story. The Constitution gives the voters the exclusive power to select replacement representatives. And it will take months before a series of special elections will return 435 living members to the makeshift Capitol. Nevertheless, in 2005 the Republican leadership foresaw the potential problem, and convinced the House to pass new rules specially designed for "catastrophic circumstances," under which a "provisional quorum" is determined by the number of representatives who show up on the floor within 72 hours after being summoned.

Three days have now passed, revealing the devastating success of the terrorist onslaught—only 50 House members have managed to answer the call, making 26 a quorum under the emergency rules, and allowing the body to act on majority votes as small as 14 to 12. Before the blast, the House was narrowly under Democratic control, and this remains true in the rump House. Because none of the old House leaders have survived, as their first action, Democrats elect a new speaker, a relatively unknown female representative from Indiana.

In the meantime, the new acting president has fired the Democratic defense secretary and replaced him with a Republican protégé, giving him a recess appointment valid through the end of the congressional session. This dynamic young man aggressively follows through on his predecessor's declaration of martial law. He tells TV cameras that his troops will be sweeping thousands of suspects—aliens and Americans alike—into military custody, beyond the reach of any civilian court.

Day 5. The new speaker considers her options under the presidential succession statute. Just as the Senate president could bump the defense secretary out of the acting presidency, it gives her the right to bump him. What is more, she is the "unbumpable bumper": The speaker will serve until the next election (subject only to impeachment). Nevertheless, she hesitates when she takes a glance at the Constitution: "A majority of each [House] shall constitute a quorum to do business." Does this provision imply that she isn't really the speaker, since she had been elected on a vote of 31 to 19, and the Constitution implies that 218 members must be present in the chamber before a valid election can take place?

After weighing the pros and cons, she decides that the framers would have supported the decision by the Republican 109th Congress to create an exception for emergency conditions—otherwise the nation would be unable to make any laws to respond to the ongoing crisis. She decides that she is the rightfully elected speaker of the House, takes the oath of office as acting president, and demands that the Senate president recognize her authority.

But he refuses—and no less importantly, so does the dynamic new Republican defense secretary, who denounces Ms. Speaker as a weakling unfit to govern the country at its most perilous hour. Democrats respond by praising the wisdom of Dennis Hastert in promulgating the new rules. Republicans insist on obedience to the plain meaning of the Founding Fathers' commands.

Meanwhile, the country pays homage to the fallen president and vice president in solemn rites in Arlington.

Day 6. The new speaker sues to obtain the presidency, and the case is expedited to receive rapid treatment by the reconstituted Supreme Court (See Day 1).

Day 10. The Supreme Court hears oral argument and ponders the briefs. The nation waits. The secretary of defense pushes onward: Rumors suggest that more than 50,000 Americans are in custody, but the exact number is a national security secret.

Day 11. The country waits. Rumors of an impending terrorist strike generate widespread panic.

Day 12. The Supreme Court, by a vote of six to three, decides that the speaker is now acting president, and orders the present incumbent to recognize her authority.

Republicans are outraged at the defiance of the Founding Fathers, and point to the ringing denunciation of the majority by the three dissenters (who happen to be the Supreme Court's three Republican members).

Day 13. Silence from the provisional presidential office in Richmond, Virginia.

Day 14. Live from Richmond: "My fellow Americans, after considering my obligations to you and to the Constitution of the United States, I hereby accept the judgment of the Supreme Court and recognize Madame Speaker as acting president of the United States."

Day 15. An anthrax attack kills 7,000 in Chicago.

We have a problem—but not one that can't be solved. All it will take is some foresight and institutional creativity, and a bit of political leadership—not a lot, since only praise will come to those hardy politicians who lead the country to think about the unthinkable.

How likely is it that a doomsday scenario will occur, say, over the next half-century: one chance in a thousand, or five hundred, or one hundred? Hard to say, but it isn't one in a million, and that should be enough to lead us to take action.

I will begin with the presidency, move on to the Supreme Court, and conclude with the House. (The Senate only needs minor fixes.) As my opening scenario suggests, piecemeal solutions won't do the trick. Although formal constitutional amendments are not required, we do need to engage in serious constitutional thought, designing each part in light of the emerging institutional whole. We need an "emergency constitution."

The Presidency

We owe the present succession statute to Harry Truman, who, upon succeeding Franklin Roosevelt, was dismayed to learn that the secretary of state was next in line to succeed him. Truman believed that his successor should be an elected official with deep political experience, and he successfully lobbied Congress to enact his position into law. But the statute needs serious retooling.

The bumping mechanism must be radically truncated. Whoever is acting president 48 hours after the blast should stay acting president (with impeachment as a last resort).

The line of succession should be revised. Truman was right to prefer seasoned political leaders to cabinet officers, but there are two problems with the current designations. Although the speaker of the House is almost invariably a leading politician, the central figures in today's Senate are the majority and minority leaders. The statute should take this into account, and replace the president pro tem with a Senate official whose leadership skills have gained the support of his colleagues.

My next change may prove more controversial, but it shouldn't be. By putting the speaker first in line after the vice president, the current statute assures us that a skilled politician will assume the presidency, but he may well be a member of the opposing political party. This is a mistake: Terrorists should not be allowed to overrule the decision of America's voters and generate a sharp swing in public policy. A statutory tweak will suffice to assure that the party that won the last presidential election remains in control.

The new succession statute should instruct each president, at the start of each congressional session, to designate either the speaker or the minority leader as the successor to the vice president; and the president should have the same privilege when it comes to choosing between the Senate majority and minority leaders. He will, of course, choose the leader of his political party, assuring policy continuity at a time of crisis.

We run into serious trouble only if some unspeakable disaster eliminates the leaders of both houses, as well as the secretaries of state and the treasury. This puts the secretary of defense next in line, since the War Department was created immediately after the Treasury Department when George Washington set up the executive branch. This accident of history should no longer rule us. The principle of checks and balances is far more important, and it suggests that the defense secretary should be placed at the bottom of the list of Cabinet officers. As civilian chief of the military, he will inevitably—and justifiably—have a large role in emergency decision making, but he should be obliged to make his case to an acting president whose past experience has exposed him to different perspectives. If the defense secretary is made president and promotes his deputy to his old job, their conversations in the executive suite will be dangerously parochial—one Pentagon guy talking to another. The succession statute should skip to the next officer in line, the attorney general.

We then confront a problem. The attorney general, as well as the secretaries of state and treasury, are obliged to take a large view of national problems, and as a consequence, these officers regularly become prominent figures in American political life. But the other departmental secretaries have more parochial interests (Interior, Transportation), and are typically unknown to the general public. It would be terrible if any of these worthies were called upon to exercise presidential power.

My colleague Akhil Amar has suggested the creation of a new position—minister without portfolio—whose sole function would be to serve as acting president in the case of a dreadful decapitation. Once confirmed by the Senate, the minister would live outside Washington, D.C., and receive regular briefings that would enable him to act effectively if disaster struck. Amar hopes that the president would appoint a retired senior statesmen—a George Mitchell, a Colin Powell—to this post and give the country a figure in whom it has confidence at its hour of need. The danger, of course, is that the president could use the appointment to score points with a particular interest group or to reward a crony. And there is always the risk that the senior statesman will suffer a sudden decline in vigor before he is suddenly placed in command.

We should use this device only as a last resort, when a terrorist attack has taken out all six of the officials at the top of our lineup. Whatever the differences between the speaker of the House and the attorney general, all of them are wielding serious power on a day-to-day basis—and you don't stay in this position unless you are in the prime of your political life. But if it's a choice between Amar's minister and, say, the secretary of agriculture, I go with the minister.

Finally, the acting president should only serve until the next regularly scheduled biennial election: In my scenario, he would serve through 2010, not through 2012. This will assure the earliest feasible return of a president with the explicit backing of the American people. This change in the calendar might readily be accomplished without a formal constitutional amendment—indeed, for the first 150 years of American history, there was a statute on the books that did provide for a special election in cases when both the presidency and vice presidency had become vacant. We should renew this tradition.

The Supreme Court

The decapitation of the Supreme Court will predictably generate two sequential responses—both terrible, but only one suggested by my earlier scenario. Recall that my acting president, on the first day of the attack, exercised his constitutional authority to refill the Supreme Court with recess appointments valid until the end of the congressional session. This would set the stage, however, for a series of confirmation struggles over permanent appointments. The entire affair will be a giant distraction during a tragic period, diverting the president, the Senate, and the country from many pressing matters.

This is not the worst of it. The entire two-wave cycle—first interim, then permanent, appointments—threatens two great constitutional values. The first is judicial independence. The interim appointees will be on probation at a time when they will be confronting crucial constitutional problems. If the interim justices exercise their oversight powers with vigor, they may easily antagonize key politicians on Capitol Hill, jeopardizing their future careers on the Supreme Court. If they roll over and rubber-stamp, constitutional safeguards will crumble, with long-lasting consequences.

There is a second big problem. Ordinarily, the Supreme Court's membership turns over slowly—over the past half-century, a position has opened up about every three years, on average. This all-too-deliberate pace is getting to be a problem, creating the prospect of a Supreme Court that has lost touch with its many publics. But the decapitation scenario promises something worse: A problematic acting president, together with a Senate—composed, remember, of gubernatorial appointees—makes a series of lifetime appointments that will decisively shape constitutional law for decades. Even if the acting president contents himself with interim appointments and waits for an elected Senate to come to Washington, the country will still be reeling from the tragedy. This is hardly a propitious moment for selecting all nine justices, freezing the doctrinal orthodoxy of the day into a rigid pattern for 30 or 40 years.

We confront a paradox—loss of judicial independence over the short run, excessive rigidity over the long run. This is a recipe for trouble, especially in a country that depends so heavily on the Supreme Court in its governing arrangements. Once again, it won't be necessary to change the Constitution in order to get us out of this hole. A statute will be enough, and here is what it should say: If the Supreme Court is deprived of its quorum, some of the chief judges of the courts of appeal should immediately be reassigned to the high court to serve as justices. The reassignment would take place through a lottery: There are 12 regular courts of appeal; the names of each chief judge would be dropped into a hat, and the identity of the new justices will be called out after a random draw. Judges become chief of their appellate circuits through seniority, and they must resign this position when they reach 70. By promoting them to the Supreme Court, we are guaranteed experienced jurists whose powers have not yet been dulled by great age—and who will not sit on the court for 30 or 40 years.

Randomized selection will minimize the political spin—most judges on a particular circuit might be appointed by Democratic presidents, but this won't prevent the chief judge from being a Republican if seniority marks him out, and vice versa. Finally, the replacements won't occupy their seats for extremely long periods. Chief judges of the appeals courts are almost invariably in their middle or late 60s, and even in this day of medical miracles, the grim reaper can't be delayed indefinitely. The statute, however, might go further and require the chief judges to return to their circuit courts on a staggered schedule—guaranteeing the president and Senate at least one appointment every two years, say, if a vacancy doesn't otherwise arise through death or resignation.

But we are now descending into (important) details, and it is more crucial to see how the basic proposal resolves the egregious difficulties of the status quo. Rather than diverting the president and the Senate into a protracted battle over the Supreme Court at a time of emergency, the statute renews the court immediately with the nation's surviving senior jurists, without any partisanship involved. And it immediately assures judicial independence—in contrast to recess appointments by the president, the tenure of the new justices won't depend on pleasing the powers-that-be in the White House and the Senate. At the same time, the happenstance of a successful terrorist assault won't freeze constitutional jurisprudence for 30 or 40 years: The Supreme Court will evolve with the changing temper of public opinion. Is there any fair question that this is *a lot* better than we can hope from the status quo?

The House

This problem requires a little more institutional imagination. The Constitution says "The House of Representatives shall be composed of Members chosen every second Year *by the People* of the several States" (emphasis mine). These words inscribe a constitutional understanding that is deeply engraved on the national consciousness: Membership in the "People's House" is, and should be, based on a direct connection between voters and representatives. No formal amendment challenging this idea has a ghost of a chance, and I, myself, am firmly committed to retaining a direct linkage between the House and the people.

Nevertheless, there is a way to maintain existing constitutional commitments and still get the House back in business within days of a devastating attack: Congress should create a new office of vice representative, who will serve in Congress if the district's principal representative is either killed or disabled in a catastrophic attack. Henceforth, the major political parties would regularly nominate a two-person "ticket" in each House race, and voters would cast ballots for *both* positions at each election, enabling the vice representative to take over immediately in the event of a decapitating strike.

This system transparently complies with the constitutional text, since both representative and vice representative will be "chosen every second Year by the People." Rather than violating this command, Congress would be complying with its literal terms. It is simply changing the mode of compliance—replacing the current system of special elections with a more regularized mechanism for filling potential vacancies in advance.

My proposal may be novel, but it conforms to the Founders' decision to create the position of the vice president to serve as an immediate stand-in for the president. The framers could have dispensed with the vice presidency entirely, designating some interim figure, like the secretary of state, to call a special election to fill the office. But the death of the president seemed sufficiently likely, and sufficiently disturbing, to warrant the selection of a replacement in advance. Although they didn't give the vice president very much to do, they thought it was important to have him hanging around.

During the 18th century, the technology for a massive sneak attack wasn't available—nobody thought that the House, like the presidency, could be wiped out in a single blow. So the framers didn't seriously consider the creation of vice representatives on analogy with the vice president. But there is no reason to suspect that they would have objected as a matter of principle. So far as the Constitution is concerned, Congress has ample authority to pass a statute creating the office of vice representative as "necessary and proper" for assuring the continuing existence of government in the United States.

Turning to policy, the new system has its share of problems. For starters, the House candidate at the top of the ticket won't be interested in giving a platform to somebody with sufficient stature to launch a primary challenge during the next election cycle. Nevertheless, he won't choose an obvious incompetent. As presidential candidates have learned, the selection of a bad vice presidential nominee starts the campaign off on a very bad note—giving opponents a field day in the press. This will restrain the selection of a spouse or a child, or a notorious fool. While a House of vice representatives will contain its share of loyal hacks, so will the makeshift Senate dominated by interim members selected by state governors.

Not a pretty picture, I confess, but surely a lot less grim than a scene in which the acting president must rule by decree, or a rump House sits in defiance of bitter challenges to its constitutional legitimacy.

There will always be one disadvantage to the office of "emergency vice representative." It will serve as a constant reminder of the real possibility of a devastating terrorist attack and provide a demoralizing undertone to ordinary politics. But demoralizing or not, the truth is that we do face a low-level but palpable risk. Rather than burying our heads in the sand, isn't it better to deal with the truth in a sober fashion, and in a way that seeks best to sustain our democratic ideals?

There are two kinds of emergency: one is created by a terrorist attack; another when the attack paralyzes our government. The first kind is almost inevitable—it will be a miracle if we can stop the burgeoning traffic in increasingly powerful weapons, and I don't believe in miracles. But the second is entirely of our own making. It is the product of an ostrich-like refusal to confront the obvious inadequacies of our present arrangements. This is a matter on which all Americans should agree: However much we hope that our precautions will prove unnecessary, we should act now to create an adequate emergency Constitution.

BRUCE ACKERMAN is Sterling Professor of Law and Political Science at Yale. This essay is adapted from his new book, *Before the Next Attack: Preserving Civil Liberties in An Age of Terrorism,* to be published by Yale University Press in March.

Pursuit of Habeas

To justify Gitmo, the Bushies kept monkeying around with the Constitution. But by trying to kill the right of habeas corpus, they only made it stronger.

JACK HITT

The era of Guantanamo Bay will come to an end, according to Joseph Margulies, a lawyer who has represented some of the detainees, when a judge utters the following words to George W. Bush: "Call your first witness."

Margulies is not alone in believing that the only thing administration officials are more zealous about than fighting the Global War on Terrorism is any attempt to make public the murky processes they've cobbled together to wage it. The intricate legal scaffolding constructed by the Bush administration replaced something simple, basic, and beautiful: habeas corpus. Most Americans probably don't know the meaning of that creaky Latin phrase and have been left with the impression that it is some boutique legalism that just ends up coddling terrorists. Actually, habeas is perfectly straightforward. It is the ancient right of anyone seized by the king to cry out from the dungeon and say, "I've been wrongly jailed!" Then you get a chance to prove your claim before a neutral judge, or back to the pokey you go. Habeas puts a basic check on the most fearsome power of the state and any citizen's most primal fear—being locked away and forgotten, the civil equivalent of being buried alive.

This fundamental right was most famously codified in 1215 when, in the meadow of Runnymede, King John was forced to set his royal seal upon the Magna Carta, the seminal document that declared the rule of law above any man, including the king. The habeas hearing was among the first checks and balances. Habeas is an affront to the royalist impulse to consolidate all power under one king, or as Beltway ideologues call it these days, "the unitary executive."

The problem with opposing habeas corpus now is no different than it was eight centuries ago: You're siding with the Sheriff of Nottingham.

The problem with opposing habeas now is no different than it was eight centuries ago: You're siding with the Sheriff of Nottingham.

Since 9/11, Bush's officials have played a seven-year game of legal keep-away: filing new motions, changing jurisdictions, improvising legal proceedings on the fly, stalling, appealing, amending, and then appealing some more. So much so that the matter of habeas has now become a hot-button issue on the presidential trail. Barack Obama applauded the high court's recent decision to extend habeas to detainees in Guantanamo; former POW John McCain said it was "one of the worst decisions in the history of this country."

Many defenders of the Bush administration point out that detainees at Gitmo shouldn't be receiving a habeas hearing because they are foreign combatants. To the Supreme Court, however, the key issue is not the rights of aliens but separation of powers. It challenged Congress' audacity to limit this basic judicial power when the Constitution is clear that habeas can be suspended in only two situations—rebellion or invasion.

Another reason why habeas is being debated goes back to the original sin of the Bush administration's catastrophic decisions on the battlefield. Ever since World War II, when the military has rounded up people after a battle, it has held brief hearings to determine if a prisoner was a legitimate POW or somebody picked up in error. Lots of mistakes get made in wartime, and commanders typically don't want to be burdened with unnecessary detainees, so dealing with this matter right away—separating those who've taken up arms from those who got caught up in a raid—is essential. In the wake of the Geneva Conventions these battlefield tribunals have been referred to as Article 5 hearings.

In Vietnam, Article 5 hearings were typically held right there in the jungle. In the first Gulf War, 1,196 Article 5 hearings were held and only 310 detainees were classified as POWs. And that's typical. But not after 9/11.

Early on, White House Counsel Alberto Gonzales dismissed the Geneva Conventions as "quaint." So everybody swept up was sent en masse to the camps. Then, the civilian leadership of the Pentagon made matters even more difficult. We bloated the enemy combatant population with a new technique: We started *buying* combatants.

We dropped leaflets out of planes, offering Afghans and Pakistanis as much as $25,000 to turn in Taliban and Al Qaeda fighters. Many of these leaflets landed in areas where an annual salary might be a few hundred dollars. This made it very tempting to turn in that neighbor whose goats always harassed your sheep. And that kind of feud settling happened. It will probably be years before we entirely understand just what kind of mishmash we made of our prisoner population by turning the fire hose of turbocapitalism on the Afghan outback.

Yet from the beginning, we've always had a clue. Donald Rumsfeld announced that the detainees were the "worst of the worst," and General Richard Myers warned they "would gnaw hydraulic lines in the back of a C-17 to bring it down." But as early as 2002, the commander at Gitmo, Maj. General Michael Dunlavey, complained that he was receiving too many "Mickey Mouse" prisoners. A 2004 *New York Times* investigation found numerous officials who said that of the 595 detainees then held at Gitmo, maybe two dozen possessed any useful information. In 2006, a study of Pentagon filings on 517 detainees led by Seton Hall law professor Mark Denbeaux quantified it with hard numbers: Only 5 percent of the men at Gitmo had been scooped up by US forces, and only 8 percent were fighters of any kind.

Overstating the number of hydraulic-line chewers at Gitmo has been a routine rhetorical tactic of Bush apologists. In his dissent in the latest case, Justice Antonin Scalia (who can't get over the fact that other people can't get over *Bush v. Gore*) hysterically noted that at least 30 released detainees "have returned to the battlefield." Seton Hall's Denbeaux looked at the evidence behind that number and found that the Pentagon counted as "returning to the battlefield" detainees who had participated in the documentary *The Road to Guantanamo* or had written a pro-habeas op-ed in the *New York Times*. When you narrow it down to those who've left Gitmo and actually taken up arms against the United States, according to Denbeaux, the number is five. And among those, it would be interesting to examine the use of the word "return." What evidence does Scalia have that they weren't goatherds radicalized by years of undeserved dungeon time?

Of course, there's no better confirmation than the actions of the Pentagon itself. Even without abiding by habeas, the Pentagon has quietly released some 500 of the 770 detainees held at Guantanamo.

Over the years, as the courts have ordered the Bush administration to provide some kind of habeas-like hearing to the remaining detainees, the government's lawyers ginned up something called a "combatant status review tribunal." During a CSRT, however, you can't have a lawyer, know the evidence against you, or call witnesses except those "reasonably available." The result? Hearings that are simply bizarre. Take the case of German-born detainee Murat Kurnaz, picked up in 2001. (See "Inside Gitmo With Detainee 061") At his CSRT, he learned that one of the official reasons for holding him was because two years *after* he was seized a friend blew himself up, except that because of bureaucratic incompetence, it wasn't his

friend at all, who was alive and well and living nonterroristically back in Germany.

Paging Terry Gilliam.

The CSRTs have become such a fiasco that one-fourth of the division of Justice Department lawyers charged with executing these tribunals have opted out. In the case of actual military commissions (the improvised "trials" that follow a CSRT hearing), last year the chief prosecutor, Colonel Morris Davis, denounced the commissions as rigged, quit his job, and offered to testify on behalf of a detainee.

The reasoning for these complicated, shadowy processes—seizing prisoners in unorthodox ways, isolating them outside US jurisdiction, never bringing charges, then offering makeshift legal proceedings—is usually explained with the argument that 9/11 changed everything. Actually, Guantanamo is a case of history repeating itself.

Habeas corpus was the law of the land in England until the mid-17th century when royalist Cavaliers found themselves in a holy war with Protestant Roundheads. To the royalists it appeared that England was beset with terrorists, crazy fundamentalists who had no regard for human life—a.k.a. the Puritans. We remember them as folksy pilgrims with a garish taste in buckles. The British had other impressions. Even though the royalists themselves didn't much care for Charles I, the idea of publicly executing the king was seen as an act of bloodthirsty terrorism on a par with, say, crashing a plane into a tower. When the pendulum swung back to royalism more than a decade later, King Charles II ascended the throne. Needless to say, the king's lord chancellor—the head of day-to-day governing—a man named Edward Hyde, Earl of Clarendon, was suspicious of Puritans, suspicious of everybody. Terrorism makes you that way. So he seized anyone he fancied to be a potential threat and held them at detainment camps. And in order to avoid the bother of habeas hearings, he put them on an island off the British shore—some historians say it was the isle of Jersey—in order to deprive them of the protection of English common law.

Sound familiar?

In the end, Clarendon was impeached and fled in disgrace. Parliamentarians who thought Clarendon had gone too far—particularly one Lord Shaftesbury—passed the Habeas Corpus Act of 1679, reestablishing a balance between an executive who must make arrests in order to keep the peace and the individual's right to challenge that arrest in court. Having learned the lessons of Guantanamo Bay more than 300 years ago, the 1679 act forbade the king from removing a prisoner to "Scotland, Ireland, Jersey, Guernsey, Tangier, or into Parts, Garrisons, Islands or Places beyond the Seas, which are or at any time hereafter shall be within or without the Dominions of his Majesty."

And that was our inherited position, until George W. Bush became president. But the assault on habeas will end. Other Bush-era presidential powers will be challenged and debated. But not only will habeas be fully restored as a centerpiece of American jurisprudence, one might ultimately credit Bush indirectly for internationalizing the right, since that is a likely long-term outcome of his attempt to subvert it. The most recent court ruling broadened the reach of habeas—suggesting that no democracy should leave home without it.

Habeas is among the first great checks and balances in the very system of powers that we are said to be fighting for. With each Supreme Court reversal, with each appellate court smackdown, America walks the issue back, back to this elegant idea, back to this ancient right, back to habeas corpus. Even some of our most conservative judges have stepped up to affirm it. It's only a matter of time before Congress does the same, restraining future presidents from ever again sending prisoners "into Parts, Garrisons, Islands or Places beyond the Seas."

Is Judicial Review Obsolete?

Stuart Taylor Jr.

The big decision on June 26 that the Second Amendment protects an individual right to keep a loaded handgun for self-defense at home is the high-water mark of the "original meaning" approach to constitutional interpretation championed by Justice Antonin Scalia and many other conservatives. At the same time, the decision may show "originalism" to be a false promise.

Scalia's 64-page opinion for the five-justice majority was a tour de force of originalist analysis. Without pausing to ask whether gun rights is good policy, Scalia parsed the Second Amendment's 27 words one by one while consulting 18th-century dictionaries, early American history, the 1689 English Bill of Rights, 19th-century treatises, and other historical material.

And even the lead dissent for the Court's four liberals—who are accustomed to deep-sixing original meaning on issues ranging from the death penalty to abortion, gay rights, and many others—all but conceded that this case should turn mainly on the original meaning of the 217-year-old Second Amendment. They had little choice, given the unusual absence of binding precedent.

But in another sense, *District of Columbia v. Heller* belies the two great advantages that originalism has been touted as having over the liberals' "living Constitution" approach. Originalism is supposed to supply first principles that will prevent justices from merely voting their policy preferences and to foster what Judge Robert Bork once called "deference to democratic choice." But the gun case suggests that originalism does neither.

Even though all nine justices claimed to be following original meaning, they split along liberal-conservative lines perfectly matching their apparent policy preferences.

First, even though all nine justices claimed to be following original meaning, they split angrily along liberal-conservative lines perfectly matching their apparent policy preferences, with the four conservatives (plus swing-voting Anthony Kennedy) voting for gun rights and the four liberals against.

These eight justices cleaved in *exactly* the same way—with Kennedy tipping the balance from case to case—in the decision the same day striking down a campaign finance provision designed to handicap rich, self-funded political candidates; the June 25 decision barring the death penalty for raping a child; the June 12 decision striking down the elected branches' restrictions on judicial review of Guantanamo detainees' petitions for release; and past decisions on abortion, affirmative action, gay rights, religion, and more.

This pattern does not mean that the justices are *insincerely* using legal doctrines as a cover for politically driven votes. Rather, it shows that ascertaining the original meaning of provisions drafted more than 200 years ago, in a very different society, is often a subjective process on which reasonable people disagree—and often reach conclusions driven consciously or subconsciously by their policy preferences. And some of us have trouble coming to confident conclusions either way.

I wrote approvingly of the federal Appeals Court opinion striking down the District of Colombia's strict handgun ban 15 months ago, and found Scalia's argument for the same result equally persuasive. But then I studied the dissents by liberal Justices John Paul Stevens and Stephen Breyer, and found them pretty persuasive too. Scalia and the two dissenters all made cogent arguments while papering over weaknesses in their positions. I think that Scalia may have won on points. But more study might tip me the other way.

The reason is that the justices' exhaustive analyses of the text and relevant history do not definitively resolve the ambiguity inherent in the amendment's curious wording: "A well-regulated militia, being necessary to the security of a free state, the right of the people to keep and bear arms, shall not be infringed."

And even if there is a clear right answer evident to people more discerning than I, the voting pattern suggests that conservative and liberal justices will never agree on what it is. More broadly, even when there is no dispute as to original meaning, it is often intolerable to liberals and conservatives alike. For example, no constitutional provision or amendment was ever designed to prohibit the federal government from discriminating based on race (or sex). This has not stopped conservatives from voting to strike down federal racial preferences for minorities (by seeking to extend liberal precedents) any more than it stopped liberals from striking down the federal laws that once discriminated against women.

Second, the notion that originalists would defer more to democratic choices than would the loosey-goosey liberals has come to ring a bit hollow. The originalists began with a compelling critique of the liberals' invention of new constitutional rights to strike down all state abortion and death-penalty laws, among others. But the current conservative justices have hardly been models of judicial restraint.

They have used highly debatable interpretations of original meaning to sweep aside a raft of democratically adopted laws. These include federal laws regulating campaign money and imposing monetary liability on states. And in last year's 5-4 decision striking down two local school-integration laws, the conservative majority came close to imposing a "colorblind Constitution" vision of equal protection that may be good policy but which is hard to find in the 14th Amendment's original meaning.

In the gun case, as Justice Breyer argued, "the majority's decision threatens severely to limit the ability of more knowledgeable, democratically elected officials to deal with gun-related problems." (Of course, Breyer's solicitude for elected officials disappears when the issue is whether they should be able to execute rapists of children or ban an especially grisly abortion method.)

If originalism does not deliver on its promises to channel judicial discretion and constrain judicial usurpations of elected officials' power, what good is it?

Indeed, it seems almost perverse to be assessing what gun controls do allow based not on examining how best to save lives but on seeking to read the minds of the men who ratified the Bill of Rights well over 200 years ago.

The originalist approach seems especially odd when it comes down to arguing over such matters as whether 18th-century lawyers agreed (as Scalia contends) that "a prefatory clause does not limit or expand the scope of the operative clause" and whether (as Stevens contends) the phrase " 'bear arms' most naturally conveys a military meaning" and "the Second Amendment does not protect a 'right to keep *and* to bear arms,' but rather 'a right to keep and bear arms' " (emphasis in original). The justices may as well have tried reading the entrails of dead hamsters.

Is the answer to embrace liberals' "living Constitution" jurisprudence, which roughly translates to reading into the 18th-century document whichever meaning and values the justices consider most fundamental?

By no means. Rather, in the many cases in which nothing close to consensus about the meaning of the Constitution is attainable, the justices should leave the lawmaking to elected officials. To borrow from an article I wrote in 1986: "Those who work so hard to prove that the Constitution cannot supply the values for governance of modern society seem to think that judges must do it, with a little help from their friends in academia. But the argument rebounds against the legitimacy of judicial review itself. Bork poses a question for which they have no good answer: 'If the Constitution is not law [that] tells judges what to do and what not to do—. . . what authorizes judges to set at naught the majority judgment of the American people?' "

Now it seems that the originalist view of the Constitution is indeed incapable of telling today's judges what to do—not, at least, with any consistency from one judge to the next. So is judicial review itself obsolete?

Not quite. Judicial review remains valuable, perhaps indispensable, because it helps provide the stability and protection for liberty inherent in our tripartite separation of powers, with the legislative, executive, and judicial branches serving as the three legs of a stool and with each potent enough to check abuses and excesses by the others.

The June 12 decision rebuffing President Bush's (and Congress's) denial of fair hearings to Guantanamo detainees proclaiming their innocence is a case in point. But the broad wording of Kennedy's majority opinion, joined by the four liberals, went too far by flirting with a hubristic vision of unprecedented judicial power to intrude deeply into the conduct of foreign wars. *(See my column, 6/21/08, p. 15.)*

For better or worse, what Scalia has called the imperial judiciary—sometimes liberal, sometimes conservative—seems here to stay.

Indeed, not one of the nine justices seems to have a modest understanding of his or her powers to set national policy in the name of enforcing the Constitution. But the other branches, and most voters, seem content with raw judicial policy-making—except when they don't like the policies. For better or worse, what Scalia has called "the imperial judiciary"—sometimes liberal, sometimes conservative—seems here to stay.

Given this, the best way to restrain judicial imperialism may be for the president and the Senate to worry less about whether prospective justices are liberal or conservative and more about whether they have a healthy sense of their own fallibility.

Two Takes

Pulpit Politics Is Free Speech

To what extent should religious leaders be able to incorporate political endorsements into their preaching? Some pastors are protesting IRS restrictions preventing them from backing specific candidates. Should religious leaders be allowed to endorse candidates from their pulpits?

RON JOHNSON JR.

Pro Who is in charge of the pulpit? The church or the IRS? That is the question that recently led me and other pastors to deliver sermons on the subject of the upcoming elections, despite tax rules used to stifle speech about candidates. The sermons were part of a broader effort, the Alliance Defense Fund's Pulpit Initiative, which is designed to protect pastors' First Amendment rights.

I wish to be clear from the outset. I have no desire to turn my pulpit into a Christian version of the Chicago political machine. My church will not be writing large checks to candidates, or to anyone else for that matter. We have plenty to do educating Christians about tithing to support the church, let alone political campaigns.

I have no intention of selecting my sermon topics by watching CNN or Fox News. I have no secret dream of becoming president or even running for dogcatcher. To suggest, as some have, that somehow we are being seduced by political power or that we are looking to government to be America's "savior" is silliness. And no, the Pulpit Initiative is not about encouraging pastors to endorse candidates from the pulpit.

Free speech. The purpose of the Pulpit Initiative is to restore the right of pastors to speak freely from the pulpit without fear of punishment by the government for doing what churches do: speak on any number of cultural and societal issues from a biblical perspective. Christians believe that civil government owes its existence to God and is therefore accountable to him to behave righteously in serving the common good. A significant role of the church is—and always has been—to encourage the civil magistrate to do what is good and not what is evil.

"Why does the IRS get to judge the political content of a pastor's sermon?"

—Ron Johnson Jr. is the senior associate pastor of the Living Stones Fellowship Church in Crown Point, Ind.

The Internal Revenue Service has placed itself in the role of evaluating the content of a pastor's sermon to determine if the message is "political." We need to ask: Where did this authority come from? And why should Americans be willing to submit to this unconstitutional power grab without even a whimper? Why are pastors the only people who have allowed the IRS to censor their First Amendment rights for a tax exemption they have enjoyed since the founding of our nation—a tax exemption that existed long before the IRS did?

Erik Stanley, the head of the Pulpit Initiative, has rightly pointed out that pastors spoke freely about the policy positions of candidates for elective office throughout American history, even endorsing or opposing candidates from the pulpit, without anyone ever questioning whether churches should remain tax exempt. It was common-place—even expected—for pastors to speak in support of or in opposition to candidates until the tax code was amended in 1954 with no legislative analysis or debate.

Churches are tax exempt because they are churches, not because the government decided to bless them with a "subsidy." The church is not a profit-making business or individual. It is not getting a pass on taxes; it is simply outside the government's appropriate tax base.

Secularists often create a false sacred/secular dichotomy that conveniently silences our message. While it's true that pastors need to stop letting others tell us to keep Jesus inside of the church and out of the world he died to redeem, this particular battle is about whether we as pastors even have the right to speak as we feel led to within our own four walls.

The Pulpit Initiative is not about promoting political parties or agendas or establishing a "theocracy." It's about our right to bring kingdom principles and solutions to bear on contemporary social problems if we so choose. A pastor may choose not to, but it's the pastor's choice, not the choice of the IRS.

If we cannot discuss any and all topics, including those the IRS may deem "political," even within our communities of faith, we will become what Martin Luther King Jr. called an "irrelevant social club without moral or spiritual authority."

Simply put, it's time for the church to be the church.

Campaigns Can Split Churches

REV. BARRY W. LYNN

Con Most Americans who go to church expect to hear about salvation, morality, and scripture. They don't anticipate hard-ball political endorsements.

Congress made it clear in 1954 that nonprofit groups, religious or secular, may not endorse or oppose any candidate for public office.

That doesn't mean pastors, priests, rabbis, or imams cannot criticize government policies. It doesn't mean clergy cannot express views on specific pieces of legislation or ballot initiatives. Nor does it even mean they cannot participate in partisan political activities in their own personal capacity.

What it does signify is that pastors cannot make declarations to favor or oppose any candidate from the pulpit. They cannot take money from the collection plate and give it to support a candidate. And if they want to participate in any partisan activity in their personal capacity, they must make sure it is done in a manner indicating it is separate from their religious institution.

Put simply, the tax code prevents religious institutions from serving as political machines, a concept in keeping with the separation of church and state our founding fathers envisioned.

Now a group called the Alliance Defense Fund is working to alter that vision. The group recently urged pastors around the country to violate tax law and promote candidates from the pulpit. Thirty-three pastors participated. But we all know churches in America are already free to engage in religious speech. Tax law doesn't take that freedom away.

We know this because the Revs. Jerry Falwell (on the right) and William Sloane Coffin (on the left) weren't silenced from speaking from the pulpit on moral issues. And the regulation never prohibited the Rev. Martin Luther King Jr. from speaking passionately of the need for social change in our country—while never once endorsing a candidate from the pulpit.

"The law affords an astounding amount of freedom for the clergy to preach."

—Barry W. Lynn of Americans United for Separation of Church and State is an ordained minister in the United Church of Christ.

It's clear that the law as it is provides those of us in the clergy with an astounding amount of freedom to express a wide array of opinions from the pulpit. But we cannot turn sermons into political ads for candidates, nor should we have that "freedom." In a recent survey on this issue, 87 percent of Americans agreed that pastors shouldn't endorse candidates during worship services. Americans clearly see that churches should not become cogs in anybody's political machine.

Church schisms. Americans also recognize politics can split congregations.

Take, for example, the church in Waynesville, N.C., where the Rev. Chan Chandler told congregants during a sermon in October 2004, "If you vote for John Kerry this year, you need to repent or resign." This comment tore apart the congregation, initially leading to the ouster of nine Democratic members. Following a congregational meeting, they were invited back to the church and Chandler was forced to resign.

More recently at High Point Church in Arlington, Texas, Pastor Gary Simons showed a video that depicted the views of Barack Obama and John McCain on abortion. His sermon gave God's alleged view on abortion and told the congregation how to vote accordingly. Some congregants said the pastor seemed to be comparing Obama to King Herod, the biblical monarch who ordered the mass murder of infants. Several members just walked out.

Frankly, a tax exemption is a privilege, not a right. The IRS can strip a church of its tax exemption for egregious violations of law. It did just that to the Church at Pierce Creek in Binghamton, N.Y. In 1992, the church spent $44,000 on an ad in *USA Today* that called Bill Clinton a sinner and warned Christians against voting for him. The congregation contested the revocation in court but lost at every level. Not one judge agreed the church had some sort of "free speech" or "free exercise" right to engage in partisan activities.

This is not a First Amendment concern but a ploy for groups like the Alliance Defense Fund to use churches to push a political agenda. If a church doesn't want to follow IRS law, it can refuse the tax exemption. But churches that want this privilege have to play by the same rules as everyone else.

From *U.S. News & World Report*, November 17/24, 2008, pp. 10–11. Copyright © 2008 by U.S. News & World Report, L.P. Reprinted by permission.

UNIT 2

Structures of American Politics

Unit Selections

Key Points to Consider

- Read Articles I, II, and III of the U.S. Constitution to get a picture of the legislative, executive, and judicial branches as painted by the words of the Framers. How does that picture compare with the reality of the three branches as they operate today?

- How might the presidency and Congress change in the next 100 years? What about the judicial branch?

- What advantages and disadvantages do each of the following have for getting things done: The president? The vice president? A cabinet member? The speaker of the House of Representatives? The Senate majority leader? The chief justice? A top-ranking bureaucrat in an executive branch agency? A congressional aide?

- Which position in American government would you most like to hold? Why?

Student Web Site
www.mhcls.com

Internet References

Department of State
http://www.state.gov

Federal Reserve System
http://www.federalreserve.gov

Supreme Court/Legal Information Institute
http://supct.law.cornell.edu/supct/index.html

United States House of Representatives
http://www.house.gov

United States Senate
http://www.senate.gov

James Madison, one of the primary architects of the American system of government, observed that the three-branch structure of government created at the Constitutional Convention of 1787 pitted the ambitions of some individuals against the ambitions of others. Nearly two centuries later, political scientist Richard Neustadt wrote that the structure of American national government is one of "separated institutions sharing powers." These two eminent students of American politics suggest an important proposition: the very design of American national government contributes to the struggles that occur among government officials who have different institutional loyalties and potentially competing goals.

This unit is divided into four sections. The first three treat the three traditional branches of American government, and the last one treats the bureaucracy. One point to remember when studying these institutions is that the Constitution provides only a bare skeleton of the workings of the American political system. The flesh and blood of the presidency, Congress, judiciary, and bureaucracy are derived from decades of experience and the shared expectations of today's political actors.

A second relevant point is that the way a particular institution functions is partly determined by the identities of those who occupy relevant offices. The presidency operates differently with Barack Obama in the White House than it did when George W. Bush was president. Similarly, Congress and the Supreme Court function differently according to who serve as members and who hold leadership positions within the institutions. There were significant changes in the House of Representatives after Democrat Nancy Pelosi succeeded Republican Dennis Hastert as speaker in 2007 and, before that, when Hastert took over from Newt Gingrich in 1999. In the Senate, over a two-year period beginning in January 2001, Republican majority leader Trent Lott was succeeded by Democrat Tom Daschle, who in turn was succeeded by Republican Bill Frist. These changes in leadership brought obvious changes in the operation of the Senate. Changes were evident once again when Democrat Harry Reid succeeded Frist in 2007.

A third point about today's American political system is that in recent decades traditional branch-vs.-branch conflict has been accompanied, and perhaps even overshadowed, by increasing partisanship between the two major parties. In the first six years of George W. Bush's presidency, Republican members of Congress seemed to be substantially more influenced by the party affiliation that they shared with President Bush than the institutional loyalties that, in Madison's eyes, would and should pit Congress against the president. In turn, many observers think that during the first six years of the twenty-first century, Congress did not satisfactorily perform its traditional function of "checking" and "balancing" the executive branch.

The November 2006 elections brought Democratic majorities to both houses of Congress. For Democrats in the 110th

© The McGraw-Hill Companies, Inc./Jill Braaten, photographer

Congress, party affiliation and a belief in institutional or branch prerogatives reinforced one another. Both their party differences with President Bush *and* their belief that Congress is and should be co-equal to the executive branch fueled opposition to the Iraq war and to other Bush initiatives. And President Bush no doubt had both party loyalties and executive branch prerogatives in mind as he contended with Democratic leaders and Democratic majorities in the 110th Congress. The 2008 elections brought Democratic control to all three elective institutions of the national government (Presidency, House of Representatives, and Senate), a situation that political scientists call "unified government." Some observers of the American political system, Woodrow Wilson among them, have argued that "unified government" is likely to be more effective and efficient than its counterpart, "divided government" (in which neither major party controls all three elective institutions). Others, most notably Professor David Mayhew of Yale University, arguably the most respected contemporary political scientist specializing in the study of American politics, have concluded that "unified governments" vary very little, if at all, from "divided governments" in what gets accomplished. For nearly two-thirds of the six decades since World War II, Americans have lived under "divided government." But in January 2009, a new period of "unified government" (under Democratic control) began, and time will tell how well the country is served.

The first section of this unit contains articles on the contemporary presidency. They include both assessments of the presidency of George W. Bush, and articles written before Barack Obama took office, addressing how he might perform as president.

Eight months after Bush became president in the aftermath of the controversial 2000 election, terrorist attacks on the World Trade Center and the Pentagon on September 11, 2001, abruptly transformed the context of his presidency. Americans of both parties rallied around President Bush in his efforts to respond decisively to the attacks, and Congress passed a resolution that authorized President Bush to invade Iraq. The resulting war in Iraq began in early 2003, and within a few weeks President Bush triumphantly declared the success of the invasion that overthrew the regime of Iraqi president Saddam Hussein.

But the situation in Iraq grew worse instead of better in the next few years, and by the start of 2006, the majority of Americans opposed the Iraq war and disapproved of Bush's performance as president. The November 2006 congressional elections gave voters the chance to express their views forcefully on the Bush administration and they did so, handing majority control of both houses of Congress to the Democrats. It is in this context that articles in the first section of this unit assess the presidency of George W. Bush.

The second section of this unit treats Congress, which has undergone noteworthy changes in the past four decades after over a half-century of relative stability anchored by an enormously powerful seniority system instituted in the early twentieth century. In the 1970s, reforms in that seniority system and the budgetary process brought an enormous degree of decentralization to Capitol Hill. The unexpected Republican takeover of the House of Representatives as a result of the 1994 congressional elections brought even more changes. The new Republican speaker, Newt Gingrich, reduced the power of committees and the importance of the seniority system, imposed term limits on committee chairs, consolidated power in the Speaker's office, and became a prominent figure on the national scene. The 2006 congressional elections, of course, led to Democrats regaining majority control of both houses. A woman, Representative Nancy Pelosi of California, became Speaker of the House for the first time in history, and Republicans controlled neither house of Congress for the first time in a dozen years. Democrats increased their majorities in both houses of Congress in the 2008 elections, and, of course, a fellow Democrat, Barack Obama, won the White House. As mentioned above, it remains to be seen whether the first instance of "unified government" under Democratic control since the first two years of the Clinton administration in the early 1990s will lead to noteworthy accomplishments.

The Supreme Court sits at the top of the U.S. court system and is the main focus of the third section in this unit. The Court is not merely a legal institution; it is a policymaker whose decisions can affect the lives of millions of citizens. The Court's decisive role in determining the outcome of the 2000 presidential election showed its powerful role in the American political system. Like all people in high government offices, Supreme Court justices have policy views of their own, and observers of the Court pay careful attention to the way the nine justices interact with one another in shaping decisions of the Court. Membership of the nine-member Court—and, in turn, operation of the institution as a whole—was unusually stable between 1994 and 2005, one of the longest periods in American history during which no Supreme Court vacancies occurred. In July 2005, Justice Sandra Day O'Connor announced her intention to resign and a few months later Chief Justice William Rehnquist died. President Bush's nominees to fill the two vacancies, John Roberts and Samuel Alito, became Chief Justice and Associate Justice, respectively. Most observers expect more vacancies to occur during the Obama presidency and the new president is expected to nominate justices with quite different judicial and policy views from those of Bush's two nominees.

The bureaucracy of the national government, the subject of the fourth and last section in this unit, is responsible for carrying out policies determined by top-ranking officials. Yet the bureaucracy is not merely a neutral administrative instrument, and it is often criticized for waste and inefficiency. Even so, government bureaucracies must be given credit for many of the accomplishments of American government.

As a response to the September 11 terrorist attacks, Congress in 2002 passed a bill establishing the Department of Homeland Security, the biggest reorganization of the executive branch since the Department of Defense was founded in the aftermath of World War II. In the summer of 2004, the 9/11 Commission issued its report recommending the restructuring of the government's intelligence community. In response, Congress passed a bill in December 2004, establishing the position of Director of National Intelligence in an attempt to bring a clearer hierarchy and better communication to the government's intelligence establishment. More effective and efficient functioning of the bureaucracy has clearly become an important concern since the destruction of the World Trade Center, and efforts to improve government bureaucracy's performance in the areas of homeland security and intelligence gathering are continuing.

Some observers have attributed the home mortgage crisis and related credit and banking problems that signaled a dramatic economic downturn in 2008 to ineptly functioning bureaucracies of the national government. Fannie Mae and Freddie Mac, two relatively obscure government-related agencies, began to receive unfavorable scrutiny as the nation's home mortgage system faltered, with catastrophic consequences for Wall Street and the economy as a whole. Critics suggested that too generous lending by banks under the auspices of Fannie Mae and Freddie Mac was responsible for the credit problems that touched off the global economic downturn.

What Bush Got Right

For the next president, simply reversing this administration's policies is not the answer.

FAREED ZAKARIA

Compared with the flutters and flurries of the near-daily polls in the presidential race, one set of numbers has stayed fixed for months, even years. President George W. Bush now enters his 23rd consecutive month with an approval rating under 40 percent. (It currently stands at 32 percent.) No matter what he does, or what happens in the world, the public seems to have decided that Bush has been a failure. As a result, both candidates are promising a change from the Bush presidency. Barack Obama, of course, promises a wholly different approach to the world. But even Bush's fellow Republican, John McCain, has on several issues suggested that he would depart from the administration's policies. McCain was last seen with the president at a fund-raiser more than two months ago at which no reporters or photographers were allowed.

A broad shift in America's approach to the world is justified and overdue. Bush's basic conception of a "global War on Terror," to take but the most obvious example, has been poorly thought-through, badly implemented, and has produced many unintended costs that will linger for years if not decades. But blanket criticism of Bush misses an important reality. The administration that became the target of so much passion and anger—from Democrats, Republicans, independents, foreigners, Martians, everyone—is not quite the one in place today. The foreign policies that aroused the greatest anger and opposition were mostly pursued in Bush's first term: the invasion of Iraq, the rejection of treaties, diplomacy and multilateralism. In the past few years, many of these policies have been modified, abandoned or reversed. This has happened without acknowledgment—which is partly what drives critics crazy—and it's often been done surreptitiously. It doesn't reflect a change of heart so much as an admission of failure; the old way simply wasn't working. But for whatever reasons and through whichever path, the foreign policies in place now are more sensible, moderate and mainstream. In many cases the next president should follow rather than reverse them.

Consider as a symbol of this shift—Bush's appointment of the World Bank's president. His first choice for the job was Paul Wolfowitz, an arch neoconservative with little background in economics. But by the time Wolfowitz was forced to resign and the post opened up again, Bush realized that he needed a less ideological choice, and he picked the highly qualified and respected Robert Zoellick. Where Dick Cheney was once the poster child for the administration, today policy is being run by Condoleezza Rice, Robert Gates, Stephen Hadley and Hank Paulson—all pragmatists. Change has not extended to all areas, and in many places it's been too little, too late. But that there has been a shift to the center in many crucial areas of foreign policy is simply undeniable.

The most obvious case is Iraq. For many people—a clear majority of those polled—the decision to go to war is now seen as a mistake. But wherever one stands on that issue, it is overwhelmingly clear that the administration made a series of massive blunders in Iraq in 2003 and 2004. It went in with too few troops, dismantled Iraq's Army, bureaucracy and state-owned factories, arrested tens of thousands of Iraqis, mistreated and tortured some of them, and used overwhelming military force against all perceived threats. The outcome? Chaos; an angry, dispossessed and armed Sunni community; a sullen and restless Shiite population; an insurgency; a jihadist terrorist movement, and spreading sectarian violence. In addition, foreign forces were destabilizing the country because both the invasion and the occupation were undertaken without first gaining support from neighboring Arab states or winning international legitimacy. The result was a perfect storm in international affairs, a failure that kept getting worse.

For years, even after it was apparent to almost everyone that the Iraq strategy was not working, the administration stuck to its guns. But by 2005, the failure was simply too large to ignore, so some efforts to repair the situation were made—mostly tactical and incremental moves, like searching for a better Shiite leader and trying to slow down the process of de-Baathification. Some U.S. officials in Iraq freelanced—for example, Ambassador Zalmay Khalilzad began the outreach to Sunni leaders and militants in 2006, even while his bosses in Washington were steadfastly condemning them as terrorists. American generals in Iraq were also learning from their own failures and advocating changes in tactics. (One of them was to support efforts by tribal sheiks in Anbar to take on their Qaeda rivals, which is why the Sunni Awakening actually preceded the surge.) By 2006, Bush told *The Weekly Standard*'s Fred Barnes that he was searching for new approaches. But it was only after the 2006 midterm-election debacle that Secretary of Defense Donald Rumsfeld was fired and a new politico-military strategy was put in place with a commander who understood the need for sweeping change.

It took a long time, but the turnaround in our policy in Iraq has been significant. The United States has made broad overtures to the Sunni community, and now actively supports Sunni fighters it had once jailed. We've concentrated on stabilizing Shiite neighborhoods, helping to free them from dependence on militias. We have abandoned dreams of a pure, free market, instead trying to jump-start Iraq's state-owned enterprises in order to create jobs. And we've even been pursuing a more regional approach, trying to get neighboring countries to open embassies in Baghdad and commit to help stabilize Iraq. None of this has changed some of the basic gruesome realities of Iraq—a country from which 2.5 million people have fled (mostly the professional class), thugs and militias rule in too many places, dysfunction and corruption are utterly endemic, and religious theocrats still wield immense power. But given where things were in 2005, the administration has moved firmly in the right direction.

On Afghanistan, there is a more compelling case to be made that the administration mishandled the most important front in the War on Terror. The central critique that Barack Obama makes—that American attention, energy, troops and resources were wrongly diverted from Afghanistan to Iraq—is devastating and hard to dispute. But it's a criticism of Bush policy in 2003. The policy that the administration is currently pursuing is less vulnerable to easy attacks.

Like Obama, Defense Secretary Gates has talked about sending more troops to the region. But the problem is bigger than a lack of American soldiers. European countries haven't contributed enough troops to the effort, and have put absurd restrictions on the forces they do have in theater. Afghanistan itself is extremely complex. The country contains vast swaths of mountainous territory that have never been ruled effectively by the central government, where levels of illiteracy and unemployment are stunningly high, and where Pashtun nationalism has got mixed up with Islamic extremism. Many serious scholars and local politicians argue that more troops would not solve the problem—particularly since the Taliban's back bases are located across the border in Pakistan. And the administration has ramped up spending in the region considerably. Whereas in 2003 it spent $737 million on reconstruction and equipping the Afghan Army, by 2007 it was spending $10 billion.

On North Korea, the administration's reversal has been near total. Within months of entering the Oval Office, Bush publicly repudiated his secretary of State, Colin Powell, for even suggesting that the administration would continue Bill Clinton's efforts to negotiate with Kim Jong Il. But since July 2005, Bush has pursued a very similar approach, in fact an even more multilateral one than Clinton's—four additional parties are now at the table. Bringing in the Chinese has been crucial because they are the only ones who have any real leverage with Pyongyang. Bush began by describing North Korea as part of the Axis of Evil. Today he is considering taking the country off the terror list and has offered economic aid to its regime.

On Iran, the third charter member of the Axis of Evil, the administration has performed a similar about-face. Forget the muttering of various proponents of military action, periodically leaked to newspapers. The efforts of the administration have been diplomatic and multilateral. Its point-person for most of the second term was Nicholas Burns, a veteran diplomat who is viewed with great suspicion by neoconservatives. Last month one of the State Department's seniormost officials, William Burns (no relation), joined the Europeans at the table with Iranian negotiators, the first physical American involvement in these talks. One could argue—I would—that the administration's diplomacy is half-hearted and lacks ambition. An offer of direct engagement and negotiations would be a bolder step. But that's not a silver bullet. Such an offer could well prove fruitless. The principal obstacles to a negotiated settlement are Iranian intentions, suspicions and dysfunctions. The general thrust of Bush administration policies has now evolved into the correct one.

The same could be said for the Israeli-Palestinian peace process. Bush began his term in office vowing that he would not involve himself in Clinton-style efforts at peacemaking. His administration adopted a hands-off approach, allowing resentments to build and conditions to worsen. It gave free rein to irresponsible policies from all parties, encouraging, for example, a thoughtless and ill-planned Israeli attack on Lebanon that ended up weakening Israel, devastating Lebanon and empowering Hizbullah. This year Bush has plunged into the process, holding an international conference in Annapolis at which, for the first time, both Israel and the Palestinians accepted that the purpose of the exercise was to create a Palestinian state. Since that meeting, Rice has made a half dozen visits to the region. All this hasn't produced much yet, may be seven years too late, and perhaps is not the right approach (what is?). But few would argue that U.S. policy is currently on the wrong track.

The ones who would are revealing. Disgruntled conservative hardliners have been dismayed by the administration's policy in many areas, particularly North Korea, Iran and Israel. John Bolton, formerly Bush's U.N. ambassador and a superhawk, publicly makes the case for betrayal. When Burns joined the talks with Iran, Bolton fumed sarcastically on television that the State Department was obviously "doing its best to ensure a smooth transition to the Obama administration." (Obama has long advocated American negotiations with Tehran.) He described Bush's handling of North Korea as a capitulation, comparing him to Jimmy Carter and Bill Clinton. John Bolton is absolutely right that Bush has changed course fundamentally in many of these areas. Of course, I would celebrate that fact rather than condemn it.

Other reversals have drawn less opposition. In its early years the Bush administration seemed intent on confirming the conservative stereotype of being utterly uninterested in assistance to poor countries, especially if the money was going to treat AIDS patients. In each of its first two years it spent less than $1 billion on global HIV projects. This year the United States will spend almost $6 billion, most of it in Africa. The president's signature program, PEPFAR, has been a bipartisan success story (although the requirement that some of the money be spent on abstinence programs dilutes the program's effectiveness). Bush's overall efforts on disease prevention and aid have won him praise from an unusual assortment of figures—Bono, Bob Geld, and *New York Times* columnist Nicholas Kristof, who wrote that "George Bush has done much more for Africa than Bill Clinton ever did."

Politically the picture in Africa is more mixed. Bush put time, a presidential envoy, and considerable effort behind the negotiations to broker a peace between north and south in Sudan, and he's made some similar attempts in Darfur. (These haven't yielded much, though mostly for reasons that cannot be blamed on the administration.) More generally, however, the administration has been far too focused on the threat of terrorism, providing aid and military assistance to any and every regime—from Ethiopia to Equatorial Guinea—that claimed to be battling Al Qaeda. In a sad replay of the cold war, the United States has allied itself with unscrupulous dictators for no particular gain, only because they have learned to mouth the language of the global War on Terror.

An obsession with terrorism has also made the administration devote too little time and energy to the defining feature of the new world order—"the rise of the rest," by which I mean the growth in economic and political power of countries like China, India, Russia, Brazil and a series of regionally prominent nations like South Africa, Nigeria, Mexico and Kazakhstan. In some cases its policy positions are divided and incoherent, as in the case of Russia. But in several crucial instances, they've pursued extremely sensible strategies.

The most important one, without question, is China. The bilateral relationship between China and America will be the most significant one in the 21st century. Bush began his term poorly on the subject. During the campaign, when asked by Larry King for the single most important area where he would depart from Clinton foreign policy, he cited China. "The current president has called the relationship with China a strategic partnership," Bush said. "I believe our relationship needs to be redefined as one as competitor." The initial months of the administration suggested that Bush would adopt a confrontational approach to Beijing, just as many neoconservatives and Pentagon strategists hoped.

Then in April 2001, four months into Bush's presidency, a U.S. reconnaissance aircraft collided with a Chinese fighter plane about 70 miles from the Chinese island of Hainan, and was forced to make an emergency landing. The Chinese claimed that the American plane had entered and violated Chinese airspace; Washington argued that it was in international airspace. In order to recover the aircraft and crew, Washington had to negotiate with Beijing and—despite much conservative grumbling—Bush agreed to send the Chinese a "letter of two sorries," in which the United States offered some carefully worded expressions of regret about the incident and death of the Chinese pilot.

Since then the administration's China policy has moved toward recognizing the centrality of the relationship. If China can be brought into the existing world order—in some fashion and to some extent—that will greatly improve the prospects for future peace and stability. Bush, despite his grand rhetoric about spreading democracy around the world, has been practical in his relations with the Chinese regime. On the most important issue to Beijing—that of Taiwan—Bush not only sided with the Chinese but has done so in a more direct manner than any previous president. He made clear to the then Taiwanese President Chen Shui-bian that were Taiwan to make any moves toward independence, the island would lose the support of the United States. More recently, unlike some heads of government in Europe, Bush chose to attend the opening ceremony of the Beijing Olympics, a move that will earn the United States much good will not just with the Chinese government but also with its people.

Of course, the administration recognizes that the rise of China upsets the strategic balance in Asia. That's led Washington to deepen the strategic relationship with Japan and to develop a new one with India. In the latter case, Bush deserves credit for having transformed the relationship. While Indo-U.S. ties were warm under Bill Clinton, they were always limited by the controversy over India's nuclear program. The Clintonites refused to legitimize India's nuclear program, but for Indians their nukes were absolutely vital. Bush broke the deadlock by accepting, in large measure, that India would have to be treated as an exception and be brought into the nuclear nonproliferation regime as a nuclear power, not a renegade. Now India and America are developing a strategic relationship at many levels of government, which will stand both countries in good stead no matter what the future balance of power in Asia looks like.

If the United States hasn't engaged with this emerging world actively enough, other countries have done even less. In an essay in Foreign Affairs, political scientist Daniel Drezner points out that the administration has sought to give China, India and Brazil more weight in international institutions like the International Monetary Fund, the World Bank, the G8 and other such bodies. Timothy Adams, the undersecretary of Treasury, told *The New York Times* in August 2006 that "by re-engineering the IMF and giving China a bigger voice, China will have a greater sense of responsibility for the institution's mission."

The fiercest resistance to such reforms comes from Europe. If power in international organizations is going to be allocated on the basis of the current configuration of power, European nations, which are shrinking as a percentage of global GDP, will lose influence. If the U.N. Security Council were to be set up today, would 40 percent of the vetoes be given to European powers?

All this is not meant as a defense of George W. Bush. The administration made monumental errors in its first few years, ones that have cost the United States enormously. The shift in impressions about America's intentions across important sections of the globe, the sense in much of the Islamic world that America is anti-Muslim, the vast and counterproductive apparatus of homeland security—visa restrictions, arrests and interrogations—are lasting legacies of the Bush administration. Its dysfunction and incompetence have left a trail of misery in countries like Iraq and Lebanon, which have been destabilized for decades. The embrace of torture and other extralegal methods has violated America's noblest traditions and provided little in return.

And then there is the administration's record outside of foreign policy. Bush 43 has surely been the most fiscally irresponsible president in American history, taking surpluses that equaled 2.5 percent of GDP and turning them into deficits that are 3 percent. This is a $4 trillion hit on the country's balance sheet. On the central issue of energy policy—the greatest economic challenge and opportunity of our times—Bush has been utterly obstructionist, recycling the self-serving arguments of industry lobbyists. On the whole, Bush's record remains one of failure and missed opportunities.

So why offer this corrective? Because we cannot go back to 2001. The next president will inherit the world as it is in 2009. He will have to examine the Bush administration's policies as they stand in January 2009—not as they were in 2001 or 2002 or 2003—and decide how to accept, modify and alter them. There was a U.S. president who came into office convinced that everything his predecessor had done was feckless, stupid, ill-informed and venal. He rejected and tried to reverse everything that he could, almost as an article of faith. Before he had even examined the policies carefully, he knew that they had to be changed. The base of his party was delighted by his clarity and fighting spirit.

That president, of course, was George W. Bush. His decision to blindly repudiate anything associated with Bill Clinton is what got us into this mess in the first place. Let's hope that the next president, no matter how much he despises Bush, will take a careful look at his administration's policies, America's interests, and the world beyond and do the right thing for the country and its future.

Small Ball after All?

Both supporters and critics of George W. Bush tend to view him as a game-changing president. But it's possible he may be remembered another way—as a comparatively minor figure.

Jonathan Rauch

"Worst. President. Ever." That succinct judgment, received not long ago via e-mail from a political scientist, sums up a good deal of what conventional wisdom has to say about President Bush. In an unscientific online poll of 109 historians conducted in April and published by the History News Network at www.hnn.us, more than 60 percent rated Bush's presidency as the worst in U.S. history. In his 2007 book, *Second Chance: Three Presidents and the Crisis of American Superpower,* former National Security Adviser Zbigniew Brzezinski titles his chapter on Bush "Catastrophic Leadership." "A calamity," Brzezinski wrote. "A historical failure."

And he was referring to just the Iraq war. The litany of disasters and failures commonly attributed to Bush has grown familiar enough to summarize in checklist format: WMD; Guantanamo; Abu Ghraib; waterboarding; wiretapping; habeas corpus; "Osama bin Forgotten"; anti-Americanism; deficits; spending; Katrina; Rumsfeld; Cheney; Gonzales; Libby. In this view, George W. Bush is at least as destructive as was Richard Nixon, a president whose mistakes and malfeasances took decades to undo.

Though a smaller band, Bush's defenders parry that he will look to history more like Harry Truman, a president whose achievements took decades to appreciate. In this view, Bush will be remembered as the president who laid the strategic groundwork for an extended struggle against Islamist terrorism; who made democratization the centerpiece of foreign policy; who transformed the federal-state relationship in education; who showed that a candidate can touch the "third rail" of Social Security and still get elected (twice).

Antithetical as these two views are, notice what they assume in common: Bush has been a game-changing president. For better or worse, he has succeeded in his ambition of being a transformative figure rather than one who plays "small ball," in Bush's own disdainful phrase. Hasn't he?

Perhaps not. Today's debate overlooks another possibility: Bush may go down in history as a transitional and comparatively minor figure. His presidency, though politically traumatic, may leave only a modest policy footprint. In that sense—though

by no means substantively or stylistically—Bush's historical profile may resemble Jimmy Carter's more than Truman's or Nixon's. Recall that in 1980 many people wondered if the country would ever recover from Carter. Five years later, he was all but forgotten.

In other words, Bush may have accomplished something that seemed out of the question in January 2002, when he touched greatness, and in January 2007, when he touched bottom. Bush may have achieved mediocrity.

If that hypothesis sounds snide, it is not intended to. Had Bush left office at the beginning of last year, his tenure might indeed have gone down as calamitous. Winding up in the middling ranks, then, would be no mean accomplishment. Far from being happenstance, such a finish would reflect an unusual period of course correction that might be thought of as Bush's third term.

From Uniter to Divider

Odd as it may sound today, this president entered office as a proponent of bipartisanship. In his December 13, 2000, victory speech after Vice President Gore conceded the election, Bush called for a new politics of conciliation. Speaking from the chamber of the Texas House of Representatives, he said, "The spirit of cooperation I have seen in this hall is what is needed in Washington, D.C."

To be sure, Bush was capable of aggressive partisanship and brusque unilateralism, as when in 2001 he pushed through large tax cuts with little Democratic support and tore up an assortment of treaties. But in the early days, he also brought off a bipartisan education reform, and after the September 11 terrorist attacks, he did what even his critics agreed was a masterful job of rallying the country. His public approval rose to a dizzying 90 percent.

The fruits of this early period of two-party government were considerable: a new campaign finance law, the USA PATRIOT Act's revisions to domestic-security law, the Sarbanes-Oxley corporate accountability law, the creation of the Homeland

Security Department, and more. "Seventeen major legislative acts were passed in the first two years of the Bush presidency—the second-highest among first-term presidents in the post-World War II period," writes Charles O. Jones, a presidential historian.

Had Bush left office in January 2003, his reputation as our era's Truman might have been assured. His successor would have inherited not only the aforementioned laws but also a successful military campaign in Afghanistan, a set of broadly accepted policies for combating terrorism, and a United Nations still following America's lead in efforts to confront Iraq's Saddam Hussein.

But 2002 also marked the Bush administration's transition to a more rigidly partisan governing style. That January, Karl Rove, Bush's top political adviser, signaled that Republicans would "make the president's handling of the war on terrorism the centerpiece of their strategy to win back the Senate," as *The Washington Post* reported. This represented a distinct change in tone: "Until now," *The Post* noted, "Bush has stressed that the fight against terrorism is a bipartisan and unifying issue for the country."

It was in this period, says Steven Schier, a political scientist at Carleton College and the author of a forthcoming book on Bush's presidency, that "you get the idea of permanent political advantage based on national security, which becomes intoxicating to Republicans." That year's midterm election, which gave Republicans control of the Senate and consolidated their margin in the House, vindicated their strategy but also trapped the party within it.

In firm control of both branches, Bush and congressional Republicans embarked on an experiment in one-party government. Thanks to superbly honed party discipline, the plan worked for a while, but the price was high. Republicans had to govern from the center of their party, rather than the center of the country; Democrats were absolved from responsibility for the results.

What followed was a period of substantive excess and stylistic harshness that came to define Bush's presidency in the public's mind, obliterating memories of the "compassionate conservative." The list of setbacks in this period is long, merely beginning with Iraq's disintegration, North Korea's test of a nuclear bomb, and Iran's growing boldness and influence.

At home, profligate spending and a major Medicare expansion disgusted conservatives. Rising deficits troubled centrists, as did Bush's (unsuccessful) intervention in a dispute over ending the life of Terri Schiavo. His efforts to reform Social Security and immigration policy collapsed embarrassingly; his sluggish response to Hurricane Katrina cratered Americans' faith in his competence. Abroad, Abu Ghraib, Guantanamo, waterboarding, and extrajudicial detentions called the country's basic decency into question. One could go on.

Whatever you may think of the administration's policies on those issues individually, their cumulative effect on Bush and his party are not in doubt. By 2006, the president's approval rating was in the 30 percent range and falling. The Democrats swept control of Congress in November. If Bush's presidency

had ended in January 2007, his reputation as our era's Nixon might have been assured.

But, of course, Bush did not leave office then. Instead he embarked on what history may come to regard as the most surprising and interesting period of his presidency. Many presidents have had good first terms and troubled second ones; the pattern is conventional, and Bush's presidency approximately fits it. But Bush has used his last two years as, in effect, a third term, behaving as if he were his own successor.

Bush's Third Term

He began with some significant personnel changes. In 2006, Bush replaced the second of two mediocre Treasury secretaries with Henry Paulson Jr., whose performance has been lauded by the likes of House Financial Services Committee Chairman Barney Frank, D-Mass., and New York City Mayor Michael Bloomberg—neither of them Bush fans.

Shortly afterward, ending what seemed an interminable wait, Bush got around to replacing the dysfunctional Donald Rumsfeld at the Defense Department with the far more adept Robert Gates. At Justice, Michael Mukasey, a respected federal judge, set about re-professionalizing a department whose independence and credibility had been compromised under Alberto Gonzales. At State, the president gave Condoleezza Rice her head, a trust that her predecessor, Colin Powell, had never been allowed.

"There was unquestionably a sharp change in their approach to the world and in their policies," says Kenneth Pollack, a senior fellow at the Brookings Institution's Saban Center for Middle East Policy. Frequently cited examples include:

- **The Iraq surge.** Against conventional wisdom, the administration sent more troops to Iraq and gave them a new commander with a new strategy. Even Bush's critics now acknowledge that Iraq is in far better shape than it was two years ago. The gains may or may not be sustainable, but if they can be preserved, Iraq has a shot at peace and stability. That seemed a pipe dream before the surge.
- **Iran.** Bush has been patient but, many critics have said, rigid in his dealings with this charter "axis of evil" member. Lately, however, he has softened his posture and attempted to cultivate new openings, notably by authorizing what *The New York Times* called "the most significant American diplomatic contact with Iran since the Islamic revolution in 1979."
- **The Israeli-Palestinian conflict.** After years of keeping his distance from what he seemed to regard as a morass, Bush changed course in 2007, authorizing Rice to pursue diplomacy vigorously and presiding over a relaunch of Israeli-Palestinian peace talks last November.
- **North Korea.** Over hawks' objections, Bush struck a denuclearization deal with Pyongyang much like the one that conservatives, including some Bushies, derided the Clinton administration for making. "That

is the really dramatic example of Bush doing toward the end of his presidency something he would never have contemplated or tolerated early on," says Strobe Talbott, who was deputy secretary of State in the Clinton administration and is now the president of Brookings.

- **Global warming.** Repudiating the Kyoto climate treaty was among Bush's first presidential acts, and he maintained his disengagement from the issue through most of his presidency. But in July he joined the other major industrial countries in promising to halve greenhouse-gas emissions by 2050. A European environmental official told *The Washington Post,* "President Bush has moved considerably over the past one to two years."

What changed? "I think we learned a bit," Stephen Hadley, Bush's national security adviser, told reporters in June. He was speaking of U.S. forbearance in dealing with the always obstreperous North Koreans, but to outsiders the statement appears to have broader applicability. Liberals say that the administration became more flexible because it ran out of alternatives, conservatives that its resolve weakened, Kremlinologists that (as one aide told Carla Anne Robbins of *The New York Times*) "Condi wins."

Ever protective of Bush's trademark steadfastness, the White House takes issue with any talk of U-turns. "I think there's actually remarkable continuity," says Tony Fratto, the deputy press secretary. He asserts that reality has caught up with the administration rather than the other way around. It took time to draw China, India, and other major emerging economies into global-warming negotiations, a prerequisite for any ambitious U.S. commitment; it took time to persuade China to lean on the North Koreans to make a nuclear deal; it took time to weather leadership changes and factional struggles so that Middle East peace negotiations could resume. The surge in Iraq, Fratto says, "was clearly a change of course. It was a new strategy." Elsewhere, he argues, the administration has been reaping the fruits of patient effort.

Whatever the explanation (the various versions may all be partially right), in the past couple of years Bush has significantly changed the starting point for his successor. He now hands President McCain or President Obama a healing rather than a broken Iraq, diplomatic processes rather than deadlocks in the Middle East and the Korean Peninsula, and a position on global warming that is widely viewed as moving the United States past obstructionism. Both Republican John McCain and Democrat Barack Obama, it seems fair to guess, would rather follow than precede Bush's late-term adjustments. Whatever you may think of Bush's abilities as a sailor, he has proved pretty good at bailing.

Meanwhile, despite his abysmal popularity and the Democrats' control of Congress, Bush managed to win approval, on essentially his own terms, of a new wiretapping law and funding for the war in Iraq, the last things anyone expected a Democratic Congress to give him. "I think what you see here is a guy who has learned to be as effective as possible in reduced circumstances," says Schier, the Carleton College political

scientist. Paradoxically, this chief executive who prided himself on assertive, even aggressive, leadership proved to be a weak strong president but a surprisingly strong weak one.

Back to the Future

To what end?

That Bush has improved his legacy over the past couple of years is an easy case to make. True, the economy has declined, oil prices have risen, and the mortgage crisis has loosed a Category 4 storm on Wall Street. But the economy and oil prices are not under Bush's control, and both he and Congress have leaned aggressively into the financial gale, adopting a bipartisan stimulus package and intervening forcefully to support the mortgage market. With unemployment rising and Wall Street wondering where the mortgage fallout may end, no one much likes the economy's condition today, but not many people would trade the *policies* of late 2008 for the *policies* of late 2006.

The harder question is where Bush will leave matters after eight years, not after just the past two. The only honest answer is: It depends. What do you measure? How do you think a President Gore would have done? Those are the sorts of questions that keep historians and journalists in business. You will find no definitive answers here.

But you will find a hypothesis, one at odds with the prevailing wisdom that Bush, whatever you think of him, has been a president of major consequence. Consider, again, the five problems mentioned earlier, this time comparing their likely status in January 2009 with where things stood in January 2001.

- **Iraq.** The situation in January 2001 was unstable and dangerous but not critical. Then, for a time, affairs in Iraq became critical, verging on catastrophic. Now the situation is again unstable and dangerous but not critical. Obviously, Iraq today is a very different kind of problem than it was eight years ago, one more pregnant with both promise and risk. But the U.S. preoccupation with Iraq that Bush inherited in 2001, and that he intended to dispose of once and for all, will instead continue into its fourth presidency, if not beyond. (Iraq will soon have been a sinkhole for U.S. foreign-policy energy for 20 years, almost half the length of the Cold War.)
- **Iran.** This rogue nation was a problem in 2001 and remains a problem now. In the interim, Iran has raced ahead with uranium enrichment, elevated an apocalyptic demagogue to its second-highest office, and expanded its regional influence. At the same time, however, Western powers have edged toward a consensus on confronting Iran, and the United Nations has imposed several sets of sanctions, some of which—the financial ones—appear to be biting.
- **The Israeli-Palestinian conflict.** As Bill Clinton left office, the United States was struggling against long odds to broker a peace deal; as George W. Bush leaves office, the United States is struggling against long odds to broker a peace deal. Whether the situation is more

intractable today than it was eight years ago is an open question, but Bush's reluctant conclusion that the U.S. must mediate an agreement all but guarantees that no future president will try to walk away from the problem. If Bush couldn't walk away, no one can.

- **North Korea.** A tenuous denuclearization agreement was in place eight years ago; a tenuous denuclearization agreement is in place again today. Now, as then, the agreement may or may not be worth the paper it is written on. In the interim, Pyongyang acquired a few more nuclear bombs and tested one, but the two sides are still playing the same game.

- **Global warming.** Eight years ago, the United States had committed itself to reducing greenhouse-gas emissions, though rhetorically rather than substantively; today the United States has again committed itself to reducing greenhouse-gas emissions, though rhetorically rather than substantively. As with the Israeli-Palestinian conflict, Bush's attempt to disengage from the climate-change issue merely established that the United States cannot do so. The next president will pick up more or less where the Clinton-era Kyoto Protocol left off.

Bush may have made these problems harder or easier to solve, a question that partisans can contest to their hearts' delight. What is clear, however, is that all five were large and difficult challenges in 2000 and all five remain large and difficult challenges in 2008.

Two other areas, the war on terrorism and fiscal policy, deserve a closer look. Bush's defenders stake their claims heavily on the former, his detractors on the latter. Has Bush built a lasting architecture for the "long war"? Has he wrecked the country's finances?

The War on Terrorism

September 11, 2001, it is often said, "changed everything." It certainly changed Americans' attitudes, convincing the public that Al Qaeda and its affiliates are a threat rather than a nuisance, and that the United States must apply military as well as civilian tools to confront terrorism. September 11 thereby triggered a cascade of policy changes, ranging from the PATRIOT Act to the Iraq war.

The threat was pre-existing, however, as Bush's supporters tirelessly repeat (adding that the Clinton administration failed to deal with it). The Qaeda-Taliban-jihadi nexus has relocated its headquarters from Afghanistan to the nearby borderlands of Pakistan, but whether and how much it has been weakened is hard to say. The absence of attacks on the American homeland is to the Bush administration's credit, but it seems only fair to guess that a Gore administration would have worked domestic security just as hard. And to the extent that the United States is safer because jihadists shifted their attention to the softer targets of Iraq and Afghanistan, that is not altogether reassuring. Might a different administration have attained better results with less damage to the American brand overseas? Maybe.

A more intellectually interesting question is whether Bush, like Truman, has set up a lasting strategic and institutional architecture for managing the conflict. Bush's defenders argue that a return to either the pinprick responses of the 1990s or the cynical realism of the Cold War is inconceivable. "If we wait for threats to fully materialize, we will have waited too long," Bush said in June 2002. That statement, the core of the Bush Doctrine, is hardly controversial today.

"None of the key elements of the Bush Doctrine—[U.S.] primacy, prevention [of terrorist attacks], coalitions of the willing, and democracy promotion—will be abandoned in practice by successor administrations, whatever their rhetorical recalibrations and tactical adjustments," write Timothy J. Lynch and Robert S. Singh in their new book, *After Bush: The Case for Continuity in American Foreign Policy.* Similarly, the Detainee Treatment Act, the Military Commissions Act, the PATRIOT Act, and the new Foreign Intelligence Surveillance Act have put in place mechanisms that subsequent presidents may revise but will not repudiate.

Such is the strongest upside case for Bush as a turning-point president, and it may well prove correct. The retort, however, is also strong: What was most striking about Bush's attitude toward the long war was his perverse *reluctance* to create a sustainable institutional architecture. In marked contrast to Truman, Bush treated Congress and U.S. allies as afterthoughts, running the war on jihadism as a permanent emergency in which the president could single-handedly make up the rules as he went along. He regarded the war as an opportunity to build a political base, not an institutional one.

Result: It took nearly seven years to finish the first trial of a Guantanamo detainee. The courts have shredded Bush's claim that he could detain almost anyone practically forever, leaving the presidency, in some respects, with less power than it had before. (George H.W. Bush and Bill Clinton both used Guantanamo Bay to hold detainees without judicial oversight; the Supreme Court recently revoked that authority.) The country still lacks coherent and indisputably constitutional structures governing the detention and treatment of terrorism suspects. The sad fact, in this view, is that it will be largely up to the next president to construct the durable, consensus-based structures for the war on terrorism that Bush could and should have built.

As for strategy, this retort continues, what is new about the Bush Doctrine is not sustainable, and what is sustainable is not new. President Gore would likely have moved toward preemption and democratization, but without the rhetorical and military excesses that have widely discredited both approaches. Indeed, Bush has been forced to become a reluctant realist, collaborating with exactly the sorts of tyrannies—in the Middle East, Africa, and Asia—that he has condemned. The Bush Doctrine's worst enemy, in this view, has been Bush.

This argument can't be settled any time soon, if ever. What seems fairly clear, however, is that the jihadist threat is still very much present and that Bush's role has been ambiguous, erecting while also partially discrediting a militarily focused, executive-driven approach that may prove more vigorous than sustainable.

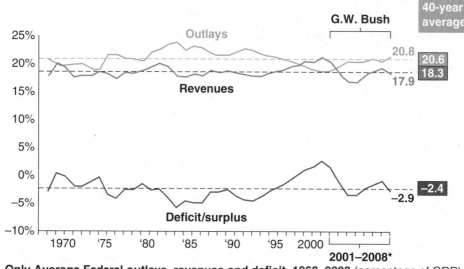

Only Average Federal outlays, revenues and deficit, 1968–2008 (percentage of GDP).

Source: Congressional Budget Office.

Red Ink Rising

Bush's critics, meanwhile, argue that he trashed the country's finances. He cut taxes steeply, waged an expensive war without paying for it, engineered a costly expansion of Medicare (also without paying for it), and untethered federal spending, thus turning healthy surpluses into chronic deficits—all while failing to come to grips with an imminent crisis in entitlement programs.

"We're in much worse fiscal shape today than we were in 2001," says David Walker, who until recently headed the Government Accountability Office and is now president of the Peter G. Peterson Foundation. According to GAO figures, the country's fiscal exposure—the long-term shortfall in its finances, in present-value terms—more than doubled between 2000 and 2007 from $20.4 trillion to $52.7 trillion. Walker says, moreover, "Our $53 trillion hole grows $2 trillion to $3 trillion a year even with a balanced budget," because of rising health care costs, demographic changes (fewer workers supporting more retirees), and accumulating interest on the national debt.

Fiscal recklessness is probably the strongest downside case for Bush as a turning-point president. Here again, however, there is a challenging counterargument.

Thanks mainly to a growing economy, but also partly to tighter budgets, the deficit shrank relative to the economy in Bush's second term. (See Chart, this page.) In fiscal 2007, the deficit was 1.2 percent of gross domestic product, which was below the average of the last 40 years. The 2008 deficit will rise to about 2.9 percent of GDP, according to administration projections; but that is still only slightly above the 40-year average, and the cause is primarily cyclical rather than structural, because the economy is slowing down.

For all the talk of runaway spending, moreover, outlays are also right at the 40-year norm. The exceptional federal spending policies were Ronald Reagan's and Bill Clinton's, not Bush's.

As for Bush's tax cuts, viewed in historical perspective they were a blip, not a turning point. Overall, taxes went down early in this decade but then bobbed back up again, though not all the way. In 2007, federal receipts were 18.8 percent of GDP, slightly *above* the 40-year average of 18.3 percent. Even assuming that Bush's tax cuts are all extended when they expire after 2010, *and* assuming that Congress "fixes" the alternative minimum tax by permanently stopping its upward creep, the Congressional Budget Office forecasts that taxes will stay at about 19 percent of GDP.

Bush and Congress, then, didn't smash the revenue base; they just returned it to its well-worn groove. That groove seems to track the public's comfort zone, as suggested by the nonpartisan Tax Policy Center's recent report that Obama's tax program would keep revenues at about 18.4 percent of GDP through 2018—again, right at the historical norm.

As for how the tax burden is allocated, Obama promises to cut taxes at the bottom and increase them at the top. He would raise the top income-tax rate to 39.5 percent, right back where Bill Clinton left it. You can make a plausible case that the end result would approximate what would have been President Gore's tax code.

No question about it: Bush failed to deal with the long-term entitlement problem. He left the ledger in worse shape than he found it, and his botched effort to reform Social Security may have made entitlement reform more difficult politically. "I think we've lost a tremendous opportunity during the Bush period and, really, over the last part of the Clinton period," says Stuart Butler, an analyst at the Heritage Foundation.

Still, as Butler's comment implies, Bush's failure in this regard is not unique. His predecessors ducked the entitlement problem and his would-be successors are all but promising to do the same. McCain's pledges to reduce taxes, and Obama's to increase spending, would likely make the problem worse.

Bush's fiscal failing, in short, arguably lies not in being exceptional but in being all too ordinary.

Disaster, or Detour?

The point of this article is not that the Bush years were uneventful or barren. Far from it. In the realm of foreign policy, the last eight years have seen a nuclear pact with India, a passel of bilateral trade agreements, a redoubled commitment to fight HIV/AIDS, and an innovative foreign-aid program (the Millennium Challenge Account). In social policy, the Bush presidency has brought education reform, restrictions on embryonic-stem-cell research, and incentives for faith-based programs. In finance, the 2002 Sarbanes-Oxley law and the government's current scramble to contain the mortgage-market turmoil have arguably done more to extend Washington's control over Wall Street than anything since the Depression era. The creation of the Homeland Security Department represents the biggest bureaucratic reorganization that Washington has seen in two generations. Bush's two Supreme Court appointments have nudged the Court to the right.

None of those changes is trivial. But few if any are outside the boundaries of ordinary policy-making in an eventful eight-year presidency. It seems fair to guess that most will get sentences or paragraphs, rather than chapters, in the history books.

Indeed, what is most striking about the Bush presidency is not the new problems it has created (though Iraq may yet change that verdict) or the old problems it has solved (though Iraq may yet change that verdict, too). What is striking, rather, is that Bush will pass on to his successor all the major problems and preoccupations he inherited: Iraq, Iran, Israel and the Palestinians, North Korea, global warming, Islamist terrorism, nuclear proliferation, health care, entitlement costs, immigration. What is remarkable, in other words, is not how much Bush has done to reshape the agenda but how little.

Reagan removed inflation from the agenda; he and George H.W. Bush (still sadly underrated) removed the Cold War; Clinton removed welfare and the deficit. Bush, as of now, ends up more or less where he started—not exactly, of course (he resurrected the deficit, for example), but about as close as history's turbulence allows. The biggest surprise of the Bush presidency is its late-breaking bid to join the middling ranks of administrations that are judged not by their triumph or tragedy but by their opportunity cost: What might a greater or lesser president have done with Bush's eight years?

In his recent book *The Bush Tragedy,* Jacob Weisberg, the editor-in-chief of the Washington Post Co.'s Slate Group, mentions the he was "originally going to call this book *The Bush Detour,* thinking of the Bush presidency simply as lost time for the country." His original title may have been closer to the mark. If so, history's ironic judgment on this singularly ambitious president will be that his legacy was small ball, after all.

A Liberal Shock Doctrine

History teaches us that presidents have to move quickly to enact progressive reforms before the window of opportunity closes forever. It's a lesson Barack Obama should take to heart.

RICK PERLSTEIN

Progressive political change in American history is rarely incremental. With important exceptions, most of the reforms that have advanced our nation's status as a modern, liberalizing social democracy were pushed through during narrow windows of progressive opportunity—which subsequently slammed shut with the work not yet complete. The post–Civil War reconstruction of the apartheid South, the Progressive Era remaking of the institutions of democratic deliberation, the New Deal, the Great Society: They were all blunt shocks. Then, before reformers knew what had happened, the seemingly sturdy reform mandate faded and Washington returned to its habits of stasis and reaction.

The Oval Office's most effective inhabitants have always understood this. Franklin D. Roosevelt hurled down executive orders and legislative proposals like thunderbolts during his First Hundred Days, hardly slowing down for another four years before his window slammed shut; Lyndon Johnson, aided by John F. Kennedy's martyrdom and the landslide of 1964, legislated at such a breakneck pace his aides were in awe. Both presidents understood that there are too many choke points—our minority-enabling constitutional system, our national tendency toward individualism, and our concentration of vested interests—to make change possible any other way.

Reforms such as Social Security, Medicare, and desegregation happened fast. Otherwise they wouldn't have happened at all.

That is a fact. A fact too many Democrats have trained themselves to ignore. And it sometimes feels like Barack Obama, whose first instinct when faced with ideological resistance seems to be to extend the right hand of fellowship, understands it least of all. Does he grasp that unless all the monuments of lasting, structural change in the American state—banking regulation, public-power generation, Social Security, the minimum wage,

the right to join a union, federal funding of education, Medicare, desegregation, Southern voting rights—had happened fast, they wouldn't have happened at all?

I hope so. Because if Barack Obama is elected president with a significant popular mandate, a number of Democrats riding his coattails to the House, and enough senators to scuttle the filibuster of his legislative agenda—all of which seem entirely possible—he will inherit a historical opportunity to civilize the United States in ways not seen in a generation. To achieve the change he seeks—the monumental trio of universal health care, a sustainable energy policy, and a sane and secure internationalism—he has to completely reverse the way Democrats have habituated themselves to doing business. If they want true progress, they have to be juggernauts. American precedent gives them no other way.

Let Franklin Roosevelt be our guide. We take for granted now one of his signature political innovations: the idea of an executive "legislative agenda," a specific set of White House proposals, by which the success or failure of a presidency can be judged. FDR's was the first and most spectacular. He understood that the New Deal would pass quickly or it would not pass at all. And so, politically, he yoked Congress' willingness to pass his program without obstruction to Congress' willingness to address the national emergency *tout court.*

We're not facing a Great Depression–level emergency now. But with an unprecedented 77 percent of respondents in an Associated Press poll saying they believe the nation is on the "wrong track," and 9 percent telling the Gallup organization they approve of Congress' job performance, Obama is not without leverage. Ideally, Obama's Washington would resemble FDR's in 1935. "The stories of that period always seemed to follow the same pattern," Thomas Frank writes in his new book, *The Wrecking Crew: How Conservatives Rule,* "how the bright young man arrived in the city, fresh from law school, where he was put to work immediately on business of utmost urgency; how he went for days without sleep."

One of those exhausted bright young men, of course, was bright-eyed Lyndon B. Johnson of the Texas Hill Country. The 1930s Washington culture in which LBJ thrived was not merely a function of the New Dealers' scramble to redeem a national emergency. It was a function of the fact that they understood the reality of America as "the frozen republic," as Daniel Lazare has called it. By the time Johnson got his accidental opportunity to occupy his hero FDR's chair, progressives understood implicitly that the unique constitutional system, conceived to protect the minority interests of slaveholders, gives the upper hand to obstructers. This, and not the supposed necessity of trimming ideological sails to placate some notional conservative majority, guided their strategizing. James MacGregor Burns' book on the subject, *The Deadlock of Democracy,* was not merely what every progressive in Washington was reading during the Kennedy years, it was what every progressive was living. The House Rules Committee, dominated by reactionary Southerners, kept Kennedy from passing even an increase in the minimum wage, let alone his campaign promise—the cornerstone of *his* legislative agenda—to extend Social Security to cover medical care for the elderly. It was, as historians G. Calvin Mackenzie and Robert Weisbrot write in their fine recent study, *The Liberal Hour: Washington and the Politics of Change in the 1960s,* "a lesson fully understood by the Southerners in Congress. They didn't need to have majorities on their side, they didn't need to have public opinion on their side, they didn't need the president on their side. They only needed to have the rules on their side."

Three accidents of history followed in quick succession to break the deadlock. First, in the most important turning point in history you've never heard of, Kennedy narrowly won a vote to dynamite the House Rules Committee's role as a tar pit for liberal legislation by expanding its membership. Second, the Supreme Court's first "one man, one vote" decision, *Baker v. Carr* (1962), outlawed Southern electoral systems, which, for instance, gave the three smallest counties in Georgia, with a total population of 69,800, as much voting strength as the largest county in the state, with a population of 556,326. And finally, Kennedy was shot. The national trauma was a blunt political opportunity from whose import Johnson did not flinch. "Let us continue," he intoned in his first address to a joint session of Congress. Then, before this tragic but miraculous once-in-a-lifetime store of political capital drained away, he started passing the liberal legislative agenda that had been little more than a shadow during Kennedy's lifetime.

"I'm not going to cavil, and I'm not going to compromise," Lyndon Johnson said of the Civil Rights Act of 1964.

Less than a month into his presidency, Johnson wrangled from a recalcitrant Congress a loan guarantee to help our mortal enemies, the Soviets, buy grain before he had been in office a month, convincing 38 legislators to return to Washington during their Christmas vacations to approve the loan. The Economic

Opportunity Act of 1964—the "war on poverty"—passed by a nearly two-to-one margin. Johnson advocated for a tax cut that conservatives called a budget-buster, bringing Dwight D. Eisenhower out of retirement to campaign against it. But Johnson passed that, too. Then came Medicare. Then the Civil Rights Act. "I'm not going to cavil, and I'm not going to compromise," Johnson told Sen. Richard Russell of Georgia as the landmark bill Kennedy introduced to no avail in the summer of 1963 was steamrolling its way to completion.

In 1965 Johnson passed new legislation for preschool for poor children, college prep for poor teenagers, legal services for indigent defendants, redevelopment funds for lagging economic regions, landmark immigration reform, a new Department of Housing and Urban Development, and national endowments for the humanities and art. He even added a whole new category to the liberal agenda with the passage of the Highway Beautification Act, the Water Quality Act, and the Clean Air Act. He insisted to his congressional leadership that the House's bill for federal aid to education pass the Senate "literally without a comma changed," aide Eric Goldman recalled. It did indeed, two weeks later, with only 18 votes in opposition.

His insistence on ramming through bills "without a comma changed" wasn't a function of Johnson's natural aggressiveness or ego (or at least not only that). It was, in the American legislative context, a necessary sort of pragmatism. The 36th president saw that his opportunity to move the country forward could end any day and that he must act before America lurched back into a state of fearful reaction. He was right. During the span of just a few weeks in the summer of 1965, Johnson flew to Independence, Missouri, to sign Medicare—the reform JFK had run on in 1960—and to Washington to sign the Voting Rights Act. Five days later, on Aug. 11, the Watts Riots brought down the curtain on the liberal hour. After that, he couldn't even get Congress to approve $60 million for rodent control in the slums.

The right and Democratic centrists have taught us to think of the Great Society in terms of its failures, like the War on Poverty's Community Action Program, which drove a wedge between Washington and local Democratic municipal administrations and supposedly empowered all manner of swindlers and "poverty pimps." We should focus instead on Johnson's remarkable number of broad-based accomplishments in those first 22 months. We now take for granted the notion that the elderly have a right to medical care, that the government should provide aid for education, that immigration policy should not discriminate on the basis of race, and that the government should concern itself with clean air. It would be unimaginable to see them reversed—in part because of the constitutional inertia that made them so difficult to achieve in the first place. They are the kind of things Republicans now pretend they were in favor of all along. This is the way social change works. It is the responsibility of the next progressive president to crash through a similar set of reforms for the *next* generation to take for granted.

Conservatives understand these stakes, which is why obstructionism is the rock upon which they have built their political church. Not for nothing was Jesse

Helms celebrated so unequivocally by conservatives upon his death this summer: He was "Senator No." They know that a single well-placed roadblock, whether within the news cycle or behind closed doors in the legislative process, can stop progress *cold*—even in the face of a Democratic Congress united with a Democratic president and a friendly judiciary. They understand that in America, Democratic (and democratic) mandates are tailor-made for sabotage and that the sabotage must come early, quick, and hard.

This was the reliable formula that brought down such progressive initiatives as Clinton's health-care program. But it was Jimmy Carter's attempt to fix American energy policy that really set the precedent for failed reform. It is easy to forget how progressive hopes were soaring on January 20, 1977. A Republican president had resigned in disgrace. His replacement had proven hapless and tainted. A slew of young liberal lions had been swept into office in 1974 on the wave of disgust, and Jimmy Carter was elected to give America "a government as good as its people." Even the pundits' affection was in his pocket.

In retrospect, of course, we remember how badly Carter mishandled the job of pushing his own legislative agenda. He couldn't work with Congress. He alienated key Democratic constituencies. Maybe such deficiencies won't hobble Barack Obama, who appears an infinitely more skilled politician. But despite his skill, Obama will not be available to avoid the fact that the right also learned from the early years of FDR and LBJ. They know the lessons in their bones: Strike hard and fast by any means necessary to degrade a popular new Democratic president's capability to pass anything big right away, because once something is passed, it might never go away.

Carter started out with a bang, just as FDR and LBJ would have counseled. He immediately proposed, as Sean Wilentz records in his new book, *The Age of Reagan,* "an enormously ambitious legislative agenda on matters ranging from national energy policy to streamlining the federal government." He "demanded and received emergency authorization to deregulate natural gas prices," then handed down unconditional amnesty for draft evaders and "weathered the storm and enhanced his reputation for decisiveness and independence"—shades of the bold strokes of Roosevelt's First Hundred Days. Through April, his approval rating was 75 percent. "For the moment," Wilentz concludes, "it looked as if the country had found the leader it had been searching for since Richard Nixon's downfall." And it also looked as if that something big might happen before circumstances slammed shut the window of opportunity. The energy program, an effort Carter announced as "the moral equivalent of war," passed the House comfortably in April. But by the end of the year, the Senate eliminated it with extreme prejudice. Partly, again, it was Carter's poor political skill. It also had plenty to do with the fact that Republicans managed to destroy Carter's public goodwill in his first year as president.

A literary assassin played an outsize role in this project. Former Nixon operative William Safire was ensconced on *The New York Times* op-ed page. Sloppy record-keeping and the sort of petty favoritism endemic to provincial banking had brought Carter's close friend and budget director Bert Lance, a former banker in Georgia, before a Senate subcommittee for minor

questioning. Safire raised a series of where-there's-smoke-there-must-be-fire insinuations. He hinted that the Teamsters Central States Pension Fund (which "the Labor Department says corruptly bankrolls Las Vegas mobsters," Safire helpfully reminded readers) played a role, along with, of course, the Chicago Democratic Machine—and Arabs!

Safire penned eight Lance columns over the next four months, sometimes twice a week. He repeated the original charges, dropping ones others debunked, ever implying that the charges he still mentioned were the only ones he had made all along, counting on the public's short memory to cover the fact that his original case was falling apart. Most often, his columns baited reporters: Why were they "refusing" to investigate Lance like they had hounded past Republicans? More cunningly, Safire larded the columns with less-than-subliminal linguistic references to Watergate. "Lancegate," he implied, was *exactly the same.* He even declared a memo by the Manufacturers of Hanover Trust was "the smoking gun." (Readers were counted on to vaguely recall that the "smoking gun" tape that had brought down Nixon two years earlier *also* involved the derailing of an FBI investigation.)

It worked, at least where it counted: in the court of political cartoons. *Washington Post* editorial cartoonist Herblock gave Carter a "Checkers Award," after the infamous cocker spaniel Richard Nixon used to save his hide in a famous 1952 speech. Syndicated cartoonist Pat Oliphant went with a more straightforward depiction of Carter as Nixon: "Stonewall it. . . . They're out to get us." Lance resigned; the Justice Department handed down indictments. Even though Lance was eventually completely exonerated, the damage was done. Carter, like Obama, had run as a "different kind of Democrat"—pure, unsullied. So saboteurs like Safire had a clear challenge: "prove" that Carter was just another impure politician, if even on the shakiest of pretexts.

That, of course, is what the right will try on the next Democratic president. They will take the possibility that Obama might break through the icy seas of conservative stasis and try to render it an absurdity. There is now an army of Safires and a Republican Party full of Senator No's. Recall William Kristol's famous memo enjoining congressional Republicans to refuse to deal with President Clinton's proposed health-care reforms. "The plan should not be amended," he wrote, "it should be erased." The right might not be at its strongest, but it certainly understands that the American system favors fell swoops, on offense as well as on defense. The system provides conservatives with opportunities for obstruction in profusion—no matter how low their approval ratings.

Barack Obama has not run as a policy maximalist. By and large, his big proposals have all been in that safe spot where liberals can't quite get mad and the Beltway wise men can't quite get scared. He has advocated for not-quite-universal health care rather than single-payer, and promised tax cuts, not massive new social outlays. But this shouldn't worry progressives. There may be no better way to achieve an operational liberalism than to appeal to America's rhetorical conservatism. That, after all, was how the balanced-budget-promising Franklin Roosevelt ran in 1932 and how the let-us-continue Lyndon Johnson was elected in 1964.

But when it comes time to govern, an ingrained habit of incrementalism may be a very profound problem indeed. Stopped in our tracks time and time again in attempts to assure Americans the basic social rights taken for granted by citizens of every other industrialized nation, progressives have made virtue of necessity—we have learned to think of strategic incrementalism as a positive good, even an end in itself. If, on the morning of January 20, 2009, Barack Obama should wake up to find himself president, with 60 senators and 250 representatives, plus 60 percent of the public firmly in favor of passing universal health care, would his instincts direct him to ram the legislation through as quickly as possible? No one can say for sure. This attitude is so dormant in progressive thinking that it's hard to know whether we can revive it.

Weisbrot and Mackenzie's *The Liberal Hour* is a very aptly named book: a splendid evocation of just how evanescent American moments of reform truly are. They are not unlike an action movie starring Bruce Willis, who has 60 minutes left to defuse a time bomb before everything blows up. Take immediate action, and you might just get reforms that had seemed impossible the day before but are impossible to imagine America without just one and two generations later. Take it slow, however, and you might not get anything at all.

RICK PERLSTEIN is the author of *Nixonland: The Rise of a President and the Fracturing of America,* and is a senior fellow at the Campaign for America's Future.

From *The American Prospect,* September 2008, pp. 22–26. Copyright © 2008. Reprinted with permission from Rick Perlstein and The American Prospect, 11 Beacon Street, Suite 1120, Boston, MA 02108. All rights reserved.

Living History

Occasionally America turns out to be every bit as good as its hype. It's thrilling to be around to witness one of those moments.

ANNA QUINDLEN

The American Museum of Natural History threw a spectacular party on New Year's Eve 1999, but perhaps the millennium really arrived there just a few weeks ago. A group of New York City schoolchildren were at an event marking the 150th birthday of Theodore Roosevelt, naturalist and president, and at the end of the visit one of the kids raised his hand. "I have a question," he said. "Was he black?"

History will record that on Nov. 4, 2008, Barack Hussein Obama was elected the first black president of the United States. It is impossible to overstate what that means to this nation.

America is as much a concept as it is a country, but it is a concept too often honored in the breach. The Statue of Liberty welcomes with the words "Give me your tired, your poor." Yet generation after generation of immigrants arrived here to face contempt and hatred until the passage of time, the flattening of accents, turned them into tolerated natives. The Declaration of Independence states unequivocally that all men are created equal. Yet for years the politicians and the powerful seemed to take the gender of that noun literally and denied all manner of rights to women.

But no injustice or prejudice brought to bear by this country against its own people can compare with how it has treated black men and women. Humiliation, degradation, lynchings, beatings, murders. The rights the United States pretended to confer upon all were unthinkingly and consistently denied them: the right to the franchise, to representation, to protection by the justice system.

Literal ownership gave way to something not so different: "When we are moved to better our lot," Richard Wright wrote in 1941, "we do not ask ourselves 'can we do it?' but 'will they let us do it?'" Henry Louis Gates Jr., in the memoir "Colored People," says simply, "For most of my childhood, we couldn't eat in restaurants or sleep in hotels, we couldn't use certain bathrooms or try on clothes in stores." Alice Walker left home for college on a bus and was ordered to move after a white woman complained that she was too near the front.

None of this was so very long ago.

Time passed. Things changed. John Lewis, a boy who loved books but was not permitted to enter the public library, a man whose skull was fractured by Alabama state troopers when he led a peaceful march across a bridge, now sits in Congress. Gates is a professor at Harvard, Walker a revered writer. Segregation as a matter of law has given way to segregation as a matter of class and custom. As President-elect Obama said when he gave a speech about race earlier this year, speaking of systemic poverty, bad schools and broken families, "Many of the disparities that exist in the African-American community today can be directly traced to inequalities passed on from an earlier generation that suffered under the brutal legacy of slavery and Jim Crow."

But Obama said something else in that speech, something both simpler and more profound that has special resonance now that his improbable candidacy has prevailed. He made the political spiritual. "In the end, then," he said, "what is called for is nothing more, and nothing less, than what all the world's great religions demand—that we do unto others as we would have them do unto us." He asked the American people to be fair and just, to be kind and generous, to put prejudice behind them and be one people because that is, not a legal or social imperative, but a moral one.

There will be learned discussion in the years to come about the specific meaning of this moment, about whether it will be more symbolic than substantive, about whether having a black president will lull Americans into believing that racism is a thing of the past. But for just a moment consider this small fact: for a long time a black man in many parts of the United States was denied even the honorific "Mister" by the white community, and was instead called by his first name, like a child, no matter how elderly and esteemed he might be.

Now a black man will be called Mr. President.

They never thought they would see the day, people said, especially the older ones, who could remember the murders of Martin Luther King Jr., Medgar Evers and Malcolm X. They wept, some of them, and so did I. Perhaps it was because this man seems so young and vigorous in a nation that seems old and tired. Perhaps it is because he promises change and hope, and both are so badly needed. He is the president for our children's generation, a more tolerant and diverse society, so insensible of bright dividing lines that one of them would idly wonder whether Theodore Roosevelt was a black man. They belie a time when there was a crayon labeled "flesh" in my Crayola box, a crayon that was a pale pink.

But I suspect that, like many others, I wept for myself, too, because I felt I was part of a country that was living its principles. Despite all our prejudices, seen and hidden, millions of citizens managed, in the words of Dr. King, to judge Barack Obama by the content of his character and not the color of his skin. There were many reasons to elect him president, but this was one collateral gift: to be able to watch America look an old evil in the eye and to say, no more. We must be better than that. We can be better than that. We are better than that.

The Two Obamas

STUART TAYLOR JR.

When John McCain and many other Republicans ask, "Who is the real Barack Obama?" there is an implication that maybe he is somehow sinister or extremist.

I don't believe that. But I do think that there are two very different Obamas. Both are extraordinarily intelligent, serene under pressure, and driven by an admirable social conscience—albeit as willing to deploy deception as the next politician. But while the first Obama would be a well-meaning failure, the second could become a great president.

While the first Obama would be a well-meaning failure, the second could become a great president.

An ultraliberal in moderate garb? The first Obama has sometimes seemed eager to engineer what he called "redistribution of wealth" in a 2001 radio interview, along with the more conventional protectionism, job preferences, and other liberal Democratic dogmas featured in his campaign. I worry that he might go beyond judiciously regulating our free enterprise system's all-too-apparent excesses and stifle it under the dead hand of government bureaucracy and lawsuits.

This redistributionist Obama has stayed in the background since he set his sights on the presidency years ago, except when he told Joe the Plumber that his tax plan would help "spread the wealth." This Obama seems largely invisible to many supporters. But he may retain some attachment to the radical-leftist sensibility in which—as his impressive 1995 autobiography, *Dreams From My Father,* explains with reflective detachment—he was marinated as a youth and young man.

Obama spent much of his teenage years searching for his black identity. He was mentored for a time by the poet Frank Marshall Davis, a black-power activist who had once been a member of the Communist Party, and who was (according to Obama's book) "living in the same Sixties time warp" as Obama's mother, a decidedly liberal free spirit.

In college, lest he be "mistaken for a sellout," Obama "chose my friends carefully," according to his book: "The more politically active black students. The foreign students. The Chicanos. The Marxist professors and structural feminists and punk-rock performance poets." After college, his social conscience steered him to become a community organizer and "organize black folks" in Chicago, from 1985 to 1988.

It was then that Obama met the Rev. Jeremiah Wright, who as head of Trinity United Church of Christ did many good things but had a now-famous penchant for America-hating, white-bashing, conspiracy-theorizing, Farrakhan-honoring rants. A central theme of the first Wright sermon that Obama attended—the one titled "the audacity of hope"—was that "white folks' greed runs a world in need."

After graduating near the top of his Harvard Law School class in 1991, Obama could easily have landed a prestigious Supreme Court clerkship and gone on to a big law firm where partners make well over a $1 million a year. Instead, he followed his social conscience and political ambition back to Chicago, joining a small law firm.

Obama became more than casually acquainted with Bill Ayers, the Weather Underground bomber with whom he served on the boards of two Chicago philanthropic groups. In 1995, Ayers and his wife, Bernardine Dohrn—the same Dohrn who in a blood-curdling 1969 speech had cited the Charles Manson gang of murderers as role models for the Weather Underground—co-hosted a political fundraiser for Obama at their home. By then, the still-unrepentant Ayers had become a respected member of an academic establishment in which far-left views are fashionable.

I dwell on these much-debated associations not because I think that Obama sympathizes with what he has called Ayers's "detestable acts 40 years ago, when I was 8" or identifies with Wright's wild ravings. But I do think that Obama has understated (at best) his involvement with Wright and Ayers. And I wonder about the worldview of a man who was so comfortable with such far-left extremists and whose wife, Michelle, asserted earlier this year that America is "just downright mean" and "guided by fear" and that most Americans' lives have "gotten progressively worse since I was a little girl."

Obama's voting record as an Illinois and then U.S. senator is not extremist or radical. But it is not a bit bipartisan, either. He has hardly ever broken with his party, and he famously had the most liberal record of any senator in 2007 (although not in 2006 or 2005), according to *National Journal*'s vote ratings.

This Obama has endorsed a long list of liberal restrictions on free enterprise that could end up hurting the people they are supposed to help, along with the rest of us: statist remedies for our broken educational system; encouraging unionization by substituting peer pressure and an undemocratic card-check process for secret ballots; raising the wages of women or lowering those of men who have dissimilar jobs that are declared by bureaucrats to be of comparable worth; renegotiating NAFTA; and more.

I wonder how far Obama wants to go down the road suggested by his lament in that 2001 radio interview that the civil-rights movement had failed to engineer "redistribution of wealth" and "economic justice." Would he be content with the moderately redistributive, Clintonesque increase in taxes on high-earning Americans that he proposes now? Or would he end up pushing for confiscatory taxes that could stifle entrepreneurship and job creation?

And would Obama's declared desire to appoint judges and justices driven mainly by "empathy" for "the powerless," rather than by fidelity to the law, lead to judicially invented constitutional rights to welfare, to ever-more-rigid preferences based on race and gender, and to other novel judicial overrides of democratic governance?

A pragmatic reformer? The pragmatic, consensus-building, inspirational Obama who has been on display during the general election campaign is a prodigious listener and learner. He can see all sides of every question. He seems suffused with good judgment. His social conscience has been tempered by recognition that well-intentioned liberal prescriptions can have perverse unintended consequences. His tax and health care proposals are much less radical than Republican critics suggest.

This Obama has surrounded himself not only with liberal advisers but also with mainstream moderates such as Warren Buffett and former Fed Chairman Paul Volcker. He has won the support of moderate Republicans, including Colin Powell and Susan Eisenhower, and conservatives, including Kenneth Adelman and Charles Fried.

This is the Obama who said in his dazzling 2004 Democratic convention speech that "there is not a liberal America and a conservative America; there is a United States of America." This is the Obama who distanced himself not only from Jeremiah Wright but also—more subtly—from the rest of the racial-grievance crowd in a March 18 speech deploring as "profoundly distorted" the view that "sees white racism as endemic."

The pragmatic Obama is smart enough to know that reforms take root only if they enjoy broad public support and that self-identified conservatives vastly outnumber self-identified liberals in America. He also understands that while we need more-effective regulation, "America's free market has been the engine of America's great progress. It's created a prosperity that is the envy of the world. It's led to a standard of living unmatched in history." He has said that "we don't want to return to marginal tax rates of 60 or 70 percent." He wants to expand the armed forces and to send more troops to Afghanistan.

The pragmatic Obama is not just a made-for-the-campaign creation. He was elected president of the Harvard Law Review in 1990 not only because he was one of the most brilliant students but also because the handful of conservatives whose votes helped tip the balance saw him as fair-minded and open to their point of view. And they were not disappointed.

Obama has dipped his toe in the water of questioning Democratic interest-group orthodoxies. He has supported charter schools (while opposing vouchers) and merit pay for teachers; he offended trial lawyers by voting in 2005 to curb unwarranted class-action lawsuits; and last year he questioned whether affluent black children such as his daughters should continue to get racial preferences over more needy whites and Asians.

To be sure, apart from these less-than-bold gestures, Obama's down-the-line liberal voting record does not give a centrist like me much basis for hope that he would resist pressure from Democratic interest groups, ideologues, and congressional leaders to steer hard to the left.

The best thing for the country would be for Obama to take on the interest groups and to govern from the center.

But I do hope that if Obama wins, the enormity of the economic and international crises facing him will accelerate his intellectual evolution and convince him that simply replacing dumb Bush policies with dumb Democratic policies will only drive the country deeper into the ditch. The best thing for the country would be to take on the interest groups and govern from the center. That would also be the best way for Obama to win re-election and have a truly historic presidency.

Veto This!

When presidents veto a bill, they're exercising strength—or showing weakness. They usually win the override battles but sometimes lose the war for public approval.

CARL M. CANNON

The first presidential veto in American history was exercised, fittingly enough, by George Washington. He informed Congress in writing on April 5, 1792, that having "maturely considered the Act passed by the two Houses," he felt obligated to send it back on the grounds that it was unconstitutional. The legislation had to do with the number of citizens that each member of the House would represent. Having defeated the British on the field of battle—thereby giving the members of Congress their jobs to begin with—President Washington was accorded a high level of deference. No serious attempt to override the veto transpired, and Congress rewrote the measure to satisfy his objections.

Washington issued a single veto in his second term as well. This time, the dispute was on policy grounds, as the former general didn't cotton to the minutiae of a congressional plan for reorganizing the armed forces. He issued that veto on February 28, 1797; again, the veto stood. With these two actions, Washington initiated a tug-of-war between the executive and legislative branches of the federal government that persists to this day. The veto, a forgotten power during George W. Bush's first term, has now emerged as a prime battleground in the twilight months of his presidency.

"One thing that needs to be underscored is that because President Bush is a 'lame-duck' president, it doesn't mean that he is no longer powerful," said Chris Kelley, a political science professor at the University of Miami in Ohio. "The veto is a powerful weapon that the president simply must use from time to time."

Alexander Hamilton would have agreed. At the dawn of the Republic, Hamilton told his fellow Founders that the presidential veto (Latin for "I forbid") was "a qualified negative" that would serve as a brake on the passions of a popularly elected legislature. For five years, Bush did not avail himself of this authority, making him the only president except for John Quincy Adams to go an entire four-year term without vetoing anything that Congress sent him.

Was Bush practicing good government, or bad government? The answers to that question—and to the questions about Bush's newfound fondness for the veto—are partly political, partly theoretical. The political portion of the question is the voters' to answer. It will be addressed on the 2008 campaign trail, where presidential and congressional candidates from both parties are parsing Bush's recent vetoes to boost their candidacies. The theoretical component has even more movable parts and is the continuation of an argument more than 200 years old.

The first U.S. president to use the prerogative to veto *major* legislation solely over policy objections was Andrew Jackson. He was also the first to see the veto's potential as a political tool: In 1832, Jackson vetoed the enabling legislation to extend the charter of the villified Second Bank of the United States. Although his economic reasoning was specious, his political antenna was flawless, and the 1832 bank veto helped to assure Jackson's re-election.

For the better part of two centuries, political scientists and constitutional scholars have debated the propriety of Jackson's willingness to use the veto as a political tool, even while the principle became the standard for all subsequent presidents. Two rival theories of what constitutes a good-government use of the veto emerged.

The first, in the words of Stephen Skowronek, a political science professor at Yale University, is that the Jackson veto precedent "made a mockery of the premier operating principle" of Jeffersonian democracy, that is, deference to people's representatives in Congress. Jackson's veto was an artifice, these critics have said over the years, that short-circuited the separation of powers and contributed to the rise of the "imperial presidency" so disfavored by the Founders. In substituting the whims of one person for the will of the people, the veto also—and inevitably— soured relations between the branches of government.

"The veto tilts the balance of power in Washington too far toward the status quo."

—Sanford Levinson,
University of Texas professor

This was the precise complaint leveled against Bush last week when he vetoed a $35 billion, five-year expansion of the State Children's Health Insurance Program that passed both chambers of Congress with comfortable majorities and enjoyed bipartisan support.

"You [had] consensus across party and ideology, and a unity on the most important domestic issue, health care," Rep. Rahm Emanuel, D-Ill., said. "Except for one person."

But one person is all it takes—if that person is the president.

"I think that this is probably the most inexplicable veto in the history of the country," Sen. Edward Kennedy, D-Mass., declared on the Senate floor. "It is incomprehensible: It is intolerable. It's unacceptable."

But accept it Congress must—unless Democrats can muster a two-thirds vote in each chamber to override. And that's where critics of the veto say that the system goes off the rails. "Put simply, the veto tilts the balance of power in Washington too far toward the status quo," says Sanford Levinson, professor of law and government at the University of Texas (Austin).

Levinson, author of a recent book, *Our Undemocratic Constitution: Where the Constitution Goes Wrong (and How We the People Can Correct It)*, asserts that anyone who thinks that judicial review of legislation passed by majorities has an autocratic tinge to it ought to be more worried about the presidential veto. He says that the Supreme Court has invalidated some 165 laws throughout U.S. history, while presidents have vetoed about 2,550 bills—only 106 of which Congress has managed to override. "If judicial activism is anti-democratic," he wrote recently, "then the presidential veto is, well, *very* anti-democratic."

There is, however, a second school of thought, represented by such scholars as Ronald C. Moe and Louis Fisher, who wrote about separation-of-powers issues for the Congressional Research Service. In this view, the presidential veto has a positive impact on the political process. For starters, the threat of a veto gives Congress an incentive to draw legislation more carefully, encouraging compromise. The veto can serve, as Alexander Hamilton suggested it might, as an additional brake against "improper laws" passed in the heat of the moment. "It establishes a salutary check upon the legislative body, calculated to guard the community against the effects of faction, precipitancy, or of any impulse unfriendly to the public good, which may happen to influence a majority of that body," Hamilton wrote.

Implicit in this view of checks and balances is a sophisticated notion: namely, that bad ideas, once signed into law, are more difficult to repeal than they were to enact. A contemporary illustration of Hamilton's fear may be the innocent sounding "Anti-Drug Abuse Act." Congress passed it hurriedly in 1986 without hearings, partially as a response to the cocaine-induced death of University of Maryland basketball star Len Bias. Coming as cheap crack, cocaine was turning urban streets into shooting galleries, the law prescribed far harsher sentences for possessing or dealing crack than it did for having powder cocaine.

That provision has put tens of thousands of young African-Americans in federal prison for far longer terms than white drug abusers, who tend to traffic in powder cocaine. President Reagan signed the law a week before the 1986 election. Eric Sterling, then a Democratic House aide who helped to draft the

bill, wistfully recalls wishing that Reagan had vetoed it. Sterling, who now heads the Criminal Justice Policy Foundation, has been trying for the better part of two decades to persuade Congress to repeal the 1986 statute that mandates harsh terms for low-level cocaine dealers. "The Framers would have offered this law as a perfect example of the proper use of the presidential veto," Sterling said. "The problem is that by virtue of [these laws'] popularity, they are the hardest vetoes to cast."

Who's in Charge?

Mirroring the ongoing philosophical discussion about the proper role of presidential vetoes, another conversation is taking place on a more practical political level: Are vetoes a sign of strength or weakness in a chief executive? Does it help a president to issue vetoes, or hurt him and his party? These, as Bush and his suddenly fractious Republicans are discovering during the current term of Congress, are not academic questions. Once again, there are two sides to the equation; and once again, it is clear that the dispute won't be settled in Bush's presidency.

Let's call the first viewpoint the Rodney King school of thought. Why *can't* we all get along? This argument holds that presidential vetoes are, almost by definition, a sign that the chief executive lacks power, leadership ability, and a large enough following to shape events. In other words, a president who has to veto has failed to persuade, can't compromise, can't get the White House's own legislation through Congress, and is unable to take the issue over the heads of Congress to the people.

"A strong president needs fewer vetoes because he's able to exercise sufficient control over the congressional agenda, whether through decisive influence over legislative formulation or judicious use of veto threats that make it unlikely bills the president would oppose would land on his desk," says Robert Spitzer, professor of political science at the State University of New York (Cortland).

Framed this way, Capitol Hill has more say-so in setting the veto-agenda than is generally acknowledged these days in Washington. In an influential 1978 book on the politics of the veto, political scientists Thomas Romer and Howard Rosenthal explored this point. The authors outlined a "monopoly agenda control model" in which Congress, not the president, determines the fate of veto threats. In their theory, the agenda-setter is the pivotal legislator on any given issue, who presents the White House with take-it-or-leave-it proposals. Thus, the president is essentially in a reactive, and therefore, subordinate, position. This is something of a postmodern (or, at least, post–Franklin Roosevelt) view, and it probably is not a coincidence that Romer and Rosenthal were doing their research when Gerald Ford was president.

Ford was a creature of the House, but as president he was also a captive of the huge Democratic majorities he inherited as voters in 1974 reacted against the Republican Party of Richard Nixon, Spiro Agnew, and Watergate. Despite serving as president for barely half a term, Ford has the distinction of tying for second place on the all-time list of presidential vetoes that were overridden by Congress. Ford, overridden 12 times, shares that dubious silver medal with President Truman, who recorded the lowest Gallup Poll job-approval rating in history. The record-holder is Andrew Johnson, overridden 15 times, who was impeached by the House and nearly convicted in the Senate. The precipitating act of impeachment was Johnson's veto of a bill he believed—correctly, the Supreme Court later ruled—was unconstitutional.

"Many conventional presidency scholars argue that the use of a veto indicates a weak president, since the power of the presidency resides in his ability to bargain and persuade the Congress to go along with his policies," Kelley said. "Thus if he uses a veto, it means that his credibility with the Congress is low. Those who point to Ford as a failed president often will examine both his vetoes and the overrides."

Nolan McCarty, acting dean of the Woodrow Wilson School of Public and International Affairs at Princeton University, has described two other models for vetoes. In one, the White House and Congress have incomplete information about exactly what will precipitate a veto. Bush, for example, threatened to veto an expansion of the student loan program, but then didn't, perhaps leading wishful Democrats to believe that he would feel

Presidents Usually Win

Congress is rarely able to muster the two-thirds majority of votes in both chambers to override a presidential veto. This list, based on a compilation by the Congressional Research Service, does not include pocket vetoes after Congress adjourned.

President	Vetoes	Overrides	Vetos that Stuck	Major Overrides
TRUMAN	180	12	Natural-gas deregulation 1950 Coastal tidelands 1946, 1952	Taft-Hartley labor relations 1947 Income-tax cuts 1947, 1948 McCarran Internal Security 1950 McCarran-Walter immigration quotas 1952
EISENHOWER	73	2	Natural gas 1956 Farm spending 1956, 1958 Housing programs 1959 Pollution control 1960	TVA spending 1959 Federal pay 1960
KENNEDY	12	0	Federal pensions 1961	
JOHNSON	16	0	Cotton quotas 1968	
NIXON	26	7	Minimum-wage increase 1973	Water Pollution Control 1972 War Powers Act 1973
FORD	48	12	Oil price controls 1975	Freedom of Information Act 1974
CARTER	13	2	Nuclear reactor 1977	Oil import fee 1980
REAGAN	39	9	Textile quotas 1988	South Africa sanctions 1986 Water projects 1987 Highway funding 1987
G.H.W. BUSH	29	1	Minimum-wage increase 1989 Job discrimination 1990 China trade status 1992 Family-medical leave 1990, 1992 Taxes 1992 Stem-cell research 1992 Campaign finance 1992	Cable TV 1992
CLINTON	36	2	Spending reductions 1995 Appropriations 1995 Bosnia arms embargo 1995 "Partial-birth" abortion 1996, 1997 Product liability 1996 Tax culs 1999 Estate-tax repeal 2000	Line-item vetoes 1998 Securities litigation 1995
G.W.BUSH	4	0	Stem-cell research 2006, 2007 Iraq war limits 2007	

pressured to sign the SCHIP bill. The absence of a dominant legislative actor is what leads to the impasse. "When there is such uncertainty," McCarty wrote, "vetoes may occur because the Legislature overestimates its ability to extract concessions from the president."

In the wake of Bush's SCHIP veto, perhaps the nation's capital finds itself in that fluid state of affairs—meaning that, eventually, compromise legislation will emerge. The president has left the door open, and Congress is home to a handful of moderate Republicans who hope that Bush and the Democrats will walk through that door together. Of course, there is another, less pleasant, place to be. McCarty describes this model as "Blame-Game Vetoes."

When one party accuses the other of making "war on children," it is a safe bet that partisan advantage, not meaningful negotiation, is at the frontal cortex of the party's collective brain. Not that the Democrats tried to hide it. "We're not going to compromise," Senate Majority Leader Harry Reid said flatly after Bush's recent veto. House Speaker Nancy Pelosi vowed that Democrats would try to override and to make the issue "a hard vote for Republicans." New Jersey's Democratic governor, Jon Corzine, said, "I hope we override the veto before we start worrying about compromise."

To produce legislation, the process usually needs to work the other way around. But this is the blame game. SCHIP "has got to be up there with motherhood and apple pie," Rep. Jim Cooper, D-Tenn., told the *Los Angeles Times,* apparently with a straight face. "This is Tiny Tim. And who is against Tiny Tim? The only person in all of literature was Ebenezer Scrooge."

So who is winning the blame game? The early signs were a thumbs-down for George W. Scrooge and a thumbs-up for the Democrats. Public opinion polls showed that the voters, egged on by Democrats and media editorialists, thought that Bush's veto was wrongheaded, if not heartless. Eventually, White House aides and a few Republicans joined the fray, raising various arguments to support Bush's position: Some of the "children" covered under this bill would be nearly 25 years of age; the earning power of some eligible families tops $80,000 a year; some people opting into the program already have private health insurance; the Democrats' plan would be funded with a regressive $1-a-pack tax on cigarettes—that kind of thing. There was truth (or some truth, anyway) to all of these assertions, but Bush did not make them in the days leading up to the veto. Speaking to reporters at the White House, Bush simply said he had "philosophical" differences with the Democrats.

That was code, pure and simple, intended for the ears of fiscal conservatives, who have grown disenchanted with the GOP leader who has run up huge budget deficits in each year of his presidency. Translated, Bush's words meant: "OK, OK, I'll quit spending tax dollars like a drunken sailor."

In this new spirit, Bush has threatened to veto 10 of 11 pending appropriations bills. Until now, nobody knew for sure whether he was serious. In his first term, Bush vetoed nothing. In year five of his presidency, despite threatening 133 vetoes, Bush issued a single one, on embryonic-stem-cell research. This year, he vetoed a similar stem-cell bill, along with a spending measure aimed at curbing escalation of the Iraq war. Now Bush

has issued his fourth veto. Has he found his groove? Perhaps. But some believe that he waited too long.

"It's an hour too late," says Frank Luntz, the Republican communications guru who helped fashion the 1994 Contract with America. "And a dollar too short."

Situational Ethics

Until Democrats reclaimed Congress in the 2006 elections, the premium in Bushworld was indeed on getting along. Rodney King would have approved. In the first term, Nicholas Calio, then-White House director of legislative affairs, told *National Journal* that the two top Republicans in the House, Speaker Dennis Hastert and Majority Leader Tom DeLay, made it a point of pride to send no bill to 1600 Pennsylvania Avenue that would be vetoed. "It's a real principle with the speaker and DeLay," Calio said. John Feehery, Hastert's spokesman at the time, went further, asserting that his boss believed that to invite a presidential veto signaled "a breakdown in the system."

"We don't want to make political points with this president," Feehery added, "because we agree with him on almost everything." Congressional Republicans challenged Bush's veto threats only once, in 2002, on a campaign finance overhaul. Bush didn't like the bill, but he put his signature on it anyway, the overt evidence of his displeasure was that he didn't invite one of its principal authors, Sen. John McCain, R-Ariz., to the signing ceremony.

Another reason that Bush hasn't relied on the veto is that he routinely uses "signing statements" to assert that he will implement new legislation in ways that conform with his thinking and that of White House lawyers and policy makers. On other occasions, particularly as regards national security, this president hasn't even given that much deference to congressional intent: If White House lawyers deem a law, such as the statutes regarding the wiretapping of suspected foreign terrorists, to be technologically out-of-date, well, this administration just writes its own hall pass.

Thus, Bush's first term featured an odd combination of co-operating closely with Capitol Hill Republicans on some occasions and simply ignoring Congress on others. Along the way, Team Bush overlooked historic examples showing that sometimes a veto—along with a healthy dose of chutzpah—is just what it takes to make a president look strong. Truman, in his first term, lamented during several crippling national strikes that he lacked the executive authority to force trade union leaders to the bargaining table. Congress gave Truman that power in the Taft-Hartley Act. He promptly vetoed it, putting himself at long last in organized labor's good graces. Congress overrode the president's veto, and Truman happily used the power vested in him some dozen times. Moreover, he turned around and won re-election in 1948, with, yes, the help of labor. For a president, this is as good as it gets—veto nirvana.

Republicans were in charge of both ends of Pennsylvania Avenue during most of the first six years of Bush's presidency, so the chances for such showdowns were small. But Democrats ran the show when Franklin Roosevelt was president—and he vetoed 635 of their bills. According to presidential scholar William Leuchtenburg, Roosevelt would instruct White House aides to look for legislation that he could veto, "in order to remind Congress that it was being watched."

Alan Greenspan, who is old enough to remember FDR, believes that Bush—and the country—would have been well served if this president had done the same. "My biggest frustration remained the president's unwillingness to wield his veto against out-of-control spending," Greenspan wrote in his new book, *The Age of Turbulence: Adventures in a New World.* "Not exercising the veto power became a hallmark of the Bush presidency. . . . To my mind, Bush's collaborate-don't-confront approach was a major mistake."

Many movement conservatives couldn't agree more. They think that Bush's belated embrace of the veto might save the GOP's soul and give the Republican base a principle to be excited about. "The GOP needs to regain its brand on spending," says Grover Norquist, president of Americans for Tax Reform. "The Democrats are acting now in 2007 and 2008 as they did in 1993 and 1994: taxing, spending. And here the GOP can highlight its differences with vetoes and veto-upholding. It is a truly selfless act by Bush as he isn't running, but the GOP House and Senate guys are, and they need their brand back. This autumn's fight, which I hope to be long and drawn out and repetitive, will do for the GOP what they should have been doing over the past six years."

Other Republicans, most notably moderates who face tough re-election fights next year, are unnerved by Bush's newfound fiscal conservatism, and especially by his willingness to veto a children's health bill to prove it. "I believe this is an irresponsible use of the veto pen," said Sen. Gordon Smith, an Oregon Republican who faces a spirited challenge in 2008. "It's the White House that needs to give," added another Senate GOP centrist, Susan Collins of Maine.

The noises emanating from the White House don't give these worried Republicans much reassurance. "Good policy is good politics," said White House spokesman Tony Fratto last week. "If members stand on principle, they'll be just fine."

Principles can be in the eye of the beholder, however, especially in Washington, where situational ethics are routinely on display. Dan Mitchell of the libertarian Cato Institute points out that the money at stake in the health care initiative is small compared with the excess spending that Bush accepted when Republicans controlled Congress. "There certainly does seem to be a legitimate argument that the president only objects to new spending when Democrats are doing it," Mitchell said.

Bush might have more moral sway had he, back in 2002, vetoed a bipartisan and pork-laden $190 billion farm bill. Half a century ago, Dwight Eisenhower did just that. The Democrats pounced, thinking they had Ike right where they wanted them. "The veto of the farm bill," then-Senate Majority Leader Lyndon Johnson said, "can be described only as a crushing blow to

the hopes and the legitimate desires of American agriculture." That was one description. Another was "fiscal restraint," something that Eisenhower had managed to make sexy—with his veto pen.

By the end of the 1959 Christmas recess, an unnamed White House aide was telling *Time* magazine, "When those congressmen come back in January, they're going to be so anxious to find something to cut that they'll cut their own wrists if necessary." On his way out of office, with high approval ratings and a federal budget nearly in balance, Eisenhower was *Time's* "Man of the Year."

Similar battle lines are drawn for the upcoming year, during which Democrats will try to hold their congressional majorities and recapture the White House. Will they succeed? They will if Sen. Hillary Rodham Clinton has anything to say about it. "With the stroke of a pen, President Bush has robbed nearly 4 million uninsured children of the chance for a healthy start in life and the health coverage they need but can't afford," the New York Democrat and 2008 presidential front-runner said after Bush's veto.

"This is vetoing the will of the American people," Clinton added. "I was proud to help create the Children's Health Insurance Program during the Clinton administration, which today provides health insurance for 6 million children."

Hillary Clinton was right about her role in SCHIP. The part of the story that she may be forgetting, however, is that her husband got traction as president after the Republicans took over Congress and he began wielding his veto pen—36 times before leaving office.

"Clinton's skillful and aggressive use of the veto was a hallmark of his domestic presidency after the Republicans gained control of Congress in 1994," wrote Charles Cameron, a political science professor at Princeton and the author of *Veto Bargaining: Presidents and the Politics of Negative Power.* "In some respects, he was more successful opposing Congress than he had been leading it, when the Democrats controlled the institution."

Reagan faced a House controlled by the opposition party and he, too, issued a spate of vetoes, 78 (half of them pocket vetoes). Congress overrode nine—matching Roosevelt's tally. The overrides didn't hurt either man's legacy. At least one of the 2008 presidential candidates has apparently taken this lesson to heart. Republican Mitt Romney, who as Massachusetts governor faced an overwhelmingly Democratic Legislature for four years, boasts of vetoing hundreds of appropriations while serving in Boston— and says he'd happily do it all over again in Washington.

"If I'm elected president, I'm going to cap nondefense discretionary spending at inflation minus 1 percent," he said recently. "And if Congress sends me a budget that exceeds that cap, I will veto that budget. And I know how to veto. I like vetoes."

ccannon@nationaljournal.com.

When Congress Stops Wars
Partisan Politics and Presidential Power

WILLIAM G. HOWELL AND JON C. PEVEHOUSE

For most of George W. Bush's tenure, political observers have lambasted Congress for failing to fulfill its basic foreign policy obligations. Typical was the recent *Foreign Affairs* article by Norman Ornstein and Thomas Mann, "When Congress Checks Out," which offered a sweeping indictment of Congress' failure to monitor the president's execution of foreign wars and antiterrorist initiatives. Over the past six years, they concluded, Congressional oversight of the White House's foreign and national security policy "has virtually collapsed." Ornstein and Mann's characterization is hardly unique. Numerous constitutional-law scholars, political scientists, bureaucrats, and even members of Congress have, over the years, lamented the lack of legislative constraints on presidential war powers. But the dearth of Congressional oversight between 2000 and 2006 is nothing new. Contrary to what many critics believe, terrorist threats, an overly aggressive White House, and an impotent Democratic Party are not the sole explanations for Congressional inactivity over the past six years. Good old-fashioned partisan politics has been, and continues to be, at play.

It is often assumed that everyday politics *stops* at the water's edge and that legislators abandon their partisan identities during times of war in order to become faithful stewards of their constitutional obligations. But this received wisdom is almost always wrong. The illusion of Congressional wartime unity misconstrues the nature of legislative oversight and fails to capture the particular conditions under which members of Congress are likely to emerge as meaningful critics of any particular military venture.

The partisan composition of Congress has historically been the decisive factor in determining whether lawmakers will oppose or acquiesce in presidential calls for war. From Harry Truman to Bill Clinton, nearly every U.S. president has learned that members of Congress, and members of the opposition party in particular, are fully capable of interjecting their opinions about proposed and ongoing military ventures. When the opposition party holds a large number of seats or controls one or both chambers of Congress, members routinely challenge the president and step up oversight of foreign conflicts; when the legislative branch is dominated by the president's party, it generally goes along with the White House. Partisan unity, not institutional laziness, explains why the Bush administration's

Iraq policy received such a favorable hearing in Congress from 2000 to 2006.

The dramatic increase in Congressional oversight following the 2006 midterm elections is a case in point. Immediately after assuming control of Congress, House Democrats passed a resolution condemning a proposed "surge" of U.S. troops in Iraq and Senate Democrats debated a series of resolutions expressing varying degrees of outrage against the war in Iraq. The spring 2007 supplemental appropriations debate resulted in a House bill calling for a phased withdrawal (the president vetoed that bill, and the Senate then passed a bill accepting more war funding without withdrawal provisions). Democratic heads of committees in both chambers continue to launch hearings and investigations into the various mishaps, scandals, and tactical errors that have plagued the Iraq war. By all indications, if the government in Baghdad has not met certain benchmarks by September, the Democrats will push for binding legislation that further restricts the president's ability to sustain military operations in Iraq.

Neither Congress' prior languor nor its recent awakening should come as much of a surprise. When they choose to do so, members of Congress can exert a great deal of influence over the conduct of war. They can enact laws that dictate how long military campaigns may last, control the purse strings that determine how well they are funded, and dictate how appropriations may be spent. Moreover, they can call hearings and issue public pronouncements on foreign policy matters. These powers allow members to cut funding for ill-advised military ventures, set timetables for the withdrawal of troops, foreclose opportunities to expand a conflict into new regions, and establish reporting requirements. Through legislation, appropriations, hearings, and public appeals, members of Congress can substantially increase the political costs of military action—sometimes forcing presidents to withdraw sooner than they would like or even preventing any kind of military action whatsoever.

The Partisan Imperative

Critics have made a habit of equating legislative inactivity with Congress' abdication of its foreign policy obligations. Too often, the infrequency with which Congress enacts restrictive statutes is seen as prima facie evidence of the institution's failings. Sometimes it is. But one cannot gauge the health of the U.S. system of governance strictly on the basis of what Congress does—or does not do—in the immediate aftermath of presidential initiatives.

After all, when presidents anticipate Congressional resistance they will not be able to overcome, they often abandon the sword as their primary tool of diplomacy. More generally, when the White House knows that Congress will strike down key provisions of a policy initiative, it usually backs off. President Bush himself has relented, to varying degrees, during the struggle to create the Department of Homeland Security and during conflicts over the design of military tribunals and the prosecution of U.S. citizens as enemy combatants. Indeed, by most accounts, the administration recently forced the resignation of the chairman of the Joint Chiefs of Staff, General Peter Pace, so as to avoid a clash with Congress over his reappointment.

To assess the extent of Congressional influence on presidential war powers, it is not sufficient to count how many war authorizations are enacted or how often members deem it necessary to start the "war powers clock"—based on the War Powers Act requirement that the president obtain legislative approval within 60 days after any military deployment. Rather, one must examine the underlying partisan alignments across the branches of government and presidential efforts to anticipate and preempt Congressional recriminations.

During the past half century, partisan divisions have fundamentally defined the domestic politics of war. A variety of factors help explain why partisanship has so prominently defined the contours of interbranch struggles over foreign military deployments. To begin with, some members of Congress have electoral incentives to increase their oversight of wars when the opposing party controls the White House. If presidential approval ratings increase due to a "rally around the flag" effect in times of war, and if those high ratings only benefit the president's party in Congress, then the opposition party has an incentive to highlight any failures, missteps, or scandals that might arise in the course of a military venture.

After all, the making of U.S. foreign policy hinges on how U.S. national interests are defined and the means chosen to achieve them. This process is deeply, and unavoidably, political. Therefore, only in very particular circumstances—a direct attack on U.S. soil or on Americans abroad—have political parties temporarily united for the sake of protecting the national interest. Even then, partisan politics has flared as the toll of war has become evident. Issues of trust and access to information further fuel these partisan fires. In environments in which information is sparse, individuals with shared ideological or partisan affiliations find it easier to communicate with one another. The president possesses unparalleled intelligence about threats to national interests, and he is far more likely to share that information with members of his own political party than with political opponents. Whereas the commander in chief has an entire set of executive-branch agencies at his beck and call, Congress has relatively few sources of reliable classified information. Consequently, when a president claims that a foreign crisis warrants military intervention, members of his own party tend to trust him more often than not, whereas members of the opposition party are predisposed to doubt and challenge such claims. In this regard, Congressional Democrats' constant interrogations of Bush administration officials represent just the latest round in an ongoing interparty struggle to control the machinery of war.

Congressional Influence and Its Limits

Historically, presidents emerging from midterm election defeats have been less likely to respond to foreign policy crises aggressively, and when they have ordered the use of force, they have taken much longer to do so. Our research shows that the White House's propensity to exercise military force steadily declines as members of the opposition party pick up seats in Congress. In fact, it is not even necessary for the control of Congress to switch parties; the loss of even a handful of seats can materially affect the probability that the nation will go to war.

The partisan composition of Congress also influences its willingness to launch formal oversight hearings. While criticizing members for their inactivity during the Bush administration, Ornstein and Mann make much of the well-established long-term decline in the number of hearings held on Capitol Hill. This steady decline, however, has not muted traditional partisan politics. According to Linda Fowler, of Dartmouth College, the presence or absence of unified government largely determines the frequency of Congressional hearings. Contrary to Ornstein and Mann's argument that "vigorous oversight was the norm until the end of the twentieth century," Fowler demonstrates that during the post–World War II era, when the same party controlled both Congress and the presidency, the number of hearings about military policy decreased, but when the opposition party controlled at least one chamber of Congress, hearings occurred with greater frequency. Likewise, Boston University's Douglas Kriner has shown that Congressional authorizations of war as well as legislative initiatives that establish timetables for the withdrawal of troops, cut funds, or otherwise curtail military operations critically depend on the partisan balance of power on Capitol Hill.

Still, it is important not to overstate the extent of Congressional influence. Even when Congress is most aggressive, the executive branch retains a tremendous amount of power when it comes to military matters. Modern presidents enjoy extraordinary advantages in times of war, not least of which the ability to act unilaterally on military matters and thereby place on Congress (and everyone else) the onus of coordinating a response. Once troops enter a region, members of Congress face the difficult choice of either cutting funds and then facing the charge of undermining the troops or keeping the public coffers open and thereby aiding a potentially ill-advised military operation.

On this score, Ornstein and Mann effectively illustrate Bush's efforts to expand his influence over the war in Iraq and the war on terrorism by refusing to disclose classified information, regularly circumventing the legislative process, and resisting even modest efforts at oversight. Similarly, they note that Republican Congressional majorities failed to take full advantage of their institution's formal powers to monitor and influence either the formulation or the implementation of foreign policy during the first six years of Bush's presidency. Ornstein and Mann, however, mistakenly attribute such lapses in Congressional oversight to a loss of an "institutional identity" that was ostensibly forged during a bygone era when "tough oversight of the executive was common, whether or not different parties controlled the White House and Congress" and when members' willingness to challenge presidents had less to do with partisan allegiances and more to do with a shared sense of institutional responsibility. In the modern era, foreign-policy making has rarely worked this way. On the contrary, partisan competition has contributed to nearly every foreign policy clash between Capitol Hill and the White House for the past six decades.

Divided We Stand

Shortly after World War II—the beginning of a period often mischaracterized as one of "Cold War consensus"—partisan wrangling over the direction of U.S. foreign policy returned to Washington, ending a brief period of wartime unity. By defining U.S. military involvement in Korea as a police action rather than a war, President Truman effectively freed himself from the constitutional requirements regarding war and established a precedent for all subsequent presidents to circumvent Congress when sending the military abroad. Although Truman's party narrowly controlled both chambers, Congress hounded him throughout the Korean War, driving his approval ratings down into the 20s and paving the way for a Republican electoral victory in 1952. Railing off a litany of complaints about the president's firing of General Douglas MacArthur and his meager progress toward ending the war, Senator Robert Taft, then a Republican presidential candidate, declared that "the greatest failure of foreign policy is an unnecessary war, and we have been involved in such a war now for more than a year. . . . As a matter of fact, every purpose of the war has now failed. We are exactly where we were three years ago, and where we could have stayed."

On the heels of the Korean War came yet another opportunity to use force in Asia, but facing a divided Congress, President Dwight Eisenhower was hesitant to get involved. French requests for assistance in Indochina initially fell on sympathetic ears in the Eisenhower administration, which listed Indochina as an area of strategic importance in its "new look" defense policy. However, in January 1954, when the French asked for a commitment of U.S. troops, Eisenhower balked. The president stated that he "could conceive of no greater tragedy than for the United States to become involved in an all-out war in Indochina." His reluctance derived in part from the anticipated fight with Congress that he knew would arise over such a war. Even after his decision to provide modest technical assistance to France, in the form of B-26 bombers and air force technicians, Congressional leaders demanded a personal meeting with the president to voice their disapproval. Soon afterward, Eisenhower promised to withdraw the air force personnel, replacing them with civilian contractors.

Eventually, the United States did become involved in a ground war in Asia, and it was that war that brought Congressional

opposition to the presidential use of force to a fever pitch. As the Vietnam War dragged on and casualties mounted, Congress and the public grew increasingly wary of the conflict and of the power delegated to the president in the 1964 Gulf of Tonkin resolution. In 1970, with upward of 350,000 U.S. troops in the field and the war spilling over into Cambodia, Congress formally repealed that resolution. And over the next several years, legislators enacted a series of appropriations bills intended to restrict the war's scope and duration. Then, in June 1973, after the Paris peace accords had been signed, Congress enacted a supplemental appropriations act that cut off all funding for additional military involvement in Southeast Asia, including in Cambodia, Laos, North Vietnam, and South Vietnam. Finally, when South Vietnam fell in 1975, Congress took the extraordinary step of formally forbidding U.S. troops from enforcing the Paris peace accords, despite the opposition of President Gerald Ford and Secretary of State Henry Kissinger.

Three years later, a Democratic Congress forbade the use of funds for a military action that was supported by the president— this time, the supply of covert aid to anticommunist forces in Angola. At the insistence of Senator Dick Clark (D-Iowa), the 1976 Defense Department appropriations act stipulated that no monies would be used "for any activities involving Angola other than intelligence gathering." Facing such staunch Congressional opposition, President Ford suspended military assistance to Angola, unhappily noting that the Democratic-controlled Congress had "lost its guts" with regard to foreign policy.

In just one instance, the case of Lebanon in 1983, did Congress formally start the 60-day clock of the 1973 War Powers Act. Most scholars who call Congress to task for failing to fulfill its constitutional responsibilities make much of the fact that in this case it ended up authorizing the use of force for a full 18 months, far longer than the 60 days automatically allowed under the act. However, critics often overlook the fact that Congress simultaneously forbade the president from unilaterally altering the scope, target, or mission of the U.S. troops participating in the multinational peacekeeping force. Furthermore, Congress asserted its right to terminate the venture at any time with a one-chamber majority vote or a joint resolution and established firm reporting requirements as the U.S. presence in Lebanon continued.

During the 1980s, no foreign policy issue dominated Congressional discussions more than aid to the contras in Nicaragua, rebel forces who sought to topple the leftist Sandinista regime. In 1984, a Democratic-controlled House enacted an appropriations bill that forbade President Ronald Reagan from supporting the contras. Reagan appeared undeterred. Rather than abandon the project, the administration instead diverted funds from Iranian arms sales to support the contras, establishing the basis for the most serious presidential scandal since Watergate. Absent Congressional opposition on this issue, Reagan may well have intervened directly, or at least directed greater, more transparent aid to the rebels fighting the Nicaraguan government.

Regardless of which party holds a majority of the seats in Congress, it is almost always the opposition party that creates the most trouble for a president intent on waging war. When, in the early 1990s, a UN humanitarian operation in Somalia devolved into urban warfare, filling nightly newscasts with scenes from Mogadishu, Congress swung into action. Despite previous declarations of public support for the president's actions, Congressional Republicans and some Democrats passed a Department of Defense appropriations act in November 1993 that simultaneously authorized the use of force to protect UN units and required that U.S. forces be withdrawn by March 31, 1994.

A few years later, a Republican-controlled Congress took similar steps to restrict the use of funds for a humanitarian crisis occurring in Kosovo. One month after the March 1999 NATO air strikes against Serbia, the House passed a bill forbidding the use of Defense Department funds to introduce U.S. ground troops into the conflict without Congressional authorization. When President Clinton requested funding for operations in the Balkans, Republicans in Congress (and some hawkish Democrats) seized on the opportunity to attach additional monies for unrelated defense programs, military personnel policies, aid to farmers, and hurricane relief and passed a supplemental appropriations bill that was considerably larger than the amount requested by the president. The mixed messages sent by the Republicans caught the attention of Clinton's Democratic allies. As House member Martin Frost (D-Tex.) noted, "I am at a loss to explain how the Republican Party can, on one hand, be so irresponsible as to abandon our troops in the midst of a military action to demonstrate its visceral hostility toward the commander in chief, and then, on the other, turn around and double his request for money for what they call 'Clinton's war.'" The 1999 debate is remarkably similar to the current wrangling over spending on Iraq.

Legislating Opinion

The voice of Congress (or lack thereof) has had a profound impact on the media coverage of the current war in Iraq, just as it has colored public perceptions of U.S. foreign policy in the past. Indeed, Congress' ability to influence executive-branch decision-making extends far beyond its legislative and budgetary powers. Cutting funds, starting the war powers clock, or forcing troop withdrawals are the most extreme options available to them. More frequently, members of Congress make appeals designed to influence both media coverage and public opinion of a president's war. For example, Congress' vehement criticism of Reagan's decision to reflag Kuwaiti tankers during the Iran-Iraq War led to reporting requirements for the administration. Similarly, the Clinton administration's threats to invade Haiti in 1994 were met with resistance by Republicans and a handful of skeptical Democrats in Congress, who took to the airwaves to force Clinton to continually justify placing U.S. troops in harm's way.

Such appeals resonate widely. Many studies have shown that the media regularly follow official debates about war in Washington, adjusting their coverage to the scope of the discussion among the nation's political elite. And among the elite, members of Congress—through their own independent initiatives and through journalists' propensity to follow them—stand out as the single most potent source of dissent against the president. The sheer number of press releases and direct feeds that members of Congress produce is nothing short of breathtaking. And through carefully staged hearings, debates,

and investigations, members deliberately shape the volume and content of the media's war coverage. The public posturing, turns of praise and condemnation, rapid-fire questioning, long-winded exhortations, pithy Shakespearean references, graphs, timelines, and pie charts that fill these highly scripted affairs are intended to focus media attention and thereby sway the national conversation surrounding questions of war and peace. Whether the media scrutinize every aspect of a proposed military venture or assume a more relaxed posture depends in part on Congress' willingness to take on the president.

Indeed, in the weeks preceding the October 2002 war authorization vote, the media paid a tremendous amount of attention to debates about Iraq inside the Beltway. Following the vote, however, coverage of Iraq dropped precipitously, despite continued domestic controversies, debates at the United Nations, continued efforts by the administration to rally public support, and grass-roots opposition to the war that featured large public protests. Congress helped set the agenda for public discussion, influencing both the volume and the tone of the coverage granted to an impending war, and Congress' silence after the authorization was paralleled by that of the press.

Crucially, Congressional influence over the media extended to public opinion as well. An analysis of local television broadcast data and national public-opinion surveys from the period reveals a strong relationship between the type of media coverage and public opinion regarding the war. Even when accounting for factors such as the ideological tendencies of a media market (since liberal markets tend to have liberal voters and liberal media, while conservative districts have the opposite), we found that the airing of more critical viewpoints led to greater public disapproval of the proposed war, and more positive viewpoints buoyed support for the war. As Congress speaks, it would seem, the media report, and the public listens.

As these cases illustrate, the United States has a Congress with considerably more agenda-setting power than most analysts presume and a less independent press corps than many would like. As the National Journal columnist William Powers observed during the fall of 2006, "Journalists like to think they are reporting just the facts, straight and unaffected by circumstance." On the contrary, he recognized, news is a product of the contemporary political environment, and the way stories are framed and spun has little to do with the facts. In Washington, the party that controls Congress also determines the volume and the tone of the coverage given to a president's war. Anticipating a Democratic Congressional sweep in November 2006, Powers correctly predicted that "if Bush suffers a major political setback, the media will feel freed up to tear into this war as they have never done before."

With the nation standing at the precipice of new wars, it is vital that the American public understand the nature and extent of Congress' war powers and its members' partisan motivations for exercising or forsaking them. President Bush retains extraordinary institutional advantages over Congress, but with the Democrats now in control of both houses, the political costs of pursuing new wars (whether against Iran, North Korea, or any other country) and prosecuting ongoing ones have increased significantly.

Congress will continue to challenge the president's interpretation of the national interest. Justifications for future deployments will encounter more scrutiny and require more evidence. Questions of appropriate strategy and implementation will surface more quickly with threats of Congressional hearings and investigations looming. Oversight hearings will proceed at a furious pace. Concerning Iraq, the Democrats will press the administration on a withdrawal timetable, hoping to use their agenda-setting power with the media to persuade enough Senate Republicans to defect and thereby secure the votes they need to close floor debate on the issue.

This fall, the Democrats will likely attempt to build even more momentum to end the war in Iraq, further limiting the president's menu of choices. This is not the first instance of heavy Congressional involvement in foreign affairs and war, nor will it be the last. This fact has been lost on too many political commentators convinced that some combination of an eroding political identity, 9/11, failures of leadership, and dwindling political will have made Congress irrelevant to deliberations about foreign policy.

On the contrary, the new Democratic-controlled Congress is conforming to a tried-and-true pattern of partisan competition between the executive and legislative branches that has characterized Washington politics for the last half century and shows no signs of abating. Reports of Congress' death have been greatly exaggerated.

WILLIAM G. HOWELL and **JON C. PEVEHOUSE** are Associate Professors at the Harris School of Public Policy at the University of Chicago and the authors of *While Dangers Gather: Congressional Checks on Presidential War Powers.*

The Case for Congress

According to opinion polls, Congress is one of the least esteemed institutions in American life. While that should come as a shock, today it's taken for granted. What can't be taken for granted is the health of representative democracy amid this corrosive— and often unwarranted—distrust of its central institution.

LEE H. HAMILTON

Several years ago, I was watching the evening news on television when the anchorman announced the death of Wilbur Mills, the legendary former chairman of the House Ways and Means Committee. There was a lot the newscaster could have said. He might have recounted the central role Mills had played in creating Medicare. Or he might have talked about Mills's hand in shaping the Social Security system and in drafting the tax code. But he did not. Instead, he recalled how Mills's career collapsed after he was found early one morning with an Argentine stripper named Fanne Foxe. And then the anchorman moved on to the next story.

One of the perks of being chairman of an influential committee in Congress, as I was at the time, is that you can pick up the telephone and get through to a TV news anchor. Which I did. I chided the fellow for summing up Mills's career with a scandal. And much to my surprise, he apologized.

Americans of all stripes like to dwell on misbehavior by members of Congress. They look at the latest scandal and assume that they're seeing the *real* Congress. But they're not. They hear repeatedly in the media about missteps, but very little about the House leader who goes home on weekends to pastor his local church, or the senator who spends one day a month working in a local job to better understand the needs of constituents, or the many members who labor behind the scenes in a bipartisan way to reach the delicate compromises needed to make the system work.

I don't want to claim that all members are saints and that their behavior is always impeccable. Yet I basically agree with the assessment of historian David McCullough: "Congress, for all its faults, has not been the unbroken parade of clowns and thieves and posturing windbags so often portrayed. What should be spoken of more often, and more widely understood, are the great victories that have been won here, the decisions of courage and the visions achieved."

Probity in Congress is the rule rather than the exception, and it has increased over the years. When I arrived in Congress, members could accept lavish gifts from special interests, pocket campaign contributions in their Capitol offices, and convert their campaign contributions to personal use. And they were rarely punished for personal corruption. None of that would be tolerated now. Things still aren't perfect, but the ethical climate at the Capitol is well ahead of where it was a couple of decades ago. And, I might add, well ahead of the public's perception of it.

During my 34 years in the House of Representatives, I heard numerous criticisms of Congress. Many seemed to me perceptive; many others were far off the mark—such as when people thought that as a member of Congress I received a limousine and chauffeur, or didn't pay taxes, or was entitled to free medical care and Social Security coverage. When people are upset about Congress, their distress undermines public confidence in government and fosters cynicism and disengagement. In a representative democracy such as ours, what the American people think of the body that's supposed to reflect their views and interests as it frames the basic laws of the land is a matter of fundamental importance. I certainly do not think Congress is a perfect institution, and I have my own list of ways I think it could be improved. Yet often the public's view is based on misunderstanding or misinformation. Here are some of the other criticisms I've heard over the years:

Congress is run by lobbyists and special interests. Americans have differing views of lobbyists and special-interest groups. Some see them as playing an essential part in the democratic process. Others look at them with skepticism but allow them a legitimate role in developing policy. Most, however, see them as sinister forces exercising too much control over Congress, and the cynicism of this majority grew during the recent wave of corporate scandals, when it was revealed how extensively companies such as Enron and Arthur

Andersen had lobbied Congress. The suspicion that Congress is manipulated by powerful wheeler-dealers who put pressure on legislators and buy votes through extensive campaign contributions and other favors is not an unfounded concern, and it will not go away, no matter how fervently some might try to dismiss it.

That said, the popular view of lobbyists as nefarious fat cats smoking big cigars and handing out hundred-dollar bills behind closed doors is wrong. These days, lobbyists are usually principled people who recognize that their word is their bond. Lobbying is an enormous industry today, with billions of dollars riding on its outcomes. Special-interest groups will often spend millions of dollars on campaigns to influence a particular decision—through political contributions, grassroots lobbying efforts, television advocacy ads, and the like—because they know that they'll get a lot more back than they spend if a bill contains the language they want. They're very good at what they do, and the truth is, members of Congress can sometimes be swayed by them.

But the influence of lobbyists on the process is not as simple as it might at first appear. In the first place, "special interests" are not just the bad guys. If you're retired, or a homeowner, or use public transit or the airlines, or are concerned about religious freedom, many people in Washington are lobbying on your behalf. There are an estimated 25,000 interest groups in the capital, so you can be sure your views are somewhere represented. Advocacy groups help Congress understand how legislation affects their members, and they can help focus the public's attention on important issues. They do their part to amplify the flow of information that Thomas Jefferson called the "dialogue of democracy."

Of course, Congress often takes up controversial issues on which you'll find a broad spectrum of opinions. Public attention is strong, a host of special interests weigh in, and the views of both lobbyists and legislators are all over the map. In such circumstances, prospects are very small that any single interest group or lobbyist can disproportionately influence the results. There are simply too many of them involved for that to happen, and the process is too public. It's when things get quiet—when measures come up out of view of the public eye—that you have to be cautious. A small change in wording here, an innocuous line in a tax bill there, can allow specific groups to reap enormous benefits they might never have been granted under close public scrutiny.

The answer, it seems to me, is not to decry lobbying or lobbyists. Lobbying is a key element of the legislative process—part of the free speech guaranteed under the Constitution. At its heart, lobbying is simply people banding together to advance their interests, whether they're farmers or environmentalists or bankers. Indeed, belonging to an interest group—the Sierra Club, the AARP, the Chamber of Commerce—is one of the main ways Americans participate in public life these days.

When I was in Congress, I came to think of lobbyists as an important part of the *public discussion* of policy. I emphasize "public discussion" for a reason. Rather than trying to clamp down on lobbying, I believe we'd be better off ensuring that it happens in the open and is part of the broader policy debate. Our

challenge is not to end it, but to make sure that it's a balanced dialogue, and that those in power don't consistently listen to the voices of the wealthy and the powerful more intently than the voices of others. Several legislative proposals have been made over the years that would help, including campaign finance reform, tough restrictions on gifts to members of Congress, prohibiting travel for members and their staffs funded by groups with a direct interest in legislation, and effective disclosure of lobbyists' involvement in drafting legislation. But in the end, something else may be even more important than these proposals: steady and candid conversation between elected officials and the people they represent.

Members of Congress, I would argue, have a responsibility to listen to lobbyists. But members also have a responsibility to understand where these lobbyists are coming from, to sort through what they are saying, and then to make a judgment about what is in the best interests of their constituents and the nation as a whole.

Congress almost seems designed to promote total gridlock. People will often complain about a do-nothing Congress, and think that much of the fault lies in the basic design of the institution. When a single senator can hold up action on a popular measure, when 30 committees or subcommittees are all reviewing the same bill, when a proposal needs to move not just through both the House and the Senate but through their multilayered budget, authorization, and appropriations processes, and when floor procedures are so complex that even members who have served for several years can still be confused by them, how can you expect anything to get done? This feeling is magnified by the major changes American society has undergone in recent decades. The incredible increase in the speed of every facet of our lives has made many people feel that the slow, untidy, deliberate pace of Congress is not up to the demands of modern society.

It is not now, nor has it ever been, easy to move legislation through Congress. But there's actually a method to the madness. Basic roadblocks were built into the process for a reason. We live in a big, complicated country, difficult to govern, with enormous regional, ethnic, and economic differences. The process must allow time for responsiveness and deliberation, all the more so when many issues—taxation, health care, access to guns, abortion, and more—stir strong emotions and don't submit easily to compromise. Do we really want a speedy system in which laws are pushed through before a consensus develops? Do we want a system in which the views of the minority get trampled in a rush to action by the majority? Reforms can surely be made to improve the system, but the basic process of careful deliberation, negotiation, and compromise lies at the very heart of representative democracy. Ours is not a parliamentary system; the dawdling pace comes with the territory.

We misunderstand Congress's role if we demand that it be a model of efficiency and quick action. America's founders never intended it to be that. They clearly understood that one of the key roles of Congress is to slow down the process—to allow tempers to cool and to encourage careful deliberation, so that unwise or damaging laws do not pass in the heat of the moment and so that the views of those in the minority get a fair hearing. That basic vision still seems wise today. Proceeding carefully to develop consensus is arduous and exasperating work, but it's the only way to produce policies that reflect the varied perspectives of a remarkably diverse citizenry. People may complain about the process, but they benefit from its legislative speed bumps when they want their views heard, their interests protected, their rights safeguarded. I recognize that Congress sometimes gets bogged down needlessly. But the fundamental notion that the structure of Congress should contain road blocks and barriers to hasty or unfair action makes sense for our country and needs to be protected and preserved. In the words of former Speaker of the House Sam Rayburn, "One of the wisest things ever said was, 'Wait a minute.'"

There's too much money in politics. When people hear stories about all the fundraising that members of Congress must do today, they come to believe that Congress is a "bought" institution. I've often been told that in our system dollars speak louder than words, and access is bought and sold. By a 4 to 1 margin, Americans believe that elected officials are influenced more by pressures from campaign contributors than by what's in the best interests of the country. But in fact, the problem of money in politics has been with us for many years. It's become so much more serious in recent years because of the expense of television advertising. The biggest portion of my campaign budget in the last election I faced—$1 million, for a largely rural seat in southern Indiana—went for TV spots.

Having experienced it firsthand, I know all too well that the "money chase" has gotten out of hand. A lot of money from special interests is floating around the Capitol—far too much money—and we ignore the problem at our own peril. To be fair, many of the claims that special interests can buy influence in Congress are overstated. Though I would be the last to say that contributions have no impact on a voting record, it's important to recognize that most of the money comes from groups that already share a member's views on the issues, rather than from groups that are hoping to change a member's mind. In addition, many influences shape members' voting decisions—the most important of them being the wishes of their constituents. In the end, members know that if their votes aren't in line with what their constituents want, they won't be reelected. And *that,* rather than a campaign contribution, is what's foremost in their minds.

Still, it's an unusual member of Congress who can take thousands of dollars from a particular group and not be affected, which is why I've come to the view that the influence of money on the political process raises a threat to representative democracy. We need significant reform. We have a campaign finance system today that's gradually eroding the public's trust and confidence. It's a slow-motion crisis, but it is a crisis. It's not possible to enact a perfect, sweeping campaign finance bill today, and perhaps not anytime soon. Yet the worst abuses can be dealt with, one by one.

LEE H. HAMILTON is director of the Wilson Center and director of the Center on Congress at Indiana University. He was U.S. representative from Indiana's Ninth District from 1965 to 1999, and served as chairman of the House Committee on International Relations, the Joint Economic Committee, and several other committees. This essay is adapted from his new book *How Congress Works and Why You Should Care,* published by Indiana University Press.

From *Wilson Quarterly,* Spring 2004, pp. 12–17. Copyright © 2004 by Lee H. Hamilton. Reprinted by permission of Lee H. Hamilton.

This Is What a Speaker Looks Like

From a row house in Baltimore to the pinnacle of the House of Representatives: Nancy Pelosi has finally cracked the marble ceiling of the Capitol. Soon after she was named speaker, our 2002 Woman of the Year—now more powerful than any U.S. woman politician has ever been—took time from her demanding schedule for an exclusive interview with *Ms.*

MARIE COCCO

To trace Nancy Pelosi's political lineage, you follow a path of prominent titles. Father: Thomas D'Alesandro Jr., member of Congress and Baltimore mayor, a local legend and loyal acolyte of FDR. Brother: Tommy, Baltimore mayor and city councilman. Nancy: speaker of the U.S. House of Representatives.

To hear Pelosi tell it, the strongest root of this powerful tree didn't hold an official title at all. "My mother was sort of the driving force," Pelosi told *Ms.* "My mother was very committed and passionate about the issues—about fairness in the economy, and housing." When her father was mayor and her mother, also named Nancy, was Baltimore's first lady, "She always said, 'How can we teach children love and respect without giving them a place to live?' "

The strands of Pelosi's political DNA—her father's technical skills and people's touch, her mother's passion for economic justice and potency as a grassroots organizer—now have intertwined with Pelosi's own dogged work and personal ambition to put her at the pinnacle of American politics. As House speaker, she will be the most powerful woman in American history.

Yet, parse the testimonials to her, and a remarkable absence becomes apparent. She's not described as an icon, in the manner of Hillary Rodham Clinton. She is never—ever—portrayed as an accidental candidate, in the mold of Washington's Patty Murray, who first ran for Senate as "just a mom in tennis shoes." In truth, Pelosi is rarely compared with other political women, and no other woman has ever been in a comparable position. She is likened instead to Tip O'Neill.

Perhaps it is a good omen for congressional Democrats that the speaker, a woman of impeccable style, is seen as a natural heir to that rumpled old Irish pol. The late Thomas P. "Tip" O'Neill helped lead Congress for years. When he finally retired as House speaker, he'd emerged from the political vicissitudes of the Reagan years as a revered figure.

Pelosi and O'Neill share the New Deal philosophy that sees government as an instrument for bettering people's lives. "I believe that my parents were working on the side of the angels," Pelosi told *Ms.* "I always say that. That's part of my motivation in politics." In the precincts of big-city ethnic neighborhoods where both Pelosi and O'Neill cut their teeth, politics was defined as the principled—and pragmatic—lending of a hand to those in need. Payback came in the currency of votes.

The words so often spoken about O'Neill by those who worked with him—and against him—now are used to describe Pelosi: generous, tough, gracious. A committed partisan who gives, and expects, loyalty. And Pelosi is willing to say the hardest word for any politician to utter: No. "She's fully prepared to tell people no. Most leaders only want to say yes," says Rep. George Miller of California, a longtime Pelosi friend and political ally.

It was Pelosi's firm *no* to President Bush's 2005 plan to change Social Security from a system of guaranteed benefits to one dependent on private savings accounts that bound normally fractious congressional Democrats together and was, in fact, the first step on their path toward November's victories. The president had just won re-election, and boasted he had "political capital" to spend. Conventional wisdom on Capitol Hill—and in the echo chambers of television's talking heads—was that Democrats had to offer their own plan for shoring up Social Security. Failure to do so, the thinking went, would allow Bush to claim that Republicans were its true protectors.

"She stiffed the Republicans," chuckles former Texas Rep. Martin Frost, who lost a high-profile contest to Pelosi for the Democratic leader's slot in 2002. "She understood instinctively that you couldn't negotiate with these people on that kind of issue. She knew there was no middle ground there. Strategically, that was very important."

But victory did not come without struggle—or grousing. Pelosi demanded that Democrats put nothing forward until details of the president's plan were exposed, and Democrats in both chambers were jittery about the repeated accusations that they had no plan. Ambitious lawmakers craved the prominence that would come from putting forward a Social Security revision of their own. "Members would run up in a panic and say, 'They're asking me, they're telling me,'" Miller recalled. "And she would just say, 'Hold your fire, hold your fire, hold your fire, hold your fire.' She walked up and down the line and told people, 'Hold your fire.'"

Pelosi believed Bush's privatization plan would wither under public scrutiny—she understood how intricately Social Security is woven into the fabric of millions of American lives. "If we'd lost that fight, we as a party should be in the dustbin of history," Pelosi said during a breakfast with journalists last May.

Instead, Bush's top domestic priority collapsed under the weight of public disapproval. Republican lawmakers ran from it. The episode was an early indicator that Democrats could succeed not by accommodating Bush, but by taking him on. "That's when we got up and said, 'We're not your doormats anymore,'" says New York Rep. Louise Slaughter.

That showdown, as much as anything, revealed Pelosi's instincts as a political thoroughbred.

Her father's base of political operations was the family row house. As a little girl, Pelosi would stuff envelopes and make the rounds with her father at public appearances and political meetings. Though her father was the patriarch, Pelosi credits her mother's acute political instincts. She would welcome any visitor or favor-seeker to dinner, Pelosi says her brother always claimed. "She would just expand the pasta and the stew and everything else." More impressive, Pelosi says, were her mother's leadership skills. "She always had a whole band of women, whether it was to support candidates, to walk precincts, to make the phone calls. This was before the age of money in politics . . . She had a whole army of women that she could mobilize who could act upon any of the issues. She was *organization!*"

The power of the warm gesture exemplified at her mother's dinner table has helped propel Pelosi to the height of American politics. It's a cornerstone of her leadership style, fellow lawmakers say—one reason she's able to draw philosophically disparate Democrats into her corner. Former Connecticut Rep. Sam Gejdenson, who ran Pelosi's first leadership race for Democratic whip, said he was impressed with the broad ideological and regional spectrum of Democrats who already were onboard before the hard campaigning had begun. "Oftentimes, later in a political process the base grows and broadens. But in Nancy's race, right from the beginning, she had a very broad base in the Congress," Gejdenson says. "And it wasn't an accident. She works very hard at keeping in touch with a lot of people and she makes them feel comfortable."

Once a leader, Pelosi made sure that during late-night sessions, food was available in her offices at the Capitol—rank-and-file lawmakers have offices a short walk away. Her suite would become a gathering spot for weary members in need of coffee and a sandwich. The informal klatches were a way for Pelosi to catch up on their concerns and get word on issues critical to their districts.

Last October, in the final frenzy of the 2006 campaign, Pelosi was jetting between back-to-back fundraisers, incessant strategy sessions and briefings on get-out-the-vote operations. She also was on watch for her youngest daughter, Alexandra—who directed the 2002 documentary about George W. Bush's presidential campaign—to give birth to her sixth grandchild.

Pelosi's political instincts may be second nature, but she pursued them only as a second career. Her first was as a stay-at-home mother who raised five kids. She didn't expand her political involvement beyond grassroots activism until Alexandra was about to graduate from high school.

Amid the whirl of carpooling, bake-sale organizing and chaperoning field trips, Pelosi still nourished her love of politics. She opened her elegant San Francisco home (her husband, Paul, had become a wealthy investor) to Democrats for soirees to discuss issues such as the environment and economics. She encouraged other women to run for office, supporting their campaigns with organizational and fundraising help as if they were her own.

I guess they're called women's issues because if women did not focus on them there really wouldn't be any chance of [getting something done].

Most significantly, she dedicated herself to the art of raising money, accumulating a deep roster of donors and earning a reputation as one of the Democratic Party's premier fundraisers. Pelosi finally entered and won her first congressional race in a 1987 special election after the death of Sala Burton, who'd held the seat previously occupied by her husband, Phil Burton—one of Pelosi's closest political mentors. Once on Capitol Hill, Pelosi's fundraising prowess and the enormous amount of time she spends on the money circuit were keys to her climb. Loyalty in leadership races often is purchased with campaign cash that the best fundraisers dispense to other lawmakers.

Now Pelosi has taken everything she's learned—from the brick stoops of Baltimore to the feigned niceties of fundraising parties to the hard-fought battles of the feminist movement to the chummy conversations of the cloakroom—to become poised for unprecedented power. She is acutely aware of her role in history, having first felt its weight when she began attending the high-level White House meetings as minority leader. "For an instant, I felt as though Susan B. Anthony, Lucretia Mott, Elizabeth Cady Stanton—everyone who'd fought for women's right to vote and for the empowerment of women in politics . . . were there with me in the room," Pelosi has written.

As the first woman speaker, Pelosi will be the first woman in the line of succession to the presidency, after the vice president. But that hypothetical ascension is less significant than the tangible power Pelosi will wield. The House speaker picks select and conference committee chairs, and decides what legislation comes to a vote. Pelosi and her team will set the agenda. It promises progress on issues of deep concern to women. She voted against the Iraq

War, and understands that dissatisfaction with the Iraq War drove voters—especially women—to choose Democrats in November.

The intensity of her commitment to ending the military entanglement led to a high-profile decision most of Washington considered an inexcusable early blunder: Pelosi backed John Murtha, the Pennsylvania defense hawk who came out early for withdrawing troops from Iraq, in his failed bid to become the No. 2 Democratic leader. Whether a gesture of loyalty—Murtha ran Pelosi's hard-fought campaign for minority leader four years ago—or a damaging lapse of political judgment, the Murtha endorsement reflected Pelosi's style.

"I have to be who I am, not who the chattering class thinks I am," Pelosi told *Ms.* "The chattering classes would say you don't do these things, you don't take risks." But the punishing hours and grueling travel she endures are meaningless without passion to support them. And, she vowed, "I will never turn into what Washington's expectation is, which is 'Play it safe.'"

Democratic leaders agree on pushing measures that matter to families—and help women's pocketbooks. Because women are the majority of minimum wage workers, raising the wage floor to $7.25 as the Democrats promise would boost their incomes. Changing the Medicare prescription-drug program so that the government can negotiate lower prices stands to benefit elderly women, who make up the majority of Medicare beneficiaries and have lower incomes than elderly men.

If none of this has to do with sex, condoms, abortion or other scorching debates, it's not because Pelosi shies from defending reproductive rights—she's always been a firm advocate. But she's never believed women's concerns are so constricted. National security, the economy and the environment, she says, are women's natural preoccupations, while those issues usually identified with women—quality child care and the like—"should be everybody's issues . . . I guess they're called women's issues because if women did not focus on them there really wouldn't be any chance of [getting something done]."

Pelosi has the chance to get a lot done. That is likely to be the easy part of her job, as she is entirely competent at massaging votes into line. But she's often better in the cloakroom than before the cameras.

"I've always said I can bake the pie or sell your pie, but it's hard for me to sell my own pie," Pelosi says. "That's what I have to go out there and do." Now she must embrace the higher public profile that comes with the power she's earned—and learn to flourish under the glare of political klieg lights.

Marie Cocco is a syndicated columnist on political and cultural topics for *The Washington Post Writers Group.*

For more commentary about Pelosi from former Rep. Patricia Schroeder and other leaders, see www.msmagazine.com.

Life on Capitol Dunghill

NORMAN J. ORNSTEIN

Is there a culture of corruption in the U.S. Congress? As my kids might have said to me when they were in third grade, "Do bears poop in the forest?" On November 7, voters reacted to their own palpable sense of the ubiquity of the corruption by pooping on enough majority party incumbents in Congress to turn both the House and Senate over to the Democrats. Of course, the scandal and sense of the culture of corruption was not the only, or even the major, issue driving the vote—that distinction goes to Iraq. But corruption was significant enough to make a real difference, helping to oust several lawmakers with their own ties to scandals, including Senator Conrad Burns of Montana, Rep. Curt Weldon of Pennsylvania and Rep. Richard Pombo of California, along with the loss of the otherwise strongly Republican open seats vacated by Tom DeLay and Mark Foley.

The assumption that money distorts democratic politics is so old that by now it has deeply rooted itself in American folklore. It was Mark Twain himself who famously said, well over a century ago, "It could probably be shown by facts and figures that there is no distinctly native criminal class except Congress." More recently, a variety of tart humor messages circulating on the Internet have set out to prove Twain right: To wit, members of the House of Representatives are far more likely than any average group of 435 adult Americans to have declared bankruptcy, been delinquent in alimony and child support payments, had their taxes audited, flunked or been thrown out of college, and been arrested for drunk driving—among other tawdry adventures. Urban legend or not, the frequency of these assertions underscores the widespread belief in the culture that politicians are by nature corrupt, and that any scandal is just business as usual—only this time, they got caught.

In the past, we could admire Twain's irascible wit, chuckle at the e-mail humor, lap up the scandal du jour in the morning paper, roll our eyes and get on with life. But these days political corruption is so diverse and abundant that it demands not just disgust, but serious attention. We are not faced merely with a series of isolated miscreants—the garden-variety corruption that inevitably crops up when human beings, power and money intersect. Things today are well below and beyond the norm. Just consider the news from this past October, as I wrote this article:

- Susan Ralston, a senior White House aide and top assistant to Karl Rove, resigned on October 6 after a House Government Reform Committee investigation showed nearly 500 contacts between White House

officials and convicted lobbyist Jack Abramoff and his staff. During the investigation it came out that on numerous occasions Ralston asked Abramoff, her former employer, for expensive tickets to sporting and entertainment events. The committee investigation also showed that several non-profit organizations, including one run by conservative activist Grover Norquist, had actively connived with Abramoff to launder money in order to evade the laws and rules preventing lobbyists from paying for congressional travel, and to disguise the sources of millions of dollars of income going to Christian Coalition founder Ralph Reed, among others.

- On October 11, the *Wall Street Journal* detailed the millions of dollars Rep. Charles Taylor (R-NC) had made from real estate deals enhanced by earmarks he aggressively pursued for North Carolina.

- On October 13, Rep. Bob Ney (R-OH) pled guilty to a variety of offenses stemming from his relationship with Jack Abramoff that included favors to Ney in return for official actions on his part, with a sentence to follow of 27 months in jail. On October 15, a *Los Angeles Times* story outlined e-mail traffic showing that Abramoff had asked White House Political Director Ken Mehlman (recently departed chairman of the Republican National Committee) to arrange for government official Alan Stayman to be fired. At the U.S. State Department, Stayman had long been an advocate for improving labor practices in the Northern Marianas Islands, where sweatshop operators had hired Abramoff as their chief lobbyist. The e-mail exchange suggested that Mehlman complied with Abramoff's request: Stayman was fired.

- In mid-October, Rep. John Sweeney (R-NY) fell into the Abramoff morass when it was revealed that he failed to disclose that his trip to the Northern Marianas in 2001 with Abramoff staffer (and former Tom DeLay aide) Tony Rudy was paid for by the Saipan Chamber of Commerce in violation of House ethics rules.

- On October 16, FBI raids targeting the daughter of Weldon undercut vociferous denials that he was under investigation for steering lucrative lobbying contracts to his daughter from Russian and Serbian interests. *Washington Post* investigations suggested a series of aggressive actions on Weldon's part for several of these interests even as his daughter was garnering large fees from them. The next day, *USA Today*'s lead story, "Relatives have 'inside track' in lobbying for tax dollars," noted:

Lobbying groups employed 30 family members last year to influence spending bills that their relatives with ties to the House and Senate appropriations committees oversaw or helped write, a *USA Today* investigation found. Combined, they generated millions of dollars in fees for themselves or their firms. The connections are so pervasive that, in 2005 alone, appropriations bills contained about $750 million for projects championed by lobbyists whose relatives were involved in writing the spending bills.

- On October 17, Rep. Jane Harman (D-CA), the ranking Democrat on the House Intelligence Committee, released—over the objections of the committee chair Peter Hoekstra (R-MI)—an investigative report indicating that former Rep. Randy "Duke" Cunningham (R-CA) had steered $80 million in intelligence-related contracts to two individuals in return for hefty bribes, in the process bullying and coercing staff and others to achieve the goal.
- In the fall of 2006, investigations of several lawmakers besides Bob Ney were ongoing, including former House Majority Leader Tom DeLay (R-TX), Senator Conrad Burns (R-MT) and Rep. John Doolittle (R-CA), as was the investigation of allegations involving senior Interior Department officials. Rep. William Jefferson (D-LA) skyrocketed to notoriety when the FBI discovered $90,000 in cash, tied via wiretaps to bribes, hidden in his freezer, and followed up with an aggressive raid on Jefferson's congressional office.
- Senate Majority Leader Harry Reid (D-NV) faced controversy over his failure to record or disclose a land transfer to a corporation until well after the land was sold for a substantial profit, and used leadership PAC funds to pay for Christmas gifts for employees at the Ritz Carlton condominium where he lives (he subsequently revised his disclosure statement and paid for the gifts out of personal funds).
- David Safavian, another Abramoff associate who had been the Chief of Staff of the General Services Administration, was convicted and sentenced to 18 months in prison on charges including obstruction of justice and making false statements under oath.

Incredibly, only the tawdriness of the Mark Foley (R-FL) page scandal seemed to finally spur the House Ethics Committee to serious action, as a stream of staffers and lawmakers appeared in some cases to give clearly contradictory stories about a possible cover-up. Rep. Dale Kildee (D-MI) emerged from a closed-door session with the Ethics Committee to tell reporters on October 17 that the Page Board, of which he was the only Democratic member, had held recent conference calls on other accusations of impropriety with pages, but *not* those concerning Foley. Such is life on Capitol Dunghill.

These scandals are not just a series of isolated, one-off events. To be sure, some of the allegations and investigations might be attributed to overzealous Federal prosecutors or reporters' voracious appetite for scandalmongering. But the sheer weight of the allegations, the breadth of the scandals and the evidence already in hand of serious chicanery make it clear that the problem is a systemic one: "Regular order" on Capitol Hill—the web of norms and rules that regulate legislative conduct—has collapsed. It has done so for two overlapping and mutually reinforcing reasons: First has been the astonishing level of majority-party hubris and entitlement, the likes of which America hasn't seen since the fabled Gilded Age of the 1870s; second is the virtual disappearance of the ethics enforcement process.

Hubris and Entitlement

The story of Congress' dealings with lobbying groups like the Investment Company Institute (ICI) paint a clear picture of the rise of Republican hubris and entitlement. According to the *Washington Post,* in 2003 staff members and possibly Rep. Mike Oxley (R-OH), the chairman of the House Financial Services Committee, demanded that the ICI, the major trade association for mutual fund companies, fire its Democratic chief lobbyist and replace her with a Republican designated by the committee. The demands were backed up by the threat of hearings scheduled on whether mutual funds had overcharged their customers and withheld important information. If the committee's demands were not met, the staffers told ICI, the hearings could turn ugly.

This was not the first time Republicans in Congress had made this kind of threat. In 1998, Republican leaders bristled at a decision by the Electronic Industries Association (EIA) to hire former Congressman Dave McCurdy (D-OK) as its head instead of their choice, former Republican Congressman Bill Paxon (R-NY). They struck back by postponing a vote favored by the EIA that was also required to implement two international treaties about intellectual property rights. The EIA eventually got its treaties, but that series of events resulted in a rebuke by the House Ethics Committee of then-Majority Whip Tom DeLay (R-TX)—the first of his several run-ins with the committee.

But the threats against the ICI were about more than just delaying a vote. In this case, Republicans were brandishing a stick of embarrassing hearings followed by punitive legislation, intimidating an entire industry for partisan gain. It's difficult to see this as anything other than a fundamental abuse of power.

To be sure, sweetheart relationships between lobbyists and lawmakers are nothing new. When he was Senate majority leader, Lyndon Baines Johnson was in deep with a number of lobbyists in Austin, Texas, and Washington, DC, including Thomas G. "Tommy the Cork" Corcoran, the former FDR braintruster who became a top lobbyist, and with whom Johnson had a long-standing relationship. In her 1992 book *Scandal,* Suzanne Garment noted that if modern standards had been applied to Corcoran, "he would probably have been under continuous indictment for offenses such as attempted bribery and conspiracy to make illegal campaign contributions." In *The Path to Power* (1981), Robert Caro described how Johnson received bags of cash that had been channeled through lobbyists and oilmen for his first Senate campaign. Other career politicians like Jack Brooks (D-TX) could stand toe-to-toe with Johnson in intimidating lobbyists. And Brooks Jackson's *Honest*

Graft: Inside the Business of Politics (1988) documents efforts by House Democrats like California's Tony Coelho to siphon off campaign funds and key job postings from lobbyists in the mid-1980s. But by and large, lobbyists didn't need encouragement from the likes of Tony Coelho to cozy up to a party that had had a lock on the majority for more than forty years. It was all Coelho could do to keep up with the offers.

In 1994, the Republicans swept into power with a manifesto for change—the Contract with America—that pledged "to restore accountability to Congress; to end its cycle of scandal and disgrace; to make all of us proud again of the way free people govern themselves." It sounded great, but the systematic plan key Republican leaders brought with them to power soon made Johnson's and Coelho's offenses, and Jack Brooks' meanness, seem almost innocent by comparison. Republican efforts harnessed a climate ripe for corruption and abuse of power. The cases of the ICI and the EIA, discussed above, are just two stories out of many about pressure brought to bear by the Republican leadership against trade associations, companies and lobbying firms to place former colleagues and allies in top and mid-level lobbying posts. These well-placed individuals, who often earned five to ten times their previous salaries as congressional or party staffers, contributed handsomely to individual Republicans' political campaigns, campaign committees, outside campaign groups and leadership PACs—thus perpetuating the Republican lock on power. These efforts were called "the K Street Project" by their Republican progenitors, including Abramoff, DeLay, Norquist, Senator Rick Santorum (R-PA) and others in their circle.

This machinery was about more than just winning elections; it was about changing laws, too. Yes, of course, lobbyists have always had a hand in slipping language into legislation—an amendment to a tax bill here, an earmark there—but in the past few years their influence increased by orders of magnitude. Lobbyists have had a much more direct role in drafting legislation, including the major energy and bankruptcy statutes recently passed and signed into law. The relationship has clearly been two-way, however. Much of the initiative has come from leaders in Congress who have pushed lobbyists for support and have shaken them down for more campaign funding.

In March 2001, Juliet Eilperin of the *Washington Post* illustrated the matter well: "Just last week, Senate GOP Conference Chairman Rick Santorum held a meeting with several lobbyists in which they agreed to come up with a list of candidates for several high-profile vacancies, including ones at AARP, the Business Roundtable and the U.S. Telecom Association." Among the attendees at that meeting was Jack Abramoff, the lobbyist who in January 2006 followed his former partner, one-time DeLay press secretary Michael Scanlon, in pleading guilty to conspiring to defraud clients out of millions of dollars. Scanlon has also admitted to conspiring to corrupt public officials. Other former DeLay staffers, including Tony Rudy and Ed Buckham, were also trapped directly in the corruption net. Abramoff further confessed to evading Federal taxes and running a wire fraud in Florida, and has agreed to pay $26.7 million in restitution, penalties and back taxes, and to serve almost six years in prison.

The many sordid press accounts of Abramoff's dealings have made him into the poster child for congressional corruption

and insider dealings. But his chicanery and amoral approach to Washington were clear a decade ago, long before it came to light that he and Scanlon had charged Indian tribes $82 million to help them get licenses to build casinos or to block other tribes from getting their licenses approved. Abramoff first drew the attention of Washington watchers when he helped operate a foundation that was secretly funded by intelligence forces in apartheid South Africa to keep track of apartheid opponents. Abramoff then parlayed his close relationships with key conservatives like DeLay, Norquist, Reed and Dennis Hastert (R-IL) into a lobbying machine that sloshed money around town to and through key lawmakers and cronies with arrogance, greed and venality. In one such case, Abramoff used $2 million from eLottery, an Internet gambling firm, to try to stop a bill that would have curtailed the firm's business. Among other things, the money was used to pay a consulting fee to the wife of DeLay aide Tony Rudy at the same time that Rudy was secretly helping direct the eLottery lobbying effort from inside DeLay's Capitol Hill office. Money was also spent to persuade conservative anti-gambling groups led by Louis Sheldon and Ralph Reed to attack the bill, incredibly, as *pro-gambling*. In Reed's case, elaborate efforts were made to channel the money in ways that would make it seem as if it weren't coming from a gambling group.

Lend Me Your Earmark

Abramoff & Co.'s flagrant corruption could easily make one forget that his dealings represented just one aspect of a broader culture cultivated by the majority in order to extend their hold on power (often while making a quick buck in the process). Consider the Republican majority's perfection of the art of the earmark—multimillion-dollar contracts glommed on to defense, transportation, education and appropriations bills to benefit specific causes, communities or companies. Since 1994, earmarks have increased at least tenfold. The 2005 highway bill alone had 6,371 earmarks worth more than $23 billion. Include defense and education earmarks, and the total is well above $50 billion—all of which bypassed any cost/benefit analysis, independent review or priority test. And most members of Congress vote on bills without the slightest idea of what earmarks have been added by their colleagues, often at or near the last hour before a vote.

The ease with which lawmakers can introduce earmarks has created a particularly tempting climate for bribery. It was taking bribes in exchange for earmarks that got "Duke" Cunningham in trouble. Marcus Stern, a Copley News Service reporter, grew suspicious of a Cunningham real estate transaction and, after further investigation, discovered that the deal was a funnel for a bribe. The bribe was used to get Cunningham, a member of the Defense Appropriations Subcommittee, to steer a huge contract to a fledgling defense contractor. In November 2005, Cunningham pleaded guilty to taking $2.4 million in bribes from the contractor and resigned; he is currently in Federal prison.

Yet straight-up bribery is only one, obviously illegal, way that lawmakers use earmarks to enrich their personal fortunes. To illustrate another method, let's turn to none other than former Speaker Hastert.

The basic facts about the Hastert case were first reported in the *Chicago Tribune* and the *Chicago Sun-Times*. (Scott Lilly and I amplified on them in an October 6, 2006 article for the *New Republic*.) In essence, Hastert aggressively pushed to add to the recent, pork-laden highway bill an earmark funding construction of the Prairie Parkway Corridor, west of Chicago. Neither the public nor the state government supported construction of the highway; a majority of area residents favored using the money to make improvements to existing roads instead. But the highway was very convenient to one constituency: It was located a little more than a mile from land Hastert had bought for $5,200 per acre in August 2002 and used to get in on a real estate trust 18 months later. Four months after the highway bill with Hastert's earmark was signed in December 2005, the real estate trust sold its newly valuable land to a housing developer for $36,152 per acre. Hastert cleared $3,118,000 on the deal. When all was said and done, low-end estimates placed the Speaker's net worth at $6.2 million—virtually all of it from these earmark-enriched land transactions.

Hastert was not the only House member to make real-estate investments aided by earmarks on the highway bill. In 2005, Rep. Ken Calvert (R-CA) and a business partner purchased land near March Air Reserve Base in Riverside County, California, and then snagged handsome Federal funding worth about $10 million for both a freeway interchange and commercial development. Within the year, they sold the land for a nice $500,000 profit, doubling their investment. Rep. Gary Miller (R-CA) secured more than $1 million in highway funding near a commercial development he co-owns in Diamond Bar, California. Of course, Republicans aren't the only ones making out like bandits from earmarking. Rep. Alan Mollohan (D-WV) has also benefited personally from earmarks. Mollohan secured $179 million in government contracts for West Virginia companies that in turn gave $225,000 to his family charity, accounting for nearly half the charity's revenue.

Breakdown of Ethics Enforcement

According to the Constitution, only Congress has the power to police its members in their official conduct. It has always been reluctant to do so without an outside prod or substantial public pressure, however. This reluctance has grown in the past decade as a result of two changes in House rules, the first to block outside groups from initiating ethics complaints against lawmakers, and the second a pact between the major parties not to launch complaints from the other side of the aisle. This pact was broken when Chris Bell, a Democrat who lost his seat in 2004 after Texas' redistricting, raised a series of complaints against then-Majority Leader Tom DeLay—the man who had engineered his defeat. These complaints led to a triple rebuke of DeLay by the House Ethics Committee, as well as the indictments brought against him for violations of Texas campaign finance laws.

After the committee issued its admonitions, Hastert fired the committee chair, Rep. Joel Hefley (R-CO) and two of the committee's strongest Republican members, replacing them with members who had given substantial sums to the DeLay legal defense fund. The new chair, Rep. Doc Hastings (R-WA), knew which master he served. He flouted the committee's long-standing rules

by appointing a partisan staff leader, igniting a controversy that shut down any meaningful ethics process for more than a year, until the Mark Foley scandal forced it back into action. And even when the committee did finally bestir itself to investigate the performance of Hastert and his top aides in the Foley matter, it broke precedent with past investigations of speakers by failing to hire a respected, independent counsel to work with it. There is still no sign that the committee will move beyond a passive, reactive role in any case besides the Foley scandal.

The breakdown of the Ethics Committee comes in the midst of a much broader breakdown of regular order. One only needs to look at the embarrassing bipartisan antics displayed during the House debate this past spring about ethics and lobbying reform. The debate was only scheduled in the first place due to a barrage of criticism growing out of the Abramoff scandal. As the process began, the Rules Committee actually held a model hearing. But the bill it eventually considered in May had been diluted to meaninglessness. The committee then acted to quash virtually all reasonable amendments designed to restore some substance, including several broadly bipartisan ones. For example, Reps. Christopher Shays (R-CT) and Marty Meehan (D-MA) sponsored an amendment to create an Office of Public Integrity to oversee lobbying disclosure reports and investigate allegations of ethics violations, reporting any violations to the Ethics Committee for action. No vote was allowed. Nor was a vote allowed on an amendment to strengthen the Ethics Committee sponsored by ousted chairman Joel Hefley (R-CO) and Kenny Hulshof (R-MO), one of the panel's stronger former members.

Meanwhile, the House Government Reform Committee, in a striking burst of bipartisanship, approved by a 32-0 vote (repeat: *thirty-two to nothing*) the Executive Branch Reform Act of 2006, which proposed revolving door bans, protection for whistleblowers on administration staffers working for lobbyists, and an end to secret meetings between Executive Branch officials and lobbyists. The House Republican leadership refused to incorporate these provisions into the reform package. Further, the Rules Committee refused to allow a floor vote on an amendment including reforms offered by Reps. Tom Davis (R-VA) and Henry Waxman (D-CA), the chairman and ranking member of the Government Reform Committee, respectively. All told, every meaningful amendment was summarily rejected. The rule on the final bill was so restrictive that a sizable group of Republicans voted against it, but eight Democrats supported it, allowing it to pass.

There was one more golden opportunity to get real reform at the end of the debate: The House voted on a "motion to recommit with instructions," a usually pro forma effort in which the minority party has a chance at an alternative. The motion would have adopted the Democrats' ethics and lobbying reform bill, a reasonably tough package of ethics reforms put forward by the Democratic leadership. On every other occasion when a motion to recommit with instructions had been offered, it had failed on party lines; the majority Republicans treated such efforts as procedural, not substantive, and cracked the party whip. This time, however, driven by a bipartisan disgust with the failure to deal with corruption, the motion to recommit garnered an astonishing twenty Republican votes. But it still came up short by two, when four Democrats cast their ballots against it.

One of those Democrats was John Murtha of Pennsylvania. Murtha traded his vote, and possibly other votes, in return for earmarks! If this is how a top Democratic contender for majority leader, and a man frequently lauded in the press as speaking "truth to power," behaves, what should we expect from congressmen who are literally breaking laws? Murtha showed his stripes during the post-election campaign for majority leader when he met with a group of Democratic colleagues to campaign for the post and called ethics reform "pure crap." At least he lost the opportunity to lead the new majority, with its incoming Speaker's pledge to create the most ethical House in history.

Cleaning House

What is to be done? Even more significant than discrete legislative reforms are a change in attitude by those running Congress and a sustained sense of outrage by the public. The breakdown of regular order was the result of conscious decisions to disregard or bypass existing norms of conduct, so a conscious commitment to once again abide by those rules would do more to restore Congressional credibility than any reform package. The support from reformist Democrats like Marty Meehan for the ethically challenged Murtha, who has his own long and controversial relationship to scandal (the 1980 Abscam) as well as to earmarks, shows that the change in attitude will not come easily and will require constant pressure from inside and outside the institution.

Nevertheless, reforms will play an important role in cleaning the House, and they should start with the ethics process. By now it ought to be clear that having current members police themselves entails a conflict of interest: When they're aggressive they're called "partisan," but when they're passive they're just another part of the "good old boy network." Congress needs to find a way to build credibility for the internal investigations it undertakes (and for those it doesn't, as well).

The best approach is through an independent Office of Public Integrity of the kind proposed by Shays and Meehan, but with enhancements. Such an office would work in conjunction with existing ethics committees, moving investigations out of the partisan morass and into a new and more independent venue—not one of special prosecutors, independent counsels or people unfamiliar with the legislative process, but one that engages former members such as Reps. Lee Hamilton (D-IN), David Skaggs (D-CO), Mickey Edwards (R-OK) and John McCollister (R-NE) to determine when the House (or Senate) ethics panel should engage in a fuller investigation of allegations against a member or staffer. Indeed, the best move that Speaker Nancy Pelosi could make would be to name retiring Rep. Joel Hefley to take charge of the outside element of the ethics process—picking a conservative Republican of impeccable integrity and institutional honesty. A proposal by Senator Barack Obama (D-IL), drawn directly from the largely successful independent ethics commissions in Florida and Kentucky, contains the best overall approach.

We must also address some of the malodorous dynamics of money and politics in the nation's capital. Leadership Political Action Committees (PACs), fundraising schemes used by increasing numbers of members to raise money to distribute to other candidates, have become the "price of admission" to attain leadership posts. In 2004 House Republicans engaged in an embarrassing open contest to choose a chairman of the Appropriations Committee from three senior members. The criterion for the contest was the amount of money raised for "the team" via their leadership PACs, not their legislative skills. The winner, Jerry Lewis of California, is now—big surprise—deeply embroiled in controversy over his fundraising networks and their links to official actions. All such leadership PACs should be abolished.

In addition, Congress should adopt a rule now in force in many state legislatures that prohibits fundraising in Washington when Congress is in session. Combining that with a pledge that Congress will be in session for at least 26 five-day weeks each year would make the legislative process much more deliberative, build a greater sense of institutional identity among members, and create a stronger sense of commitment to integrity, compared to the near drive-by quality of activity in Congress in recent years.

We are never going to remove the main catalyst of corruption in politics—money—from the process. It would be a mistake to demand that members of Congress and staffers live ascetic or penurious lives. In fact, lawmakers (and judges, for that matter) ought to be paid at least as much as second-year associates in big law firms, and probably more, if we are to get the best people. (Right now, they are on a par with 25-year-old entering associates with court clerkships.) Still, low pay doesn't justify one whit of the misbehavior of the recent Congress.

While money will always remain a temptation to ignoble behavior, we can put limits on it. Most money-grubbing is not undertaken for personal gain but for campaign bankrolling. If decent campaign financing reform could be agreed upon—reform that actually makes the problem smaller rather than the other way around—that would certainly help.

In the end, however, the congressional swamp will never be drained without a sharp change in behavior outside Congress. The response by voters this past November to throw at least some of the rascals out will help. But the fact is that many Democrats would be delighted to change only the flow of dollars from the GOP to them; one reformist House Democrat said of this variety of his colleagues, "They want to get rid of the K Street Project—and to replace it with Project K Street." The only way to prevent the return to business as usual, this time with a Democratic majority flavor, is a continuing major reaction by voters against the culture of corruption. When we have a level of honest outrage that is commensurate with the manifest justification for it, we'll start to really clean house. If the American people show instead that they just don't care, they will get the government they so richly deserve.

Remote Control

The Supreme Court's greatest failing is not ideological bias—it's the justices' increasingly tenuous grasp of how the real world works.

STUART TAYLOR JR.

I've been working on some questions in case the makers of Trivial Pursuit ever decide to put forth a Supreme Court edition: Now that Sandra Day O'Connor has announced her retirement, how many remaining justices have ever held elected office? How many have previously served at the highest levels of the executive branch of government? How many have argued big-time commercial lawsuits within the past thirty-five years? How many have ever been either criminal defense lawyers or trial prosecutors? How many have presided over even a single criminal or civil trial? The answers are zero, zero, zero, one, and one, respectively. (David Souter was a New Hampshire prosecutor once upon a time, and later served as a trial judge.)

The answers would have been starkly different fifty years ago. Five of the nine justices who decided *Brown* v. *Board of Education,* in 1954, had once worked as trial prosecutors, and several had substantial hands-on experience in commercial litigation. More famously, that Court included a former governor, three former senators, two former attorneys general, two former solicitors general, and a former SEC chairman.

That Court, in other words, was intimately familiar with the everyday workings of the political and judicial systems, and with the beliefs and concerns of everyday Americans. Not so the Court that recessed in June, eight of whose members (in addition to their long tenure in the splendid isolation of the Supreme Court's marble palace) have been drawn from judgeships on appellate courts, and sometimes from academic law before that—places already far removed from the hurly-burly of our judicial and political systems. The current justices are smart and dedicated. But they're not like you and me.

Debates over the Court's "balance"—ideological, ethnic, gender—will doubtless heat up as Congress considers the current vacancy. Yet there is likely to be little discussion about the greatest imbalance—the one in the collective real-world experience of its justices. The Court's steady homogenization by professional background has gone largely unremarked.

Should we be concerned? After all, the Supreme Court is supposed to sit above politics and apart from popular whims. But when a large majority of the Court's justices have never

cross-examined a lying cop or a slippery CEO, never faced a jury, never slogged through the swamps of the modern discovery process, something has gone wrong. As the Court has lost touch with the real-world ramifications of its decisions, our judicial system has clearly suffered.

The Court's slow disengagement from practicality was visible by the 1970s, when, for example, in a well-intentioned effort to protect students from unwarranted suspension and tenured public school teachers from arbitrary dismissal, the Court issued a series of decisions requiring hearings before such action. The justices presumably imagined simple, cursory hearings to guard against egregious abuses of power. Predictably, that's not what happened. Hearings quickly became clogged with lawyers, witnesses, trial-type formalities, multiple administrative and judicial appeals, and years of delay. To avoid such ordeals, many principals and administrators have simply stopped trying to remove thuggish students and inept teachers from our schools.

Over time the justices have failed ever more conspicuously to understand what messes their decisions might make. In 1997, while forcing Bill Clinton to give a sworn deposition in the Paula Jones sexual-harassment lawsuit, the Court stunned litigators and trial judges by predicting that this was "highly unlikely to occupy any substantial amount of [President Clinton's] time." Only Justice Stephen Breyer seemed to appreciate that the realities of modern discovery practice "could pose a significant threat to the President's official functions." Sure enough, the district court ordered Clinton to answer detailed, tangential questions about his relations with various women. The rest is history.

In a string of decisions since 2000 the Court has thrown the criminal-justice system into utter confusion by repeatedly changing the rules on the roles of judges and juries in sentencing, while providing minimal guidance on how the new rules should be implemented. In response to the rulings, thousands of current inmates have requested re-sentencing, to the consternation of federal trial and appellate judges, who are all over the lot on how to handle these requests. (The judges also have major differences of opinion on how much weight they should now give sentencing guidelines in new cases.) We'll be hearing more about this confusion—it's a clear recipe for an onslaught of additional appeals down the road, which will further tax our already overburdened criminal-justice system.

Then there's the Court's recent Janus-faced pair of rulings on governmental displays of the Ten Commandments. The gist: recently installed, framed copies must be stripped from courthouse walls; forty-year-old, six-foot-high monuments can stay on the grounds outside. The logic: well, for that you'll have to read ten separate opinions totaling 140 pages. In announcing part of this mess, Chief Justice William Rehnquist said, "I didn't know we had that many people on our Court." Chief Justice John Marshall once observed (in *Marbury* v. *Madison*) that "it is the province and duty of the Judicial Department to say what the law is." Government officials and lower-court judges often find the law difficult to ascertain today. But at least they do know—in minute detail—what each justice thinks it ought to be.

As our Supreme Court justices have become remote from the real world, they've also become more reluctant to do real work—especially the sort of quotidian chores done by prior justices to ensure the smooth functioning of the judicial system. The Court's overall productivity—as measured by the number of full, signed decisions—has fallen by almost half since 1985. Clerks draft almost all the opinions and perform almost all the screening that leads to the dismissal without comment of 99 percent of all petitions for review. Many of the cases dismissed are the sort that could be used to wring clear perversities and inefficiencies out of our litigation system—especially out of commercial and personal-injury litigation.

Traditionally the Court decided major questions of federal commercial law, adapting to the changing nature of business and the increasing complexity of litigation. Yet according to Michael Greve, the head of the American Enterprise Institute's Federalism Project, this Court has "resolutely refused to tackle the inconsistencies and absurdities that, after decades of neglect, afflict nearly every area of commercial litigation." One reason, Greve argues, is that with the exception of Justice Breyer, "the Court has absolutely no idea what business litigation in America now looks like."

What accounts for the Court's drift? There are two factors—one political and one biological. Politically the appointment of Supreme Court justices has become more contentious as it has focused on a small number of polarizing issues—most notably abortion. The ideal candidate today is predictable enough to suit the president and his political base, yet not so predictable as to be an easy target for critics. Appellate-court judges simply fit the bill better than other candidates. Their legal opinions signal ideological leanings (providing more of a track record than would exist for, say, a prominent litigator or a prosecutor). But because they are bound to follow Supreme Court precedents, they ordinarily don't say whether they would overturn those precedents if, as justices, they got the chance. (Elected officials, in contrast, must take specific stands on abortion and other hot issues—all but disqualifying them from consideration for the Court.) Past justices took many roads to the Supreme Court. Today, almost invariably, there appears to be just one.

Moreover, that road is receding further in the rear-view mirror. Longer life spans and justices' increasing reluctance to retire have raised their average tenure from fifteen years before 1970 to twenty-five years since then. Until this summer no justice had retired in eleven years. Real-world experiences gained before their years on the appellate and Supreme courts have become distant memories for today's justices.

Will future appointees bring more diversity of experience? Alas, the political incentives to pick appellate judges seem likely to persist. But one proposed reform—which, after a phase-in, would limit judicial terms to eighteen years, and allow each president to appoint a new justice every two years—would create more opportunities to diversify the Court over time.

The proposal, which is backed by some forty-five leading legal scholars, both liberal and conservative, would (among other benefits) ensure frequent and regular infusions of new blood, and with it more recent experience with the practical aspects of judicial decisions. And because more appointments would lower the political stakes for each one, presidents might be willing to look beyond the usual suspects.

That would be welcome. Quietly our Supreme Court has become a sort of aristocracy—unable or unwilling to clearly see the workings, glitches, and peculiarities of the justice system over which it presides from such great altitude.

STUART TAYLOR JR. is a *National Journal* columnist and a *Newsweek* contributor.

Court Approval

Will John Roberts ever get better?

JEFFREY ROSEN

At the end of a bitterly divided Supreme Court term, liberals are by turns fighting mad and full of despair. Although Chief Justice John Roberts began the term by calling for greater consensus, a third of cases were decided by five–four votes, the highest percentage in more than ten years. The polarization inspired the four liberal justices to write some of their most passionate, incisive, and memorable dissents. But how pessimistic should liberals really be about the future of the Court? Just after the term ended, I had an opportunity to interview Justice Stephen Breyer about the Court's role in American democracy at the Aspen Ideas Festival.

Breyer made no bones about his disappointment with the divisions on the Court. He began by discussing his 77-page dissenting opinion in the Seattle case forbidding public schools to use race in student assignments. The dissent is a tour de force. It combines a passionate defense of judicial restraint with blistering criticism of the majority for distorting precedents. "Of course, I got slightly exercised, and the way I show this is that I wrote seventy-seven-page opinions," he joked. "I think the color-blind view is *very* wrong, I think it's *never* been in the law, it's never been accepted by a majority of this Court, and, my goodness, if ever there was a decision that should be made locally, it's this one."

In several of the term's important cases, Roberts and Justice Samuel Alito declined to join Justices Antonin Scalia and Clarence Thomas in calling for the open overruling of previous precedents. Scalia even accused Roberts of "judicial obfuscation" and "faux judicial restraint" for his refusal to overturn the entire structure of campaign finance law rather than dismantling it incrementally. But Breyer, too, seemed unimpressed by conservative incrementalism: He suggested that it was better to overturn precedents cleanly than to pretend to preserve them while distorting them beyond recognition. "There were ten cases listed as important cases in the newspapers. I was in the majority twice—that was better than nothing," he said. "In three of the other cases, the majority of the Court said it was overruling prior precedents, and, in four other cases, the minority of the Court said you are overruling prior precedents. I thought there was quite a lot of precedent overruled, but the people on

the other side, who are very good judges, thought they weren't overruling. I do think it's better to be open."

Breyer noted that the number of unanimous opinions has fallen from 32 percent in 2004, Justice Sandra Day O'Connor's last year on the Court, to 22 percent this year, and the five–four decisions rose from about 25 to 33 percent. Moreover, he noted, the number of five–four decisions where what he called "the usual suspects—me and John Stevens and Ruth Ginsburg and David Souter" were joined in a bloc has risen from 55 to 80 percent. He admitted that he had looked up another statistic: "In the 2004 term, I was in the majority eighty percent of the time, and I looked at this term: It's dropped to about thirty-five percent, so I was in dissent quite a lot."

I asked Breyer why Roberts had failed in his efforts to achieve consensus and whether he might ever come closer to achieving these goals. "Will he do better in the future? He can join my dissents!" Breyer replied with a chuckle. But then Breyer said he was always hopeful that new justices will change. "This is a job that people who are appointed have for a long time. . . . It takes a while before you have enough experience with the cases in front of you, before you have a view of what this document is, and a view of the institution." That's why, he said, "[I]t's very hard to predict how a person will decide things five or ten years in the future."

Breyer's cautious hope that the Court might become less polarized in the future, combined with disappointment at the polarization of the present, seems like the right attitude. It is a far more productive model for liberals than self-pity or shock about the unsurprising fact that, now that Alito has replaced O'Connor, the Court has moved right. For example, Emily Bazelon of *Slate* has demanded that liberals and moderates who supported Roberts as a potential unifier (including me) recant. This is premature. Bush won the 2004 election, and the opportunity to replace O'Connor with Alito ensured that he would change the direction of the Court. Those of us who supported Roberts never denied his conservatism. The question was: Who among the candidates President Bush was plausibly inclined to appoint as chief justice would be most likely to avoid the radicalism of Scalia and Thomas and try to unify the Court? In his first term, which began in October 2005, Roberts entirely vindicated these hopes. He embraced bipartisan consensus as his highest goal and presided over more unanimous opinions in a row than at any point in the Court's modern history.

This term, by contrast, Roberts notably failed in his efforts to achieve consensus, although he continued to distinguish himself from Scalia and Thomas with his commitment to incrementalism. The Court's shift to the right was driven by the fact that it took up controversial issues, such as race, abortion, and campaign finance, which it had avoided while waiting for O'Connor's replacement. On all these issues, Alito and Anthony Kennedy are more conservative than O'Connor. And, most important of all, Kennedy, who is less pragmatic than O'Connor, refused to embrace Roberts's invitation to converge around narrow, unanimous opinions. Asked by Stuart Taylor Jr. and Evan Thomas of *Newsweek* what he thought of Roberts's effort after the term ended, Kennedy laughed. "I guess I haven't helped much," he said. "My initial reaction was going to be, 'Just let me write all the opinions.'" Roberts acknowledged from the beginning that he couldn't succeed without his colleagues' support, and he understood that, in the face of resistance to his vision from the median justice, even the most strenuous efforts to achieve consensus would be doomed.

It's too soon, as Breyer suggests, to tell whether Roberts will ultimately be more successful in achieving consensus. But, since he has embraced this as the standard by which his tenure should be judged, Roberts presumably understands that he can't preside over a decade of five–four decisions. Far from going down in history as a unifier in the tradition of John Marshall, he would be perceived as the leader of a partisan conservative Court, one that may be increasingly at odds with a more liberal president and Congress.

For the foreseeable future, however, the political composition of the Court won't likely change. And that has put some liberals in a despairing mood. On *The New Republic's* website, Cass R. Sunstein has lamented "the absence of anything like a heroic vision on the Court's left" to counteract "the existence of such a vision on the Court's right," embodied by Scalia and Thomas. Here I respectfully disagree. There is, in fact, a heroic vision on the Court's left, and it is squarely in the tradition of previous liberal visionaries like Oliver Wendell Holmes and Louis Brandeis. This vision, championed by TNR

since its founding in the Progressive era, is rooted in strenuous bipartisan judicial restraint. It is today defended most eloquently and systematically by Breyer and Ginsburg, who have voted to strike down fewer state and federal laws combined than any of their colleagues.

In our conversation, Breyer self-consciously embraced the mantle of restraint. "To a very large measure, judges have to be careful about intruding in the legislative process," he said. "[R]uth and I have been among the ones less likely to strike down laws passed by the legislature, and, by that measure, we're not very activist." Far from being a cautious or defensive posture, bipartisan restraint has always been rooted in liberal self-confidence—confidence that, given a fair opportunity, liberals can fight and win in the political arena. The fact that conservatives now rely on the Court to win their battles for them—striking down democratically adopted campaign finance laws and integration programs—is a sign of their weakness.

Breyer and his liberal colleagues were not unwavering in their restraint this term: They dissented from the partial-birth abortion decision, despite the fact that bans on the procedure are supported by bipartisan majorities in Congress and in most states. When I asked Breyer how he reconciled this dissent with his commitment to judicial deference, he demurred. "The only question for me was, am I suddenly going to overrule a whole lot of precedent? No. That's a strong basis." Liberals, in fact, could have reconciled their commitment to precedent and judicial restraint by upholding the partial-birth law while insisting it include a health exception. But no one is consistent in every case; and the activism of liberals here was an exception, not the rule.

Judged by their willingness to defer to legislatures, liberals are now the party of judicial restraint. Conservatives have responded to this embarrassing turnabout by trying to rob the term of any neutral meaning. In a series of unintentionally hilarious editorials, *The Wall Street Journal* praised the Roberts Court for "restoring business confidence in the rule of law and setting limits on the tort bar and activist judges." Spare us the twistifications. For more than 50 years, conservatives have insisted that judges should defer to legislatures and let citizens resolve their disputes politically. But, at the very moment they consolidated their Supreme Court majority, they have abandoned this principle and embraced the activism they once deplored. I hope that Chief Justice Roberts, over time, will achieve his welcome goal of transcending the Court's divisions and helping conservatives rediscover the virtues of modesty and deference. But, for now, the party of judicial restraint has a convincing spokesman in Justice Breyer.

The Power Broker

In an exclusive interview, Justice Kennedy discusses life, center stage.

STUART TAYLOR JR. AND EVAN THOMAS

In 19 cases during the past year, the Supreme Court split down the middle along ideological lines. The court's four conservatives—Chief Justice John Roberts Jr. and Justices Antonin Scalia, Clarence Thomas and Samuel Alito—lined up on one side, and the four liberals—Justices Stephen Breyer, John Paul Stevens, Ruth Bader Ginsburg and David Souter—lined up on the other. Each time, the tie was broken by a fifth vote belonging to Justice Anthony Kennedy. On 13 occasions, Kennedy aligned himself with the conservatives. While the court is clearly moving to the right, it's obvious that Kennedy holds the balance of power.

Kennedy is known for examining his conscience as well as the law books when he decides a difficult case. And justices caught in the middle of fierce ideological disputes sometimes agonize or brood over their opinions. But sitting with a *Newsweek* reporter in his chambers overlooking the U.S. Capitol on the day after the court's final decision of the 2006–07 term, Kennedy seemed cheerful, even enthusiastic, about his role. True, "the cases this year were more difficult than I thought they would be," he said. In closely divided cases when time is short, he added, the court's "tone becomes somewhat more acrimonious." But he laughed and held up his hands and said, "Hey, I'm a lawyer. I'm trained to argue. I love it."

He does not love being called a "swing vote." He told *Newsweek* that he and earlier denizens of the court's center—Justice Sandra Day O'Connor and the late Justice Lewis Powell— "never liked the term 'swing vote' because it indicates that you elect to swing for the purpose of accommodating one side or the other." Indeed, in the court's most important case of the year, Kennedy refused to accommodate either side. He voted with the four conservatives to strike down racial-integration plans championed by school districts in Seattle and Louisville, Ky. But he refused to go along with the conservatives in joining an opinion by Chief Justice Roberts that exuded hostility to all race-based solutions to racial inequalities. Kennedy suggested that school boards might be able to assign students based on their race as a last resort, though only if they could show that other methods proved ineffective. At the same time, Kennedy reproached the liberals on the high court for supporting racial engineering that "may entrench the very prejudices we seek to overcome."

More than a half century after the Supreme Court required school desegregation in *Brown* v. *Board of Education*, Americans remain divided over race and by race. In the latest *Newsweek* Poll, 35 percent of whites and 23 percent of nonwhites approved of the court's decision to limit the use of race for school-integration plans, while 29 percent of whites and 54 percent of nonwhites disapproved. The court's decision provoked an emotional dissent from Justice Breyer, who thundered that the ruling would "threaten the promise of Brown" by hindering progress toward "true racial equality." Some commentators attacked Kennedy's middle-way opinion for leaving school officials with no idea what they can legally do.

In his interview with *Newsweek*, Kennedy did not seem much disturbed by the hubbub. He recalled how, as a Stanford undergraduate in the mid-1950s, he was given the privilege of helping escort around campus the nation's greatest civil-rights lawyer, Thurgood Marshall, who later became a Supreme Court justice. Marshall had, a couple of years earlier, successfully argued Brown. "I thought that we had solved the race problem," Kennedy recalled. "I mean, that's how little I knew about it." But he seemed more bemused than rueful about "how naive many of us were," and he went on to talk enthusiastically about the "whole heap of fascinating, difficult problems" the court faces each year.

Kennedy's critics say he is perhaps a little too eager to play the role of Wise Man in the Middle. In a biting *New Republic* cover story last month, Jeffrey Rosen, a George Washington University Law School professor and a widely noted court watcher, portrayed Kennedy as a pretentious moralizer with a "self-aggrandizing conception of the court's role." A few of Kennedy's former clerks interviewed by *Newsweek* allow that he can be a little pompous. "He thinks he is the living embodiment or transmitter of the nation's bedrock values," says one, who refused to be identified criticizing his former boss. But this clerk—and all the others interviewed—portrayed him as gracious, decent, fair-minded and intellectually curious about many things ranging far beyond the law. "I would put him in the top rank intellectually," says Washington lawyer Richard Willard, who became the then Judge Kennedy's first clerk in 1975 and has remained close.

In a partisan age, Kennedy is almost bound to disappoint. "Liberals don't like him because he is conservative most of the time and extreme conservatives don't like him because he is not conservative all of the time," says Willard. Not just right-to-lifers but many conservatives were bitter when Kennedy, a Ronald Reagan appointee, voted in a 1992 decision, *Planned Parenthood v. Casey,* to uphold what he, O'Connor and Souter called "the essential holding of *Roe* v. *Wade,*" the Supreme Court's 1973 decision giving women a right to abortion.

Kennedy can, in fact, paint with a broad brush. "At the heart of liberty is the right to define one's own concept of existence, of meaning, of the universe and of the mystery of human life," declared an opinion signed by Justices Kennedy, Souter and O'Connor in the Casey decision. Kennedy (who, it later turned out, drafted the language) quoted the same passage in a 2003 majority opinion striking down laws against gay sodomy. In a dissent to the court's gay-rights decision, Justice Scalia mockingly referred to this language as the "famed sweet-mystery-of-life passage." Another federal judge, Robert Beezer of the U.S. Court of Appeals, wrote in 1996 that Kennedy's formulation is "so broad and melodramatic as to seem almost comical in its rhetorical flourish."

Kennedy, 70, is tall, dapper and shows no sign of slowing down. Chief Justice Roberts has tried, so far without much success, to get the justices to speak with fewer voices. He wants them to write fewer concurrences judicial opinions that, like Kennedy's in the school-desegregation case, reach the same conclusion as the majority but articulate different reasons. Asked by *Newsweek* about this effort, Kennedy laughed and interjected, "I guess I haven't helped much. My initial reaction was going to be, 'Just let me write all the opinions'."

Marking Time
Why Government Is Too Slow

BRUCE BERKOWITZ

In recent years we have been witness to a portentous competition between two determined but dissimilar rivals on the international scene. In one corner we have al-Qaeda, founded in the early 1990s, the transnational Islamic terrorist organization led by Osama bin Laden. In the other corner, we have the government of the United States of America, established in 1787, at present the most powerful state on the planet. The key question defining this competition is this: Who has the more agile organization? Al-Qaeda, in planning and executing a terrorist attack, or the United States, in planning, developing and executing the measures to stop one?

Let's look at the record. Sometime during the spring of 1999, Khalid Sheikh Mohamed visited bin Laden in Afghanistan and asked if al-Qaeda would fund what came to be called the "planes operation"—the plan for suicide attacks using commercial airliners. (Mohamed had been mulling the plot since at least 1993, when he discussed it with his nephew, Ramzi Yousef, one of the terrorists behind the first World Trade Center bombing and the attempted Philippine-based effort to bring down a dozen U.S. airliners over the Pacific in 1995.) Bin Laden agreed, and by the summer of 1999 he had selected as team leaders four al-Qaeda members—Khalid al-Mihdhar, Nawafal-Hazmi, Tawfiq bin Attash (also known as "Khallad") and Abu Bara al-Yemen.

These four team leaders entered the United States in early 2000 and started taking flying lessons that summer. The so-called "muscle" hijackers, the 15 terrorists tasked with overpowering the crews on the targeted flights, began arriving in April 2001 and spent the summer preparing for the September 11 attack. So from the point in time that a government contracting official would call "authority to proceed" to completion, the operation took approximately 27 months.

Now let's track the U.S. response. U.S. officials began debating options for preventing future terrorist attacks immediately following the September 11 strike. Congress took a year to debate the statute establishing the Department of Homeland Security. George W. Bush, who originally opposed creating a new department, changed his mind and signed the bill into law on November 25, 2002. A joint House-Senate committee finished the first investigation of intelligence leading up to

the attack in December 2002. The 9/11 Commission issued its report on July 22, 2004, recommending among other things the establishment of a Director of National Intelligence and a new National Counterterrorism Center. President Bush established the NCTC by Executive Order on August 27, 2004.

Adoption of the Intelligence Reform and Terrorism Prevention Act, which embodied most of the Commission's other proposals, took another three months. The measures it authorized—including the creation of a Director of National Intelligence—lay fallow until a second commission, investigating intelligence prior to the war in Iraq, issued its own report four months later. The new Director was sworn in on April 21, 2005. Total response time, charitably defined: about 44 months, and implementation continues today.

Obviously, planning an attack and adjusting defenses to prevent a subsequent attack are not comparable tasks. Still, it is hard to avoid concluding that organizations like al-Qaeda are inherently nimbler than governments, especially large and highly bureaucratized governments like ours. As things stand now, terrorists can size up a situation, make decisions and act faster than we can. In military terms, they are "inside our decision cycle."

Recall July 7, 2005, for example, when terrorists bombed three London Underground trains and a double-decker city bus, killing 52 commuters. The four bombs exploded within a minute of each other, an operationally and technically challenging feat that is a hallmark of al-Qaeda attacks. A "martyrdom video" proclaiming allegiance to al-Qaeda and taped months earlier by one of the bombers, Muhammad Sidique Khan, soon surfaced on al-Jazeera. Khan apparently made the video during a visit to Pakistan, and investigators concluded that an earlier trip to Pakistan in July 2003 also had something to do with the attack. If so, then the planning of the London attack required two years, possibly less.

Organizations like al-Qaeda are inherently nimbler than governments, especially large ones like ours.

Again, it may seem unfair to compare a government bureaucracy, American or British, with a network of loosely organized, small terrorist cells. But unfairness is the point: Terrorists will *always* make the conflict between us as "unfair" as possible, avoiding our strengths and exploiting our vulnerabilities however they can. So will insurgency leaders and rogue dictators, who also happen to be surreptitious WMD proliferators; narco-traffickers and money launderers, who aid terrorists either wittingly or inadvertently. The U.S. government and similarly arrayed allies will simply lose battle after battle if our adversaries absorb information, make decisions, change tactics and act faster than we can.

Reading the 9/11 Commission Report one cannot help but be struck by how often simple delay and chronic slowness led to disaster on September 11. President Clinton told the Commission that he had asked for military options to get rid of bin Laden in late 1999. But General Hugh Shelton, Chairman of the Joint Chiefs of Staff, was reluctant to provide them. Secretary of Defense William Cohen thought the President was speaking only hypothetically. The one person who could have given a direct order to cut through the resistance and ambiguity, President Clinton himself, did not do so. He thought that raising his temper wouldn't accomplish anything, so he allowed himself to be slow-rolled, and the issue went essentially unaddressed.

The problem wasn't just at the top, however. Down below in the bureaucracy, things were just as bad—case in point, the Predator. The now-famous robotic aircraft was originally built for battlefield reconnaissance and was later modified to carry missiles. The U.S. Air Force had flown Predators in the Balkans since 1996, but Afghanistan was trickier. The aircraft had a limited range and thus needed a remote base and data uplinks to get the information back to Washington. It took until July 2000 to work our these details, and two more months to deploy the Predator over Afghanistan.

Predator operators thought they spotted bin Laden in September 2000, but U.S. officials disagreed over rules of engagement. National Security Advisor Samuel Berger wanted greater confidence in bin Laden's location before approving a strike, and he worried about civilian casualties. At the same time, Air Force leaders were reluctant to carry out what looked to them, not unreasonably, like a covert operation, and the CIA was reluctant to undertake a direct combat operation—or to violate the Executive Order prohibiting assassination.

These disagreements dragged into 2001 as the Bush Administration took office. Then President Bush put everything on hold while National Security Advisor Condoleezza Rice directed a comprehensive plan to eliminate al-Qaeda. George Tenet, the Director of Central Intelligence, deferred the legal over whether the CIA could take part in an attack until the Administration had prepared its new strategy. So it went, until the clock ran out and the terrorists killed nearly 3,000 people.

Or take the inability of the Immigration and Naturalization Service (INS), as it existed on September 11, 2001, to track the whereabouts of known terror suspects and to report relevant information about their attempts to enter the country to other Federal agencies. The INS failed to meet its homeland security responsibilities partly because Congress systematically underfunded it. But even worse, the INS had failed to disentangle its different functions; keeping some people out of the country while letting others in. Meanwhile, everyone—the White House, Congress, the bureaucracy—failed to agree on a solution that both dealt with illegal immigration while also allowing entry to laborers essential to the American economy. The security problem flowing from this failure is obvious: As long as underfunded bureaucrats are unable to regulate the enormous flow of illegal immigrants seeking work, they will never be able to detect and track the few truly dangerous people trying to enter the country.

Of course, the story of the run-up to 9/11 is an oft-told one. Yet almost everyone seems to miss the core problem from which all others followed: There was always time for another meeting, another study, another round of coordination. Virtually no one was worrying about the clock—about whether *time itself mattered.* It's not that every concern raised didn't have some legitimate rationale (at least within the legal-bureaucratic culture that characterizes the U.S. government). It's the fact that, while we were working out legal issues, al-Qaeda was developing and executing its plan.

This same problem surfaced again a year later. Just about everyone agrees now that the United States was unprepared for the insurgency in Iraq, but most overlook that someone else was also unprepared: the insurgents. U.S. analysts who interviewed captured Iraqi officials and military officers for the Defense Department have concluded that Iraqi leaders had not prepared a "stay-behind" or "rope-a-dope" strategy. They had never planned to forfeit the conventional war in order to win a guerrilla war later on. Iraqi military leaders believed they would lose the war and just wanted to get it over with quickly. Saddam Hussein's security services and core Ba'ath Party operatives kept the lid on the various sects, tribes and ethnic groups so that they could not plan a guerrilla war either. The result was that *no one* was prepared for an insurgency. The United States, its coalition partners, Ba'athis who had escaped capture, tribal leaders, religious authorities, foreign fighters—everyone was starting from scratch. So when Saddam's statue came down in Firdos Square on April 9, 2003, the question that mattered most was who could organize and execute faster, the would-be insurgents or the U.S. government?

Alas, we were left in the starting blocks. The insurgents organized much faster than U.S. officials could recognize and respond. We were playing catch-up from the beginning, which is another way of saying we were losing.

Things would perhaps not be so bad if the war on al-Qaeda and the war in Iraq were exceptional. In truth, the problem is pervasive and getting worse. "Organizational agility" sounds abstract, but it really boils down to specific questions: How long does it take to deliver a critical weapon or information system? How fast can an agency bring new people on board? How fast can it change its mix of people if it needs to? In short, *how fast can government agencies act—and is this fast enough to stay ahead of the competition?*

The U.S. government is not always woefully slow. The response to the December 2004 Southeast Asian tsunami, for example, was admirably quick and reasonably effective under the circumstances. So was the relief mission that the United States effectively led following the massive earthquake that rocked northern Pakistan in October 2005. However, these few exceptions aside, the U.S. government has become an increasingly ponderous beast, unable to act quickly or even to understand how its various parts fit together to act at all.

Once, When We Were Fast

It was not always so. After the surprise attack at Pearl Harbor, one of the most heavily damaged ships was the battleship USS *West Virginia.* Most of its port side had been blown away. The ship sank rapidly, but on an even keel on the bottom of the harbor. The Navy needed every 16-inch gun it could muster, so Navy leaders decided to repair the ship. It was not easy, but the USS *West Virginia* steamed into Puget Sound in April 1943 to be refitted and modernized. It rejoined the fleet in June 1944, thirty months after it was sunk, took part in several operations and was present for the surrender ceremonies in Tokyo Bay in September 1945. By comparison, after al-Qaeda agents in Yemen damaged the USS *Cole* far less severely with a single improvised bomb in October 2000, it took 16 months to retrieve the still-floating destroyer and complete repairs in Pascagoula, Mississippi. The ship did not then leave its home port in Norfolk, Virginia, for its first deployment until November 2003—37 months later.

World War II offers many examples like the recovery of the *West Virginia* in which organizations worked with remarkable alacrity. Take the effort to build the first atomic bomb. Albert Einstein wrote to Franklin D. Roosevelt on August 2, 1939, alerting him to the possibilities of nuclear weapons. He met with FDR about a month later, which led Roosevelt to establish the Uranium Committee to research military applications of nuclear fission. Vannevar Bush, Roosevelt's science adviser, persuaded the President to accelerate the project in October 1941, as war with Germany and Japan seemed likely. On September 14, 1942, Brigadier General Leslie Groves was appointed director of the new Manhattan Project, marking the formal start of the project to build the atomic bomb. The Trinity test, the world's first nuclear explosion, took place on July 16, 1945, and Hiroshima was bombed on August 6, less than a month later. The entire effort, costing $21 billion in today's dollars, developed three different means of producing fissile material, two bomb designs and three devices.

Or consider the Office of Strategic Services, the predecessor of today's CIA. President Roosevelt appointed William Donovan as his "Coordinator of Information" in July 1941, and the OSS was itself established in June 1942. Harry Truman disbanded it in September 1945. In other words, the entire history of the OSS—what many consider the Golden Age of American intelligence—spanned just 37 months. In that short time it recruited, trained and deployed a workforce of about 13,000 people. William Casey, directing OSS espionage in Europe, stood up his entire network in about 18 months. By comparison, after 9/11 Tenet said on

several occasions that it would require five years to rebuild the CIA's clandestine service.

Or recall the war in the Pacific. The Battle of the Coral Sea was fought in May 1942, the Battle of Midway a month later. Within six months of Pearl Harbor, the U.S. Navy had destroyed five Japanese carriers, along with most of Japan's naval aircraft and aviators. It has taken us longer just to get organized for the so-called War on Terror (to the extent that we *are* organized for it) than it did to fight and win World War II.

Delivering the Product

Everything else today is moving faster, thanks to jet airliners, interstate highways, the computer and the Internet. But government, including the parts responsible for national security, is moving slower, and it's getting worse.

Everyone knows, for example, that weapons have been getting more expensive per unit, but few realize that it now also takes much longer to get a weapon into the hands of the warfighter. In the early 1940s, it took 25 months to get a new fighter like the P-47 Thunderbolt into action from the time the government signed a contract for a prototype. In the late 1940s, this delay had grown to about 43 months for an early jet fighter like the F-86 Sabre. By the 1960s, the F-4 Phantom required 66 months, and its 1970s replacement, the F-15 Eagle, 82 months. The latest fighter to enter service, the F-22 Raptor, traces its development to a prototype built under a contract signed in October 1986. The prototype first flew in September 1990, and the production model entered service in December 2005—a total of 230 months, or about 19 years. Put another way, that comes to slightly longer than the typical career of an officer in the U.S. Air Force. (The new F-35 Lighting II, which will replace the F-16, is slated to require "just" 15 years from signing the contract for the prototype to when it enters service. We'll see.)

One might think the problem with jet aircraft is a result of the growing technical complexity of modern fighter aircraft, but that argument does not hold up. No rule says that the more complex a technology is, the longer it takes to deliver. Government aircraft of *all* kinds take longer to develop, and longer than their commercial counterparts. Compare a military transport, like the C-17 Globemaster III with the new Boeing 787 Dreamliner. The C-17 required 12 years to enter service, while the 787—more complex than the C-17 in many respects—will take just four. And the 787, for example, will require a little *less* time to develop than its predecessor from the early 1990s, the 777.[1]

The problem holds for most weapons other than airplanes, too—ships, tanks, electronic systems and so on. Threats are changing much faster than we can develop the means to counter them. This is why some officials occasionally say we have to anticipate requirements further into the future. But that's simply unrealistic. When you try to forecast two decades ahead because your weapon takes twenty years to develop, it isn't analysis: it's fortune telling.

The ever-slowing pace of government appears in other ways, as well. Simply getting a presidential administration into place is a stellar example. According a 2005 National Academy of Sciences study, every Administration since Kennedy's has taken longer than its predecessor to fill the top 500 jobs in government. In the 1960s it took just under three months; today it is three times as long. A new administration isn't up and running until almost a year after the election that put it in office. How can a team possibly win the Big Game if half the players don't show up until the end of the first quarter?

That is more or less what happened in 2001 as al-Qaeda was preparing 9/11. The Bush Administration's Cabinet Secretaries were confirmed and ready to go when the new President was sworn in on January 20, 2001, but that was about it. The Administration didn't nominate Paul Wolfowitz to be Deputy Secretary of Defense until February 5, and he had to wait until March 2 to be confirmed and sworn in. Wolfowitz's wait was comparatively short; most positions took longer to fill. Richard Armitage, nominated for Deputy Secretary of State, waited until March 23, 2001. Six months passed before the top Defense Department leadership was in place. Douglas Feith, the Under Secretary of Defense for Policy—as in "policy for combating terrorists"—was *last* to be sworn in, in July 2001.

What is so depressing about the National Academy of Science study is that the problem just keeps getting worse. If top officials have to wait two or three months at the beginning of an administration, candidates for positions at the assistant secretary level in the middle of a term can often wait six months or more. Further down the food chain, bringing on new staff is paced largely by how long it takes to obtain a security clearance. For civil servants, this can take almost a year, for government contractors, the average is about 450 days.

Why?

What explains this bureaucratic torpor? In part, government is slowing down because more people insist on getting involved. Ever more congressional committees, lobbyists and oversight organizations vie to get their prerogatives enacted in a law, regulation or procedure. As the participants multiply, workloads expand and everything slows down.

At another level, it's because there is more obligatory paperwork to handle—financial disclosure in the case of officials, cost justification in the case of contracts, quality assurance documentation in the case of hardware. At yet another level, it's because all organizations have standard procedures that never seem to get shorter or more flexible; quite the reverse. New procedures are almost always cumulative, accreting in ever thicker layers of bureaucratic hoariness. Indeed, we may be seeing a classic case of "organizational aging," a phenomenon perhaps first defined by economist Anthony Downs back in 1967.

In his classic book, *Inside Bureaucracy,* Downs observed that when organizations are first established, they have few rules, written or unwritten, and because new organizations tend to be small, they have a flat, short chain of command with little hierarchy. As time goes by, alas, organizations add personnel. Since managers can oversee only a limited number of people, they develop a reporting hierarchy, which adds to the time and difficulty of making a decision. More members are in a position to say "no," and the joint probability of "yes" diminishes. This translates into the well-known bureaucratic adage, "Where

there's a will, there's a won't." The fact that people expect promotion to positions with greater responsibility (and pay) also encourages the establishment of more management slots with the selective power to say "no," or just to kibbitz. Either way, the process takes more time.

Also, as organizations mature, they develop dogma—sometimes written, sometimes simply part of the organization's culture. This, of course, is exactly what bureaucracies are supposed to do: simplify decisions and improve efficiency by adopting rules. This is fine, until the rules become cumbersome or no longer appropriate to the situation—which is exactly what is happening today.

But the most insidious problem of all is that as organizations mature their character changes. New organizations with few rules offer lots of challenge and risk, so they tend to attract risk-takers who want to make their own rules. Mature organizations with well-defined rules and missions, on the other hand, attract the "Organization Man"—the sort who wants to plug himself in and carry out tasks as set forth in an official, approved job description.

This is why it is somewhere between ironic and pointless to hear critics complain that this or that long-established government organization needs to become less risk-averse and more innovative. Inevitably, they are speaking to people who, by self-selection, are where they are *precisely because they are risk-averse.* They *like* the way things are; they would not otherwise have joined the organization and stayed with it. Organization Men are no less patriotic, dedicated or capable than risk-takers; they're just temperamentally opposite.

If we are serious about gaining agility, we will clearly have to break some china. Improving agility means more than just rearranging boxes on an organization chart, though that is mostly what we have tried to do. There have been countless studies on how to streamline contracting, speed up background investigations, shorten the process of nominating and confirming appointees, and so on. None of these recommendations will ever amount to anything unless we find a way to produce a new mix of people who can develop new ways of doing things, and attract the kinds of recruits who thrive on doing just that.

It's easy to get lost in the day-to-day specifics of why it takes so long to get anything done in the American national security community today. It is far more important to recognize that the underlying theme connecting all the sources of our sloth is that we are trying to balance risk with speed, and there is rarely a champion for speed. The risks that concern people take many forms—that some group will be underrepresented in a decision, that a design or work task will be flawed, that a secret will be compromised, that someone will cheat the government, that an official will have a conflict of interest. Whatever the specifics, we lose agility every time we manage risk by adding a step to reduce the probability of something bad happening. Rarely does anyone with responsibility, opportunity or power say that we should accept more risks so that we can act faster.

It is easy to argue for doing something to avoid some hypothetical bad thing happening. It is much harder to argue that one can take so many precautions against some kinds of risk that other kinds of risk actually increase due to an organization's diminished capacity to act in a timely fashion. The real question is, or ought to be, how much speed do we want to sacrifice in order to reduce certain kinds of risk? There is no single, objective answer to such a question, but without advocates and mechanisms for greater speed, we will be protected against risk so well that arguably our most dangerous adversaries will beat us every time.

Examples of Speed and Success

Lest we be *too* pessimistic, there are cases—including a few fairly recent ones—in which government organizations moved out smartly on national security missions. These cases show us what we need to do if we want organizations to move fast. Consider, for example:

- *The U-2 aircraft:* In the 1950s, the United States needed a higher-flying airplane to take pictures of Soviet military facilities. The CIA gave Lockheed authority to proceed in December 1954; the aircraft flew its first reconnaissance mission over the Soviet Union in July 1956. Total time required: 18 months.
- *The Explorer 1 satellite:* Desperate to match the Soviet Sputnik I launched in October 1957, the Defense Department authorized the Army Ballistic Missile Agency to prepare a satellite for launch on November 8, 1957. Werner von Braun's team launched it three months later, on January 31, 1958.
- *The GBU-28:* At the start of Operation Desert Storm in 1991, the Air Force discovered it did not have a bomb that could penetrate Iraq's deepest underground shelters. To pack enough kinetic energy, the bomb had to be long, streamlined and heavy. The Air Force Research Laboratory took surplus gun barrels from eight-inch howitzers as a casing, filled them with explosive, bolted an existing laser guidance system to the front end, and—after assigning it an official Air Force designation—delivered a bomb in 27 days.
- *JAWBREAKER:* President Bush asked for options to respond to the September 11 attacks. The CIA presented its plan two days later to use Northern Alliance forces as a surrogate army. CIA units, called "JAWBREAKER," arrived in weeks, and Kabul was taken on November 14, 2001.

These programs are all related to national security, but they are as different from one another as one can imagine. One is an aircraft development program, one a space research mission, one a weapon system and one a covert paramilitary operation. The Army, Air Force and CIA are all represented. Two were in wartime, two in peacetime. Yet they share some common features, the most important of which seems to be that someone was willing to bend rules and take responsibility for getting things done. This is a logical—even a *necessary*—condition for speed.

Every organization has a "natural" maximum speed defined by its standard procedures, which are designed to reduce risk. Some are formal, others implicit. Together they establish the organization's operations—who has to confer with whom, who

can approve, what materials have to be prepared and so on. Organizations usually operate well below this optimum speed, but in principle one could analyze any organization and then assess whether it can act faster than its competitors. It is hard to measure maximum speed precisely, but it is easy to identify most of the "hard points" that constitute it, like the one official or office lying in the critical path of workflow. Conversely, when government organizations have moved faster than their normal maximum speeds, it's almost always because someone either bent the rules or managed to evade them. Consider the cases cited above.

In developing the U-2, the CIA avoided the constraining pace of the annual Federal budget cycle by using its special authority to spend money without a specific appropriation—the first time the CIA had used that authority to develop a major system like an aircraft. The CIA also wasn't bound to Defense Department regulations, so rather than use the arduous military acquisition and contractor selection process, the CIA simply chose Lockheed.

Lockheed's famous "Skunk Works," in turn, shortened or eliminated many steps a military contractor would usually take. For example, by having all its people working in one location, an engineer could ask metal workers to adjust the design on the spot with a conversation rather than a meeting, and follow up with documentation later. This would violate normal Defense Department acquisition regulations.

The Army also broke rules in building the Explorer 1 satellite—specifically, the rule saying that the Army wasn't supposed to build satellites. The Defense Department and White House had given the Navy that mission. Major General John Medaris, the Army Ballistic Missile Agency director, "went out on a limb," as he put it, and set aside hardware that later gave the Army the ability to get off a quick shot after the Soviets launched Sputnik.

The U-2 and Explorer 1 also had something in common: They "stole" a lot of technology from other programs, using them in ways that no one had originally intended but that sped up the process. The U-2's design was in many ways just like that of the F-104 Starfighter that Lockheed had designed earlier for the Air Force, but with longer wings and a lot of weight cut out. The rocket that launched Explorer 1 was based on an Army Redstone ballistic missile, which, in turn, was an updated V-2 that the Army's German engineers had developed during World War II.

In the case of the GBU-28, the Air Force Development Test Center team compressed a development program that would ordinarily have taken two years into less than two weeks by taking engineering shortcuts and a more liberal approach to safety. For example, it tested the aerodynamics and ballistics of the weapon with a single drop, rather than the usual thirty.

Note that it required an individual with the *authority* and *inclination* to make the decision on how to interpret a contract or a standard. If a person could not legally give approval, the organization would not have followed his direction. If a person had not been willing to use his authority (and, in the process, accept responsibility), nothing would have happened, either—which brings us to JAWBREAKER.

CIA officers like Gary Schroen, who first went into Afghanistan to prepare the operation immediately after 9/11, had largely acted on their own initiative in the 1990s when they kept up personal contacts with Northern Alliance figures like Ahmed Shah Masoud. After the Soviets were defeated in the U.S. supported guerrilla war from 1980 to 1989, the CIA had turned its interest elsewhere. Schroen's contacts and experience in the region greased the re-establishment of the relationship when the United States decided to retaliate against al-Qaeda and the Taliban.

After the fighting started, the CIA was fortunate to have officers on hand with admitted inclinations for focusing more on results than procedures. Gary Berntsen, who took command of JAWBREAKER as the fighting began, once described himself as a "bad kid" from Long Island who graduated second from the bottom in his high school. Once in the CIA, he bragged about his "grab-'em-by-the-collar" approach.

As Admiral Ernest King supposedly said about wartime, "When they get in trouble, they send for the sons of bitches." If you don't have SOBs on staff and a way to get them to the front line, organizations will plod along at their routine pace. True, if everyone broke the rules all the time, there would be no rules. But one of the keys to a fast organization that can beat its opponent to the punch is almost always a willingness to break the rules. This is nothing new. It was said often in the 19th century that Paris sent officials into the French countryside not to enforce rules, but to decide judiciously when and how to ignore them.

How To Get Faster

If we want more speed and agility, some lessons are clear. We must: Make sure U.S. national security organizations have a legal mechanism for bending or breaking existing rules; make sure they have the means for having such rule-benders at hand; make sure these rule-benders exercise influence; and make sure they don't get out of control. (Even unofficially designated rule-benders need *some* clear lines of accountability.)

We need to allow responsible senior officials to put the government in overdrive when it's really important.

Basically, we need to allow responsible senior officials to put the government into overdrive when it's really important. With the possible exception of the operating forces of the military and their counterparts in the intelligence community, even top officials lack this ability today. This encourages other kinds of risks: workarounds. Cabinet secretaries who need to get decisions fast and begin operations expeditiously know that they cannot entrust such matters to the standing bureaucracy. But workarounds and shortcuts spite the institutional memory of an organization and court disaster from ignorance. Iran-Contra is

a good example of a workaround gone wrong. The only way to avoid such dangers is to make the responsible bureaucracies faster only when they really need to be fast.

There is always a tension between orthodoxy and innovation, and between direct command and checks and balances. There is no sure-fire way to ensure the best mix. But we don't seem to be close now, or even trying to get closer. Ultimately, our willingness to balance different sorts of risk must be a political decision, in which voters can turn incumbents out and try something else if they are dissatisfied. But if we don't at least have the foundation for rule-bending, they will never get that choice.

What then, should we do? First, to build agility into the key parts of the U.S. government, Congress will clearly have to cooperate. That's the system; that's the Constitution. It is therefore folly for any administration to try to steamroll the legislators—as the then-popular Bush Administration did from about 2002 to 2004, such as when it shunted aside congressional concerns that the Iraq insurgency was gaining steam rather than entering its "last throes," or that U.S. forces did not have the resources to deal with the worsening situation. Accepting these concerns and criticisms quickly would have both improved the situation and solidified support for the effort by getting Congress' "buy in" on the record.

Second, we should consider establishing a small number of powerful "bottleneck breakers" in the Executive Office of the President. Senior experienced officials could be designated by the White House, formally or informally. The important thing is that officials down the line know that these bottleneck breakers are acting at the behest of the president to make sure his policies are carried out. Unlike the too-familiar "czars" that have been given responsibility for drug enforcement, energy conservation and, most recently, the war in Iraq, these officials would know how, and be given the authority, to work quickly and quietly with the Office of Management and Budget. It would take only a few examples of a sequestered budget line, a dismissed appointee or a transferred senior executive to give these bottleneck-breaker envoys the implicit power they require. The very existence of such EOP envoys, and the only occasional demonstration of their authority, would work wonders with hidebound, risk-averse bureaucrats.

Other measures that would counter the natural tendency of bureaucracies to slow down come readily to mind:

- Requiring senior civil service executives to periodically do a tour in a different Executive Branch department. This would make them more familiar with conditions in other departments, so they could anticipate what might slow down an action. It would also build social networks that could help clear these impediments.
- Create an "up or out" system of promotion for senior executives resembling the approach used in the military to create a dynamic that keeps the bureaucracy from getting too settled.

- Adopt a mandatory, congressionally approved, periodic de-layering of bureaucracies.
- Increase the number of Schedule C appointments to give new administrations a better ability to rattle cages. We need not repeal the Pendleton Act completely, but the trend in most sectors of the economy is toward "at will" employment. As an employee rises higher in the organization, it should be easier to move or remove him or her.

One could think of other measures in the same vein, and some have. The point, however, is that if we do not do *something* to increase the speed of government, we will be sure to fall behind future events, get beaten to the punch, and lose ground to our most ruthless competitors. Given the stakes in today's world, that is a loss we cannot afford.

Note

1. Also consider today's automobiles, which are much more complex than earlier models. Like jet fighters, cars today go faster and handle better. They can also locate their current position and tell you how to reach your destination—all while meeting ever-tougher safety and emissions standards. Yet the time required to develop a car and get it into the showroom *is getting shorter all the time.* Toyota is best at about two years, and it is trying to cut this time to 12 months. Ford and GM are trying to keep up, but still take one to two years longer than Toyota—one reason they have been taking a beating in the market.

BRUCE BERKOWITZ is a research fellow at the Heaver Institution at Stanford University. He was Director of Forecasting and Evaluation at the Department of Defense from 2004–05.

From *The American Interest,* September/October 2007, pp. 59–70. Copyright © 2007 by American Interest. Reprinted by permission.

Worse than You Think

What went wrong at Fannie and Freddie—and what still might.

PETER J. WALLISON AND EDWARD PINTO

The government's takeover of Fannie Mae and Freddie Mac in the middle of a presidential race—coupled with the fact that their activities contributed significantly to the current financial crisis—has brought these "government-sponsored enterprises" (GSEs) into unusual prominence. One of the principal elements of the story is its similarity to the savings-and-loan (S&L) collapse of only 20 years ago, and the failure of Congress to understand and apply the lessons of that debacle.

Fannie began life as a government agency, commissioned to add liquidity to the housing-finance system. To perform this function, it borrowed funds in the capital markets and used them to buy mortgages from lenders. For many years it toiled quietly in this routine business.

In 1968, as a budgetary measure, the Johnson administration privatized Fannie by allowing it to sell shares to the public. But the shareholder-owned company retained many of its ties to government, and was given a congressional charter. So despite its private ownership, investors and other creditors continued to believe the government backed it—that taxpayers would come to the rescue if things went wrong.

By the late 1980s, the U.S. financial world was in turmoil. Fed chairman Paul Volcker's effort to curb inflation had resulted in high market interest rates, which in turn had devastated the S&L industry. Unlike commercial banks, S&Ls had a narrow range of permissible activities, focused primarily on housing. Their assets—principally home mortgages—were not diverse enough to keep them alive when the housing market went into one of its frequent tailspins. In a high-interest-rate environment, S&Ls had to pay more to attract and hold deposits than they were receiving in revenue from mortgages. The mismatch—high short-term liabilities, low-yielding long-term assets—was driving the industry toward insolvency.

Deposits in S&Ls, like those in commercial banks, were federally insured, and this enabled them to raise funds despite their weak financial condition. Congress broadened their investment powers, allowing the industry to invest in new and risky ventures as it "gambled for resurrection." This gamble did not pay off, and the losses continued to mount.

In 1989, the first Bush administration recognized that it had to intervene. New legislation established the Resolution Trust Corporation to acquire and sell the assets of failed S&Ls, a process that eventually cost the taxpayers $150 billion. The same legislation also "privatized" Freddie Mac—then a subsidiary agency of the Federal Home Loan Bank Board—under a charter virtually identical to Fannie's.

The prospect of huge losses for taxpayers engendered a bitter debate about causes and blame. On one side were those who argued that greed, fraud, and incompetence among S&L owners and managers were responsible. On the other were those who blamed the government for allowing an industry that was inherently vulnerable to take enormous risks with insured deposits. Both sides were partially right, but only the former explanation seemed to sink in with a Congress eager to deny its culpability.

The Super-S&L

By 1991, James A. Johnson, a politically connected former top aide to Walter Mondale, had become Fannie's chairman and CEO. He stepped into this barren landscape with an idea that would have been rejected out of hand if Congress had correctly diagnosed the S&L problem. Johnson's view was that Fannie could prosper as a super-S&L by using its low-cost, government-backed funds to buy and hold a portfolio of high-yielding mortgages. Fannie and Freddie's activities, as in the case of the S&Ls, were restricted to housing. This business model was different from the S&Ls' in but one important way: This new S&L wouldn't have to limit itself to $100,000 deposits to get government insurance; *all* of Fannie's debt had the implicit backing of the taxpayers.

Fortunately, some in Congress saw that allowing a privately owned company to borrow money with government backing required at least some form of regulation, and in 1991 Congress finally got around to considering revisions to the GSEs' charters and the creation of a regulatory agency to oversee their activities.

At about this time, Fannie, under Johnson's control, committed to loan $10 billion over two years to promote affordable housing. This initiative helped Fannie resist effective regulation in several ways. First, it showed that Fannie would share some of its gains with taxpayers—and thereby created goodwill with lawmakers. Second, members of Congress saw that they could use affordable-housing lending much the way they use earmarks: They could select projects in their states and districts, and politely request that Fannie loan money to them. Unlike the countless banks scattered across the country, Fannie was conveniently centralized in D.C., and talks with it did not require (or receive) much public scrutiny.

In the end, Johnson got a good deal: The regulatory structure that Congress adopted—which, in passing, added an affordable-housing "mission" to Fannie's charter—was seriously deficient. Not two years after the demise of the S&Ls had shown beyond question that government backing (in the form of FDIC insurance) without adequate risk controls was a prescription for disaster and taxpayer loss, Congress repeated its mistake.

The new regulator—the Office of Federal Housing Enterprise Oversight (OFHEO)—had none of the strong authorities routinely given to bank regulators; it was also subject to congressional appropriations, which made it possible for the GSEs to control their own regulator through their congressional supporters. This was an aberration from other congressional activity: The year before, the same Congress had adopted the Federal Deposit Insurance Corporation Improvement Act, which significantly toughened the regulation of banks and gave their regulators more independence.

Jim Johnson lost no time in using the affordable-housing initiatives to cement congressional support into place. The principal element of this bargain was that Congress would allow the GSEs to retain federal backing, and the absence of a strong regulator would permit Fannie and Freddie to grow without serious restriction. The lack of regulation would also make it possible for the GSEs to meet the demands of Congress on the allocation of affordable-housing funds.

In 1994, Johnson announced another affordable-housing initiative, this time with a goal of $1 trillion in loans—intended to enable 10 million families to buy homes by the end of 2000. At the same time, he created local partnership offices (eventually totaling 51) in urban areas across the country. These offices were overtly political, and performed a grassroots lobbying function, assuring congressional backers of Fannie and Freddie that they could tap into supportive local groups when it came time for reelection—or to beat back initiatives that might clip the GSEs' wings.

In 2000, after succeeding Jim Johnson as chairman and CEO of Fannie Mae, Franklin Raines, head of the Office of Management and Budget in the Clinton administration, announced Fannie's "American Dream Commitment," a ten-year, $2 trillion pledge to support affordable housing. It made another huge, taxpayer-backed program available for manipulation and political patronage.

In 2003 and 2004, when Fannie and Freddie were found to have been practicing Enron-style accounting, their friends in Congress rushed to their defense, citing affordable housing. At a House Financial Services Committee meeting in September 2003, Massachusetts Democrat Barney Frank—then ranking minority member and now chairman—observed: "I do think I do not want the same kind of focus on safety and soundness. . . . I want to roll the dice a little bit more in this situation towards subsidized housing." Charles Schumer of New York, then a powerful member of the Senate Banking Committee, stated the next month: "My worry is that we're using the recent safety and soundness concerns, particularly with Freddie, and with a poor regulator, as a straw man to curtail Fannie and Freddie's [affordable-housing] mission."

An Attempt to Regulate

By the end of 2004, things had gotten a great deal bleaker for the GSEs. Their accounting frauds had prompted bad publicity and some serious challenges from within the government. The Bush administration sought the stronger, bank-like regulatory regime that Congress had failed to adopt in the early '90s. Alan Greenspan—then at the height of his authority as Federal Reserve chairman—called for controls on the growth of the GSEs' hugely profitable mortgage portfolios. Fed economists had determined that the GSEs did not, as they'd claimed for years, reduce interest rates for middle-class homebuyers. Franklin Raines had resigned under fire for his participation in Fannie's false accounting. Republicans had introduced stronger regulatory legislation in both the House and the Senate. Drastic steps were needed to rebuild the bond with Congress and prevent the adoption of tough new regulations.

The GSEs made it clear that such regulations would make it harder to get affordable-housing pork to Congress's constituents. A strong regulator could make the GSEs' portfolios less profitable—and without these profits, it would not be possible for Fannie and Freddie to continue to subsidize affordable housing. Worse, a strong regulator might scrutinize their affordable-housing investments, including ones members of Congress had requested.

Beginning in 2005, Fannie and Freddie put more than $1 trillion in junk loans on their books. The unprecedented rate of defaults on this $1 trillion is what precipitated the takeover of Fannie and Freddie by the federal government in September, and will burden taxpayers with tremendous costs. But it worked politically. The GSEs' supporters (and beneficiaries) in Congress held off on any new regulation. The Senate Banking Committee adopted a strong regulatory bill in 2005—with the unanimous support of committee Republicans and over the unanimous opposition of committee Democrats—but it could not be brought to a vote on the Senate floor. Not a single Democrat, including Barack Obama, supported it. The benefits that Fannie and Freddie offered to Congress continued to flow. In 2006, Chuck Schumer's office issued a press release headlined "Schumer Announces up to $100 Million Freddie Mac Commitment to Address Fort Drum and Watertown Housing Crunch." The release boasted that the senator had "urged" the company to "step up" and make this commitment.

Congress thus repeated with Fannie and Freddie the error that had produced the collapse of the S&L industry in the late 1980s. It gave government backing to inadequately supervised private companies. But the case of Fannie Mae and Freddie Mac is far worse than the S&L debacle. First, taxpayers' losses this time will be enormously larger. Second, in the case of the S&Ls, the missteps of Congress can be understood and to some extent excused: It had never encountered anything quite like the S&L collapse, and the banking failures of the Depression were 50 years in the past. Third, while individual lawmakers received favors from the S&L industry, these were the petty graft that tends to go along with political power—not to be condoned, of course, but nothing new. But Congress's failure to create a strong regulatory regime for Fannie Mae and Freddie Mac *was* something new. Coming as it did on the heels of the passage of tough new banking regulation, it had to be a conscious choice by the GSEs' supporters in Congress—most of them liberal Democrats—to continue using the GSEs' financial resources for political purposes.

Perhaps worst of all, the takeover of Fannie and Freddie by a government conservator does not end the problem. In fact, it might open a new and more costly era. In a statement to the House Financial Services Committee on September 25, James B. Lockhart III, director of the agency that serves as both regulator and conservator of Fannie and Freddie, insisted on meeting the affordable-housing goals required by HUD regulations: "The market turmoil of this year resulted in a tightening of underwriting criteria . . . thereby reducing the availability of traditionally goal-rich, high loan-to-value home-purchase loans. . . . I will expect each enterprise to develop and implement ambitious plans to support the borrowers and markets targeted by the goals."

If this is what a Republican administration says about the use to which Fannie and Freddie will be put in conservatorship, one can only imagine what a Democratic administration might do.

MR. PETER J. WALLISON holds the Arthur F. Burns chair at the American Enterprise Institute. **MR. EDWARD PINTO** held various positions at Fannie Mae from 1984 to 1989, and now provides consulting services to the mortgage-finance industry.

From *The National Review,* November 3, 2008, pp. 36–38. Copyright © 2008 by National Review, Inc, 215 Lexington Avenue, New York, NY 10016. Reprinted by permission.

UNIT 3

Process of American Politics

Unit Selections

Key Points to Consider

- In comparison with other political systems, how "democratic" is the American political system?

- How do the political views and behavior of young Americans compare and contrast with those of their parents?

- Do you think that our current procedures for choosing the president are good ones? In light of the Florida controversy in the 2000 presidential election, do you think that electoral reforms are necessary? What do you think about the big influence that people in Iowa and New Hampshire have in the presidential nomination process? Explain your answers.

- Do you think that interest groups have too much influence in the American political system? Why or why not?

- What do you think about the way elections are financed in the American political system? Do you think that there ought to be limits on how much a presidential candidate can spend to try to get elected? Do you think that the government should provide money ("public financing") to candidates or that they should have to raise money on their own?

- What do you think about candidate Barack Obama pledging in the summer of 2007 to accept public financing for the general election if he were his party's nominee, and then changing his mind in the summer of 2008 and becoming the first presidential candidate to decline public financing (and the accompanying spending limits) because he realized that he could raise a great deal more money from supporters? (As it turned out, Obama spent more than three times as much in the general election campaign as his opponent, John McCain, who accepted public financing.)

Student Web Site

www.mhcls.com

Internet References

The Gallup Organization
http://www.gallup.com

The Henry L. Stimson Center
http://www.stimson.org

Influence at Work
http://www.influenceatwork.com

LSU Department of Political Science Resources
http://www.lsu.edu/politicalscience

NationalJournal.com
http://nationaljournal.com

Poynter Online
http://www.poynter.org

RAND
http://www.rand.org

Real Clear Politics
http://www.realclearpolitics.com

According to many political scientists, what distinguishes more democratic political systems from less democratic ones is the degree of control that citizens exercise over government. This unit focuses on the institutions, groups, and processes that are supposed to serve as links between Americans and their government.

The first three sections address parties, elections, voters, interest groups, and the role of money in campaigns and governing. Recent changes in these areas will likely affect American politics for decades to come, and these changes are the focus of many of the readings in these sections.

One noteworthy development in the past few decades has been growing polarization between the two major parties. Republicans and Democrats in Congress have both become more likely to toe their party's line in opposition to the other party, with partisan voting increasingly becoming the norm on Capitol Hill. Some decry this increase in partisanship, while others think that sharper and more consistent policy differences between Democrat and Republican officeholders will make elections more meaningful.

The advantages of incumbents in winning re-election in both the House of Representatives and the Senate have also grown in recent years, so much so that, despite Americans' dissatisfaction with President Bush and his Republican supporters in Congress, most observers emphasized how difficult it would be for Democrats to regain majority control of the House and Senate in the 2006 congressional elections. But, as almost everyone knows by now, Democrats *did* win control of both houses, illustrating what many consider a good example of American democracy at work. Despite the 2006 results, however, incumbency advantages—including the way House districts are drawn, name recognition, and easier access to campaign contributions—are likely to remain a concern for those who would like to reform the democratic process in the United States.

Over and above the way House district lines are drawn, American elections suffer from all sorts of difficulties. Many of these problems became apparent during the controversy over the outcome of the 2000 presidential election, and reform measures were enacted both in Congress and in many states. Despite some improvements in the way elections are conducted in the American political system, many aspects of U.S. election mechanics still seem inferior to the mechanics of elections in many other western democracies.

Campaign financing became a major concern after the 1972 presidential election. Major campaign finance reform laws passed in 1974 and 2002 (the latter is the so-called McCain-Feingold Act) have been aimed at regulating the influence of campaign contributions in the electoral process, but they have met, at best, with only partial success. As recent bribery and corruption scandals make clear, the fundamental challenge of how to reconcile free speech, the freedom of an individual to

White House photo by Chris Greenberg

spend money as he or she wishes, the costs of campaigns, and the fairness of elections remain. In the summer of 2007, Barack Obama publicly pledged to accept public financing—and the accompanying condition that a candidate who accepts public financing can spend only the sum provided by the government—if he became his party's nominee. A year later, Obama changed his mind, and became the first and only presidential candidate to decline public financing since it became available beginning with the 1976 election. Obama made this decision because he realized that he could expect to raise more than three times as much money from supporters than the sum provided through public financing. As it turned out, candidate Obama *did* raise and spend more than three times as much money as his general election opponent, John McCain, who accepted public financing and the accompanying spending limit. One irony is that Democrats have traditionally been stronger proponents of campaign finance regulation and public financing than Republicans, notwithstanding John McCain's long-standing and much praised leadership in the area.

This unit also treats the roles of interest groups in the American political process and their impact on what government can and cannot do. While "gridlock" is a term usually applied to a situation that some observers think results from "divided government," in which neither major party controls the presidency and both houses of Congress, it seems that gridlock—and perhaps favoritism in policymaking—also may result from the interaction of interest groups and various government policymakers. The weakness of parties in the United States, compared to parties in other Western democracies, is almost certainly responsible for the unusually strong place of interest groups in the American political system. In turn, one can wonder whether the current era of stronger, more disciplined parties in government will eventually contribute to the weakening of interest groups.

The fourth and fifth sections in this unit address, among other topics, news and other media, which may play a more important role in the American political system than do their counterparts in other political systems. Television news broadcasts and newspapers are not merely passive transmitters of information. They inevitably shape—or distort—what they report to their audiences, and greatly affect the behavior of people and organizations in politics. Television talk shows, radio talk-back shows, and thirty-minute "infomercials" have entered the political landscape with considerable effect. In 2004, televised attack ads paid for by so-called 527 committees targeted both presidential candidates and seemed to affect voters' views. In 2008, Barack Obama's campaign perfected and improved some of the Internet fund-raising techniques pioneered by candidate Howard Dean in 2004, who unsuccessfully sought the Democratic party's presidential nomination. Obama's remarkable run for the presidency included his vanquishing—and outspending—Democratic rival Hillary Clinton, who herself raised and spent more money on her nomination campaign than any candidate in history, *except* Obama. Then, as mentioned above, Obama outspent John McCain by a more than three-to-one margin in the general election campaign. One key to Obama's extraordinary fund-raising prowess was the Internet, the relatively new medium that has revolutionized so many aspects of American life. In addition to facilitating fund-raising, the Internet played another role in the 2008 campaign by hosting political YouTube segments that played to large segments of the population, including some who tended to avoid traditional news media outlets. Selections in the fourth and fifth sections cover how media, old and new, shape political communication and political behavior in the American political system.

The fifth and concluding section in this unit focuses on the 2008 elections. Besides addressing the media's role in the campaigns, the selections report and assess Barack Obama's remarkable and historic candidacy; noteworthy campaign techniques and innovations, and the like.

The Weakness of Our Political Parties

WILFRED M. MCCLAY

No doubt it is the height of hubris to think that one could, writing in the waning days of spring 2008, make accurate predictions about the November presidential election and its aftermath. Predictions are always chancy. Six months is an eternity in American electoral politics, and given the multitude of factors already in play, and fresh ones arising out of contingencies we now can only faintly imagine, it is quite possible that, by the time this article appears in print, we will already be operating in a dramatically changed political universe. The one thing that always remains the same is our inability to count on things always remaining the same, or to count on present trends continuing undisturbed.

But still, the exercise is far from being pointless. The immediate future is very hard to anticipate. But sometimes longer trends will emerge with clarity if one stands back at sufficient distance from the present scene. I would like to focus here on one of those trends: the steady decline in power and authority of the political parties, a development that has had serious and almost entirely negative consequences. This is, of course, an old lament, even if one hears it less these days. A Lexis-Nexis search could probably produce a hundred articles in the past few decades that have borne the title "Is the Party Over?" or some variant on that theme.

But the familiarity of the complaint does not make it any less valid. The steady growth in numbers and influence of independent voters undoubtedly reflects the growth of individualism in American culture. No thinking person these days wants to be labeled as a "straight ticket" voter. But it also is hard to deny that the broad American electorate has become deeply distrustful of both political parties. As a consequence, American voters have, since the fall of Lyndon Johnson, seemed to prefer the frustrations of divided government to the specter of domination by a single political party.

This trend has only been boosted by the appalling disarray of the presidential nomination process, a monument to misguided "reform." In those states that rely on party caucuses to nominate a candidate, power is acquired by small cadres of activists, at the expense of broader constituencies. Worse yet has been the calamitous spread of open primaries, which have the effect of allowing voters to have a significant hand in selecting the candidates of parties to which they do not belong; and rules of Byzantine complexity governing the assignment of delegates. And worst of all have been the futile efforts to rein in campaign spending, notably the McCain–Feingold legislation, measures that have succeeded only in weakening the ability of parties to steer and discipline their members, and greatly strengthened the hand of unaccountable (and often extreme and irresponsible) interest groups that may or may not act as proxies for the legitimate campaigns, but surely work to intensify and polarize the messages those campaigns feel constrained to offer.

There is no end in sight for these trends, because the American public does not yet understand why such trends themselves, and not a surfeit of partisanship, are an important source of the problems of which they complain in the American political system. There is a kind of innocence, not to mention an invincible ignorance, behind the independent voter's declaration that "I vote for the man, not the party." Such dismissiveness is, in a sense, nothing new. The Framers of the Constitution earnestly hoped that America could be spared the corrupting indignity of political parties, and even so clever and realistic a man as James Madison did not reckon with the inexorability with which they would affix themselves to the American political system.

But the fact of the matter is that healthy parties are necessary vehicles for organizing, clarifying, taming, filtering, and even sublimating the nation's political conflicts. Mr. Smith may have gone to Washington in the movies, but in the real world, we need Mr. Smiths far less than we need a system with healthy political parties, where political conflict is channeled into predictable and accountable channels. Especially endangered is the fundamental idea of a loyal opposition. As Richard Hofstadter well put it in his *Idea of a Party System* (1970), legitimate democratic opposition is "responsible, effective, constitutional opposition" which offers a "critique of existing policies" that "is not simply a wild attempt to outbid the existing regime in promises, but a sober attempt to formulate alternative policies which it believes to be capable of execution within the existing historical and economic framework, and to offer as its executors a competent alternative personnel that can actually govern."

Notice the emphasis upon *responsibility* in Hofstadter's account. In a world where campaign rhetoric and spending emanate primarily from political parties, we can know that when candidate X is running for president as the nominee of party A, extreme advertisements attacking candidate Y from party B will be traceable to X's campaign and party, not to some other shadowy source which may or may not be operating independently. Candidate X will not be able to disavow with one hand what he is tacitly encouraging with the other. Nor will he be unable to silence sources of "information" that may be inimical to his actual strategies and interests. The current mounting disorder in our domestic politics resembles the forces impinging upon our world order, in which the visible authority and accountability of legitimate nation-states is increasingly threatened by the invisible coercions of shadowy and illegitimate groups, which sometimes operate as proxies for those nation-states but often operate entirely on their own. In both cases, the problem is with forces that no longer have a home address.

The election in the fall of 2008 will, in all likelihood, put forward two candidates who will both owe their nominations, to a very considerable extent, to people who are not loyal rank-and-file members of their respective parties. Both will be triangulating nonstop in their campaigns, targeting independent voters to an unprecedented degree. Both will pretend to be above partisanship, while trying to manipulate, and avoid being at the mercy of, 527s and other unaccountable organizations which will be driving much of the debate.

This is especially true of the anomalous candidacy of John McCain. This is a man with many admirable personal virtues, but also a man who (like so many career military men) seems almost oblivious to the role of successful political parties in a representative democracy. McCain has for most of his career as a legislator been known as a "maverick" who was unafraid to buck his own party's leadership, and its most important base constituencies, and strike out on a stubbornly independent path regarding a very long list of key issues, ranging from immigration to global warming to campaign-finance reform. How bizarre, then, that he should have become the presumptive party leader of the Republican Party, the very party he has made his reputation in bucking; for whatever else a "maverick" may be, he is not, by definition, a leader. If McCain nevertheless succeeds in outgrowing his "maverick" persona and becoming a credible leader of his party, it will only be because of a resurgence of national-security issues, quite possibly due to a rash of terror incidents at home or abroad. Otherwise, he can expect to get precisely the measure of party loyalty that he has given.

Barack Obama has energized supporters with an idealistic vision of a post-partisan and post-racial America, deemphasized his party identification, repeatedly praised Ronald Reagan, promised to "restore" bipartisanship and even to appoint Republicans to his administration. But amid all this happy talk about post-partisanship, voters might fruitfully remember that, although Thomas Jefferson famously declared that "we are all republicans, we are all federalists" in his First Inaugural Address in 1801, he proceeded to run a fiercely partisan administration, intent upon driving the Federalist party out of existence (and enjoying remarkable success in doing precisely that).

Or, assuming that Obama's desire is more sincere than Jefferson's, it might be well for him to remember that George W. Bush came into office in 2001 talking sincerely about how effectively he had worked with Democrats in Texas, proposing to "change the tone in Washington," and proclaiming sincerely that he was a "uniter, not a divider." And before him, Bill Clinton, George H. W. Bush, and Jimmy Carter all attempted (with greater or lesser degrees of sincerity and subtlety) to split the difference between ideologies and parties, and the end result was much the same. By contrast, the most successful presidency since the 1960s was that of Reagan, whose famously propounded 11th commandment, "Thou shalt not speak ill of another Republican" has not, to put it mildly, been the motto of John McCain.

Similarly, Obama will likely ascend to the Democratic nomination (the final outcome being undecided as of this writing) without strong support from some of his party's most influential constituencies, most notably feminists and rank-and-file workers, and without significant support from his party's remarkably feckless leadership. In addition, his lurching and often amateurish campaign was dogged relentlessly by the indefatigable Hillary Clinton, whose appeal to working-class white voters in Ohio, Pennsylvania, West Virginia, Indiana, and Kentucky was augmented by crossover votes from Republicans taking advantage of open primaries and lax registration rules to influence the Democratic race. There is little doubt that, should he be elected to the Presidency, the antiwar constituency will be only the first of many Democratic constituency groups to find itself not only disappointed but enraged by the inability of Obama's actions to match his sweeping rhetoric. Once Obama's star power starts to fade, as it already has begun to do, he will have little by way of party cohesiveness to fall back upon. Divided government would almost certainly return to Washington with the Congressional elections of 2010.

Chances are that, for the foreseeable future, our Presidents will have to operate within a nearly evenly divided electorate, with political debate driven by hard and vocal (and disproportionately influential) ideological minorities, soft silent majorities, weak and fractious parties, and hostile, irresponsible mass media. Whether we get Obama or McCain, we will have a President who does not owe his election chiefly to his party, who will not want to have to depend upon his party, and who does not regard the conflict between strong and healthy parties as one of the safeguards of a constitutional democracy. I expect that to be one of the aftereffects of the election of 2008, even though it will merely be continuing a trend of long standing.

WILFRED M. MCCLAY, an Advisory Editor of *Society,* holds the Sun-Trust Bank Chair of Excellence in Humanities and is professor of history at the University of Tennessee at Chattanooga. He is author most recently of *Figures in the Carpet: Finding the Human Person in the American Past* (Eerdmans).

America the Liberal

The Democratic majority: It emerged!

JOHN B. JUDIS

Even before the final results showing a Democratic sweep were in, Washington's pundits were declaring that nothing had really changed politically in the country. In a cover story labeled "AMERICA THE CONSERVATIVE," *Newsweek* editor Jon Meacham warned that, "[s]hould Obama win, he will have to govern a nation that is more instinctively conservative than it is liberal." Meacham's judgment was echoed by Peter Wehner, a fellow at the Ethics and Public Policy Center. "America remains, in the main, a center-right nation," Wehner wrote in *The Washington Post.*

These guys—and the others who are counseling Barack Obama and the Democrats to "go slow"—couldn't be more wrong. They are looking at Obama's election through the prism of Jimmy Carter's win in 1976 and Bill Clinton's victory in 1992. Both Carter and Clinton did misjudge the mood of the electorate. They tried unsuccessfully to govern a country from the center-left that was moving to the right (in Carter's case) or that was only just beginning to move leftward (in Clinton's case)—and they were rebuked by voters as a result.

Obama is taking office under dramatically different circumstances. His election is the culmination of a Democratic realignment that began in the 1990s, was delayed by September 11, and resumed with the 2006 election. This realignment is predicated on a change in political demography and geography. Groups that had been disproportionately Republican have become disproportionately Democratic, and red states like Virginia have turned blue. Underlying these changes has been a shift in the nation's "fundamentals"—in the structure of society and industry, and in the way Americans think of their families, jobs, and government. The country is no longer "America the conservative." And, if Obama acts shrewdly to consolidate this new majority, we may soon be "America the liberal."

Realignments—which political scientist Walter Dean Burnham called "America's surrogate for revolution"—are not scientifically predictable events like lunar eclipses. But they have occurred with some regularity over the last 200 years—in 1828, 1860, 1896, 1932, and 1980. The two most recent realignments were essentially belated political acknowledgments of tectonic changes that had been occurring in the country's economic base. In the case of the New Deal, it was the rise of an urban industrial order in the North; in the case of Reagan conservatism, it was the shift of industry and population from the North to the lower-wage, non-unionized, suburban Sunbelt stretching from Virginia down to Florida and across to Texas and southern California.

The new Democratic realignment reflects the shift that began decades ago toward a post-industrial economy centered in large urban-suburban metropolitan areas devoted primarily to the production of ideas and services rather than material goods. (In *The Emerging Democratic Majority,* Ruy Teixeira and I called these places "ideopolises.") Clustered in the regions that have undergone this economic transition are the three main groups that constitute the backbone of the new Democratic majority: professionals (college-educated workers who produce ideas and services); minorities (African Americans, Latinos, and Asian Americans); and women (particularly working, single, and college-educated women).

As late as the 1950s, professionals were the most Republican of all occupational groupings, but they were also relatively small in number—about 7 percent of the labor force. Today, professionals (who are the brains, so to speak, of the new post-industrial economy) make up 20 percent of the labor force and are a quarter or more of the electorate in many northern and western states. They range from nurses to teachers to TV producers to software programmers to engineers. They began voting Democratic in 1988 and have continued to do so ever since.

Using census data, Teixeira and I calculated that, between 1988 and 2000, professionals voted for the Democratic presidential candidate by an average of 52 to 40 percent. I don't know exactly what percentage of professionals voted for Obama this week because exit polls don't include professionals as a category. Still, as an approximation, I can use a somewhat smaller (and maybe even slightly more conservative) group: people with advanced degrees. Obama won these voters by a whopping 58 to 40 percent. He even won college graduates as a whole, 50 to 48 percent. (It may be the first time that a Democrat has ever accomplished this. In 1996, for instance, Clinton, even while beating Bob Dole handily, failed to carry college graduates.) Moreover, if you look at states Obama carried and compare them to the states that have the highest percentage of people with an advanced degree, you find that he won the top 19 states—*all of them,* which together account for 234 electoral votes. He also won 21 of the top 24, accounting for 282 electoral votes. McCain, by contrast, won the six states that have the lowest percentage of people with advanced degrees.

As for minorities: Most—with the exception of Cubans, Chinese-Americans, and Vietnamese-Americans—have voted Democratic since the 1930s. But, with the shift of the economy and the liberalization of immigration laws, the number of Latinos and Asian Americans has expanded. Some of the new immigrants are professionals, but others form the working class of the post-industrial economy. They are orderlies, child-care workers, janitors, fast-food cooks, and servers. As late as 1972, minorities accounted for just 10 percent of the electorate. In this election, they made up 26 percent. Blacks, of course, went overwhelmingly for Obama, but he also won Hispanics by 66 to 31 percent and Asians—who as a group used to split their vote between Democrats and Republicans—by 62 to 35 percent.

Women, too, were once disproportionately Republican—in 1960, Richard Nixon won the women's vote. But their voting patterns began to change as they entered the labor force. In 1950, only one-third of women worked; today, 60 percent of women work, making up 46 percent of the total labor force. Over 70 percent of working women have white-collar jobs, and 24 percent work as professionals—compared to 17 percent of men. In 1980, women began disproportionately backing Democrats, and the trend has continued. This year, Obama enjoyed a 13-point edge among women voters and only a one-point edge among men. He carried working women by 21 points. If you add these numbers to the Democrats' advantage among professionals and minorities, that is a good basis for winning elections.

To be sure, Obama and the Democrats needed to win about 40 percent of the white working class that used to be d financial crisis certainly helped bring these voters home. But the heart of the new majority is no longer blue-collar workers. While the ranks of professionals, minorities, and working women are growing, the traditional white working class is shrinking—having already gone from 58 percent of the workforce in 1940 to 25 percent in 2006, according to Teixeira and Alan Abramowitz.

The new electoral map that has emerged from these demographic trends is, in some ways, the mirror image of the one generated by Republican William McKinley's 1896 presidential victory—with the Deep South now Republican rather than Democratic, and the Northeast now Democratic rather than Republican. (Vermont, today thought of as a left-wing Democratic bastion, voted for only one Democratic presidential candidate before backing Bill Clinton in 1992.)

And yet the geography of the new Democratic majority is not quite so straightforward. That's because, while the post-industrial economy is obviously strong in traditionally liberal areas like Boston, Chicago, and San Francisco, it has also taken root in parts of the South and West—areas like Charlotte (a financial center) and the Raleigh-Durham-Chapel Hill research triangle in North Carolina, the northern Virginia suburbs, Orlando and South Florida, and the Denver-Boulder region. This helps explain why North Carolina, Virginia, Florida, and Colorado all shifted from red to blue in this election.

The rise of these voting groups within the post-industrial economy has brought in its wake a new political worldview. Call it "progressive" or "liberal" or even "Naderite" (for Ralph Nader the consumer advocate, not the misbegotten presidential candidate). If unionized industrial workers were the vanguard of the New Deal majority, professionals are the vanguard of the new progressive majority. Their sensibility is reflected in the Democratic platform and increasingly in the country as a whole. It has sometimes been described as socially liberal and fiscally conservative, but that doesn't really get it right. Professionals are generally liberal on civil rights and women's rights; committed to science and to the separation of church and state; internationalist on trade and immigration; skeptical of, but not necessarily opposed to, large government programs; and gung-ho about government regulation of business, especially K Street lobbyists.

Many are children of the 1960s and '70s—heavily influenced by Martin Luther King Jr., Betty Friedan, Gloria Steinem, and Nader—but their views are clearly reflected in succeeding generations of college-educated Americans, particularly the "millennials" who grew up during the administrations of Bill Clinton and George W. Bush. UCLA's annual study of incoming college freshmen across the country found in 2006 that 28.4 percent identified themselves as "liberal"—the highest percentage since 1975.

If you compare Americans' attitudes from the 1970s and '80s with attitudes today, you can see how much the worldview of these professionals has already permeated the electorate. In March 1981, two months into the Reagan administration, a *Los Angeles Times* poll found that 54 percent of Americans thought there was "too much regulation of business and industry" and only 18 percent thought there was "too little." By October 2008, 27 percent thought there was "too much" and 45 percent thought there was "too little." In a Pew poll released in March 2007, 83 percent backed "stricter laws and regulations to protect the environment," and 66 percent supported "government guaranteeing health insurance for all citizens, even if it means raising taxes."

Attitudes on social issues have also changed dramatically. The Pew poll from March 2007 found that the percentage of Americans who believe that school boards should have the right to fire gay teachers fell from 51 percent in 1987 to 28 percent. Those who want to make it "more difficult" for women to obtain abortions dropped from 47 to 35 percent. Those who think that "it's all right for blacks and whites to date each other" rose from 48 to 83 percent. The poll also found that 62 percent of the general population—and 83 percent of college graduates—disagreed with the notion that "science is going too far and hurting society."

These opinions had become prevalent in the 1990s; but September 11 and the fear of an imminent terrorist attack temporarily revived the conservatism of the 1980s, especially on social issues. (As I wrote in THE NEW REPUBLIC last year, there is strong psychological evidence suggesting that a heightened fear of death pushes people toward traditional views on social questions.) Today, however, seven years removed from September 11, liberal views have re-emerged with a vengeance. Now, the coming recession seems likely to push voters even further left. And how Obama handles the economy will go a long way toward determining whether the new Democratic majority that has swept him into office proves to be a fleeting phenomenon or a durable one.

There have been two kinds of realignments in American history—hard and soft. The realignments of 1896 and 1932 were hard: They laid the basis for 30 years of party dominance, periods when the same party would win the bulk of national, state, and local elections. (During the New Deal realignment, from 1932 to 1968, Republicans controlled the presidency for only eight of 36 years and Congress for only four years.) The conservative Republican realignment of 1980, by contrast, was soft: It began in 1968, was interrupted by Watergate, resumed during Carter's presidency, and climaxed in Reagan's landslide. Yet, even then, Democrats retained control of the House and got back the Senate in 1986. Republicans did win Congress in 1994, but a Democrat was president and was reelected easily in 1996. Burnham characterized the '90s as a period of "unstable equilibrium" between the parties.

What made the 1896 and 1932 realignments hard was that they coincided with steep downturns in the business cycle. The political trends were present in prior elections—in 1928, for instance, Al Smith began to draw urban voters to the Democrats—but the depression of the 1890s and the Great Depression catalyzed and accelerated these trends. McKinley and the Republicans blamed the depression of the 1890s on Democrat Grover Cleveland. Franklin Roosevelt blamed the 1929 stock market crash and subsequent depression on Herbert Hoover. In both cases, the stigma remained for decades. Democrats were still running successfully against Herbert Hoover 20 years after he left office.

In 1980, Reagan and the Republicans were able to take advantage of deep divisions within the Democratic Party over civil rights (and later abortion), but, for catalysts, they had to rely on the Iranian hostage crisis and the stagflation of the late '70s, which led to a recession. By the 1992 election, the impressions created by these events had largely worn off. That prevented the Reagan Republicans from developing the kind of hard, enduring majority that the New Deal Democrats had enjoyed.

Will the Democratic realignment of 2008 be hard or soft? Initially, it seemed it would be soft. Like the Reagan realignment, it began in fits and starts—Clinton's victory in 1992 was comparable to Richard Nixon's victory in 1968, with Ross Perot playing the schismatic role that George Wallace had played in 1968. The Democratic trend was slowed by the Clinton scandals and interrupted by September 11. By this measure, 2008 seemed to be more analogous to 1980 than to 1932 or 1896.

But the onset of the financial crisis may have changed this. The coming economic downturn may more closely resemble the depression of the 1930s than the relatively shallow recessions of 1980 or 1991. There are, sad to say, striking resemblances between the circumstances that led to the Great Depression and those that led to the current emergency. In both cases, the downturn was preceded by overcapacity in an industry that had been key to growth—automobiles in the 1920s, telecommunications and computers in the 1990s. In both cases, there were mild recessions—1927 and 2002, respectively—that preceded the final downturn and were overcome by government policies. The Fed lowered interest rates in the 1920s and 2000s, and the Bush administration cut taxes. But, instead of fueling a genuine recovery, these policies fueled a speculative bonanza in the stock market of the late 1920s and in the housing market of the last years. That created a tower of toxic debt. When consumer demand and productive investment began to lag again, this tower collapsed. And, in both cases, the downturn, instead of being confined to the United States, was international, making recovery even more difficult.

There are differences, of course, between the two periods. For one thing, international cooperation to prevent a recession from becoming a global depression is much more likely this time around. Still, there is a likelihood that this recession will deepen over the next year and at least raise the specter of a new depression—something that never occurred in 1980 or in 1991.

If Obama and congressional Democrats act boldly, they can not only arrest the downturn but also lay the basis for an enduring majority. As was the case with Franklin Roosevelt's New Deal, many of the measures necessary to combat today's recession will also help ensure long-term Democratic electoral success. Many Southerners remained Democrats for generations in part because of Roosevelt's rural electrification program; a similar program for bringing broadband to the hinterland could lure these voters back to the Democratic Party. And national health insurance could play the same role in Democrats' future prospects that Social Security played in the perpetuation of the New Deal majority.

Americans, to be sure, are always reluctant to undertake ambitious government initiatives. This is a country, historian Louis Hartz once pointed out, founded on Lockean liberalism. But, as Roosevelt discovered when he was elected, a national crisis creates popular willingness to entertain dramatic initiatives. Moreover, Obama will not face the same formidable adversaries that Jimmy Carter and Bill Clinton had to confront. The Republican Party will be divided and demoralized after this defeat. And, just as the Great Depression took Prohibition and the other great social issues of the 1920s off the popular agenda, this downturn has pushed aside the culture war of the last decades. It simply wasn't a factor in the presidential election.

If, however, Obama and the Democrats take the advice of official Washington and go slow—adopting incremental reforms, appeasing adversaries that have lost their clout—they could end up prolonging the downturn and discrediting themselves. What might have been a hard realignment could become not merely a soft realignment, but perhaps even an abortive one. That's not the kind of change America needs—or wants.

America Observed

Why foreign election observers would rate the United States near the bottom.

ROBERT A. PASTOR

F ew noticed, but in the year 2000, Mexico and the United States traded places. After nearly two centuries of election fraud, Mexico's presidential election was praised universally by its political parties and international observers as free, fair, and professional. Four months later, after two centuries as a model democracy, the U.S. election was panned as an embarrassing fiasco, reeking with pregnant chads, purged registration lists, butterfly ballots, and a Supreme Court that preempted a recount.

Ashamed, the U.S. Congress in 2002 passed the Help America Vote Act (HAVA), our first federal legislation on election administration. But two years later, on November 2, more than 200,000 voters from all 50 states phoned the advocacy organization Common Cause with a plethora of complaints. The 2004 election was not as close as 2000, but it was no better—and, in some ways, worse. This was partly because the only two elements of HAVA implemented for 2004 were provisional ballots and ID requirements, and both created more problems than they solved. HAVA focused more on eliminating punch-card machines than on the central cause of the electoral problem, dysfunctional decentralization. Instead of a single election for president, 13,000 counties and municipalities conduct elections with different ballots, standards, and machines. This accounts for most of the problems.

On the eve of November's election, only one-third of the electorate, according to a *New York Times* poll, said that they had a lot of confidence that their votes would be counted properly, and 29 percent said they were very or somewhat concerned that they would encounter problems at the polls. This explains why 13 members of Congress asked the United Nations to send election observers. The deep suspicion that each party's operatives had of the other's motives reminded me of Nicaragua's polarized election in 1990, and of other poor nations holding their first free elections.

Ranking America's Elections

The pro-democracy group Freedom House counts 117 electoral democracies in the world as of 2004. Many are new and fragile. The U.S. government has poured more money into helping other countries become democracies than it has into its own election system. At least we've gotten our money's worth. By and large, elections are conducted better abroad than at home. Several teams of international observers—including one that I led—watched this U.S. election. Here is a summary of how the United States did in 10 different categories, and what we should do to raise our ranking.

1. Who's in Charge? Stalin is reported to have said that the secret to a successful election is not the voter but the vote counter. There are three models for administering elections. Canada, Spain, Afghanistan, and most emerging democracies have nonpartisan national election commissions. A second model is to have the political parties "share" responsibility. We use that model to supervise campaign finance (the Federal Election Commission), but that tends to lead either to stalemates or to collusions against the public's interest. The third, most primitive model is when the incumbent government puts itself in charge. Only 18 percent of the democracies do it this way, including the United States, which usually grants responsibility to a highly partisan secretary of state, like Katherine Harris (formerly) in Florida or Kenneth Blackwell in Ohio.

2. Registration and Identification of Voters. The United States registers about 55 percent of its eligible voters, as compared with more than 95 percent in Canada and Mexico. To ensure the accuracy of its list, Mexico conducted 36 audits between 1994 and 2000. In contrast, the United States has thousands of separate lists, many of which are wildly inaccurate. Provisional ballots were needed only because the lists are so bad. Under HAVA, all states by 2006 must create computer-based, interactive statewide lists—a major step forward that will work only if everyone agrees not to move out of state. That is why most democracies, including most of Europe, have nationwide lists and ask voters to identify themselves. Oddly, few U.S. states require proof of *citizenship*—which is, after all, what the election is supposed to be about. If ID cards threaten democracy, why does almost every democracy except us require them, and why are their elections conducted better than ours?

3. Poll Workers and Sites. Dedicated people work at our polling stations often for 14 hours on election day. Polling sites are always overcrowded at the start of the day. McDonald's hires more workers for its lunchtime shifts, but a similar idea has not yet occurred to our election officials. Poll workers are exhausted by the time they begin the delicate task of counting the votes and making sure the total corresponds to the number who signed in, and, as a result, there are discrepancies. When I asked about the qualifications for selecting a poll worker, one county official told me, "We'll take anyone with a pulse." Mexico views the job as a civic responsibility like jury duty, and citizens are chosen randomly and trained. This encourages all citizens to learn and participate in the process.

4. Voting Technologies. Like any computers, electronic machines break down, and they lose votes. Canada does not have this problem because it uses paper ballots, still the most reliable technology. Brazil's electronic system has many safeguards and has gained the trust of its voters. If we use electronic machines, they need paper-verifiable ballots.

5. Uniform Standards for Ballots, Voting, Disputes. The Supreme Court called for equal protection of voters' rights, but to achieve this, standards need to be uniform. In America, each jurisdiction does it differently. Most countries don't have this problem because they have a single election commission and law to decide the validity of ballots.

6. Uncompetitive Districts. In 2004, only three incumbent members of Congress—outside of House Majority Leader Tom DeLay's gerrymandered state of Texas—were defeated. Even the Communist Party of China has difficulty winning as many elections. This is because state legislatures, using advanced computer technologies, can now draw district boundaries in a way that virtually guarantees safe seats. Canada has a nonpartisan system for drawing districts. This still favors incumbents, as 83 percent won in 2004, but that compares with 99 percent in the United States. Proportional representation systems are even more competitive.

7. Campaign Finance and Access to the Media. The United States spent little to conduct elections last November, but almost $4 billion to promote and defeat candidates. More than $1.6 billion was spent on TV ads in 2004. The Institute for Democracy and Electoral Assistance in Stockholm reported that 63 percent of democracies provided free access to the media, thus eliminating one of the major reasons for raising money. Most limit campaign contributions, as the United States does, but one-fourth also limit campaign expenditures, which the Supreme Court feared would undermine our democracy. In fact, the opposite is closer to the truth: Political equality *requires* building barriers between money and the ballot box.

8. Civic Education. During the 1990s, the federal government spent $232 million on civic education abroad and none at home. As a result, 97 percent of South Africans said they had been affected by voter education. Only 6 percent of Americans, according to a Gallup Poll in 2000, knew the name of the speaker of the House, while 66 percent could identify the host of *Who Wants to Be a Millionaire?* Almost every country in the world does a better job educating citizens on how to vote.

9. The Franchise. The Electoral College was a progressive innovation in the 18th century; today, it's mainly dictatorships like communist China that use an indirect system to choose their highest leader.

10. International Observers. We demand that all new democracies grant unhindered access to polling sites for international observers, but only one of our 50 states (Missouri) does that. The Organization for Security and Cooperation in Europe, a 55-state organization of which the United States is a member, was invited by Secretary of State Colin Powell to observe the U.S. elections, yet its representatives were permitted to visit only a few "designated sites." Any developing country that restricted observers to a few Potemkin polling sites as the United States did would be roundly condemned by the State Department and the world.

On all 10 dimensions of election administration, the United States scores near the bottom of electoral democracies. There are three reasons for this. First, we have been sloppy and have not insisted that our voting machines be as free from error as our washing machines. We lack a simple procedure most democracies have: a log book at each precinct to register every problem encountered during the day and to allow observers to witness and verify complaints.

> **McDonald's hires extra workers at lunchtime, but this has not yet occurred to our election officials. Poll workers are exhausted by the time they start counting votes.**

Second, we lack uniform standards, and that is because we have devolved authority to the lowest, poorest level of government. It's time for states to retrieve their authority from the counties, and it's time for Congress to insist on national standards.

Third, we have stopped asking what we can learn from our democratic friends, and we have not accepted the rules we impose on others. This has communicated arrogance abroad and left our institutions weak.

The results can be seen most clearly in our bizarre approach to Iraq's election. Washington, you may recall, tried to export the Iowa-caucus model though it violates the first principle of free elections, a secret ballot. An Iraqi ayatollah rejected that and also insisted on the importance of direct elections (meaning no Electoral College). Should we be surprised that the Iraqi Election Commission chose to visit Mexico instead of the United States to learn how to conduct elections?

ROBERT A. PASTOR is director of the Center for Democracy and Election Management and a professor at American University. At the Carter Center from 1986–2000, he organized election-observation missions to about 30 countries, including the United States.

Who Should Redistrict?

DEAN E. MURPHY

Rising out of the farmland south of Sacramento, Elk Grove is a pleasant, unremarkable collection of scrubbed subdivisions with artificial lakes and velveteen lawns. What makes Elk Grove special—and of intense interest to politicians—is that in a state where political segregation is the norm, Democrats and Republicans live side by side in almost equal numbers.

When the residents of Elk Grove choose their state legislators, however, their votes are divided into two improbable assembly districts that meander into outlying rural areas and give each a Republican majority. Those districts are the legacy of a statewide redistricting in California in 2001 from which both parties benefited. The Democrats retained firm control of the State Legislature and the 53-member Congressional delegation, while Republicans were assured 20 safe seats in Congress and a spoiler's share of the seats in the state Capitol.

And so, on a sunny May afternoon, Elk Grove was the natural backdrop for the Republican governor, Arnold Schwarzenegger, to stump for Proposition 77, an ostensibly politically neutral ballot initiative that would take the power to set voting districts away from state lawmakers and give it to an independent panel of retired judges. Schwarzenegger stood in the center of a neighborhood of half-million-dollar homes where aides had put down hundreds of feet of red ribbon. The ribbon bisected the street, turning at a right angle on the asphalt in front of the governor's lectern and continuing through the sprinkler-fed turf between homes owned by Darren and Nichola Denney and Garry and Susan Darms, who were standing, Let's-Make-A-Deal fashion, in front of them. A pair of blue signs posted on either side of the red line said "15th Assembly District" and "10th Assembly District."

"The politicians have divided a neighborhood," Schwarzenegger intoned. "They have divided cities, towns and people, and this is what we want to eliminate. And this is why we need redistricting, because the district lines were drawn to favor the incumbents rather than to favor the voters." One of the assemblymen with the governor, Guy Houston, complained that his district stretched across four counties from suburban San Francisco to Elk Grove, 80 miles to the northeast. "I love Elk Grove," said Houston, who lives in San Ramon, on the western fringe of the district. "The people here are so nice, great to represent. But shouldn't we have districts that are more compact and competitive?"

The short answer to Houston's rhetorical question is yes. Politicians tend to be held to account when they represent communities where social ties and common institutions make people more likely to be politically active. Gerrymandered districts like Houston's have been blamed for a host of ills: complacent incumbents, polarized politics, cynical voters, dull elections. The arguments for taking the politics out of drawing political boundaries have been mounting. California and Ohio voters will go to the polls Nov. 8 to decide whether to let outside panels determine how electoral districts—both for State Legislature and for the United States House of Representatives—will be drawn. More than a dozen other states are thinking of doing the same.

And yet, how many of the complaints about elections would really disappear simply by taking the redistricting process out of the hands of elected officials? Houston says districts should be compact and competitive, but in California, like-minded people tend to cluster. Draw a box around San Francisco and you create a safe haven for Democrats; do the same around Bakersfield and Republicans benefit. The districts would have less sinister shapes, but they would not necessarily lead to more meaningful elections. So which is more important to democracy? Compactness or competitiveness? Or something entirely different?

The two Elk Grove districts are neither compact nor particularly competitive, so no doubt there is room for improvement there. As it turned out, the red ribbon running up Grand Point Lane did not divide the 10th from the 15th district; the real boundary was blocks away. But nobody noticed it at the time, not the elected officials nor the residents, and that can't be good for democracy either.

The drawing of legislative boundaries is one of the most politicized and corruptible practices in American-style government, and few people will say they approve of the gerrymandering it has unleashed. Boundary-rigging infamously kept blacks from gaining political power in the South. (One Mississippi district, mapped in the late 1870s with the single purpose of preventing the re-election of a black congressman, was 500 miles long and 40 miles wide.) In the early part of the 20th century, rural lawmakers held onto power by simply ignoring their obligation to draw new boundaries as people migrated to the cities and populations shifted, thus denying the swelling cities the political representation their numbers warranted.

The passage of the Voting Rights Act in 1965 and various rulings by the Supreme Court curtailed such egregious gerrymandering, but the practice endures—sometimes to favor incumbents, sometimes to favor one political party over the other. Lawmakers now use finely tuned demographic information and advanced computer programs to create "safe but slim victory margins in the maximum number of districts, with little risk of cutting their margins too thin," as the Supreme Court justice Stephen G. Breyer wrote last year in a dissenting opinion in a gerrymandering case, *Vieth v. Jubelirer.* That is what happened in California, where the deal worked out between the two parties created safe seats for incumbents. There was also, of course, the spectacle two years ago in which Tom DeLay, then the Republican majority leader in the House, orchestrated a mid-decade partisan gerrymander in his home state of Texas, which Democratic lawmakers tried to thwart by fleeing to Oklahoma and New Mexico. They failed, and of the seven incumbents defeated in Congress in 2004, four of them were Texas Democrats who had been placed in the newly rigged districts.

But while it's easy to make a case against gerrymandering, it's much harder to say how districts should be drawn. Most states require that district boundaries be revisited every 10 years, after the release of new census data and the reapportionment of the country's Congressional seats. The creation of contiguous districts is the most widely accepted and uncontroversial criterion. Every state requires contiguity, and in 1842, Congress passed the first federal law that mandated the drawing of contiguous Congressional districts. A few other rules apply: the Supreme Court decisions of the 1960s forced Congressional districts to be roughly equal in population. The Voting Rights Act also prohibits "retrogression" in minority voting rights in certain states and the diluting of the political strength of minority communities anywhere. But beyond these piecemeal and often vague criteria—contiguity, after all, can accommodate serpentine shapes—legislators are free to create the maps as they see fit.

The Supreme Court has been little help in separating raw politics from mapmaking, with the justices disagreeing on how to deal with even obvious partisan boundary-rigging. In *Vieth v. Jubelirer,* Pennsylvania Democrats asked the court to overturn the state's redistricting plan, which was drafted by a Republican-led State Legislature and signed into law by a Republican governor. The new map gave Republicans the advantage in 12 of 19 Congressional districts, even though Democrats outnumbered Republicans statewide. Four of the justices held that redistricting was a political matter that could never be decided by the courts. Five justices agreed that excessive partisanship in redistricting could be unconstitutional, but they didn't settle on a standard for deciding when a party had gone too far. Ultimately, the court allowed the Pennsylvania map to stand.

Vote or Else

A modest proposal for curing election fraud.

ALLISON R. HAYWARD

In the state of Washington, it may be that a governor will serve for the next four years who was not properly elected. Voter registration rolls and election practices are sloppy enough—not just in Washington, mind you, but in many places—that in very close elections it may be impossible to know for sure which candidate has received more properly cast votes. (In three separate counts in Washington, the margins were 261, 42, and 129 votes out of 2.9 million cast.) It is past time we address this problem, and here's a thought: Maybe the United States should require eligible citizens to register to vote, and then to vote.

For most people, this idea is radical and distasteful. Why should we want presumably uninformed, apathetic people voting? Wouldn't they be influenced by caprice, last-minute mud, or improper entreaties? Isn't it a person's right not to vote if he doesn't want to? Only nasty one-party regimes make voting mandatory, right? And Venezuela, for one, requires its citizens to register and vote, showing that mandatory voting and massive fraud can coexist.

The usual defenses for mandatory voting seem tepid in contrast. People would be more "engaged" in government. The underclass would be better represented. "We, the people"—not some motivated subset—would elect representatives. It is not obvious that any of these arguments is true or, if true, is sufficient reason to require voting.

Moreover, it would seem American elections face more urgent challenges, voting fraud and voter intimidation being the most notorious. Yet it is as a palliative to these ills that mandatory voting would have its greatest appeal. That is because a mandatory system would require government to take voter registration—including the issue of fraud—seriously.

Suppose, as in Australia, eligible citizens were required to register and to appear at the polls on Election Day. Election administrators would need to know, first, who among the throng was eligible, and ensure that they registered in the appropriate place. Duplicate registrations and obsolete addresses would have to be purged. At election time, officials would need to ascertain accurately who had voted and who hadn't. No more question of whether precautions, such as requiring identification, would be intimidating. And it would be in the interest of a voter to make sure he was correctly identified. With better

records, it would be more difficult to lard the rolls with phony registrations. Nor could the converse scam of "unregistering" valid voters be as easily perpetrated. For those voting absentee, the incentives would be much stronger to make sure their vote was received and cast properly, lest they face a fine for failing to vote.

The significant and sometimes mischievous role partisans now play in our current elections would diminish. Just as we don't see private interests going door to door helping people complete tax or immigration forms, the role special interests and parties now assume in registering and mobilizing voters would fade. There would be no reason to go to elaborate lengths to register or ferret out voters at election time—no more cause to slash the tires or block the phones of the other side's activists, or to pay cash bounties for registrations, subsidizing the duplicative, phony dreck that already clogs our voter rolls.

But isn't mandatory voting a little, um, totalitarian? One could argue that—although arguably no more so than having to file tax forms on a regular basis. A system of mandatory voting does not mean that individuals are forced to vote for any particular candidate, or even any candidate at all. If the United States were to follow a system like Australia's, mandatory registration and voting would be mitigated by the secret ballot. If voters do not care to vote, they can simply take a ballot and not vote it, or "undervote" by choosing some offices and not others.

Would mandatory voting favor liberals and Democrats over conservatives and Republicans? The conventional wisdom for decades has been that making voter registration and voting easier—broadening the "base," as it were—favors the Democratic party. However, people who know much more about this than I tell me that the conventional wisdom no longer necessarily obtains. When the base is broadened in some part by false and duplicative registration, as happens now, the side favored would seem to be the one willing to throw those votes into the pool, i.e., to commit fraud. That can have different partisan implications depending on where you live and what's at stake.

The main obstacle to mandatory voting in the United States is that it is beyond imagination what jurisdiction would implement it. Under the Constitution, election administration and qualifications are for the most part the province of the states.

How could one, or even a handful, of states institute mandatory voting, given the way Americans move about? It would seem impossible to assemble the essential prerequisite—the list of eligible citizens—unless other states could be relied upon to keep good records, too. The federal government might be able to work that miracle nationally (probably not), but whether the federal government could constitutionally institute mandatory voting has yet to be litigated, and would in any case mean a revolution in election jurisdiction that is unlikely to take place.

Still, that need not be the end of the story. As we see from the anti-smoking campaign, people can be made to change their behavior through moral suasion. Following the model of California's antismoking Proposition 99, states could institute taxes to pay for massive voter education efforts, shaming people into self-registering and voting, by associating nonvoting with all things ugly and slothful. Groups could receive grants for crafting an eligible-voter database, or for sanitizing the registration rolls. Hollywood-based consultants could place pro-registration and antifraud references in popular movie and television scripts. State treasuries could reward taxpayers who demonstrate they voted with a tax credit.

Or, in the alternative, states could get serious about cleaning up election rolls, educating voters, and prosecuting election fraud. Ultimately, using mandatory voting to push the system toward reform is a little like punishing the victim.

ALLISON R. HAYWARD is counsel to Commissioner Bradley A. Smith of the Federal Election Commission. The views expressed here are her own, and do not reflect the position of the commission, any of its commissioners, or its staff.

The Presidential Nomination Process: The Beginnings of a New Era

BRUCE STINEBRICKNER

L et me start with two points that provide essential context for considering significant changes occurring in the American presidential nomination process today. First, in every presidential election since 1860 (that is, in the last 37 presidential elections) either the Democratic or Republican candidate has won and become president of the United States. Thus, the presidential nomination process serves to identify the *only* two individuals who ultimately have a chance to become president of the United States. Second, since the introduction of presidential primaries in the early twentieth century, the American people have played a much bigger role in the American presidential nomination process than their counterparts in any comparable nomination process in the world.

These two points testify to the importance and uniqueness of the American presidential nomination process. But the process by which major party candidates for president are nominated has not remained static since the introduction of presidential primaries early in the twentieth century, much less since the time of President George Washington. The presidential nominating process has sometimes changed suddenly on account of deliberate and focused reform efforts, and sometimes at a more measured and evolutionary pace.

I begin this article with an overview of the history of the presidential nomination process in the United States, identifying four distinct eras and laying the groundwork for the suggestion that we are entering or about to enter a *fifth* era in the way major party presidential nominees are chosen. Second, from the vantage point of November 2007, I identify the major changes that have arrived—or are arriving—on the scene, tracing their origins back to 2004 or 2000 as needed. Third, by assessing the likely consequences of these changes, I make the case that they represent more than minor revisions or routine evolution of the presidential nomination process. Instead, I argue that a sea change—a major transformation—in the process seems to be at hand.

Four Eras in the Presidential Nomination Process
The First Era: The Congressional Caucus Era (ca. 1800–1828)

Revolutionary War hero George Washington became the first president of the United States, serving two terms in office after having been elected unanimously by the Electoral College in 1788 and again in 1792. After Washington retired, party caucuses in Congress (that is, meetings of all the members of Congress who identified with each party) assumed the function of nominating presidential candidates. In six consecutive presidential elections from 1800 through 1828, every successful candidate had first been nominated by his party's congressional caucus. This first era in the presidential nominating process—the Congressional Caucus era—came to an end in 1831–1832, when parties began to hold national nominating conventions to choose their presidential candidates.

The end of the Congressional Caucus era—which some pejoratively called the "King Caucus" era—is significant. Had members of Congress continued to control the presidential nomination process, a key distinction between the American system of government and the parliamentary system of government would probably not have emerged. At the heart of parliamentary systems such as those in Great Britain, Australia, Japan, Italy, and India lies the relationship between candidates for prime minister (and prime ministers) and members of the lower house of parliament. As these systems have come to operate today, a party's members in parliament choose their leader, and that leader becomes the party's candidate for prime minister. Voters play a decisive role in selecting the prime minister by choosing between the parties, their policy positions, and their prime ministerial candidates in general elections. The end of the Congressional Caucus era in the United States severed the direct link between Congress and presidential nominations. In turn, the relationships between Congress and American presidential candidates, on the one hand, and parliaments and prime ministerial candidates in parliamentary democracies, on the other, developed in fundamentally different ways.[1]

The Second Era: National Conventions of Party Regulars or Activists (ca. 1831–1908)

By ending the direct and controlling role of members of Congress in choosing their parties' presidential candidates, the introduction of national nominating conventions in 1831–1832 marked the beginning of the second era in the history of the nominating process. From 1831 to the early twentieth century, delegates to national nominating conventions were individuals active in party organization affairs at the state and local levels. Party officeholders such as state and county party chairs as well as other party regulars became delegates. The national conventions were gatherings of party organization people—that is, party leaders and other party activists—from all the states, with each state party sending a number of delegates roughly proportional to the population of that state in comparison with other states.

In the twentieth century, two significant changes in the methods for selecting delegates to the parties' quadrennial national conventions gave birth to the third and fourth eras in the history of the presidential nomination process.

The Third Era: The "Mixed System" for Choosing Delegates to National Conventions (ca. 1912–1968)

In the early twentieth century, state governments introduced what has been called "the most radical of all the party reforms adopted in the whole course of American history"—the direct primary.[2] Accompanying the introduction of direct primaries for such offices as member of the United States House of Representatives, governor, state legislator, and mayor, was the introduction of presidential primaries by a number of states. A key objective was to reform, revitalize, and enhance American democracy.

Presidential primaries to choose delegates to national nominating conventions were used by twelve states in 1912. From 1916 through 1968, between thirteen and twenty states used presidential primaries, with roughly 35% to 45% of delegates (a minority, but a significant minority nevertheless) to the national conventions typically being chosen in primaries.[3] Because the remaining delegates were party organization activists, this era in the history of the presidential nominating process has been called the "mixed system."

Although reformers had managed, for the first time, to introduce mass popular involvement in choosing a sizable proportion of delegates to national conventions, their efforts did not result in all delegates being selected by voters in primaries. Even this "mixed system," however, introduced mass involvement in the process for nominating presidential candidates to an unprecedented extent and to a degree unrivalled in

the nomination process for any other nation's highest elected government office.

In practice, since no candidate of either party's nomination was likely to win every delegate chosen in presidential primaries and, until 1936, Democratic convention rules required a successful candidate to win two-thirds of the delegates' votes, major party nominees during the "mixed system" era typically had to gain substantial support among those delegates coming from states that did not hold presidential primaries. Even so, "inside" and "outside" strategies for winning a party's nomination were possible. A candidate could concentrate on gaining support directly from the party organization regulars who would be attending the relevant national convention, an "inside" strategy illustrated by Hubert Humphrey's successful 1968 candidacy for the Democratic presidential nomination. Alternatively, a candidate could emphasize the primaries and seek to show sufficient electoral appeal in primary states to convince party leaders and the rest of the delegates to support his candidacy. Candidate Dwight Eisenhower used an "outside" strategy in winning the Republican presidential nomination in 1952, and candidate John F. Kennedy did likewise in winning the Democratic nomination in 1960.

The last year of the "mixed system" era, 1968, was a tumultuous and violent year in American politics. Opponents of the Vietnam War supported the anti-war candidacies of Senators Eugene McCarthy and Robert Kennedy for the Democratic presidential nomination. Kennedy was assassinated in June 1968 and, even though McCarthy or Kennedy had won virtually all the presidential primaries while taking strong anti-war positions, the "mixed system" left McCarthy with substantially less than a majority of delegates at the 1968 Democratic convention in Chicago. Adopting an "inside" strategy in seeking the Democratic party's presidential nomination that year, Vice President Hubert Humphrey did not oppose American involvement in the war being waged by his patron, President Lyndon Johnson, and did not compete in a single presidential primary. Yet Humphrey was duly nominated as his party's presidential candidate. The selection of Humphrey marked the end of the "mixed system" that had made his nomination possible.

The Fourth Era: The Plebiscitary Model for Choosing Delegates to the National Convention (1972–present)

Anti-war opponents of Hubert Humphrey waged vigorous protests in the streets of Chicago outside the 1968 Democratic convention and were violently subdued by Chicago police under the direction of Mayor Richard Daley, a Democrat and a leading supporter of Hubert Humphrey's nomination. As a consolation prize of sorts, the convention voted to establish a reform commission, which came to be known as the McGovern-Fraser Commission, reflecting the names of the two Democratic members of Congress—Senator George McGovern and Congressman Donald Fraser—who, in succession, chaired the commission.

The Commission's charge was to look for ways to make the selection of delegates to future Democratic conventions more transparent and democratic.

The McGovern-Fraser Commission uncovered and reported many interesting—some might say scandalous—points about how delegates were selected in various states and made recommendations about how to reform the system. The recommendations went into effect in 1972 and served to democratize the selection of delegates to the national conventions. (Even though the Commission was a Democratic party body, implementation of its recommendations affected the presidential nomination process for both major parties.) Presidential primaries were used to select a clear majority of delegates to national conventions. Those states not using primaries were required to open their party-run delegate selection procedures to all registered voters identifying with either party. These procedures became known as the "caucus/convention" alternative to presidential primaries, an alternative that Iowa, among other states, adopted. In effect, the McGovern-Fraser reforms completed the work of the early twentieth-century reformers, and a new era in the nominating process—the Plebiscitary Model—began in 1972, four years after the "mixed system" had led to the tumultuous and violence-marred nomination of Democrat Hubert Humphrey in Chicago. The name for this new era emphasizes the newly dominant role that the mass electorate could play in the reformed presidential nomination process, since "plebiscitarian" comes from the Latin word "plebs," which refers to the "common people."

A Closer Look at the Operation of the Plebiscitary Model

My central contention in this article is that changes in the functioning of the presidential nomination process in the first decade of the twenty-first century have been so significant that they signal or foreshadow the pending arrival of a new era, the *fifth*, in the history of the presidential nomination process. A brief examination of selected characteristics of the process in operation under the Plebiscitary Model will provide essential background for subsequently considering the major and noteworthy changes that are becoming apparent in 2007–2008.

My earlier discussion of the "mixed system" (ca. 1912–1968) and the "plebiscitary model" (1972–present) addressed changes in how delegates to national conventions were selected in the states. The "mixed system" began when a sizable minority of states introduced presidential primaries to select delegates to the national convention, thus opening the presidential nomination process to the public to an extent that was unique among the world's democracies. The "plebiscitary model" reformed the "mixed system" in ways that led a majority of states to adopt presidential primaries and required the remaining states to make their party-based caucus/convention systems accessible to all registered voters identifying with the relevant party.

Timing and Scheduling

By the 1950s, New Hampshire had established the "first-in-the-nation" status of its quadrennial presidential primary. Two decades later, Iowa successfully laid claim to scheduling its precinct caucuses, the initial stage of its caucus-convention system that operated over several months, shortly before the New Hampshire primary *and* before any other state started its delegate selection process. This Iowa-New Hampshire sequence has begun the delegate selection processes of the fifty states in every presidential election year since 1972. Candidates, news media, campaign contributors, pollsters, political activists, and the attentive public have all paid disproportionate attention to campaign activities and outcomes in these two states.

The sequence of other states' delegate selection processes has been more variable than the Iowa-first/New Hampshire-second part of the schedule, but a noteworthy phenomenon called "Super Tuesday" emerged in the 1980s. "Super Tuesday" came to refer to a Tuesday in March a few weeks after the New Hampshire primary on which a number of states (initially, mostly Southern states) scheduled their presidential primaries or caucuses. One initial objective was to increase the impact of "moderate" Southern states in the selection of the Democratic presidential nominee. With the introduction of Super Tuesday and ensuing variations in which states participated in Super Tuesday in a given presidential election year, the idea of more deliberately self-conscious and self-serving scheduling seemed to catch on. Some states (like California) that had traditionally held their delegate selection processes "late" (that is, in April, May, or June) began to schedule their selection processes earlier. These movements contributed to a phenomenon called "frontloading," which refers to crowding more and more state delegate selection processes into the months of January, February, and March, rather than having them spread out over the traditional February-through-June period.

After the Plebiscitary Model took hold in 1972, the sequence of delegate selection processes in the states seems to have become more visibly contentious among the states, the bunching of a number of states' primaries and caucuses on a single day became more prevalent (not only on "Super Tuesday," but on other single dates as well), and more delegate selection contests were "front-loaded" to the January-March period, while fewer occurred in April through June.

The "Invisible Primary"

Besides the acceptance of an Iowa–New Hampshire–Super Tuesday sequence in states' delegate selection processes, other expectations about broader matters of timing and scheduling in the presidential nomination process also developed. In the 1970s an observer coined the term "invisible primary" to refer to the activities of candidates and relevant others in the year or so *before* delegate selection processes began in Iowa and New Hampshire early in a presidential election year.[4] The "invisible primary" was, of course, not an actual presidential primary; that is, it was *not* an election run by a state government in which registered voters choose delegates to a national nominating convention. *Nor* was it "invisible." But the term, especially the word "invisible," is helpful in understanding how the presidential nomination process has been changing in the early twentieth-first century.

The term "invisible primary" conveyed the largely unnoticed—at least by the general public and to some extent news media—activities in which would-be presidential candidates engaged in the years before presidential general elections.

Would-be candidates met with party leaders, high-ranking government officials, potential campaign contributors, and the like to gain support for their possible candidacy. But typically the would-be candidates did not openly declare their candidacies until late in the year preceding a presidential general election, and media attention was sporadic and not particularly intense. To the average American, these activities were all but "invisible." Even so, the "invisible primary" was hardly irrelevant to the outcome of the presidential nomination process that culminated in the selection of the parties' presidential candidates. The resulting campaign experience, fund-raising, and endorsements, not to mention media commentators' impressions and evaluations, presumably influenced candidates' prospects when the actual state-by-state delegate selection processes began.

Campaign Financing

In 1974, in the aftermath of the Watergate scandal associated with President Richard Nixon and his 1972 re-election campaign, Congress passed the Federal Election Campaign Act, initiating a system of campaign finance regulation that continues in its broad outlines to this day. Subsequent court decisions, legislation (most notably, the Bipartisan Campaign Reform Act of 2002, otherwise known as the McCain-Feingold Act), and administrative regulations (issued mostly by the Federal Election Commission, a six-member government body established by the 1974 Act) have left a tangled and complicated set of rules that apply to the financing of campaigns for presidential nominations.

Campaigns for a presidential nomination became subject to a host of reporting and accounting requirements. The amount that individuals could contribute to a single candidate's campaign was limited, and the government provided "matching" funds to candidates if they met certain conditions in their initial fundraising and agreed to accept limits on their state-by-state and overall campaign spending. The system of matching funds was designed to prevent candidates or would-be candidates who lacked reasonably widespread support in a number of states from receiving government subsidies for their campaigns. To become eligible for matching funds, a candidate had to raise $5000 in contributions of $250 or less in each of twenty states. Thereafter, contributions of up to $250 were matched by an equal amount of government funding. These matching provisions were unique to campaigns for presidential nominations and applied to neither presidential general election nor congressional campaigns. And, to repeat for the sake of emphasis, a candidate's acceptance of matching funds brought restrictions, specifically an overall spending limit for the candidate's nomination campaign and a limit on the amount that s/he could spend in each state (based on each state's population).[5]

The era of the Plebiscitary Model began in 1972, but the matching provisions of the Federal Election Campaign Act of 1974 did not take effect until the 1976 presidential nomination contests. Approximately fifty "serious" candidates sought the Democratic and Republican presidential nominations between 1976 and 1992, and only one—Republican John Connally in 1980, who won only one delegate—did not accept matching funds while campaigning for the presidential nomination.[6] In 1996, the issue of matching funds became significant when

a very wealthy but relatively unknown candidate seeking the Republican presidential nomination, Steve Forbes, followed in Connally's footsteps and declined matching funds. In contrast, Republican Bob Dole, the well-known frontrunner for his party's nomination, accepted matching funds and their accompanying spending limits. Forbes poured millions of his own dollars into television advertising, which made Dole spend millions of dollars in response. Dole eventually and somewhat easily prevailed over Forbes and other contenders, but, by late March, 1996, he had spent almost all that he was legally allowed to spend until he was formally nominated by his party's national convention during the summer of 1996. This situation, many observers have noted, left him a sitting duck for several months of effective television advertising launched by the incumbent president, Bill Clinton, who had been unopposed for his party's renomination in 1996. In turn, Dole, who could not buy ads to respond to Clinton's barrage until the summer, fell hopelessly behind his formidable Democratic opponent before being officially nominated.[7]

Recent Changes in the Presidential Nomination Process

Three noteworthy recent changes in the presidential nomination process involve timing and scheduling, campaign financing, and interaction between the two: (1) an earlier start to campaigning and other candidate activities, (2) the introduction of "Super Duper Tuesday" in 2008, and (3) what has been termed the "collapse" of the system of matching funds in the financing of campaigns for the presidential nomination.[8] The first and third changes are not attributable solely to the 2007–2008 nominating cycle; both have their origins in earlier years, most particularly in the 2000 and 2004 contests. The second change, the introduction of "Super Duper Tuesday," stems more specifically from the 2007–08 nominating cycle. What I have termed a *sea change* in the process for nominating presidential candidates has been emerging during at least the two most recent presidential election cycles, while the extent and durability of the changes have become significantly more apparent during the on-going 2007–08 cycle.

An Earlier Start

One change in timing is straightforward and has been much reported: Candidates' serious and visible campaigning for presidential nominations was well under way by the beginning of 2007, a full calendar year before delegate selection processes were scheduled to begin early in the presidential election year of 2008. All sorts of activities associated with candidates' attempts to win their parties' nominations have been occurring earlier than in preceding nomination cycles.

Some candidates seeking to be elected president in 2008 declared their candidacies in late 2006. For example, former two-term Iowa governor Tom Vilsack, more than a political nonentity but less than a putative front-runner in the Democratic party's 2008 presidential nomination competition, announced his candidacy in November 2006 and officially withdrew on 23 February 2007. On the other hand, former Senator Fred

Thompson, whose name surfaced as a potentially formidable candidate for the Republican presidential nomination in the first half of 2007, delayed formal announcement of his candidacy until early September. Commentators wondered why he had waited so long to announce and whether it was too late. Major Democratic contenders John Edwards, Barack Obama, and Hillary Clinton, and major Republican contenders Mitt Romney, Rudy Giuliani, and John McCain all announced their candidacies before March 2007.[9]

Nationally televised debates among Republican and Democratic candidates were in full swing during the first half of 2007. By the summer of 2007, a half-dozen debates among Republican candidates and another half-dozen among Democratic candidates had been aired, with a similar number scheduled to occur in the second half of the year. Six to nine candidates participated in each of these events, which varied in sponsorship (from television stations to labor unions to Howard University) and format (from a single moderator to CNN's YouTube-based venture).

Finally, news media provided extensive coverage of nomination campaigns and the like during the period that used to be called the "invisible primary." Candidates' debate performances, poll results, policy positions, campaign fund-raising efforts, and other "horse race" aspects of the campaign were reported, and systematic comparisons of candidates' proposals on issues such as the Iraq war and health care reform were occasionally provided. In the summer of 2007, *The New York Times* conducted interviews with voters across the United States and reported that they were unusually engaged by the early campaigning as well as "flinching at the onslaught of this early politicking."[10]

The Collapse of the System of Matching Funds

In 2000, Republican candidate George W. Bush was the first presidential nominee of either major party who had not accepted matching funds during his campaign for his party's nomination. In 2003, two leading candidates for the Democratic nomination, Howard Dean and John Kerry, followed Bush's lead of four years earlier and opted out of matching funds. The 1996 predicament of Republican Bob Dole that resulted from his acceptance of matching funds and the accompanying spending limits doubtless influenced later decisions by candidates Bush, Dean, and Kerry. By the start of the 2007–2008 presidential nomination cycle, no major contender for either party's nomination was expected to accept matching funds, although eventually Democrat John Edwards decided to do so. By 2007, the path that Republican nominee Bush had taken in 2000 had become the norm for all but one major candidate. In turn, the system of spending limits that depend on candidates' acceptance of matching funds has been undermined and, in effect, probably ended, at least among major candidates.

Several additional observations about the end of the "old" system of presidential nomination financing are in order. In the absence of spending limits that would have accompanied acceptance of matching funds, fund-raising for 2007–08 presidential nomination campaigns grew enormously. Hillary Clinton's 2007 first quarter total of 26 million dollars and fellow Democrat candidate Barack Obama's close second of 25.6 million can be contrasted with 7.4 million, the total for candidate John Edwards, the leading Democratic fund-raiser in the first quarter of 2003, and 8.9 million, Democratic candidate Al Gore's total in the first quarter of 1999.

The maximum that a candidate could receive in matching funds in the 2007–08 nomination cycle was approximately 21 million dollars. When almost all of the front-running candidates of both parties opted out of the matching system, they were concluding that that amount of partial public funding was not a sufficient reason to accept matching funds. More valuable than 21 million dollars of public funding was the freedom not to abide by the spending limits that accompanied the acceptance of matching funds. Through the end of the third quarter of 2007, Clinton had raised 90.6 million dollars and Obama 80.3 million, while the two candidates who were leading the Republican field in fund-raising, Mitt Romney and Rudy Giuliani, had raised 62.8 million and 45.8 million dollars, respectively.[11]

The demise of the "matching" system for financing campaigns for the presidential nomination cannot be attributed solely to the 2007–08 presidential nomination cycle. Foreshadowed by the predicament in which Republican candidate Bob Dole found himself in March 1996, the "collapse" of the matching system is an early twenty-first century phenomenon that culminated in 2007–08.

The Money Primary

Amidst earlier declarations of candidacy (and, sometimes, withdrawals), earlier and numerous televised debates, earlier extensive media coverage, and the collapse of the system of matching funds, a new term was coined to replace "invisible primary" as a name for the early period of the presidential nomination process—the "money primary." Federal Election Commission (FEC) regulations require quarterly reports of candidates' fund-raising activities in the years preceding presidential general elections (and monthly reports in presidential election years). As 31 March 2007 approached, journalists anticipated the required candidate filings and what they would show in fund-raising prowess and contributors' support. News media reported and analyzed candidates' first-quarter filings with the FEC against a background of different fund-raising expectations for different candidates. On the Democratic side, Barack Obama was judged to have performed especially well, raising 25.6 million dollars, just a little less than front-runner Hillary Clinton and substantially more than John Edward's 14 million. On the Republican side, candidate John McCain fell short of fund-raising expectations and prospects for his candidacy were discounted accordingly, while competitor Mitt Romney's stock rose on account of his first quarter fund-raising total of 20.7 million dollars, six million more than the amount raised by the second-place finisher at that stage of the Republican money primary, Rudy Giuliani.[12]

Through all the changes, news media retained their prominent role as assessors of the nominating competition. Years earlier, when the term *invisible primary* applied, news media had been dubbed the "Great Mentioner" because of their role in identifying candidacies that should be taken seriously. For a candidate not to be mentioned by journalists was like being afflicted with a politically terminal illness. In 2007, news media assessments continued to help the attentive public gauge the ongoing horse race among candidates. Poll results—both national polls and polls in the early caucus and primary states of Iowa, New Hampshire, and South Carolina—and the results of the quarterly "money primaries" were combined with other information and intuitions to make assessments of who was winning, who was gaining or losing ground, and the like. What seemed new in 2007 was the extent of early candidate activity, including the plethora of televised debates in the first half of the year and especially the salience of the "money primary." Campaigns for the two major parties' presidential nominations seemed to be in full swing early in 2007, nearly two years before the November 2008 general election and a year before the states' delegate selection processes were set to begin in Iowa in January 2008.

Super Duper Tuesday and Related Matters

What should probably, because of the earlier start to full-scale campaigning, be called the *2007–2008* presidential nomination process also brought noteworthy change in the clustering of delegate selection processes in the states. During the 1988 presidential nominating process, sixteen mostly Southern states scheduled their delegate selection processes on a single day in early March that was called "Super Tuesday." Such clustering of many states' primaries and caucuses on a single day continued to occur in subsequent years and "Super Tuesday" became a quadrennial event. In 2004, a second, smaller clustering of states on a single Tuesday in March after Super Tuesday was dubbed "mini-Tuesday."

Prior to 2008, the sequence of delegate selection processes in the states during the era of the Plebiscitary Model typically had the following pattern: Iowa; New Hampshire; and, fairly soon thereafter, "Super Tuesday," which grew beyond its original Southern focus to include more non-Southern states. Super Tuesday was sometimes decisive—and sometimes not—in determining eventual presidential nominees, and outcomes in Iowa and especially New Hampshire continued to play disproportionately influential roles.

The phenomenon of Super Tuesday, coupled with a general tendency in the direction of more and more "frontloading," led in 2008 to what was variously dubbed "Super Duper Tuesday," "Tsunami Tuesday," and even "Unofficial National Primary Day." By mid-2007, at least twenty states that together accounted for more than 50% of the delegates to each national convention had scheduled their delegate selection processes for 5 February 2008, a short time after Iowa, New Hampshire, Nevada, and South Carolina were scheduled to hold their delegate selection processes.

As of this writing in November, 2007, the significance of Super Duper Tuesday remains to be seen, but the outcomes of twenty-odd states' delegate selection processes on that day may well be decisive. In other words, 5 February 2008 may become the functional equivalent of a national presidential primary in which, as a consequence of voters casting ballots in at least twenty states *on a single day,* the presidential nominees of both major parties will be determined.

The idea of holding a succession of regional primaries (for example, four of them, each including a contiguous bloc of states in which approximately one-fourth of the population of the United States lives) or a single national primary is not new. Both ideas have been advocated as possible reforms to the presidential nomination process, often with an eye to reducing or eliminating the disproportionate impact of Iowa and New Hampshire. The creation of "Super Duper Tuesday" on 5 February 2008 resulted from decisions by individual states and small groups of states to hold their delegate selection processes on that date, rather than from any single, coordinated reform effort. As the magnitude and implications of "Super Duper Tuesday" came into focus, California, New York, and Florida, among other states, began to re-think the scheduling of *their* 2008 delegate selection processes.

The outline of the Florida story, as of this writing (November, 2007), bears reporting. In May, 2007, the Florida legislature scheduled its presidential primaries for 29 January 2008. Doing so violated both major parties' rule that only Iowa, New Hampshire, Nevada, and South Carolina could hold delegate selection processes before 5 February 2008. In August 2007, the Democratic national party decided that any Florida delegates elected before 5 February 2008 would not be seated at the 2008 Democratic national convention. In late September, the Florida Democratic Party announced its continuing support for holding the Florida presidential primaries on the forbidden 29 January date.[13] The final outcome of this controversy remains to be seen, but one reporter suggested that it might eventually result in the end of Iowa's and New Hampshire's traditional primacy in the presidential nomination calendar.[14]

A Sea Change and a New Era

I have pointed to three recent and significant changes in the presidential nomination process: (1) earlier sustained and public campaigning by candidates, so that public declarations of candidacies and serious campaigning are well underway two years before a presidential general election, (2) the establishment of what may function as an "unofficial national primary" early in February 2008, which reflects the convergence or perhaps even culmination of two earlier trends: (i) increased "frontloading" of the states' delegate selection processes and (ii) growing inclination of states to schedule their delegate selection processes on a single day a few weeks after Iowa and New Hampshire in an attempt to reduce the disproportionate influence of those two states in the outcome of the presidential nomination process, and (3) the demise of the system of matching funds that had anchored the regulation of presidential nomination campaign financing since the passage of the Federal Election Campaign Act in 1974.

What are the implications of these changes? Why might they matter? A simple answer is that these changes will likely affect the sort of individuals who are likely to be nominated and perhaps those who are likely to run. More specifically, the new era, whose beginnings have, in my view, become clearly visible in the 2007–08 cycle, will give the "dark horse," the underdog, the relatively little-known presidential aspirant, less chance to be nominated.

"Dark horses" emerged frequently enough during the "mixed system" era (1912–1968) to make them a staple of political lore: Sometimes such candidates emerged after an unexpectedly strong showing in important primaries, sometimes after party bosses and delegates at a deadlocked convention turned their backs on the two or three leading contenders and sought a "new face" whom supporters of the leading contenders could accept.

Under the Plebiscitary Model, the dramatic increase in the number of delegates chosen by the mass electorate meant that the outcome of early delegate selection processes, especially in Iowa and New Hampshire, led to successful nominations of Democratic dark horse candidates George McGovern and Jimmy Carter in 1972 and 1976, respectively. Little known Democrat Bill Clinton's nomination in 1992 was also a largely unexpected outcome. Yet each won their party's nomination by successfully navigating the sequence of states' delegate selection processes that operated under the Plebiscitary Model. Carter's first-place finish among candidates in Iowa in 1976 ("undecided" was Iowans' first choice), followed by his win in the New Hampshire primary, put the relatively unknown former governor of Georgia on track to be nominated. McGovern's 1972 and Clinton's 1992 successful quests to be nominated followed roughly similar scripts.

Why does the current sea change in the presidential nomination process threaten such dark horse candidacies? Let me begin with the existence of "Super Duper Tuesday," which may function *almost* as a national primary in 2008. So-called retail politics can work in small states such as Iowa and New Hampshire. The little known candidate can, by dint of arduous campaigning, impress attentive Iowa and New Hampshire voters by shaking hands, attending small meetings in people's homes, knocking on doors, and the like. It has been said (almost surely apocryphally) that an Iowa or New Hampshire voter does not take a presidential nomination candidate seriously until the voter has shaken the candidate's hand at least twice! In such a "retail politics" environment, the advantages of initial name recognition, endorsements from leading national political figures, money, and even campaign organization are less important than in the "wholesale politics" required by big state primaries or multiple-state primaries held on a single day. To the extent that "Super Duper Tuesday" approximates a national primary and the wholesale politics that that would entail, the chances of a dark horse or little-known candidate are lessened. Perhaps, as some observers have suggested, the Iowa-New Hampshire-Nevada-South Carolina-Super Duper Tuesday sequence in 2008 will not result in 5 February 2008 functioning as a national presidential primary. Perhaps it will. Regardless, Super Duper Tuesday seems to constitute movement in the direction of a national primary (or at least a series of regional primaries, which would also require wholesale politics), with such a development working to undermine dark horse candidacies.

The collapse of the system of matching funds also seems to disadvantage dark horse or underdog candidacies. Well-known front-runners typically can raise more money than less well-known underdogs. Even so, the matching system worked to narrow the gap between the campaign resources of front-runners and those of underdogs.

The third change in the presidential nomination process that I have identified—the earlier start of full-scale campaigning and resulting news media attention—might on first glance seem to enhance the chances of potential dark horse candidates. The longer the campaigning, it would seem, the more likely an underdog could out-perform better known opponents and overcome their greater resources both over the long haul and in the face of simultaneous contests in a large number of states on "Super Duper Tuesday." In addition, the argument might continue, if such an underdog performed well in the early going, the resource gap between him/her and his/her better known opponents would likely be lessened.

The counter-argument would run in an opposite direction. The superior resources of the front-running candidates and the earlier start to the campaign make it all the more unlikely that an underdog can win. The front-running candidates have more time during which to effectively spend their resources on TV ads and the like, and more time for their larger and better-financed on-the-ground organizations to produce effects. Moreover, news media identification of the top tier of candidates, based partly on the results of the money primary, has longer to sink in with the mass public and, perhaps, become the received wisdom. Finally, the earlier start to serious campaigning means that an underfinanced, underdog candidate needs to compete that much longer against better known, better financed candidates without the prospect of a headline-grabbing victory or at least an unexpectedly strong showing in Iowa or New Hampshire. Instead, the demoralizing effects of the well-publicized money primary undermine underdogs' credibility, often to the point of no return.

As should be clear, I am less certain about the effects of the lengthened nomination campaign season on dark horse candidacies than I am about the effects of an "unofficial national primary" and the demise of the system of matching funds. But, taken as a whole, recent changes in the nomination process that, in my judgment, constitute—or, at the very least, foreshadow—a sea change seem destined to undermine underdog candidacies.

Before closing, let me do one more brief round of "so what?" analysis. Suppose one wanted to change the operation of the Plebiscitary Model to eliminate virtually any chance of underdog candidates such as George McGovern (1972), Jimmy Carter (1976), and, in the 2007–08 cycle, Democrats Tom Vilsack and Chris Dodd and Republicans Tommy Thompson and Sam Brownback, four seasoned politicians with relevant government experience, but little name recognition among the public. To accomplish such an objective, one might introduce the recent changes in the presidential nomination process identified in this article. The latest sea change in the presidential nomination process may relate especially to the sorts of qualities major party presidential nominees need to have. If widespread name recognition and celebrity status—both of which, to be sure, can result from high profile experience in government, a point that sometimes is overlooked—and/or moneyed connections sufficient to raise vast sums of contributions are to be essential characteristics for a presidential nominee, then the nomination process is moving in an accommodating direction.

Perhaps the fifth era in the history of the presidential nomination process will come to be known as "the post-dark horse era," "the celebrity candidate era," "the national (or regional) primary era," or even "the era after the demise of Iowa's and New Hampshire's primacy." Whatever the new era comes to be called and whatever exact shape it takes, please do not say that no one told you it was coming.

Notes

1. The overview of the history of the American presidential nomination process presented here and continued below draws substantially from Bruce Stinebrickner, "The Presidential Nominating Process: Past and Present," *World Review* 19, No. 4 (October 1980), pp. 78–102.

2. The quotation comes from Austin Ranney, as quoted in Stinebrickner, p. 80. Austin Ranney, *Curing the Mischiefs of Faction: Party Reform in America* (Berkeley, California: University of California Press, 1975), p. 121.

3. For a table displaying exact numbers of states using presidential primaries for every presidential election year between 1912 and 2004, see "Table 3-1 Votes Cast and Delegates Selected in Presidential Primaries, 1912–2004," in *Presidential Elections, 1789–2004* (Washington, D.C.: CQ Press, 2005), p. 104.

4. See Arthur T. Hadley, *The Invisible Primary* (Englewood Cliffs, NJ: Prentice Hall, 1976).

5. For more details, see David B. Magleby and William G. Mayer, "Presidential Nomination Finance in the Post-BCRA Era," in William G. Mayer, ed., *The Making of the Presidential Candidates 2008* (Lanham, Maryland: Rowman and Littlefield, 2008), pp. 141–168. The summary of the matching provisions given here is drawn largely from pp. 142–143.

6. Magleby and Mayer, p. 144.

7. This Forbes-Dole-Clinton account is taken largely from Magleby and Mayer, pp. 149–152.

8. Magleby and Mayer use the subtitle "The *Collapse* of the Matching Fund Program" on p. 149 of their chapter (emphasis added). Martin Frost, former member of the U.S. House of Representatives and former chairman of the Democratic Congressional Campaign Committee, observed early in 2007 that it would not be a surprise if the matching system for presidential nomination process financing "simply disappears" after the 2007–08 cycle. "Federal Financing of Presidential Campaigns May Be History," FoxNews.com, 8 January 2007: 23 September 2007, <http://www.foxnews.com>.

9. Announcements signaling a candidacy for a party's 2008 presidential nomination often occurred at more than a single point in time. Several candidates made a combination of announcements, presumably to increase the increments of media attention that such announcements were expected to produce. A single candidate's announcements in 2007 might include the following: that s/he was going to make an "important announcement" in a few days, that s/he was going to begin "exploring" whether to become a candidate (or that s/he was forming an "exploratory committee" to "test the waters"), that s/he had "decided" to become a candidate, and that s/he was "formally" declaring his or her candidacy.

10. Adam Nagourney. "Voters Excited Over '08 Race; Tired of It, Too." *The New York Times*, 9 July 2007, A1.

11. Federal Election Commission: 29 November 2007, http://www.fec.gov/finance/disclosure/srssea.shtml/.

12. "First Quarter 2007 FEC Filings," *Washington Post*: 30 September 2007 <http://projects.washingtonpost.com/2008-presidential-candidates/finance/2007/q1/>.

13. Abby Goodnough, "Florida Democrats Affirm an Early Primary," *The New York Times,* 24 September 2007, A12.

14. "World News", ABC, WRTV, Indianapolis, 24 September 2007, correspondent Jake Tapper: "Democrats are convinced that this is the beginning of the end of the Iowa-New Hampshire monopoly."

I want to thank Luke Beasley, Allison Clem, Annie Glausser, Christina Guzik, Kelsey Kauffman, David Parker, Amy Robinson, and Randall Smith for their helpful comments on an earlier draft of this article. I also want to thank Luke Beasley for his work in locating presidential candidates' announcement dates for the four most recent presidential elections.

Shakedown on K Street

Even in the face of the Abramoff scandal, lawmakers are still using high-pressure tactics to squeeze donations out of Washington lobbyists.

RICHARD S. DUNHAM, EAMON JAVERS, AND LORRAIN WOELLERT

The conventional wisdom: Crass corporate lobbyists lavish millions of dollars on lawmakers in a transparent attempt to buy influence on Capitol Hill. But in the carpeted corridors of K Street, the 11,500 people who earn their living in the influence-peddling profession know a different reality. More often than not, they understand that money is vacuumed up to Capitol Hill by demands from members of Congress. "Everybody thinks it's the interest groups buying the members," says John J. Pitney Jr., a political scientist at Claremont McKenna College in Claremont, Calif. "A lot of the time it's the members shaking down the interest groups."

Despite the guilty plea of fallen superlobbyist Jack Abramoff, Capitol Hill doesn't hesitate to turn to K Street for campaign cash. One prominent business lobbyist was so aggravated by attacks on his brethren by money-raising members of Congress that he collected every fund-raising invitation letter he received for a month. The total for January: more than 60. He dutifully sent checks for most even though he says that he has never asked half of those lawmakers for anything. "I'm doing it because it's expected," he laments. "If you want to be in the game, you've got to pay."

That game can be expensive. One Washington lobbyist who asked not to be identified says he gave money to the unsuccessful Democratic candidate for a House seat. After the election, the Republican winner called to demand a check—bigger than the original gift. Why? "The late train is a hell of a lot more expensive than the early train," the lobbyist says he was told.

Lawmaker solicitations are legion and often quite creative. Take the case of House Financial Services Chairman Michael G. Oxley (R-Ohio) and his book club. Each month a junior member of Oxley's committee picks a book and distributes copies to financial lobbyists to read and discuss. The price of admission is a contribution to the featured member. The lobbyists get face time with Oxley, who largely controls the Washington agenda for their industries. Oxley, who is retiring after 2006, wins the loyalty of his low-ranking colleagues by helping them score contributions. But the sessions are hardly educational: Panel members' tastes run more to motivational screeds than to tomes on finance, attendees say. "I've never read one of the books," says a regular. "Are you kidding me? Read? I went to law school."

Advancing literacy in the legal profession isn't the point. While Oxley has never personally pressured him to ante up, says another financial-services lobbyist, he feels compelled to attend. "I feel like I have to give, even though I never otherwise would, because it's coming from Oxley," the lobbyist says. Oxley aides did not return repeated calls for comment.

If Oxley has created a group of reluctant bookworms, House Energy & Commerce Committee Chairman Joe Barton (R-Tex.) has revived the charm of an old-fashioned ride on the rails at newfangled prices. For just $2,000 a person (or $5,000 per PAC), lobbyists were given the opportunity on Jan. 20 to spend almost eight hours with the chairman aboard a train bound for San Antonio from Fort Worth. In a glossy brochure Barton described the event, which included a rolling game of Texas Hold 'Em and an after-hours visit to the Alamo, as "a hot ticket." Barton's campaign consultant did not respond to repeated requests for comment.

A not-so-movable feast was hosted by Senate Judiciary Committee Chairman Arlen Specter (R-Pa.). Lobbyists for warring sides of the asbestos trust fund legislation were invited to a $500-a-head, $1,000-per-PAC event at Specter's Georgetown apartment on Feb. 6. Specter says it was coincidental that his annual birthday fund-raiser was scheduled one day before the Senate debated the asbestos bill, which Specter co-sponsored. "No special group has been targeted," Specter says.

Republicans have no monopoly on Washington's fund-raising bazaar. One lobbyist recently received an invitation for a Mar. 8 fund-raiser for Representative William J. Jefferson (D-La.) at Democratic National Committee headquarters. The invitation prominently noted Jefferson's service on the tax-writing House Ways & Means Committee. It did not mention that a federal grand jury may be probing his dealings with U.S. businesses trying to land contracts in Africa. A former Jefferson aide has pleaded guilty to aiding and abetting bribery of a federal official. Jefferson has denied wrongdoing. Both his congressional office and campaign fund-raiser declined to comment.

Such invitations are the rule, not the exception, in Washington, where campaign shops churn out fancy engraved invitations and spam e-mail targeting K Street. One GOP lobbyist says that in prime fund-raising season he receives five to six e-mails a

Deep Pockets

Top 10 Corporate Political Givers* in the 2004 Election Cycle

Company	Millions
Goldman Sachs	$6.5
Microsoft	3.5
Morgan Stanley	3.4
Time Warner	3.4
JPMorgan Chase	3.1
Citigroup	2.9
Bank of America	2.7
UBS Communications	2.5
SBC Communications	2.4
United Parcel Service	2.4

*Includes corporate PAC contributions and gifts of $200 or more by individuals reporting a relationship with the company

Data: Center for Responsive Politics, from Federal Election Commission filings
The McGraw-Hill Companies, Copyright 2006

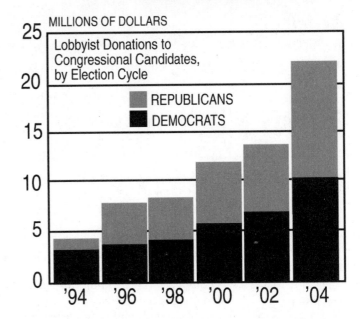

Figure 1 Capital Investment (Lobbyist Donations to Congressional Candidates, by Election Cycle, '94 to '04).

Source: Data Center for Responsive Politics.

day from the Bellwether Consulting Group, a GOP fund-raising firm in Washington. "I don't open 'em. Delete, delete, delete," he says.

Sometimes the squeeze isn't the least bit subtle. One lobbyist, who requested anonymity, returned from a meeting with a Democratic senator to find a message on the office voice mail saying where the check could be sent.

Capitol Hill's high-pressure tactics aren't new. Former House Majority Leader Tony Coelho (D-Calif.) first targeted the lobbying community in the mid-1980s when he chaired the Democratic Congressional Campaign Committee. But the squeeze tightened after the Republicans won control of Congress in 1994 and launched the K Street Project to reverse the lobbying community's pro-Democrat tilt. Tactics masterminded by Representative Tom DeLay (R-Tex.) and Senator Rick Santorum (R-Pa.) fueled a tenfold increase in lobbyists' donations to Republicans over a decade, from $1.2 million to $11.6 million, according to the Center for Responsive Politics.

Lawmakers strongly deny exerting undue pressure. They say they need to solicit lobbyists because of the skyrocketing cost of campaigns, particularly television advertising. "Unless and until we stop the outrageous expense of political campaigning in America, we're going to continue to be beholden to those who are well-off and well-connected," says Senator Dick Durbin (D-Ill.). "You've got to spend a lot of time on the phone begging for money."

But grasping politicians can't put all the blame on expensive campaigns. Most incumbents choose to raise oodles of cash to discourage serious competition and to create bulging war chests to pass along to colleagues. The benefit: They collect chits for future leadership contests.

Some lobbyists are having second thoughts about today's pay-to-play mind-set. "As a conservative, I've always opposed government involvement," says Stanton D. Anderson, a Washington business lobbyist. "But it seems to me that the real answer to this so-called lobbyist reform crisis is federal financing of congressional elections."

That kind of radical change won't happen in Republican Washington. Even proposals to bar lobbyists from donating to lawmakers or raising money for them have little chance of winning votes among the incumbents whose seats are protected by the current system. But some denizens of K Street wouldn't mind a ban. "Please, make it illegal for lobbyists to give money to political campaigns," says one Republican business rep. "Make my day."

With **LORRAINE WOELLERT,** in Washington.

Born Fighting

RONALD BROWNSTEIN

Apart from his political skills, two forces above all have propelled Barack Obama in his once-improbable quest for the presidency.

One is on vivid display this week: a wave of dissatisfaction with the country's direction that has created a visceral demand for change. That wave has reached towering heights amid the financial crisis roiling Wall Street and consuming Washington. No other candidate has drawn more power than Obama has from that desire to shift course.

With much less fanfare, this week also marked a milestone in the evolution of the second force that has lifted Obama: the rise of the Internet as a political tool of unparalleled power for organizing a vast activist and donor base.

Ten years ago this week, Wes Boyd and Joan Blades, two California-based software developers (their company created the "Flying Toaster" screensaver), posted an online petition opposing the drive by congressional Republicans to impeach President Clinton. The one-sentence petition urged Congress instead to censure Clinton and "move on." Within days the couple had collected hundreds of thousands of names. Thus was formed MoveOn.org, the first true 21st-century political organization.

Born fighting, MoveOn has become the point of the spear for the Democratic Left through eight years of combat with President Bush over issues from Iraq to Social Security. No group has been more influential, innovative, or controversial in devising the Internet-based organizing strategies that are precipitating the new age of mass political participation symbolized by Obama's immense network of contributors and volunteers. "In the evolution of this, they were there at the very beginning," says veteran Democratic strategist Joe Trippi.

MoveOn's political impact must be measured on two levels: message and mechanics. The group's techniques draw praise in both parties. Boyd and Blades, and later Eli Pariser, a young organizer who has become MoveOn's leading force, recognized that the Internet created unprecedented opportunities for organizing. Traditionally, causes and candidates faced daunting expenses in trying to find like-minded people through advertising, direct mail, or canvassing. But the Internet reversed the equation: Once MoveOn established itself at the forefront of liberal activism, millions of people who shared its views found it at little (or no) cost to the group.

"Our observation was: Whenever we fight, we get stronger."

—Wes Boyd, MoveOn.org founder

Indeed, MoveOn quickly discovered that the more fights it pursued, the more names it collected—and the more it increased its capacity to undertake new campaigns. "There's this old model of political capital: Every time you fight, you are spending something," Boyd says. "Our observation was: Whenever we fight, we get stronger."

Fueled by this dynamic, MoveOn routinely generates levels of activity almost unimaginable not long ago. Since 1998, it has raised $120 million; it mobilized 70,000 volunteers for its get-out-the-vote effort in 2004, and might triple that number this year. It now stands at 4.2 million members, after adding 1 million, mostly through social-networking sites, this year.

The purposes to which MoveOn applies these vast resources are more debatable. The group has become a favored target for Republicans and a source of anxiety for some Democratic centrists, who worry that it points the party too far left. On domestic issues, it fits within the Democratic mainstream. But on national security, it defines the party's left flank. MoveOn resisted military action not only in Iraq but also in Afghanistan. And on both foreign and domestic concerns, it often frames issues in terms so polarizing that it risks alienating all but the most committed believers. The group's lowest moment came in 2007 when it bought a newspaper ad disparaging Gen. David Petraeus, the U.S. commander in Iraq, as "General Betray Us" on the grounds that he would attempt to mislead Congress about the war. Petraeus's brilliant subsequent progress in stabilizing

Iraq has only magnified the unseemliness of that accusation. "I wouldn't have done the headline the exact same way," Pariser now concedes.

Still, as candidates and groups in both parties adapt its strategies for online organizing, MoveOn can justly claim a central role in igniting the surge in grassroots activism that is transforming American politics. "Regardless of your political convictions, you have to feel like this is a very healthy thing for democracy," Pariser says. MoveOn's causes may divide, but Democrats and even many Republicans are increasingly uniting around the bottom-up vision of political change that these ardent activists have helped to revive.

Why They Lobby

WINTER CASEY

Thank You for Smoking, the 2005 film based on a novel by Christopher Buckley, follows the life of Nick Naylor, a chief spokesman for Big Tobacco with questionable morals, who makes his living defending the rights of smokers and cigarette-makers and then must deal with how his young son, Joey, views him. Naylor may have been a fictitious character, but Washington has its share of lobbyists arguing for the interests of industries with a perceived darker side.

The cynical response in Washington is that career decisions and political give-and-take revolve around money: Greenbacks triumph over ethics. There is little argument from lobbyists that their profession's financial rewards have an undeniable allure. But those who represent socially sensitive industries such as tobacco and alcohol have a lot more to say about why, out of all the potential job opportunities, they chose and often "love" what they do.

Representing "sin" industries, such as tobacco, alcohol, or gambling, can provide a challenge like no other.

For some, the job is a result of personal history or connections. For others, lobbying on behalf of a difficult industry provides a challenge like no other. They all make it a point to note that the First Amendment sanctions lobbying: "the right of the people . . . to petition the government for a redress of grievances."

Tobacco

In the film, Naylor works for the Academy of Tobacco Studies, which Buckley based on the Tobacco Institute, the industry's former trade association. Andrew Zausner, a partner at the firm Dickstein Shapiro (which occupies some of the Tobacco Institute's old space), is a registered lobbyist for Lorillard Tobacco, the Cigar Association of America, and Swisher International. He has been working on behalf of tobacco clients for nearly 30 years, ever since he fell into the industry when he was a partner at a New York City law firm that represented Pinkerton Tobacco.

Zausner feeds off the challenge of lobbying for tobacco interests. "The more unpopular the client, the better you have to be as a lobbyist," he declares. "Believing in your client's position makes you a more forceful advocate." Although Zausner doesn't want his children to use tobacco, he notes that the "product has been continuously used in the United States before the United States existed" and says that the industry has a legitimate point of view and a constitutional right to express it.

Beau Schuyler lobbies for UST Public Affairs, a subsidiary of the holding company that owns U.S. Smokeless Tobacco and Ste. Michelle Wine Estates. A former congressional aide to two Democratic House members from his native state of North Carolina—in the heart of tobacco country—Schuyler says that the "opportunity to work internally at one of the oldest continually listed companies on the New York Stock Exchange was just too good to pass up."

Gambling

James Reeder, a lobbyist at Patton Boggs, has spent about half his time over the past decade representing the gambling industry. He insists he didn't seek out this niche, adding, "I tell my grandchildren that gambling is a bad habit . . . and to go fishing."

Shortly after Reeder joined Patton Boggs, a client named Showboat called the firm looking for someone who knew about Louisiana because the company was interested in building a casino there. Reeder happened to be from the Pelican State and was put on the case. He reasoned that Louisiana has always been a home to illegal gambling, and "if the culture of the state supports the industry, [the state] might as well make it legal and reap the benefits and get more tax money." Reeder eventually lobbied in about 17 states to get legislation passed to allow casinos—then mostly on riverboats.

"Whenever you take on one of these vices like booze or gambling and you just pass a law to say it is illegal," Reeder says, "you end up like in Prohibition, when the mob took over the liquor business."

Reeder excelled at lobbying for the gambling industry even though he avoids games of chance. "I don't gamble, because I am not a good card player," he says. "My friends would die laughing because I would go to offices to talk to clients on gambling and I would never go into a casino." If a lawmaker was morally opposed to gambling, Reeder wouldn't argue with him, he says.

John Pappas began working for the industry as a consultant for the Poker Players Alliance while at Dittus Communications. Then the alliance asked him to open its own Washington office.

Pappas calls poker a game of skill that has a rich history in America. He grew up playing cards with family members and friends, and noted during an interview that he would be playing poker with 20 lawmakers that evening at a charity tournament. "Responsibility in all aspects of life is paramount," he says.

Firearms

Richard Feldman's book, *Ricochet: Confessions of a Gun Lobbyist,* has been gaining the former National Rifle Association employee some attention recently. Feldman says that the gun control issue, like most, is not black and white. Working for the NRA, he says, "was the best job I ever had." The "huge power" he was able to wield "in the middle of major political battles" was more attractive to him at the time than the money he earned.

Feldman says he would sometimes play hardball but "didn't hit below the belt" in his pursuit of the gun industry's objectives. "Lobbying an issue that you have some special passion on (guns) is like waking up every day already having consumed a triple espresso," he said in an e-mail to *National Journal.* "On the other hand, if you can empathize with your client's position regardless of the issue, one can be a more convincing advocate, which I've always viewed as the more critical aspect of truly effective lobbying.

John Velleco ran his own painting company before he took a job in 1993 as an intern at the Gun Owners of America. Today, he is director of federal affairs for the 350,000-member group. "Most people, no matter what side of any particular issue they're on, don't always have the time to sort through what's happening in the D.C. sausage factory, so they depend on groups like GOA to keep them informed," he says. "Politicians may not like it, but my job is not to represent the views of the Congress to the people, but the views of American gun owners to the Congress."

Video Games

Because many video games contain a fair share of gunplay and other violence, Entertainment Software Association President Michael Gallagher has had to address complaints that playing violent games causes psychological harm such as increased aggression.

His group lobbies against "efforts to regulate the content of entertainment media in any form, including proposals to criminalize the sale of certain video games to minors; create uniform, government-sanctioned entertainment rating systems; or regulate the marketing practices of industry."

Gallagher, a former assistant Commerce secretary for communications and information in the Bush administration, calls video games a great form of family entertainment. The titles are responsibly rated, he says, and the gaming consoles have easy-to-use parental controls.

"I have been playing video games all my life," Gallagher says, including with his children. He contends that his industry "leads all forms of media when it comes to disclosure on what's in the game" and says that it works with retailers to "make sure minors can't buy games that are inappropriate for them."

Alcohol

Lobbyists who work for the beer, wine, and spirits industries have to deal with a host of negative images, among them drunk-driving accidents, underage drinking, and the effects of alcohol on health.

Lobbyists say their work is protected by the First Amendment—the right to "petition the government for a redress of grievances."

Mike Johnson, a lobbyist for the National Beer Wholesalers Association, acknowledges that alcohol is a "socially sensitive product" and says that is why the industry operates under strict government guidelines.

"I am blessed. I get to represent some great family-owned and -operated businesses that are very active in their communities and provide some really great jobs," Johnson says. "I am completely comfortable one day having a conversation with my son about who I work for, because I can tell him what a great job that beer distributors do in ensuring a safe marketplace and in protecting consumers from a lot of the problems we see with alcohol in other places in the world."

Craig Wolf, president of the Wine & Spirits Wholesalers, calls alcohol a "great social lubricant" that "creates great environments." Wolf got involved in wine-industry issues when he was counsel for the Senate Judiciary Committee. As his job there was ending, Wolf was offered the post of general counsel at the association; he took over as president in 2006.

"The key to advocating for a socially sensitive product is doing business responsibility," Wolf says. "We spend more time and resources [on the issue of] responsible consumption of alcohol then all other issues combined."

Distilled Spirits Council President Peter Cressy says, "I was interviewed for this position precisely because the Distilled Council wanted to continue and increase its very serious approach to fighting underage drinking." As chancellor of the University of Massachusetts (Dartmouth), Cressy says, he was active in "fighting binge drinking on campuses." The opportunity to join the council, which has lobbyists in 40 states, gave him the chance to have a national audience, he says. After nine years with the council, Cressy notes, he "has not been disappointed."

Snack Foods

Nicholas Pyle stands at the policy divide where junk food meets America's bulging waistlines. "I love my job," says Pyle, a lobbyist for McKee Foods, the makers of Little Debbie, America's leading snack-cake brand.

Many of the brand's affordable treats contain a dose of sugar, along with corn syrup, partially hydrogenated oil, bleached flour, and artificial flavor. Little Debbie "has been the target of a number of folks out there who want to paint people as a victim of the foods they eat," says Pyle, who is also president of the Independent Bakers Association. Little Debbie is a "wonderful food, great product, wholesome," with a wonderful image, he says. Pyle explains that he and his children enjoy the snacks.

"The big question of obesity is all about personal responsibility and people balancing [snacking] with a healthy and active lifestyle," Pyle insists. He contends that McKee, a family-owned business, doesn't target children in its marketing. "We market to the decision makers in the household," he says, adding that the company doesn't advertise on Saturday morning cartoon shows.

Snack Food Association President and CEO Jim McCarthy says that lobbying is one of his many duties as head of the organization. "Our belief is that all foods fit into the diet," McCarthy says, and "we don't like the term 'junk food.'" Products made by his segment of the industry—which include potato chips, party mix, corn snacks, snack cakes, and cookies—all contain natural ingredients such as vegetables, nuts, and fruit, he says.

The industry has developed healthier products over the years, McCarthy says, but at "certain times consumers haven't bought these products." He attributes the obesity problem to a lack of exercise and shortcomings in educating people about the need for a balanced diet.

Challenging Stereotypes

No matter what industry they represent, lobbyists interviewed for this article said that a good practitioner of their profession knows all sides of an issue, enabling lawmakers and their staffs to make the best-informed decision. "The system weeds out the bad actors, and the honest folks are the most successful and the longest-lasting," one lobbyist says.

Although many of the lobbyists acknowledge some familiar situations in *Thank You for Smoking*, they insist that the stereotypes are not altogether fair. "I think people don't understand the importance of lobbying to the system. If I don't explain what we do and I am not here to explain it to people, Congress will make uninformed decisions without understanding the consequences to the industry," a former liquor lobbyist says.

"Everyone draws the line in the sand about what they will or will not work on," says Don Goldberg, who leads the crisis communications practice at Qorvis Communications and was a key player on President Clinton's damage-response team. "The line is not set in stone.

"If you don't believe the points you are arguing are the best argument for your client and also that it's truthful, then you shouldn't be in this business," Goldberg continues. "I strongly believe in the First Amendment, [but] I don't believe the First Amendment is the reason to take on clients. The reason to take on clients is, they have a good story to tell and they are honest and reputable organizations."

But James Thurber, director of the Center for Congressional and Presidential Studies at American University, says that at the end of the day, money is a good explanation for why many lobbyists end up in their positions. This is especially true when it comes to tobacco, which was the leading preventable cause of disease and death in the United States in 2007, according to the Centers for Disease Control and Prevention.

For consumers, the message that lobbyists appear to be sending is that the individual is responsible for making the right choices in life. Yet the profusion of advertising, marketing ploys, political rhetoric, and seemingly conflicting studies can be bewildering. And although the financial incentive is ever-present, lobbyists believe they fill a fundamental role in society and deserve some relief from the negative stereotypes.

Starting Over

Terry Eastland

It's premature to write an obituary, but there's no question that America's news media—the newspapers, newsmagazines, and television networks that people once turned to for all their news—are experiencing what psychologists might call a major life passage. They've seen their audiences shrink, they've had to worry about vigorous new competitors, and they've suffered more than a few self-inflicted wounds—scandals of their own making. They know that more and more people have lost confidence in what they do. To many Americans, today's newspaper is irrelevant, and network news is as compelling as whatever is being offered over on the Home Shopping Network. Maybe less.

The First Amendment protects against government abridgment of the freedom of the press. But it doesn't guarantee that today's news media—some would already say yesterday's—will be tomorrow's. Though most existing news organizations will probably survive, few if any are likely to enjoy the prestige and clout they once did. So it's time to write, if not an obituary, then an account of their rise and decline and delicate prospects amid the "new media" of cable television, talk radio, and the blogosphere.

The "new media" carry the adjective because they began to emerge only in the 1980s, when the media of newspapers, newsmagazines, and network and local television news had long been firmly in place. Most newspapers had been around since the first decades of the 20th century, and though rising costs and competition caused some to be shuttered in the decades after World War II, there were still more than 1,700 papers published daily in the 1970s. *Time* and *Newsweek* were established, respectively, in 1923 and 1933. Network television newscasts were reaching most parts of the country by the 1950s, and local stations eventually provided their own news programs at various points in the day.

The most important old news organizations were the outlets that covered stories in the nation's capital and abroad. They included *The New York Times* and *The Washington Post; Time* and *Newsweek;* NBC News, CBS News, and ABC News; National Public Radio and public television's various iterations of what is now called *The NewsHour with Jim Lehrer.* When people talked about the "mainstream" or "establishment" media, these were the organizations they had in mind. They were leaders among the media generally, and shaped how regional and local outlets practiced journalism.

They were also part of America's first sizable national elite, which emerged after World War II in response to the needs of a nation whose central government was larger and more invasive, costly, and ambitious than ever before. Political leaders, lawyers, academics, businesspeople, and certain practitioners of that once-disreputable trade, journalism, populated this elite. As in the other elites, members of the media elite held degrees from many of the same (elite) universities. They believed that they had a responsibility to improve society, and they thought of themselves—as no ink-stained wretch had before—as professionals.

The most influential journalists understood that news is rarely news in the sense of being undisputed facts about people or policy, but news in the sense that it's a product made by reporters, editors, and producers. They knew that news is about facts, but that it fundamentally reflects editorial judgments about whether particular facts are "news," and if they are, what the news means and what its consequences may be. They knew, too, that those who define and present the news have a certain power, since news can set a public agenda. And they weren't shy about exercising this power. That's what made them dominant—an establishment, in fact.

At their best, the elite media pursued stories of public importance and reported them thoroughly, accurately, and in reasonably fair and balanced fashion. And they did that a great deal of the time. They were never the relentlessly vigilant "watchdogs" they congratulated themselves on being, but they did sometimes do valuable work policing the abuses and failures of government and other institutions.

And they influenced the nation, most dramatically during the 1960s and 1970s. They probably tipped the close 1960 election between Richard Nixon and John Kennedy, when, as Theodore H. White reported in *The Making of the President, 1960* (1961), the coverage clearly favored Kennedy. They early and correctly judged that the civil rights movement was news, and they turned news with datelines in the South into a national story of profound significance. They also affected the 1968 election—through what historian Paul Johnson called their "tendentious presentation" of news about the Vietnam War, which came to a head with the Tet offensive in January 1968, a major American military victory that the media cast as a defeat. Some described this portrayal as flawed reporting—notably the founding editor of this journal, Peter Braestrup, in *Big Story* (1977)—while others saw it as a product of bias. But the effect of the treatment of Tet was to help shift elite opinion decisively against the war. In

March 1968, after nearly losing the New Hampshire primary, President Lyndon Johnson decided not to run for reelection.

And then there was the presidency of Richard Nixon. Nixon was never liked by the news media, to put it mildly, and he returned the favor, calling the press "the enemy." When the judicial process exposed a "third-rate burglary" at the Watergate complex in Washington, *The Washington Post* pursued the story, with other outlets later joining in. Nixon became the only president in American history to resign the office.

The media establishment emerged at a time when Americans generally respected those in authority. But when, beginning in the 1960s, authority took a severe beating, the media establishment was the one authority that actually gained in strength. Crusading reporters and editors became cultural heroes—the rebels and nonconformists who refused to kowtow to anybody. The Watergate scandal in particular confirmed in the media the sense they had of themselves as independent guardians of the public good and the very conscience of the nation in times of crisis. Over the years, judicial decisions also went their way, securing greater protection for the exercise of media power. For the establishment media, life was very good.

The Watergate scandal confirmed the media's belief that they were independent guardians of the public good.

Since the 1980s, however, more and more Americans have stopped relying on the traditional media for news. Some have quit the news habit entirely. Newspaper circulation has been declining, and network ratings are sharply down. Mainstream outlets no longer have a monopoly on the news, their journalism is subjected to sometimes withering scrutiny, and they are ignored when they are not criticized. Life is no longer so good.

There are many explanations for why Americans have been turning away from their old news providers, including adjustments in how people now live and work (fewer have time to watch the evening news) and the lack of interest in news evident among younger generations whose tastes often carry them to MTV. But the media can also blame themselves for the change.

Here it bears noting that though journalists aspired to the status of professionals, they never acquired the self-regulatory mechanisms found in law, medicine, or even business. The nation's journalism schools, which taught—and still teach—a craft better learned on the job, never really filled the void. Those schools often tended to hire former journalists lacking both the intellectual capability and the inclination to undertake serious analysis of the institutions whence they came. Critical scholarship by those outside the guild tended to be summarily dismissed, and the field was always thin on professional journals examining its practices and guiding ideas. Most of those that were tried—for example, I edited *Forbes Media Critic* from 1993 through 1996—found no footing. Media criticism, such as it was, leaned mostly to polemics and insider chatter (news

people are happy to talk endlessly about themselves, evidently on the assumption that others are eager to listen).

Of course, the media did have critics who didn't publish articles—ordinary Americans. Too often they'd turn on the evening news and hear about conflict and controversy. It was as though news, if it were to be real, had to be boiled down to some negative essence, some clod of dirt that the subjects of a story flung at each other. Or they'd see an interview in which a correspondent would ask a nonquestion question designed to put the hapless interviewee in his or her place. Thus in 1995 did a *CBS Good Morning* host "ask" then-senator Phil Gramm of Texas, "If you really want to reduce the deficit, are you going to have to cut entitlements? But I'm sure you don't want to talk about that." Or the public would read news stories in which the writers took gratuitous shots at their subjects. Thus did Maureen Dowd, before her elevation from reporter to columnist at *The New York Times,* lead her front-page story on President Bill Clinton's 1994 visit to Oxford with a sentence stating that he was making "a sentimental journey to the university where he didn't inhale, didn't get drafted, and didn't get a degree."

Negativity in the news cause many to tune out.

The negativity in the news may have resulted from the more personalized or interpretative journalism that began appearing in the 1960s. It represented a break from the old norm of objectivity by which reporters were obliged to keep their own views out of articles, and it was thought to help in uncovering the "real story" beyond any official statements and scheduled events. Perhaps the urgent need to compete for smaller pools of viewers and readers also played a role in the rise of negative news. But to judge by opinion polls, the public wasn't impressed. The negativity, not to mention the arrogance with which it was often served up, caused many to tune out.

The public had another problem with media figures: their political and social views. Surveys taken over several decades demonstrated that most national journalists voted Democratic and were politically and socially liberal. In 1962, *The Columbia Journalism Review* published a survey of 273 Washington journalists in which 57 percent called themselves liberal and 28 percent conservative, with the rest choosing "middle of the road" or declining any label. The conservative contingent was down to 17 percent when sociologist S. Robert Lichter and Smith College political scientist Stanley Rothman conducted another survey in 1980. Most respondents said they were "lifestyle liberals," meaning that they favored abortion rights and affirmative action and rejected the notion that homosexuality was wrong. Eighty-six percent said they seldom or never attended religious services. Eighty-one percent had voted for George McGovern in 1972. In 1992, another survey of 139 Washington-based bureau chiefs and congressional correspondents found that 89 percent planned to vote for the Democrat, Bill Clinton, in the approaching presidential election.

The surveys certainly said something about the media. But they did not say that the news the media provided was biased;

that required its own demonstration. Members of the elite media often asserted that the public could count on their professionalism to ensure against bias. Yet they seldom admitted bias, even in stories in which it was all too obvious.

Today, nobody denies that most journalists are liberal in their political views and voting preferences.

Nor would they concede that they might be missing news because they were disposed to look for it only in the kinds of places people of their mindset and values thought potentially newsworthy. The news they found in those places might indeed be legitimate news. But other sorts of news, to be found in places people of a different mindset and other values might think to explore, were often neglected. A case in point was the media's failure, in the run-up to the historic 1994 congressional elections, to examine seriously the substance of the GOP's campaign manifesto, the "Contract with America." Only after the elections did the media take a much-belated look.

Whatever bias the media did not concede, and whatever places they skipped past where news might have been sought, there remained this essential fact: Most journalists were liberal in their political views and voting preferences. Today, no one really disputes that fact, nor have mainstream journalists changed much in this regard, for every new survey only confirms what all the previous ones reported. But when the mainstream media began their decline in the 1980s, they were reluctant to concede the point. In so many words, they often seemed to say, "If our liberalism is a fact—and we don't really know that it is—it's irrelevant."

The media bravely (perilously?) held that position even as the country continued a rightward movement that has now culminated, for the first time in a half century, in Republican control of both ends of Pennsylvania Avenue. An increasingly conservative public was being asked to continue getting its news from people who, by and large, held liberal views. That was a tough sell, and it got even tougher because the new media made possible by emerging technologies offered alternatives.

The Cable News Network, founded in 1980, was arguably the first new media entity, its distinguishing characteristic that it offered news 24/7. Other round-the-clock cable news providers followed, including, in 1996, the Fox News Channel. Meanwhile, national talk radio captured large audiences, with none bigger than that for Rush Limbaugh, who debuted in 1988. In 1999, the first weblog appeared on the Internet. Today the number of blogs—they make up the "blogosphere"—is growing every day.

The new media tended to be more hospitable to conservative views. And it was through the new media that a public growing more conservative in its politics began to find satisfaction. Which is not to say that the new media produced better news stories. They didn't, and still don't, because, cable news networks excepted, they don't do much in the way of original reporting. They analyze and opine on the basis of news reported not only by cable television but by the traditional media, which they daily criticize.

The Shrinking News Audience

Daily U.S. newspaper circulation
1990:	62,327,962
2003:	55,185,351

Number of daily U.S. newspapers
1990:	1,611
2003:	1,456

By age group, percentage of American adults who read a newspaper "yesterday"
18–29:	23
30–49:	39
50–64:	52
60 + :	60

Circulation of *The New York Times*
1990:	1,108,447
2004:	1,121,057

Circulation of *The Washington Post*
1990:	780,582
2004:	746,724

Circulation of *The Wall Street Journal*
1990:	1,857,131
2004:	2,106,774

Circulation of *The Los Angeles Times*
1990:	1,196,323
2004:	902,164

Time spent per day by 8-to-18-year-olds with all media: 6 hrs. 21 mins.

Time spent per day with print media: 43 mins.

Combined viewership of network evening news
1980:	52 million
2004:	28.8 million

Viewership of network evening news, by program
NBC Nightly News	11.2 million
ABC World News Tonight	9.9 million
CBS Nightly News	7.7 million
PBS *NewsHour*	2.7 million

Median age of network evening news viewers: 60

Percentage of people who believe "all or most" of what's on
Network news	24
CNN	32
Fox News	25
C-Span	27
PBS *NewsHour*	23

Percentage of radio audience listening to news/talk: 16

Percentage of news/talk listeners ages 12–34:15

Percentage of news/talk listeners age 50 or older: 65

Number of active blogs (updated in last two months): 6.8 million

Number of abandoned blogs: 13.1 million

Percentage of bloggers under age 30: 48

Percentage of Internet users who have read a blog: 27

Percentage of Internet users who don't know what a blog is: 62

Sources: Newspaper Association of America, Pew Research Center for the People & the Press, *World Almanac and Book of Facts 1992*, Audit Bureau of Circulation, Project for Excellence in Journalism, Henry J. Kaiser Family Foundation, Perseus Development Corporation, Pew Internet and American Life Project.

Yet the new media also do something else. To the traditional media, the new media have always looked awfully incomplete, as being more about politics and ideology than about news. Still, from their inception the new media have been landing blows on the old media precisely where it matters most. Remember that news is a thing made, a product, and that media with certain beliefs and values once made the news and then presented it in authoritative terms, as though beyond criticism. Thus did Walter Cronkite famously end his newscasts, "And that's the way it is." That way, period.

But the question the new media have asked is precisely, "Which way was it?" And, in answering it, they have allowed people with beliefs and values different from those dominating the old media to have their say. Though cable and radio talk shows have been derided as shoutfests, they've enabled people to think differently about the news. Historian Christopher Lasch once observed that only in the course of argument do "we come to understand what we know and what we still need to learn." The new media's chief accomplishment may well turn out to be that they opened for argument questions to which the old media alone used to provide answers.

A notable characteristic of the new media is speed (some would say haste). Their speed is another reason for the old media's travail. Consider what happened when Dan Rather reported that infamous story on CBS News's *60 Minutes Wednesday* suggesting that George W. Bush had shirked his duties while serving as a pilot in the Texas Air National Guard. The story was broadcast on September 8, 2004, and by the following morning bloggers were tearing apart documents essential to the story, revealing them to be painfully obvious fakes. Traditional media soon began picking at the CBS story, but it's not evident that, absent the blogosphere, the piece would have been deconstructed. Nor that a formal investigation by CBS itself would have ensued, which resulted in scathing criticism of the broadcast, the firing of the story's producer, the resignation of three other executives, and the earlier-than-anticipated retirement of Rather himself as anchor of the evening news.

The deeper point about the quick breakdown of the Bush National Guard story was that it revealed a media establishment without its old power and influence. CBS News and other establishment outlets wanted to determine what the news should be in the obviously important context of a presidential campaign. They had grown anxious about campaign coverage that seemed to them too influenced by "outsiders" and the new media. In early August, a group of Vietnam veterans opposed to John Kerry began running an ad that challenged his account of his Vietnam service. The establishment media ignored their claims, but the blogosphere didn't. Nor did cable and radio talk shows, on which the Swift Boat Veterans, as they were called, made frequent appearances. Once Kerry formally responded to the Swifties, the big networks and newspapers had little choice but to cover the story, despite their dislike for it.

Some establishment journalists argued that the media now had an obligation to turn the spotlight on Bush. Syndicated columnist E. J. Dionne, Jr., a former reporter for both *The New York Times* and *The Washington Post,* wrote, "Now that John Kerry's life during his twenties has been put at the heart of this campaign just over two months from Election Day, the media owe the country a comparable review of what Bush was doing at the same time and the same age. If all the stories about what Kerry did in Vietnam are not balanced by serious scrutiny of Bush in the Vietnam years, the media will be capitulating to a right-wing smear campaign. Surely our nation's editors and producers don't want to send a signal that all you have to do to set the media's agenda is to spend a half-million bucks on television ads."

Not just CBS News but several other establishment outlets were trying to reset that agenda by pursuing the National Guard story, a quest that would carry them to the door of the same man who passed the bogus documents to CBS and was described by the panel that investigated the fiasco as a "partisan with an anti-Bush agenda." CBS acted first, with fateful results, but none of the other media ever produced any authentic documents either. The story simply wasn't there.

In 1995, Jonathan Alter wrote a *Newsweek* column recognizing that the "old media order" was "in decline." The decline has only continued. Even so, it's hard to imagine an America without the news organizations that make up the old media, if only because they're still the main sources of independent reporting, and such reporting is essential in a country whose self-governing people need information to make all kinds of decisions. Yet for the old media to become newly credible, to regain respect and audience, in a country more populous and less enamored of elites than it once was, and more red than blue, they're going to have to dial down their imperial arrogance. They're going to have to learn from the best of what the new media offer, and perhaps even recruit bloggers to help with news judgment and fact-checking. And they're definitely going to have to look for news in places they formerly did not.

Occasionally you see evidence that an old media outlet is beginning to get it. Beginning, I say. Consider *The New York Times,* like CBS News a charter member of the establishment media, and, like CBS News, an institution burdened by a recent scandal (Jayson Blair's plagiarism and fabrications) which eventually cost top journalists their jobs. In January 2004 the *Times* effectively conceded the need to enlarge the field in which it looks for news when it deployed a reporter to cover, as the *Times*' press release put it, "conservative forces in religion, politics, law, business, and the media." It was as if the *Times* had decided that it should now cover some far-off, exotic country that had suddenly become a world power—and yet it was dispatching only a single correspondent to do the job! But at least that was a start. Finally, there was change. So the *Times* was right to put out a press release: This really was news.

TERRY EASTLAND is the publisher of *The Weekly Standard* and editor of *Freedom of Expression in the Supreme Court: The Defining Cases* (2000).

From *Wilson Quarterly,* Spring 2005, pp. 40–47. Copyright © 2005 by Terry Eastland. Reprinted by permission of Terry Eastland.

Sharp Pencils

How three pioneering reporters reshaped the way the press covers elections—and politics itself.

JONATHAN YARDLEY

The 1960s and early '70s were among the most tumultuous periods in American politics—assassinations, riots, the conservative uprising, Watergate—but also among the most interesting journalistically During this period three of the most influential political books of the postwar years were published, books that permanently altered the way we understand elections, the people who run them and those who report them.

All three were national bestsellers, devoured not only by political professionals but by ordinary voters: *The Making of the President 1960,* by Theodore H. White; *The Selling of the President 1968,* by Joe McGinniss; and *The Boys on the Bus,* by Timothy Crouse. They were published in 1961, 1969 and 1973, respectively. Interestingly, and oddly, the most important of the three—*The Making of the President 1960*—is the only one no longer in print, but its pervasive influence remains undiminished. Yes, influence: sales of books in this country are minuscule by comparison with sales of popular music or the audiences drawn by television and movies, but the effect of these books unquestionably was substantial and remains so to this day.

No one has assessed White's book and its influence more astutely than Timothy Crouse. In 1960, he writes in *The Boys on the Bus,* "campaign coverage had changed very little from what it had been in the 1920s." Most Americans still got their news from reading the papers, where, Crouse tells us, most reporting "remained superficial, formulaic, and dull." Then White, a journalist and novelist of wide experience if modest reputation, spent the election year bird-dogging Kennedy and Nixon, and with extraordinary speed produced his long, exhaustive account of the campaign, described on the front of its dust jacket as "A narrative history of American politics in action." Crouse writes:

"The book struck most readers as a total revelation—it was as if they had never before read anything, anywhere, that told them what a political campaign was about. They had some idea that a campaign consisted of a series of arcane deals and dull speeches, and suddenly White came along with a book that laid out the campaign as a wide-screen thriller with full-blooded heroes and white-knuckle suspense on every page. The book

hit the number-one spot on the best-seller lists six weeks after publication and stayed there for exactly a year."

As it happens, I was beginning my own career in journalism just as White's book appeared, and I vividly recall the excitement it inspired. Crouse is right: this was something totally, absolutely new. Nobody ever had done anything remotely like it. White's prose could be muddy (it seems even muddier today), his hero-worship of Kennedy was cloying and his sunny paeans to the American political system overlooked or minimized its many shortcomings, but the book had more than the drama cited by Crouse: it took readers inside politics as they'd never been before. It both demystified the process and romanticized it. Few Americans then understood how primaries worked—indeed by White's account, few even knew what they were—and few were aware that political campaigns have an inherent narrative structure and rhythm; White taught them all that.

Granted far more access to Kennedy than to Nixon, he soon became infatuated with JFK's style and intelligence. On many occasions, White had Kennedy almost entirely to himself, aboard the Kennedy plane or in hotel rooms, and the two men talked in ways that are unthinkable now, when hundreds of reporters clamor for the candidates' attention. Kennedy had White in the palm of his hand: "It was the range, the extent, the depth and detail, of information and observation that dazzled, then overwhelmed, the listener." Passages such as that—the book has a number of them—doubtless explain why it was to White that Jacqueline Kennedy turned for the first interview she granted after her husband's assassination in 1963. She told White (and the millions who eventually read his article for *Life* magazine) about her husband's fondness for the title song from *Camelot,* a disclosure that played right into White's predisposition to romanticize Kennedy.

The most lasting effect of White's book, though, isn't the Kennedy myth—for better or worse, it's been thoroughly punctured by now, leaving one to wonder what, if anything, White knew and didn't disclose about JFK's amatory adventures—but the radical changes it inspired in political coverage. First of all, as Crouse reports, "imitations and spinoffs" began to appear after the 1964 election, much to White's dismay. Four years later, "White was competing against seventeen other campaign books," with the result that none of his subsequent *Making* books generated the sales or the influence of the first, though they continued to sell respectably, despite a steady decline in quality.

By 1972, when Crouse set off to cover the press covering the race between Nixon and George McGovern, most editors, he writes, "were sending off their men with rabid pep talks about the importance of sniffing out inside dope, getting background into the story, finding out what makes the campaign tick, and generally going beyond the old style of campaign reporting." Nobody wanted to be scooped by White again. On the whole, this was a good thing, but it occurred in parallel with two more troubling developments: the rise of the "new" journalism, which valued first-person reportage, often to the extent of putting the reporter at the center of the story, and the rise of the entertainment culture, which reduced everything in public life to its power to amuse, thus rendering political campaigns even more devoid of real issues than even the image-driven 1960 campaign had been.

None of this is Teddy White's fault, and no doubt he would be horrified by the present state of political reportage, which too often treats candidates and members of their entourages as celebrities, but there is no question that he got the process started. Before he came along, there had been dramatic presidential races—after all, it was only a dozen years before 1960 that Harry S. Truman had won his cliffhanger victory over Thomas E. Dewey. White, however, conditioned people to expect drama and personality in politics: the press, now expanded exponentially by the ladies and gentlemen of television, was eager to deliver what people wanted.

One arena where drama and personality are rarely encountered any longer is the political convention. White absolutely adored conventions, as did most other journalists of his day; and believed that they "epitomize the mythology and legendry of American national politics." In 1956, not long after he'd begun writing about American politics, following years of reporting from abroad, he had been on hand for that "wild night, at the Democratic Convention [in Chicago], as John F. Kennedy and Estes Kefauver contended for the delegates' mandate for the Vice-Presidency." Thereafter, he seemed to expect every convention to reach that same fever pitch. But with the exception of 1964 in San Francisco, when Republican conservatives vilified and humiliated Nelson Rockefeller, he never again got what he hoped for.

He believed, somewhat naively, that "if the conventions have done their work well, as normally they do, then the American people are offered two men of exceptional ability," but even as early as 1960 he was able to set sentiment aside long enough to peer into the future. He understood that the rise of the primaries was changing everything—"Conventions are now less bluntly controlled by bosses, and more sharply controlled by techniques and forces set in motion outside the convention city itself." White perceived, too, that "the intrusion of television on the convention" meant that "under the discipline of the camera, conventions are held more tightly to schedule, their times adjusted for maximum viewing opportunities, their procedure streamlined, not for the convenience or entertainment of the delegates, but for the convenience of the nation" and, it goes without saying, the convenience of television.

White understood that television was changing everything, and wrote vividly about the precedent-setting 1960 televised presidential debates, but he only dimly perceived what Joe McGinniss came along eight years later to make plain: that television now ran the show. McGinniss, a young journalist working out of Philadelphia and blessed, apparently, with an abundance of charm, insinuated his way into the inner circle of Richard Nixon's media campaign, particularly those working on his advertising strategy and his carefully staged television appearances before handpicked, sympathetic audiences. He was allowed to sit in on nearly all of their meetings, traveled with them, and engaged in long, casual conversations on an ongoing basis. Whether any of them had an inkling of what lay in store for them remains unknown, but the book that resulted left no doubt that Nixon was in the hand of a small group of (mostly) amiable, cynical, hard-boiled Svengalis.

The "grumpy, cold, and aloof" Nixon, as McGinnis described him, was a public-relations nightmare, but by dint of determination and ceaseless hard work he'd recovered from his double humiliation—by Kennedy in 1960 and by Edmund G. "Pat" Brown in the 1962 California governor's race—and walked away with the 1968 Republican nomination. He commenced the fall campaign with a huge advantage handed him by the Democrats, whose riot-torn convention in Chicago was a disaster and whose nominee, Hubert Humphrey, was held in contempt by much of the party's rank and file. Nixon's handlers were resolved not to let him fritter away his lead by reverting to the humorless, graceless, calculating "Old Nixon" detested by many voters, and concentrated on projecting an image of a "New Nixon" who was, above all else, "warm."

"I am not going to barricade myself into a television studio and make this an antiseptic campaign," Nixon promised as the campaign began, but it became clear almost immediately that this was precisely what he was going to do. Psychologically, Nixon was fragile, combustible goods. His staff remembered all too well how he had flown off the handle after losing to Pat Brown, bitterly informing the press that "you won't have Nixon to kick around anymore." They were apprehensive about putting him in situations where he could not be reined in, where instead of exuding warmth he would come across as white hot. The goal, one of his advisers wrote, was "pinpointing those controlled uses of the television medium that can best convey the image we want to get across." This is how McGinniss puts it:

"So this was how they went into it. Trying, with one hand, to build the illusion that Richard Nixon, in addition to his attributes of mind and heart, considered, in the words of Patrick K. Buchanan, a speech writer, 'communicating with the people . . . one of the great joys of seeking the Presidency'; while with the other they shielded him, controlled him, and controlled the atmosphere around him. It was as if they were building not a President but an Astrodome, where the wind would never blow, the temperature never rise or fall, and the ball never bounce erratically on the artificial grass."

McGinniss' disclosures about the artificiality of the Nixonian image that his handlers presented to the electorate surprised many readers and shocked some, but they really didn't come as news. As McGinniss himself readily acknowledged, the marriage of politicians and advertising had been consummated years before—certainly by 1956, when New York City's venerable advertising agency, Batton, Barton, Durstine and Osborn, took on Dwight Eisenhower as a regular account—as was confirmed by Ike's Republican national chairman, Leonard Hall, who said unapologetically: "You sell your candidates and your programs the way a business sells its products."

No, what I think really appalled readers—especially, needless to say, those predisposed against Nixon—was what McGinniss revealed about the cynicism of the candidate and his staff toward the electorate and, even more startling, the cynicism of the staff toward the candidate. Jim Sage, one of Nixon's filmmakers, told McGinniss: "We didn't have to make cheap and vulgar films. . . . But those images strike a note of recognition in the kind of people to whom we are trying to appeal. . . . Nixon has not only developed the use of the platitude, he's raised it to an art form. It's mashed potatoes. It appeals to the lowest common denominator of American taste." Kevin Phillips, today a political pundit but then a 27-year-old Nixon staffer, struck a similar note, describing spots that featured John Wayne: "Wayne might sound bad to people in New York, but he sounds great to the schmucks we're trying to reach through John Wayne. The people down there along the Yahoo Belt."

As for how the staff regarded the candidate, Roger Ailes, who supervised the staged question-and-answer television shows (and who now runs Fox News), positively (and hilariously) dripped with contempt. "Let's face it," he said in one staff meeting, "a lot of people think Nixon is dull. Think he's a bore, a pain in the ass. They look at him as the kind of kid who always carried a bookbag. Who was forty-two years old the day he was born. They figure other kids got footballs for Christmas, Nixon got a briefcase and he loved it. . . . Now you put him on television, you've got a problem right away. He's a funny-looking guy. He looks like somebody hung him in a closet overnight and he jumps out in the morning with his suit all bunched up and starts running around saying, 'I want to be President.' I mean this is how he strikes some people. That's why these shows are important. To make them forget all that."

If there was a bombshell in *The Selling of the President 1968,* this was it. To be sure, McGinniss didn't shock enough voters to prevent Nixon from steamrolling McGovern four years later. Nevertheless, what he had to say about the campaign's scorn for the people whose votes it sought surely opened some eyes. There is no way to calibrate such matters, but I suspect that this may have contributed significantly to the cynicism that voters themselves now express about political candidates—wariness that subsequently was fed by such films as *The Candidate, All the President's Men, The War Room, Wag the Dog, Bulworth* and *Primary Colors.* If *The Selling of the President 1968* was not the crucial element in the evolution of public cynicism about politics, it certainly played a catalytic role.

This surely helps explain why the book remains in print today; for the truth is that otherwise it doesn't hold up very well. McGinniss has a keen ear and the book is full of wonderful quotes, but it's surprisingly thin—a mere 168 pages of large-type text padded out with another 83 pages of appendices—and shallow as well. With its shock value long since dissipated, *The Selling of the President* turns out to be less thoughtful than I had recalled. McGinniss learned a lot of interesting things, but he really did not have much to say about them.

The big surprise is that, of these three books, the one that holds up best is *The Boys on the Bus.* As a rule, the press exists as a subject of interest mainly to the press, and into the bargain few of the reporters and columnists about whom Crouse writes remain well-known today, the principal exceptions being R. W. Apple Jr. of the *New York Times,* David Broder of the *Washington Post* and the syndicated columnist Robert Novak. You'd think that today's reader would find the book to be journalistic inside baseball and, furthermore, yesterday's news. *The Boys on the Bus,* however, stands the test of time for two reasons: Crouse's tart, witty prose and his sharp insights into journalism, a business that takes itself far too seriously and is deeply hostile to criticism or change.

That Crouse should have been the person to produce such a book could not have been predicted. He was only three years out of college and his family's roots were in the theater: his father was the prominent Broadway producer and writer Russell Crouse *(Life With Father, Call Me Madam, The Sound of Music);* his sister is the actress Lindsay Crouse. But Crouse headed for journalism rather than the stage, persuading editors at Rolling Stone—a publication then still young, irreverent and very smart—to let him write about the journalists covering the 1972 campaign. I was in my early 30s by then, my fascination with the inner workings of journalism and politics undimmed in the dozen years since Teddy White's book; I gobbled up Crouse's articles as they appeared. But it was when they were published as a book, tightly organized and fleshed out, that their real merit became clear.

Crouse—at the time in his mid-20s—had a precocious understanding of the press, especially the big-foot press on the plane with McGovern and, far less frequently, with Nixon, whose staff, knowing the election was a lock, had isolated the candidate in the Oval Office and the Rose Garden, and kept reporters as far away as possible. Crouse—as White had done before him—found himself spending far more time with the Democrats than with the Republicans. Like Kennedy, McGovern was far more accessible to reporters than Nixon, who believed, as Crouse put it, that "the press tortured him, lied about him, hated him."

The Boys on the Bus can still be read for its portraits of the men (and the very few women) in the political press corps, portraits that are deft and (mostly) sympathetic. Crouse, for example, summed up Jules Witcover, then of the *Los Angeles Times,* in a single sentence: "He had the pale, hounded look of a small liquor store owner whose shop has just been held up for the seventh time in a year." Crouse liked and respected Witcover—"he had always been better than the paper he worked for"—but that didn't prevent him from writing honestly about him.

Indeed, honesty is the rule throughout this book. One of the dirty little secrets of the news business is that journalists travel in packs, but it's no secret here. The men and women whom

Crouse followed "all fed off the same pool report, the same daily handout, the same speech by the candidate; the whole pack was isolated in the same mobile village. After awhile, they began to believe the same rumors, subscribe to the same theories, and write the same stories." They "had a very limited usefulness as political observers, by and large, for what they knew best was not the American electorate but the tiny community of the press plane, a totally abnormal world that combined the incestuousness of a New England hamlet with the giddiness of a mid-ocean gala and the physical rigors of the Long March."

They were in a pack even before they got on the plane: "All the national political reporters lived in Washington, saw the same people, used the same sources, belonged to the same background groups, and swore by the same omens. They arrived at their answers just as independently as a class of honest seventh graders using the same geometry text—they did not have to cheat off each other to come up with the same answers." No reader needs to be told that exactly the same words could be written by an observer of American journalism today, except that the words would have to be stronger. Not only are reporters and columnists happily isolated from American reality, they now swim in the journalistic celebrity pool, where prominence and wealth have far less to do with the actual quality of one's reportage or commentary than with the ability to get on the television gong shows, travel the lecture circuit and schmooze with other members of the celebritoisie at occasions such as the annual dinners of the Gridiron Club and the White House Correspondents' Association.

It is a pity that Crouse no longer covers prominent journalists, because they badly need a critic of his acuity. His first fling with journalism, however, seems to have been his last. In the 1980s

he was co-author of a new script for one of his father's most successful shows, *Anything Goes,* with music and lyrics by Cole Porter; the revival ran for more than two years and presumably enabled Crouse to escape into early semi-retirement. He leaves us, though, with this absolutely terrific reportage, which continues to be required reading for any student of politics, the press and the internecine connections between the two.

Did *The Boys on the Bus* contribute to the suspicion and disdain in which the press is now so widely held? Not directly, would be my guess, but certainly indirectly: by describing so accurately and wittily certain truths about the press that its practitioners would just as soon not acknowledge, Crouse may have encouraged others to distort them into untruths. The pack journalism he so carefully delineates can be, and has been, distorted into conspiracy journalism by those who find the press a convenient whipping boy.

No one ever whipped it with more venom or gusto than Richard Nixon, which brings us to the Square One on which all three of these books were constructed. Teddy White tried, desperately and not very successfully, to give Nixon every benefit of the doubt; Joe McGinniss ridiculed him; Timothy Crouse mocked and reviled him. But their books could not have been written without him. They remind us that his legacy may be exceedingly ambiguous, even poisonous, but it is very large: a political system based on imagery rather than substance, a political class and a body politic that hold each other in mutual contempt, a press that labors under appallingly low public confidence. Yes, many others must share the blame for these lamentable developments in our public life, but Nixon gets a big share of it. The possibility that this would make him very happy cannot be denied.

Obama Buoyed by Coalition of the Ascendant

Winning campaign helps Democrats build formidable alliance of minorities and better-educated whites.

RONALD BROWNSTEIN

R oll over FDR and tell Hubert Humphrey the news: A new Democratic coalition has been born.

Barack Obama on Tuesday won the most decisive Democratic presidential victory in a generation largely by tapping into growing elements of American society: young people, Hispanics and other minorities, and white upper-middle-class professionals. That coalition of the ascendant—combined with unprecedented margins among African-Americans—powered Obama to a commanding victory over Republican John McCain, even though Obama achieved only modest and intermittent gains with the working-class white voters who provided the foundation of the Democratic coalition from Franklin D. Roosevelt's election in 1932 to Humphrey's defeat 36 years later.

"Obama is reimagining a Democratic coalition for the 21st century," says Simon Rosenberg, president of NDN, a Democratic group that studies electoral trends and tactics. "Democrats [are] . . . surging with all the ascending and growing parts of the electorate. He is building a coalition that Democrats could ride for 30 or 40 years, the way they rode the FDR coalition of the 1930s."

Indeed, to a striking extent, Obama's commanding victory testified to the rise of the multiracial America that he embodies with his mixed-race, mixed-nationality heritage. Compared with the performance of John Kerry, the 2004 Democratic nominee, Obama posted his most dramatic gains among African-Americans and Hispanics, with voters from both groups turning out in large numbers in important battleground states. Although Obama's gains among whites were much more limited, the Edison/Mitofsky National Election Pool exit poll conducted for a consortium of newspaper and television outlets found that whites cast only 74 percent of the vote, down from 85 percent 20 years ago. That decline has been especially steep among the white working-class voters who now constitute the core of the reduced Republican coalition.

The Democratic wave didn't reach quite as deeply into traditionally Republican territory as some had anticipated.

Republicans confined their congressional losses to the lower end of many pre-election projections by successfully defending Senate and House seats in several conservative-leaning states and districts.

Even so, Obama's victory was the most sweeping for either party since Ronald Reagan's triumph in 1980 and the broadest for any Democrat since Lyndon Johnson's in 1964. Obama didn't approach the Electoral College vote peaks of either of those landslides. But he became the first Democratic presidential nominee since Johnson, and only the second since World War II, to win more than 50.1 percent of the popular vote. Obama advanced deep into red territory by winning seven states that twice voted for President Bush, including two (Indiana and Virginia) that had not voted for any Democrat since 1964 and another two (Colorado and North Carolina) that had backed a Democrat only once since then.

And although Republicans avoided the full congressional rout that some in the party had feared, Democrats still gained at least six Senate seats (with races in Alaska, Georgia, and Minnesota still outstanding) and about 20 House seats, providing their largest majorities in both chambers since the early 1990s. Since 1948, no presidential candidate except Reagan in 1980 has carried his party to gains in both congressional chambers as large as those Obama helped produce on Tuesday, not only with his coattails but also through the massive voter persuasion and turnout operation that his campaign assembled.

Those House and Senate gains, like Obama's own advances, stretched across a strikingly wide canvas—from the Northeast and Midwest, to the outer South, to the Southwest. That breadth was another defining element of his triumph.

President Bush won his two elections more by consolidating than expanding his base—more by increasing his margins among Republicans than by converting swing voters. Obama did both. He generated a huge turnout among Democrats (particularly in urban areas) that helped increase his margin of victory by at least 3 percentage points over Kerry's in all but one of the 19 states that voted Democratic in 2004. But, according to the exit poll, Obama also won independent voters. And county-level results show that Obama substantially reduced the Republican margins in some culturally conservative and exurban GOP strongholds. The result was that he also improved on Kerry's performance in 25 of the 31 states that voted for Bush in 2004, in some cases dramatically.

A Wider Playing Field

It would be wildly premature to say that Tuesday's victory constitutes a realignment that will ensure Democrats a lasting electoral edge—if such an enduring advantage is even possible anymore in an era of loosening voter loyalty and hyperactive media scrutiny.

But there's no question that the outcome left Democrats competing on a much wider playing field than Republicans, both demographically and geographically. In the Northeast, the Pacific West, and parts of the Upper Midwest, the results consolidated formidable Democratic advantages, not only at the presidential level but also the congressional. Simultaneously, some of the Democrats' most dramatic House and Senate breakthroughs came in outer South (Florida, North Carolina, and Virginia) and Southwestern (Colorado, Nevada, and New Mexico) states where Obama also made his most impressive inroads into previously Republican territory. The Democratic gains at both levels also came behind parallel coalitions centered on minorities and better-educated whites who are often the most comfortable with the country's increasingly diverse racial and ethnic mix.

By contrast, with those losses along the Western and Southern frontiers of what had been the Republican electoral fortress since the 1980s, the GOP ends the Bush years retreating into a shrinking enclave of culturally conservative redoubts that include the Deep South, the Plains states, the northern Mountain West, and rural areas of the Midwest.

Veteran GOP consultant Bill McInturff, who served as McCain's pollster, says that the party must continue to energize those culturally conservative voters who are its modern foundation but must also find ways to restore its competitiveness in such socially cosmopolitan states as California, Illinois, New Jersey, and Pennsylvania that Democrats now dominate. "It is very difficult to try to thread the needle as we did to try to get to 270 when you are conceding that large a chunk of electoral votes," McInturff said. As Democrats extend their hold over House and Senate seats in the states they now control in presidential elections, the same can be said for Republican hopes of recapturing majorities in Congress.

A Declining Asset

In some respects, Tuesday's results testified to the stability of the demographic divides between the parties over the past 20 years. But in other ways they flashed bright warning signs for the GOP.

The stability was most evident among working-class white voters, who continued to tilt right. According to the exit poll, McCain beat Obama among these noncollege whites, 58 percent

to 40 percent. Obama's showing among those voters represented just a slight improvement over Kerry's meager 38 percent and only equaled the 40 percent that Al Gore attracted in 2000. Obama edged up among noncollege white men from 35 percent in 2004 to 39 percent. Democratic expectations of gains among economically strained noncollege white women were dashed: Obama won just 41 percent of them, hardly better than Kerry's weak 40 percent.

County-level results showed that Obama improved among working-class whites in some places. Most notably, he resoundingly carried Macomb County, a Detroit suburb considered the wellspring of blue-collar white "Reagan Democrats"; Bush had narrowly won the county in 2004. Obama also improved relative to Kerry in some other blue-collar Midwestern battleground counties such as Vigo in Indiana, Lorain in Ohio, and Jefferson in Missouri. Yet state polls showed that compared with 2004, Obama lost ground among noncollege whites in Missouri and especially in Pennsylvania. McCain exceeded Bush's margins in the blue-collar Pittsburgh suburbs of Westmoreland, Beaver, and Washington, becoming the first Republican since Richard Nixon in 1972 to carry the latter two.

But these working-class whites represent a declining asset for the GOP. According to the exit poll, they cast just 39 percent of the vote, down from 54 percent in 1988 and 46 percent as recently as 2000.

Ominously for the GOP, Obama recorded some of his strongest performances among groups that are growing in size, even as they turn away from Republicans.

First on that list are Hispanics. In 2004, Bush won about two-fifths of Hispanic voters. But after congressional conservatives derailed his proposal for comprehensive immigration reform early in his second term, the Republican vote among Hispanics plummeted to 29 percent in the 2006 House elections, exit polls found.

On Tuesday, Hispanics preferred Obama over McCain by better than 2-to-1 and simultaneously nudged their share of the vote from 8 percent in 2004 to 9 percent. Both effects were especially pronounced in states where Hispanics are most concentrated. Exit polls found that the Hispanic share of the vote increased much more than the national average in Arizona, Colorado, Nevada, and New Mexico. The Democratic share of that vote spiked by double digits in each of those states except Colorado. It also jumped in Florida. "Our party has a significant long-term structural problem with Latinos," McInturff says. Asians and other minorities, although just 5 percent of voters, likewise gave Obama nearly two-thirds of their votes.

Young and Diverse

The trends among the vast "millennial" generation now cascading into the electorate were just as daunting for the GOP. In 2004, Kerry carried 54 percent of voters younger than 30; by 2006, amid disillusionment with Bush and the Iraq war, 60 percent of them voted Democratic in House races. On Tuesday, Obama beat McCain among voters under 30 by fully 2-to-1. That lopsided result is partly explained by their increasing diversity. But even among white young people, the Republican position is eroding. Bush carried 55 percent of whites under 30 in both his elections; Obama won 54 percent of those young whites.

As in the Democratic primaries, the next pillar of Obama's coalition was white voters with college or post-graduate degrees, many of them professionals like consultants or professors. Obama won 47 percent of those highly educated whites, a higher percentage than Kerry, Gore, or Clinton. He carried 52 percent of college-educated white women (matching Gore's recent Democratic high point in 2000) and 42 percent of college-educated white men, again better than Kerry, Gore, or Clinton. While working-class whites are shrinking as a share of the vote, the exit poll found that better-educated white voters cast 35 percent of the ballots this week—largely unchanged from their slice since 1992.

Obama's strength among well-educated whites translated into crushing margins in critical white-collar suburbs that Republicans once hoped McCain, the self-described "maverick," could contest more effectively than Bush did. In fact, Obama expanded on Kerry's margins in almost all of these places—partly, some Republicans suspect, because of cultural resistance to vice presidential nominee Sarah Palin. Obama, for instance, carried Oakland County, the white-collar bookend to Macomb County outside Detroit, by a stunning 95,813 votes. He also became the first Democrat since Lyndon Johnson to carry Jefferson County outside of Denver.

Most striking were the results in the upscale Philadelphia suburbs. Four years ago, Kerry beat Bush in the four suburban Philadelphia counties—Bucks, Chester, Delaware, and Montgomery—by 87,124 votes. McCain's aides placed those four counties atop the list of places where they thought he could regain ground lost by Bush. But Obama beat McCain by nearly that many votes (86,463) in Montgomery County *alone;* overall, Obama carried the four counties by almost 200,000 votes, even storming to victory in Chester, which no Democrat since Johnson had won.

Obama ran especially well in what might be called suburban melting pots: affluent counties that contain large numbers of both well-educated whites and racial minorities. He posted big gains in diverse suburban counties from Arlington, Fairfax, and Prince William in Northern Virginia to Arapahoe outside Denver (which, like its neighbor Jefferson, had not voted Democratic since 1964) to Mecklenburg and Wake, centered on Charlotte and Raleigh, respectively, in North Carolina. In Florida's Orange County, a melange of Hispanics and better-educated whites, Obama's 86,000-vote advantage improved on Kerry's margin by a factor of *100.* That's not a typo.

Stanley Greenberg, the veteran Democratic pollster, says that Obama's strength in these melting-pot suburbs captures the essence of his new Democratic coalition. "The two biggest forces in it are the diverse racial elements and the more upscale, professional suburban white elements, who are not only comfortable with that diversity but welcome it," Greenberg says.

Just as important, Obama's victories in these Sun Belt suburbs extended onto new terrain the Democratic breakthroughs that occurred under Bill Clinton in white-collar suburbs across the Northeast, Upper Midwest, and West Coast. In essence, outer South and Southwest suburbs such as Wake or Prince William or Jefferson and Arapahoe counties in this election followed the mold cut in the 1990s by such demographic cousins as Santa Clara in California, Bergen in New Jersey, and Montgomery in Pennsylvania.

Trimming the Core

Two other types of communities provided the final ingredients for Obama's win. One was major urban centers, both those that are overwhelmingly minority (such as Philadelphia and Detroit) and those with many white professionals (such as Denver and Atlanta). Obama swelled the Democratic margin in both.

No less crucially, Obama simultaneously trimmed the Republican margins in two kinds of places central to Bush's majorities. Although McCain still won many key exurbs, Obama substantially reduced the Republican edge in such fast-growing counties as Scott in Minnesota, Henry in Georgia, and Douglas in Colorado, while capturing (for the first time since 1964) Loudoun in Virginia. Though many rural places resisted him, Obama also sliced the Republican lead in some longer-standing outposts of cultural conservatism like Springfield, Mo., and Colorado Springs, Colo.

Obama, as a mixed-race man with degrees from elite universities, embodies his coalition to an unusual extent; he personifies the change he offers. Greenberg says that unique convergence could help Obama deepen his connection to the voters he's attracted. McInturff, the McCain pollster, says that Democrats won't find it easy to construct an agenda that satisfies such a diverse alliance.

The one point on which both sides agree is that the singular new coalition Obama assembled is likely to endure only if he can meet its needs once in office. Ruy Teixeira, a political analyst at the liberal Center for American Progress, forecast the emergence of an upstairs-downstairs coalition centered on minorities and white professionals in a 2002 book that he co-authored, *The Emerging Democratic Majority.* Looking at Tuesday's results, Teixeira says that Obama has taken a first step toward constructing such a durable majority—but only that. "He succeeded with the growing groups in the Democratic coalition, and performed adequately with the declining groups that had favored the GOP," Teixeira said. "But that doesn't mean he has constructed an invulnerable majority. To keep the Republicans at bay, they are going to have to keep working."

The '08 Campaign: Sea Change for Politics as We Know It

ADAM NAGOURNEY

The 2008 race for the White House that comes to an end on Tuesday fundamentally upended the way presidential campaigns are fought in this country, a legacy that has almost been lost with all the attention being paid to the battle between Senators John McCain and Barack Obama.

It has rewritten the rules on how to reach voters, raise money, organize supporters, manage the news media, track and mold public opinion, and wage—and withstand—political attacks, including many carried by blogs that did not exist four years ago. It has challenged the consensus view of the American electoral battleground, suggesting that Democrats can at a minimum be competitive in states and regions that had long been Republican strongholds.

The size and makeup of the electorate could be changed because of efforts by Democrats to register and turn out new black, Hispanic and young voters. This shift may have long-lasting ramifications for what the parties do to build enduring coalitions, especially if intensive and technologically-driven voter turnout programs succeed in getting more people to the polls. Mr. McCain's advisers expect a record-shattering turnout of 130 million people, many being brought into the political process for the first time.

"I think we'll be analyzing this election for years as a seminal, transformative race," said Mark McKinnon, a senior adviser to President Bush's campaigns in 2000 and 2004. "The year campaigns leveraged the Internet in ways never imagined. The year we went to warp speed. The year the paradigm got turned upside down and truly became bottom up instead of top down."

To a considerable extent, Republicans and Democrats say, this is a result of the way that the Obama campaign sought to understand and harness the Internet (and other forms of so-called new media) to organize supporters and to reach voters who no longer rely primarily on information from newspapers and television. The platforms included YouTube, which did not exist in 2004, and the cellphone text messages that the campaign was sending out to supporters on Monday to remind them to vote.

"We did some very innovative things on the data side, and we did some Internet," said Sara Taylor, who was the White House political director during Mr. Bush's re-election campaign. "But only 40 percent of the country had broadband back then. You now have people who don't have home telephones anymore. And Obama has done a tremendous job of waging a campaign through the new media challenge.

"I don't know about you, but I see an Obama Internet ad every day. And I have for six months."

Even more crucial to the way this campaign has transformed politics has been Mr. Obama's success at using the Internet to build a huge network of contributors that permitted him to raise enough money—after declining to participate in the public financing system—to expand the map and compete in traditionally Republican states.

No matter who wins the election, Republicans and Democrats say, Mr. Obama's efforts in places like Indiana, North Carolina and Virginia—organizing and advertising to voters who previously had little exposure to Democratic ideas and candidates—will force future candidates to think differently.

"The great impact that this election will have for the future is that it killed public financing for all time," said Mr. McCain's chief campaign strategist, Steve Schmidt. "That means the next Republican presidential campaign, hopefully a re-election for John McCain, will need to be a billion-dollar affair to challenge what the Democrats have accomplished with the use of the Internet and viral marketing to communicate and raise money."

"It was a profound leap forward technologically," Mr. Schmidt added. "Republicans will have to figure out how to compete with this in order to become competitive again at a national level and in House and Senate races."

This transformation did not happen this year alone. In 2000, Mr. Bush's campaign, lead by Karl Rove and Ken Mehlman, pioneered the use of microtargeting to find and appeal to potential new supporters. In 2004, the presidential campaign of Howard Dean was widely credited with being the first to see the potential power of the Internet to raise money and sign up volunteers, a platform that Mr. Obama tremendously expanded.

"They were Apollo 11, and we were the Wright Brothers," said Joe Trippi, the manager of Mr. Dean's campaign.

Terry Nelson, who was the political director of the Bush campaign in 2004, said that the evolution was challenging campaign operatives who worked for every presidential campaign, and would continue in 2012 and beyond.

"We are in the midst of a fundamental transformation of how campaigns are run," Mr. Nelson said. "And it's not over yet."

The changes go beyond what Mr. Obama did and reflect a cultural shift in voters, producing an audience that is at once better informed, more skeptical and, from reading blogs, sometimes trafficking in rumors or suspect information. As a result, this new electorate tends to be more questioning of what it is told by campaigns and often uses the Web to do its own fact-checking.

"You do focus groups and people say, 'I saw that ad and I went to this Web site to check it,' " said David Plouffe, the Obama campaign manager. "They are policing the campaigns."

Mr. Schmidt said the speed and diversity of the news cycle had broken down the traditional way that voters received information and had given campaigns opportunities, and challenges, in trying to manage the news.

"The news cycle is hyperaccelerated and driven by new players on the landscape, like Politico and Huffington Post, which cause competition for organizations like The A.P. where there is a high premium on being first," he said. "This hyperaccelerates a cable-news cycle driven to conflict and drama and trivia."

Among the biggest changes this year is the intense new interest in politics, reflected in jumps in voters registration, early voting and attendance at Mr. Obama's rallies. To no small extent, that is a reflection on the unusual interest stirred by his campaign. Thus, it is hardly clear that a future candidate who appropriated all the innovations that Mr. Obama and his campaign tried would necessarily have the same success as Mr. Obama.

"Without the candidate who excites people," Mr. Plouffe said, "you can have the greatest strategy and machinery and it won't matter."

Mr. Trippi, who worked for one of Mr. Obama's rivals in the Democratic primary, former Senator John Edwards, said: "It has all come together for one guy, Barack Obama. But now that it's happened, it's a permanent change."

From *The New York Times,* November 4, 2008. Copyright © 2008 by The New York Times Company. Reprinted by permission via PARS International.

Triumph of Temperament, Not Policy

MICHAEL BARONE

The democrats' victory—and Barack Obama's—was overdetermined and underdelivered. Overdetermined: Huge majorities believe the country is on the wrong track and disapprove of George W. Bush; voters prefer generic Democrats over Republicans by 10 percent or more. But Obama beat John McCain by (at this writing) just 52 to 46 percent, running 2 points ahead of Bush in 2004 and 1 point behind George H.W. Bush in 1988. Democrats fell short of the 60 votes they need to stop filibusters in the Senate and made more modest gains in the House than the leading prognosticators expected.

To be sure, Obama ran a skillful campaign. Just as he capitalized on Hillary Clinton's weakness in party caucuses (she won more votes and delegates than he did in primaries), so in the general election he used his unprecedented ability to raise money by breaking his promise to take federal funds and by disabling the address verification system that would have screened out many illegal credit card contributions.

Such actions by a Republican, as *Washington Post* media critic Howard Kurtz has argued, would have gotten scathing coverage from mainstream media. Not so for Obama. His campaign outspent McCain's vastly on ads and organization in target states. That probably switched 1 percent or 2 percent of the vote in five key states—Florida, North Carolina, Virginia, Ohio and Indiana—which meant that Obama won a solid 364 electoral votes rather than a Bush-like thin majority of 278. All of which shows a certain ruthlessness. But ruthlessness is a useful quality for a president (see Roosevelt, Franklin; Reagan, Ronald).

Do Obama and the Democrats have a mandate? Obama got a larger percentage than any other Democrat since 1964, and Democrats have congressional majorities comparable to those in Bill Clinton's first two years. But their policies of protectionism and greater taxes on high earners seem ill-suited to a country facing a recession (see Hoover, Herbert). The public fisc does not appear to be overflowing enough to finance refundable tax credits, government health insurance or universal prekindergarten.

The half of the electorate that doesn't remember the 1970s may be more open to big government than those of us who do. But "open to" does not equal "demand." The decisive shift of public opinion came when the financial crisis hit. McCain approached it like a fighter pilot, denouncing Wall Street, suspending his campaign, threatening to skip the first debate.

Obama approached it like a law professor, cool and detached. Voters preferred law professor to fighter pilot. This was a triumph of temperament, not policy.

McCain approached the financial crisis like a fighter pilot; Obama, like a law professor.

Are we seeing a political realignment? Certainly some of the ingredients are there. As presidents, Reagan and Clinton attracted young voters to their parties; G.W. Bush signally failed to do so. Obama, before he has started governing, has inspired fervent, even quasi-religious devotion from the young and has brought millions of them into the electorate.

Judging from the polls and from my first look at the election returns, I believe he has attracted to his party many affluent, highly educated voters in metro areas running south from Philadelphia to Charlotte, N.C., and Tampa, Fla., and west to Denver and the Pacific. Democrats directed much rhetoric toward the white working class, but failed to win most of its votes. Instead, they assembled what you might call a top-and-bottom coalition: affluent suburbs plus blacks in central cities.

Alliances. The Democrats have always been a party of unlikely coalitions, capable of expansion when their leaders perform well, susceptible to disarray when they falter. The roughhewn John Murtha helps bring the designer-dressed Nancy Pelosi to power; the African-American quasi-academic Obama inspires millions in the highest- and lowest-income ZIP codes. And, as McCain handsomely acknowledged, there is something genuinely thrilling in the spectacle of Americans electing a black president.

But presidents can build majority coalitions only through performance (see Bush, G.W.). As president, Obama faces daunting problems. How to fix a financial system no one seems to fully understand. How to defeat terrorist enemies sheltered in the territory of our putative ally Pakistan. How to live up to the high expectations so visible in the cheering and tearful faces in those crowds in Berlin, Invesco Field and Grant Park. After a victory that was thrilling, but not quite what the Democrats hoped for.

The Other Winner

Howard Dean unleashed the new progressives. Can Obama deal with them?

MATT BAI

There was a moment last summer when Howard Dean's tenure as chairman of the Democratic Party seemed on the verge of a colossal failure. The party's nomination process, which was supposed to have been settled by March, was devolving into a rolling civil war without end, and Democrats grumbled that Dean—who might have stepped in and sorted out the mess before it got to the convention floor—seemed reluctant to intervene. Of all the various party entities that raise money, only Dean's national committee was getting clobbered by Republicans. For years, Democratic Congressional leaders had been mocking Dean's "50-state strategy"—his plan to rebuild local parties in every state, especially in rural areas of the South and West, by hiring organizers rather than saving that money for television ads in perennial battlegrounds like Florida and Ohio. Now they whispered that his incompetence might cost them the White House.

When I spoke to him on the day after Barack Obama swept into the White House with the largest Congressional Democratic majorities since the 1970s, Dean, characteristically defiant, refused to admit to feeling vindicated. "Everyone asks me that," he said. "Vindication is not an emotion that ever touches me, because I don't have any doubts when I'm doing it." But if election night stamped Obama indelibly into the pages of American history, then Dean's place in that history, too, should probably be revisited. Very nearly discarded by his contemporaries as a spectacularly flawed presidential candidate and a bumbling chairman, Dean may well be remembered instead as the flinty figure who bridged the distance between one generation of Democrats and the next, the man who first gave voice to liberal fury and tapped transformative technologies at the dawn of the century—and then channeled all of it into rebuilding the party's grass-roots apparatus. Just as Ronald Reagan and the conservatives learned from Barry Goldwater, just as Franklin Roosevelt and the New Dealers took inspiration from reformers like Robert La Follette, so, too, did Obama and the new progressives in America evolve from Howard Dean.

Skeptics will argue, of course, that Dean's stewardship of the party had little to do with the Democratic rout. After all, conservative states like Virginia, Indiana and North Carolina were

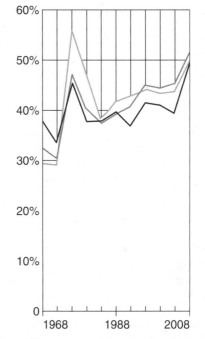

The New Blue. Percentage of the popular vote won by Democrats in North Carolina, Virginia and Indiana in the last 11 presidential elections.

in play principally because Republicans had so badly mismanaged the government and because of an economic collapse that was, to be a little crass, remarkably fortunate. And in Obama, the party fielded a nominee this time who was, for all his lack of experience, vastly more compelling than his most recent predecessors on the ticket.

And yet, it was Dean, back when Obama was still serving in the Illinois State Senate, who first introduced his party to the idea that, in the Internet age, a campaign could be built from the ground up, that door-to-door organizing could matter more than TV ads. And it was Dean who argued forcefully, as chairman, that Democrats in this new era could compete in the reddest of states and build a truly national party at a time when others in the party were belittling rural voters and agitating for a complete withdrawal from the South. Now the Republicans are the ones who find themselves reduced to regional influence, their shrinking Congressional delegations confined mostly to the South and West. (Remarkably, not a single New England Republican now remains in the House.) Dean didn't create the conditions that made that reversal possible, but he always said that if you wanted to be in a position to take advantage of favorable circumstances, then you had to at least have basic party infrastructures in place. "Chance favors the prepared mind," Dean told me, not for the first time. "You show up, you keep working and hopefully you catch a break."

That he did. Dean inherited a party so dispirited after its defeat in 2004 that few other Democrats of note expressed the least interest in running it; the party he relinquishes this January, making way for whomever Obama chooses to succeed him, will firmly control all three power centers in Washington, brandishing a decisive governing mandate for the first time since 1992. (Obama's 53 percent of the popular vote hardly qualifies as the "landslide" that some commentators said it was but, as Andrei Cherny noted on Huffington Post, Obama is only the fourth Democrat in American history to win at least 51 percent of the vote.) The important question for Democrats to consider now is what that mandate actually means.

Even before the country voted, as the contours of a Democratic wave began to come into focus, a story line of the election was taking hold among Democrats in Washington: repulsed by the incompetence of the Bush administration, American voters had at last renounced the conservative ethos of the Reagan-Bush era and had moved, en masse, to embrace the Democratic Party and its agenda. Polls showed, after all, that the number of people identifying themselves as Republicans had fallen sharply, while the ranks of those calling themselves Democrats had swelled. Surveys indicated that voters, in the wake of the credit crisis, had warmed to the idea of activist government. In fact, the election results, and especially the pivotal Democratic victories in Colorado, New Mexico and Nevada, seemed to validate the influential theory of the "emerging Democratic majority," advanced by the liberal political analysts Ruy Teixeira and John B. Judis in 2002. Combing through demographic trends, Teixeira and Judis hypothesized then that increasing numbers of nonwhite and new-economy voters would soon transform the country's electoral landscape and create new opportunities for Democrats, most notably in the West.

The cautionary note here, for jubilant Democrats, is that there is little reason to believe that the electoral trend in their favor actually reflects any widespread ideological shift. If you only look at numerical majorities, it might well seem that the story of the last 20 years in American politics is one in which voters have swerved erratically from one ideological pole to the next, embracing a harsh kind of conservatism in 1994 and then a resurgent liberalism in 2006. In reality, though, the American public doesn't seem to move very much in its basic attitudes about government, which have remained mostly pragmatic and predictable; simply put, people tend to want a little more government when times are tough and a little less when things

are going well. The number of voters who identified themselves in exit polls as conservative, liberal or moderate remained virtually unchanged between 2004 and 2008—and in fact, those numbers have been more or less steady for decades.

The real trend line in our politics—from Ross Perot and Bill Clinton in 1992 to Obama this year—speaks not to any change in governing philosophy but to a growing frustration with incumbency and dogma, a sense that both parties are more concerned with perpetuating their own power than they are with adapting government to a fast-changing world. Voters aren't really identifying more closely with one party or another when they periodically revolt; they are simply defining themselves against whoever happens to be in charge at the moment.

It now falls to Obama, as it did to Bill Clinton in 1993, to pursue a realist's agenda while somehow restraining powerful forces in his own party.

Perhaps because he is too young to have lived in a world where party affiliations were as unshakable as religious beliefs, or perhaps because he has spent so little of his life in Washington, Obama seems intuitively to understand this dynamic. (His chief strategist, David Axelrod, has long understood it, too.) Obama's entire campaign was based on the rather amorphous idea of "change" and postpartisan ideals, on an indictment of the two-party status quo, more than on any ideological argument about the role of government. It now falls to Obama, as it did to Bill Clinton in 1993, to pursue a realist's agenda while somehow restraining the forces in his own party—powerful liberal committee chairmen, sprawling interest groups—who would overreach, attempting to make of the party's mandate something that it is not.

One significant difference between then and now, however, lies in the nature of the tensions in the Democratic coalition. Clinton's party was riven, predictably enough, by geography and ideology; like Jimmy Carter before him, Clinton tried to straddle an ever-widening gap between Northern and coastal liberals whose ideal of government remained expansive and those Southern and Western Democrats who embraced a more centrist or even conservative philosophy. This was, of course, the same basic divide that underlaid the Democrats' governing coalition since Franklin Roosevelt.

Obama's landscape is less familiar. Surely there will be some residual clashes between left and center in Obama's party, but his real challenge isn't so much ideological as it is generational, a reconciling of worldviews forged in contrasting American moments. Obama's candidacy was propelled chiefly by groups that are emerging in American politics. He represents the new and ascendant service-industry unions, for instance, as opposed to the industrial-age unions that supported Hillary Clinton. He speaks more to younger voters—the 40-and-under crowd—than to their boomer parents, more to African-American families than to their leaders in churches and in Congress, who came to him only grudgingly. Obama ignites more passion among the millions of lesser-engaged, text-messaging Americans who signed up for accounts on his site (and who, in many cases, volunteered for their first political campaign) than he does among the party's older, stalwart activists.

This younger Democratic base stands less on loyalty to institutions generally, and that includes the Democratic Party itself. These voters represent a generation of Americans reared in the cynical, detached environment after Watergate rather than in the idealist, more doctrinaire atmosphere of the '60s. To keep his party unified, Obama will have to embody this modern, less-partisan ethos while at the same time respecting the power and conviction of an older set of Democrats who nurture a less-flexible liberal ideal and who aren't yet ready to step aside. Obama's task is to somehow move away from reflexively partisan solutions—no trade deals, no charter schools, no entitlement reform—even as he defers to a generation of leaders for whom ideology and partisanship are the guiding paradigms of political thought.

Voters will be watching to see how Obama achieves this balancing act within his own party—and none more so, perhaps, than those conservative voters who are waiting to see whether this young Democrat will really deliver the systemic change he promised. In a conversation not long before the end of the campaign, Obama told me he understood that these voters didn't yet feel they knew him and that, even if they voted for him because of their economic jitters, their support would represent little more than an opportunity for him to prove, as president, that he could move beyond the partisan divisions of the last generation. Howard Dean was right to insist that a Democrat in the online age could redraw the political map, and for that he deserves more than passing mention in subsequent histories of the time. But the job of creating a more lasting realignment always falls—as it did in the eras of the New Dealers and the conservative movement—to a president with the vision and temperament to pull the country forcibly into the future. For Obama and his party, the only 50-state strategy now is to govern as if they mean it.

Clicking and Choosing

The election according to YouTube.

VIRGINIA HEFFERNAN

During the presidential election, YouTube turned from a hectic mosaic of weird video clips to a first-stop source for political everything. Every gotcha moment, spoof, pundit's musing, TV clip, campaign speech, formal ad and hand-made polemic cropped up there. Star posters like Brave New Films, Barely Political and Talking Points Memo TV emerged; they cranked out parody and propaganda much faster than the campaigns themselves. Was YouTube just a new place to envision an election that would have gone the same way without it? Or does the unpredictable new form of online video carry its own ideology—a new message to go with a new medium?

YouTube didn't exist in 2004. It started up the next year. As Steve Grove, YouTube's head of news and politics, points out, the 2008 presidential election was the site's first shot at wielding influence in national politics. Sure, videos of senators dozing through hearings had always been popular on the site—and some observers even cited YouTube's gotcha videos for helping defeat the senators George Allen and Conrad Burns in the 2006 midterm elections. But YouTube wanted to do more than create mischief. The brass at the site jumped at the chance to grow up by seriously engaging voters, candidates and the mainstream media.

As MTV had done, YouTube first presented itself as a way for candidates to connect with "the youth vote." In the end, the site wound up profoundly affecting the popular perception of candidates across demographics. It showed that a video of 37 minutes—the length of Barack Obama's March speech on race—was not too long to attract more than five million views. It showed that nearly all the foot soldiers for a candidate need skills with digital technology—as editing and uploading video is now more important to a campaign than direct mail. And it showed that offhand jokes—think McCain's "bomb Iran" Beach Boys routine—can be disastrous. It's better for a candidate in the YouTube age to speak feelingly from lecterns and let voters respond chiefly to his rhetorical strategies.

In 2006, YouTube's political team came up with the idea of YouChoose, a section of the site devoted to showing videos from candidates; it began in February the next year. At first, says a spokesman for YouTube, some politicians feared that the site could only burn them with Allen-like "macaca" moments. But eventually 7 of 16 people who ran for the presidency announced their candidacies on YouTube. And as the campaign season wore on, many candidates learned to turn the site's idiosyncrasies to their advantage. They uploaded ads and permitted freewheeling—sometimes ferocious—discussion of them. Recognizing that glasnost is the key to acceptance among YouTube users, candidates virtually forfeited control over the context of their videos and allowed them to be embedded, critiqued, recut and satirized.

Some candidates also discovered, to their surprise, that they could upload vanity videos (or ones that seemed fairly parody-proof) and supporters would circulate them on social networks, amateurs would use them to make ads and they would get influential, focused advertising for nothing. Early on, the musician will.i.am used film of an Obama speech to make his "Yes We Can" music video. That video, in multiple versions, has become the most-watched political entry on the site, having been seen around 15 million times. (The campaign's upload of the actual "Yes We Can" speech has fewer than two million views.)

In the end, all the candidates opened YouTube accounts and together uploaded thousands of videos. (John McCain's channel now shows 330 videos; Barack Obama's shows 1,821.) Even after an unaffiliated user called ParkRidge47 created "Vote Different," which acidly satirized Clinton's "Hillcast" videos, the Clinton campaign kept uploading shorts, including a spoof of "The Sopranos" that won her points for sophistication and brazenness. The BarackObamadotcom account uploaded more than 150 videos during the campaign's final days, including a personal appeal by Obama's sister, Maya Soetoro-Ng, and another by Ethel Kennedy and her son Max.

Grove, who worked at *The Boston Globe* and ABC News before going to YouTube, was part of the company's political team that met with almost every candidate at the start of the campaign season. They made YouTube available to the candidates and encouraged them to start channels on YouChoose that would allow viewers to contribute money directly to campaigns via Google Checkout. Some campaigns, like Ralph Nader's, which featured a video of the candidate talking to a parrot, and Mike Gravel's, which was defined by a strange art film that could have been made by Lars von Trier, seemed to exist almost entirely on YouTube.

While some more-mainstream campaigns felt bruised by the conventions of the site—in an interview with Grove, John McCain jokingly referred to YouTube as "my sworn enemy" and expressed regret that several videos turned his "bomb Iran" quip into an earnest statement of policy—others savored the chance to talk to the electorate, talk back to the electorate, spin, campaign and upload video.

YouTube signed on as a partner for two CNN-YouTube presidential debates, at which select YouTube users had their questions for the candidates of both parties broadcast and answered on CNN. YouTube also stayed close to the Iowa caucus, the New Hampshire and Pennsylvania primaries and Super Tuesday, creating programs to allow voters to upload video that would give a sense of primary voting in their state.

What YouTube can do with these and all its other videos—how it might make money from them—is another question. But then, with advertising seeming to dry up on TV and in print media, mainstream outlets have despaired at making money off even the most captive audiences. The story of YouTube, so far, is not necessarily the story of the business of the future; it's too strange a place and too uncertain a profit model to inspire copycats. As a minicivilization, though—with heroes and villains and mores and bylaws—YouTube is a fascinating place. In 2008, a group of dogged politicos climbed its hierarchy. They created some videos that glorified the persona of the orator, and others that censured anyone playful or reckless enough to sing about bombing Iran. As he was in the election, the big winner on YouTube was Barack Obama.

From *The New York Times Magazine,* November 16, 2008. Copyright © 2008 by New York Times Syndicate. Reprinted by permission.

BHO: QED

Why Obama is scientifically certain to win in November.

JOHN BALZ

If you spend time among the chattering classes, it's easy to get caught up in Campaign '08's most tantalizing questions. Has the length and tenor of the primary campaign irreparably split the Democratic Party in half? Could the Jeremiah Wright videos hurt Barack Obama more in the general election than they did in the primary? Might improvements on the ground in Iraq make John McCain's support for the war less of a problem with voters and burnish his image as a leader on national security? Well, sure, all these things could happen. But the disinterested, square students of politics, otherwise known as political scientists, find this kind of distress silly. That's because Obama will win this fall. Period. As a political scientist, I'll stake the reputation of my profession on it. Maybe some money, too.

Over the past few decades, political scientists have come up with increasingly elaborate statistical models for predicting presidential election outcomes. The basic idea is that voters evaluate presidents largely on the basis of how the economy has fared under them. That extends to potential successors in the same party. As such, McCain basically inherits Bush's record and Obama inherits Clinton's record. These statistical models have also gotten quite accurate in their presidential forecasting. In 2004, during a very close race, eleven out of twelve studies correctly predicted a Bush win.

So why is Obama certain to prevail? Much of it boils down to what you've already heard in the press: what political scientists call the fundamentals—primarily presidential approval, the state of the economy, and incumbency—are indisputably in the Democrats' favor this year. And don't be deceived by fluctuating poll numbers, either. At this time in 1988, George H.W. Bush was solidly trailing Michael Dukakis in Gallup polls. Likewise, at this time in 1992, George H.W. Bush was solidly leading Bill Clinton. Enough said.

While political science models differ from one another in the variables they take into account and in how they weigh them, nearly all of the models are quantitative. That means they not only pick a winner—they also forecast what his or her margin of victory will be. So what are the models saying for 2008? Douglas Hibbs, who has been studying the relationship between voting and the economy since the 1970s, has predicted that the Republican candidate will win only 46.7 percent of the vote. (That means the Democrat would win 53.3 percent of the vote, since these models assume only a two-party race.) In two different models, Michael Lewis-Beck and Charles Tien of Iowa, while using quite generous assumptions for Bush's presidential popularity (35 percent) and GNP growth (3 percent annual), still predict either a narrow Republican defeat (with McCain winning 48.5 percent of the vote) or else a far more resounding one, with McCain winning only 41.4 percent. Alan Abramowitz of Emory, assuming 2 percent economic growth for the first half of the year and a 30 percent difference between the president's approval and disapproval numbers, estimates that McCain's vote total will be just under 44 percent. Ray Fair, a Yale economist, puts McCain's total at 47.8 percent. And the outlier in this crowd, Helmut Norpoth of SUNY at Stonybrook, has said that the Democratic candidate would beat McCain by only a single percentage point or less—still far from encouraging as a best-case scenario for the GOP.

So, then, if it's already been proven scientifically to be a Democratic year no matter what, why even bother to have a campaign? Or an election? Why not just hand the White House over to Obama right away? Well, here's the catch. First of all, political science isn't saying that if the election were held *today* the Democratic candidate would win. The models assume a November election. Nor are political scientists saying that Obama could win without campaigning. Indeed, their models assume that both sides will campaign. Rather, what they're saying is that the function of the campaigns will merely be to awaken the latent preferences already existing within voters. Sure, bulging campaign coffers and sky-high IQs are important assets, but they're unlikely to be significantly disparate between the two campaigns. Political scientists therefore tend to view them as a wash. (And, yes, this does tend to make us boring Beltway dinner guests.) Think of campaigning as irrigating a field in which the seeds are already planted and the weather isn't too crazy. You can't change the crop, but you do need to add the water.

And what about the worry *du jour,* the supposed split in the Democratic coalition? Again, take it from a political scientist. Don't sweat it. Democrats will come home. John Sides of

George Washington has shown that loyalty has been on the rise since the early 1970s, when only about 60 percent of Democrats voted for the Democratic nominee. Today—and since the 1990s—it's been closer to 90 percent. Sides has also dismissed the party's great education divide—college versus no college. It's "at times non-existent and, when it exists, has not 'widened' over time." More than 80 percent of Democrats with or without college degrees have supported the Democratic presidential candidate in the general election since 1988, and that number has been closer to 90 percent over the past decade. Bitter as Hillary's supporters have been, they're not going to make a meaningful dent in this trend.

Now, you may still think I'm being overly confident in my soothsaying. And I'll concede it's a strange year. For the first time since 1952, the incumbent party's candidate is neither a president nor vice president. In theory, just as Bill Clinton's strong economic record did not rub off on Al Gore, George Bush's foreign policy errors will not rub off on John McCain. But I seriously doubt it. My friends, as John McCain might say, the die is cast. As long as Democratic donors write checks, the Obama ground team performs in November as it did in February, and (let us pray) the country avoids a major terrorist attack, the story of 2008 will end happily for Democrats and for the reputation of political science. And at this point, with all the bets I plan to make, it's the only outcome I can afford.

JOHN BALZ is a political science graduate student at the University of Chicago.

UNIT 4

Products of American Politics

Unit Selections

Key Points to Consider

- What do you think is the single most important social welfare or economic policy issue facing the American political system today? The single most important national security or homeland security issue? What do you think ought to be done about them?

- What factors increasingly blur the distinction between foreign and domestic policy issues? How does "homeland security" fit into this context?

- How would you compare President George W. Bush's performance in the areas of social welfare and economic policies with the way he has handled national security and diplomatic affairs? What changes has he tried to make in each of these areas?

- What policy issues currently viewed as minor matters seem destined to develop into crisis situations?

- How important a policy issue for Americans is climate change or global warming? How important is it for you?

- What short-term and long-term effects did the events of September 11, 2001 have on the U.S. policy process and the direction of U.S. government policies?

- What do you think about the idea of devolution, which means giving state and local governments more responsibility for policymaking and policy implementation, and the national government less? What reasons are there to expect that state and local governments will do a better—or worse—job than the national government in such areas as welfare and access to health care for the old and the poor?

- How and why would you prioritize the following list of policy challenges facing American government? Which do you think need to be addressed quickly and forcefully, even if that means delaying on others? List of policy challenges: economic recovery, global warming, health care reform, homeland security, education, the budget deficit, and rapidly increasing Social Security and Medicare costs associated with the coming retirements of the baby boomer generation.

Student Web Site

www.mhcls.com

Internet References

American Diplomacy
  http://www.unc.edu/depts/diplomat/
Cato Institute
  http://www.cato.org/research/ss_prjct.html
Foreign Affairs
  http://www.foreignaffairs.org

International Information Programs
  http://usinfo.state.gov
STAT-USA
  http://www.stat-usa.gov/stat-usa.html
Tax Foundation
  http://www.taxfoundation.org/index.html

"**P**roducts" refers to the government policies that the American political system produces. The first three units of this book have paved the way for this fourth unit, because the products of American politics are very much the consequences of the rest of the political system.

The health of the American economy is almost always a prominent policy issue in the American political system. One of the most remarkable consequences of twelve years (1981–1993) under President Reagan and the first President Bush was enormous growth in budget deficits and in the national debt. During the Clinton presidency, the country enjoyed the longest period of continuous economic growth in U.S. history, accompanied by low unemployment and low inflation rates. Continuing economic growth increased tax revenues to such an extent that the long-sought goal of a balanced budget was reached in 1998 amid predictions that the entire national debt would be eliminated within a decade or so. In the last months of the Clinton administration, however, some signs of an economic slowdown appeared. President George W. Bush pushed tax cuts through Congress early in his presidency, the country entered a recession in the second half of President Bush's first year in office, and the September 11 terrorist attacks accelerated the economic downturn. Large budget deficits returned and the national debt grew accordingly. By 2007, with the costs of the war in Iraq continuing to mount and the retirement of baby boomers drawing ever nearer, the country's fiscal situation remained a cause for serious concern.

In 2008, home mortgage and other financial market problems shook the foundations of the nation's credit and banking systems, bringing Wall Street woes and a recession. Meanwhile, the national government's budget deficit soared, and growth in the national debt exceeded even that which had occurred during the Reagan administration and the first Bush presidency. By late 2008, it was unclear whether the traditional mainstays of American industry, the Big Three automakers, would avoid bankruptcy, as they publicly sought a "bail-out" from Washington in order to survive. Economic problems in the United States reverberated around the globe and many observers suggested that the economic downturn was going to be the worst since the Great Depression. This grim assessment of economic woes tended to overshadow other policy challenges as Barack Obama prepared to assume the presidency in 2009.

Domestic public policy usually involves "trade-offs" among competing uses of scarce resources. During his 1992 campaign, Bill Clinton called attention to many such trade-offs in the area of health care. As president, Clinton introduced a comprehensive health care reform proposal late in 1993. Congress never voted on that proposal, and, while various minor changes were made in the nation's health care delivery system during the Clinton administration, no comprehensive overhaul was ever achieved. In his 2007 State of the Union address, President Bush presented

www.hud.gov

several proposals relating to health care, including a change in relevant tax code provisions. Health care reform was a major priority of the two leading candidates for the Democratic presidential nomination in 2008, Hillary Clinton and Barack Obama, and change-oriented Obama's victory over John McCain would, under ordinary circumstances, suggest that some action would likely be taken. But whether even a new, energetic, and eloquent president like Obama can afford to tackle health care reform in the face of a multiplicity of other problems—a serious economic downturn, global warming, homeland security, and the wars in Iraq and Afghanistan—remains to be seen. "Trade-offs" will almost surely be an important factor in what gets done.

For most of the last half of the twentieth century, the United States and the Soviet Union each had the capacity to end human existence as we know it. Not surprisingly, the threat of nuclear war often dominated American foreign policy and diplomacy. During that same period, however, the United States used conventional military forces in a number of places, such as Korea, Vietnam, Grenada, Panama, the Persian Gulf area, and Afghanistan. The demise of the Soviet Union in 1991 left the United States as the world's sole superpower, profoundly affecting world politics and U.S. foreign policy ever since. Questions about the appropriateness of U.S. intervention in such disparate places as Bosnia-Herzegovina, Somalia, Haiti, Iraq, Kosovo, and even Russia were at the forefront of foreign policy concerns during the Clinton administration. The George W. Bush administration, of course, became preoccupied with antiterrorism efforts and homeland and national security after the September 11 terrorist attacks.

The foreign and defense policy process in the United States raises a host of related issues, including continuing struggle between legislative and executive branches for control. In 1991, Congress authorized war with Iraq, which was the first time since World War II that there has been explicit and formal congressional approval before commencement of U.S. military hostilities. In late 1995, President Clinton committed the United States to sending troops to Bosnia-Herzegovina as part of a multinational peacekeeping force. Despite some opposition, Congress passed resolutions supporting the troops. Toward the end of 1997, President Saddam Hussein of Iraq obstructed UN weapons inspection teams in his country, and President Clinton responded by increasing the readiness of U.S. military forces in the Persian Gulf. In late 1998, several days of U.S. air strikes on Iraq followed what was viewed as further provocation.

In the aftermath of the terrorist attacks in 2001, Congress supported President George W. Bush in pursuing the perpetrators and launching an assault on Al Qaeda sites in Afghanistan. In the fall of 2002, Congress authorized President Bush to wage war against Iraq if he deemed it necessary to safeguard American security. Early in 2003, U.S. forces invaded Iraq, and critics in Congress and elsewhere suggested that President Bush had made insufficient attempts to gain international support. The initial military success in toppling Saddam Hussein's government has been followed by five years of violent insurgency that threatened the legitimacy of Iraqi self-government, killed more than 4,000 U.S. troops and many multiples of that number of Iraqis, and cost billions and billions of dollars. Americans' dissatisfaction

with the Iraq war led to the Democratic takeover of the House and Senate in November 2006, which in turn set the stage for a sharp debate between President Bush and Congress about what to do next and about the proper role of each branch in shaping national security policy. Barack Obama made his early opposition to the Iraq war a cornerstone of his presidential candidacy and promised to remove American troops from Iraq in a timely manner if he became president. By late 2008, the Iraqi government declared that American troops should be removed from Iraq within three years. During the transition period between his election and his taking the oath of office on January 20, 2009, Obama announced that he would keep President Bush's Secretary of Defense, Robert Gates, one of whose responsibilities would be to oversee the safe withdrawal of American troops from Iraq. This move may suggest that, at long last, American policy-makers and the American public are moving toward a consensus about ending American military involvement in Iraq.

The traditional distinction between domestic and foreign policy is becoming more and more difficult to maintain, since so many contemporary policy decisions have important implications on both fronts. President Clinton's emphasis on the connection between domestic and international economic issues in maintaining what he called national economic security reinforced this point. In turn, he worked hard to pass the NAFTA accord of 1993, which dramatically reduced trade barriers among Canada, Mexico, and the United States. Similarly, President George W. Bush has repeatedly noted the connection between, on the one hand, military and diplomatic activities with respect to faraway places like Afghanistan, Iraq, Iran, and North Korea and, on the other, homeland security in the post-September 11 era. In his second inaugural address in 2005, President Bush declared that the liberty and security of Americans at home depends on the "expansion of freedom in all the world." Two prominent policy challenges facing the Obama administration, economic recovery and global warming, further illustrate the convergence between domestic and foreign policy. With an increasingly globalized economy, the economic health of the United States is inevitably tied to economic conditions around the world. Similarly, no unilateral action by the United States to fight global warming can be successful; strategies to combat climate change can succeed only if pursued on a multilateral, or global, level.

The Tax-Cut Con

PAUL KRUGMAN

1. The Cartoon and the Reality

Bruce Tinsley's comic strip, "Mallard Fillmore," is, he says, "for the average person out there: the forgotten American taxpayer who's sick of the liberal media." In June, that forgotten taxpayer made an appearance in the strip, attacking his TV set with a baseball bat and yelling: "I can't afford to send my kids to college, or even take 'em out of their substandard public school, because the federal, state and local governments take more than 50 percent of my income in taxes. And then the guy on the news asks with a straight face whether or not we can 'afford' tax cuts."

But that's just a cartoon. Meanwhile, Bob Riley has to face the reality.

Riley knows all about substandard public schools. He's the governor of Alabama, which ranks near the bottom of the nation in both spending per pupil and educational achievement. The state has also neglected other public services—for example, 28,000 inmates are held in a prison system built for 12,000. And thanks in part to a lack of health care, it has the second-highest infant mortality in the nation.

When he was a member of Congress, Riley, a Republican, was a staunch supporter of tax cuts. Faced with a fiscal crisis in his state, however, he seems to have had an epiphany. He decided that it was impossible to balance Alabama's budget without a significant tax increase. And that, apparently, led him to reconsider everything. "The largest tax increase in state history just to maintain the status quo?" he asked. "I don't think so." Instead, Riley proposed a wholesale restructuring of the state's tax system: reducing taxes on the poor and middle class while raising them on corporations and the rich and increasing overall tax receipts enough to pay for a big increase in education spending. You might call it a New Deal for Alabama.

Nobody likes paying taxes, and no doubt some Americans are as angry about their taxes as Tinsley's imaginary character. But most Americans also care a lot about the things taxes pay for. All politicians say they're for public education; almost all of them also say they support a strong national defense, maintaining Social Security and, if anything, expanding the coverage of Medicare. When the "guy on the news" asks whether we can afford a tax cut, he's asking whether, after yet another tax cut goes through, there will be enough money to pay for those things. And the answer is no.

But it's very difficult to get that answer across in modern American politics, which has been dominated for 25 years by a crusade against taxes.

I don't use the word "crusade" lightly. The advocates of tax cuts are relentless, even fanatical. An indication of the movement's fervor—and of its political power—came during the Iraq war. War is expensive and is almost always accompanied by tax increases. But not in 2003. "Nothing is more important in the face of a war," declared Tom DeLay, the House majority leader, "than cutting taxes." And sure enough, taxes were cut, not just in a time of war but also in the face of record budget deficits. Nor will it be easy to reverse those tax cuts: the tax-cut movement has convinced many Americans—like Tinsley—that everybody still pays far too much in taxes.

A result of the tax-cut crusade is that there is now a fundamental mismatch between the benefits Americans expect to receive from the government and the revenues government collect. This mismatch is already having profound effects at the state and local levels: teachers and policemen are being laid off and children are being denied health insurance. The federal government can mask its problems for a while, by running huge budget deficits, but it, too, will eventually have to decide whether to cut services or raise taxes. And we are not talking about minor policy adjustments. If taxes stay as low as they are now, government as we know it cannot be maintained. In particular, Social Security will have to become far less generous; Medicare will no longer be able to guarantee comprehensive medical care to older Americans; Medicaid will no longer provide basic medical care to the poor.

How did we reach this point? What are the origins of the antitax crusade? And where is it taking us? To answer these questions, we will have to look both at who the antitax crusaders are and at the evidence on what tax cuts do to the budget and the economy. But first, let's set the stage by taking a look at the current state of taxation in America.

2. How High Are Our Taxes?

The reason Tinsley's comic strip about the angry taxpayer caught my eye was, of course, that the numbers were all wrong. Very few Americans pay as much as 50 percent of their income in taxes; on average, families near the middle of the income distribution pay only about half that percentage in federal, state and local taxes combined.

In fact, though most Americans feel that they pay too much in taxes, they get off quite lightly compared with the citizens of other advanced countries. Furthermore, for most Americans tax rates probably haven't risen for a generation. And a few Americans—namely those with high incomes—face much lower taxes than they did a generation ago.

To assess trends in the overall level of taxes and to compare taxation across countries, economists usually look first at the ratio of taxes to gross domestic product, the total value of output produced in the country. In the United States, all taxes—federal, state and local—reached a peak of 29.6 percent of G.D.P. in 2000. That number was, however, swollen by taxes on capital gains during the stock-market bubble.

By 2002, the tax take was down to 26.3 percent of G.D.P., and all indications are that it will be lower still this year and next.

This is a low number compared with almost every other advanced country. In 1999, Canada collected 38.2 percent of G.D.P. in taxes, France collected 45.8 percent and Sweden, 52.2 percent.

Still, aren't taxes much higher than they used to be? Not if we're looking back over the past 30 years. As a share of G.D.P., federal taxes are currently at their lowest point since the Eisenhower administration. State and local taxes rose substantially between 1960 and the early 1970's, but have been roughly stable since then. Aside from the capital gains taxes paid during the bubble years, the share of income Americans pay in taxes has been flat since Richard Nixon was president.

Of course, overall levels of taxation don't necessarily tell you how heavily particular individuals and families are taxed. As it turns out, however, middle-income Americans, like the country as a whole, haven't seen much change in their overall taxes over the past 30 years. On average, families in the middle of the income distribution find themselves paying about 26 percent of their income in taxes today. This number hasn't changed significantly since 1989, and though hard data are lacking, it probably hasn't changed much since 1970.

Meanwhile, wealthy Americans have seen a sharp drop in their tax burden. The top tax rate—the income-tax rate on the highest bracket—is now 35 percent, half what it was in the 1970's. With the exception of a brief period between 1988 and 1993, that's the lowest rate since 1932. Other taxes that, directly or indirectly, bear mainly on the very affluent have also been cut sharply. The effective tax rate on corporate profits has been cut in half since the 1960's. The 2001 tax cut phases out the inheritance tax, which is overwhelmingly a tax on the very wealthy: in 1999, only 2 percent of estates paid any tax, and half the tax was paid by only 3,300 estates worth more than $5 million. The 2003 tax act sharply cuts taxes on dividend income, another boon to the very well off. By the time the Bush tax cuts have taken full effect, people with really high incomes will face their lowest average tax rate since the Hoover administration.

So here's the picture: Americans pay low taxes by international standards. Most people's taxes haven't gone up in the past generation; the wealthy have had their taxes cut to levels not seen since before the New Deal. Even before the latest round of tax cuts, when compared with citizens of other advanced nations or compared with Americans a generation ago, we had nothing to complain about—and those with high incomes now have a lot to celebrate. Yet a significant number of Americans rage against

taxes, and the party that controls all three branches of the federal government has made tax cuts its supreme priority. Why?

3. Supply-Siders, Starve-the-Beasters and Lucky Duckies

It is often hard to pin down what antitax crusaders are trying to achieve. The reason is not, or not only, that they are disingenuous about their motives—though as we will see, disingenuity has become a hallmark of the movement in recent years. Rather, the fuzziness comes from the fact that today's antitax movement moves back and forth between two doctrines. Both doctrines favor the same thing: big tax cuts for people with high incomes. But they favor it for different reasons.

One of those doctrines has become famous under the name "supply-side economics." It's the view that the government can cut taxes without severe cuts in public spending. The other doctrine is often referred to as "starving the beast," a phrase coined by David Stockman, Ronald Reagan's budget director. It's the view that taxes should be cut precisely in order to force severe cuts in public spending. Supply-side economics is the friendly, attractive face of the tax-cut movement. But starve-the-beast is where the power lies.

The starting point of supply-side economics is an assertion that no economist would dispute: taxes reduce the incentive to work, save and invest. A businessman who knows that 70 cents of every extra dollar he makes will go to the I.R.S. is less willing to make the effort to earn that extra dollar than if he knows that the I.R.S. will take only 35 cents. So reducing tax rates will, other things being the same, spur the economy.

This much isn't controversial. But the government must pay its bills. So the standard view of economists is that if you want to reduce the burden of taxes, you must explain what government programs you want to cut as part of the deal. There's no free lunch.

What the supply-siders argued, however, was that there was a free lunch. Cutting marginal rates, they insisted, would lead to such a large increase in gross domestic product that it wouldn't be necessary to come up with offsetting spending cuts. What supply-side economists say, in other words, is, "Don't worry, be happy and cut taxes." And when they say cut taxes, they mean taxes on the affluent: reducing the top marginal rate means that the biggest tax cuts go to people in the highest tax brackets.

The other camp in the tax-cut crusade actually welcomes the revenue losses from tax cuts. Its most visible spokesman today is Grover Norquist, president of Americans for Tax Reform, who once told National Public Radio: "I don't want to abolish government. I simply want to reduce it to the size where I can drag it into the bathroom and drown it in the bathtub." And the way to get it down to that size is to starve it of revenue. "The goal is reducing the size and scope of government by draining its lifeblood," Norquist told *U.S. News & World Report*.

What does "reducing the size and scope of government" mean? Tax-cut proponents are usually vague about the details. But the Heritage Foundation, ideological headquarters for the movement, has made it pretty clear. Edwin Feulner, the foundation's president, uses "New Deal" and "Great Society" as terms of abuse, implying that he and his organization want to do away with the institutions Franklin Roosevelt and Lyndon Johnson created. That means Social Security, Medicare, Medicaid—most of what gives citizens of the United States a safety net against economic misfortune.

The starve-the-beast doctrine is now firmly within the conservative mainstream. George W. Bush himself seemed to endorse the doctrine as the budget surplus evaporated: in August 2001 he called the disappearing surplus "incredibly positive news" because it would put Congress in a "fiscal straitjacket."

Like supply-siders, starve-the-beasters favor tax cuts mainly for people with high incomes. That is partly because, like supply-siders, they emphasize the incentive effects of cutting the top marginal rate; they just don't believe that those incentive effects are big enough that tax cuts pay for themselves. But they have another reason for cutting taxes mainly on the rich, which has become known as the "lucky ducky" argument.

Here's how the argument runs: to starve the beast, you must not only deny funds to the government; you must make voters hate the government. There's a danger that working-class families might see government as their friend: because their incomes are low, they don't pay much in taxes, while they benefit from public spending. So in starving the beast, you must take care not to cut taxes on these "lucky duckies." (Yes, that's what *The Wall Street Journal* called them in a famous editorial.) In fact, if possible, you must *raise* taxes on working-class Americans in order, as *The Journal* said, to get their "blood boiling with tax rage."

So the tax-cut crusade has two faces. Smiling supply-siders say that tax cuts are all gain, no pain; scowling starve-the-beasters believe that inflicting pain is not just necessary but also desirable. Is the alliance between these two groups a marriage of convenience? Not exactly. It would be more accurate to say that the starve-the-beasters hired the supply-siders—indeed, created them—because they found their naive optimism useful.

A look at who the supply-siders are and how they came to prominence tells the story.

The supply-side movement likes to present itself as a school of economic thought like Keynesianism or monetarism—that is, as a set of scholarly ideas that made their way, as such ideas do, into political discussion. But the reality is quite different. Supply-side economics was a political doctrine from Day 1; it emerged in the pages of political magazines, not professional economics journals.

That is not to deny that many professional economists favor tax cuts. But they almost always turn out to be starve-the-beasters, not supply-siders. And they often secretly—or sometimes not so secretly—hold supply-siders in contempt. N. Gregory Mankiw, now chairman of George W. Bush's Council of Economic Advisers, is definitely a friend to tax cuts; but in the first edition of his economic-principles textbook, he described Ronald Reagan's supply-side advisers as "charlatans and cranks."

It is not that the professionals refuse to consider supply-side ideas; rather, they have looked at them and found them wanting. A conspicuous example came earlier this year when the Congressional Budget Office tried to evaluate the growth effects of the Bush administration's proposed tax cuts. The budget office's new head, Douglas Holtz-Eakin, is a conservative economist who was handpicked for his job by the administration. But his conclusion was that unless the revenue losses from the proposed tax cuts were offset by spending cuts, the resulting deficits would be a drag on growth, quite likely to outweigh any supply-side effects.

But if the professionals regard the supply-siders with disdain, who employs these people? The answer is that since the 1970s almost all of the prominent supply-siders have been aides to conservative politicians, writers at conservative publications like *National Review*, fellows at conservative policy centers like Heritage or economists at private companies with strong Republican connections. Loosely speaking, that is, supply-siders work for the vast right-wing conspiracy. What gives supply-side economics influence is its connection with a powerful network of institutions that want to shrink the government and see tax cuts as a way to achieve that goal. Supply-side economics is a feel-good cover story for a political movement with a much harder-nosed agenda.

This isn't just speculation. Irving Kristol, in his role as co-editor of *The Public Interest*, was arguably the single most important proponent of supply-side economics. But years later, he suggested that he himself wasn't all that persuaded by the doctrine: "I was not certain of its economic merits but quickly saw its political possibilities." Writing in 1995, he explained that his real aim was to shrink the government and that tax cuts were a means to that end: "The task, as I saw it, was to create a new majority, which evidently would mean a conservative majority, which came to mean, in turn, a Republican majority—so political effectiveness was the priority, not the accounting deficiencies of government."

In effect, what Kristol said in 1995 was that he and his associates set out to deceive the American public. They sold tax cuts on the pretense that they would be painless, when they themselves believed that it would be necessary to slash public spending in order to make room for those cuts.

But one supposes that the response would be that the end justified the means—that the tax cuts did benefit all Americans because they led to faster economic growth. Did they?

4. From Reaganomics to Clintonomics

Ronald Reagan put supply-side theory into practice with his 1981 tax cut. The tax cuts were modest for middle-class families but very large for the well-off. Between 1979 and 1983, according to Congressional Budget Office estimates, the average federal tax rate on the top 1 percent of families fell from 37 to 27.7 percent.

So did the tax cuts promote economic growth? You might think that all we have to do is look at how the economy performed. But it's not that simple, because different observers read different things from Reagan's economic record.

Here's how tax-cut advocates look at it: after a deep slump between 1979 and 1982, the U.S. economy began growing rapidly. Between 1982 and 1989 (the first year of the first George Bush's presidency), the economy grew at an average annual rate of 4.2 percent. That's a lot better than the growth rate of the economy in the late 1970s, and supply-siders claim that these "Seven Fat Years" (the title of a book by Robert L. Bartley, the longtime editor of *The Wall Street Journal*'s editorial page) prove the success of Reagan's 1981 tax cut.

But skeptics say that rapid growth after 1982 proves nothing: a severe recession is usually followed by a period of fast growth, as unemployed workers and factories are brought back on line. The test of tax cuts as a spur to economic growth is whether they produced more than an ordinary business cycle recovery. Once the economy was back to full employment, was it bigger than you would otherwise have expected? And there Reagan fails the test: between 1979, when the big slump began, and 1989, when the economy finally achieved more or less full employment again, the growth rate was 3 percent, the same as the growth rate between the two previous business cycle peaks in 1973 and 1979. Or to put it another way, by the late 1980s the U.S. economy was about where you would have expected it to be, given the trend in the 1970s. Nothing in the data suggests a supply-side revolution.

Does this mean that the Reagan tax cuts had no effect? Of course not. Those tax cuts, combined with increased military spending, provided a good old-fashioned Keynesian boost to demand. And this boost was one factor in the rapid recovery from recession that developed at the end of 1982, though probably not as important as the rapid expansion of the money supply that began in the summer of that year. But the supposed supply-side effects are invisible in the data.

While the Reagan tax cuts didn't produce any visible supply-side gains, they did lead to large budget deficits. From the point of view of most economists, this was a bad thing. But for starve-the-beast tax-cutters, deficits are potentially a good thing, because they force the government to shrink. So did Reagan's deficits shrink the beast?

A casual glance at the data might suggest not: federal spending as a share of gross domestic product was actually slightly higher at the end of the 1980s than it was at the end of the 1970s. But that number includes both defense spending and "entitlements," mainly Social Security and Medicare, whose growth is automatic unless Congress votes to cut benefits. What's left is a grab bag known as domestic discretionary spending, including everything from courts and national parks to environmental cleanups and education. And domestic discretionary spending fell from 4.5 percent of G.D.P. in 1981 to 3.2 percent in 1988.

But that's probably about as far as any president can shrink domestic discretionary spending. And because Reagan couldn't shrink the belly of the beast, entitlements, he couldn't find enough domestic spending cuts to offset his military spending increases and tax cuts. The federal budget went into persistent, alarming, deficit. In response to these deficits, George Bush the elder went back on his "read my lips" pledge and raised taxes. Bill Clinton raised them further. And thereby hangs a tale.

For Clinton did exactly the opposite of what supply-side economics said you should do: he raised the marginal rate on

high-income taxpayers. In 1989, the top 1 percent of families paid, on average, only 28.9 percent of their income in federal taxes; by 1995, that share was up to 36.1 percent.

Conservatives confidently awaited a disaster—but it failed to materialize. In fact, the economy grew at a reasonable pace through Clinton's first term, while the deficit and the unemployment rate went steadily down. And then the news got even better: unemployment fell to its lowest level in decades without causing inflation, while productivity growth accelerated to rates not seen since the 1960s. And the budget deficit turned into an impressive surplus.

Tax-cut advocates had claimed the Reagan years as proof of their doctrine's correctness; as we have seen, those claims wilt under close examination. But the Clinton years posed a much greater challenge: here was a president who sharply raised the marginal tax rate on high-income taxpayers, the very rate that the tax-cut movement cares most about. And instead of presiding over an economic disaster, he presided over an economic miracle.

Let's be clear: very few economists think that Clinton's policies were primarily responsible for that miracle. For the most part, the Clinton-era surge probably reflected the maturing of information technology: businesses finally figured out how to make effective use of computers, and the resulting surge in productivity drove the economy forward. But the fact that America's best growth in a generation took place after the government did exactly the opposite of what tax-cutters advocate was a body blow to their doctrine.

They tried to make the best of the situation. The good economy of the late 1990s, ardent tax-cutters insisted, was caused by the 1981 tax cut. Early in 2000, Lawrence Kudlow and Stephen Moore, prominent supply-siders, published an article titled "It's the Reagan Economy, Stupid."

But anyone who thought about the lags involved found this implausible—indeed, hilarious. If the tax-cut movement attributed the booming economy of 1999 to a tax cut Reagan pushed through 18 years earlier, why didn't they attribute the economic boom of 1983 and 1984—Reagan's "morning in America"—to whatever Lyndon Johnson was doing in 1965 and 1966?

By the end of the 1990s, in other words, supply-side economics had become something of a laughingstock, and the whole case for tax cuts as a route to economic growth was looking pretty shaky. But the tax-cut crusade was nonetheless, it turned out, poised for its biggest political victories yet. How did that happen?

5. Second Wind: The Bush Tax Cuts

As the economic success of the United States under Bill Clinton became impossible to deny, there was a gradual shift in the sales strategy for tax cuts. The supposed economic benefits of tax cuts received less emphasis; the populist rationale—you, personally, pay too much in taxes—was played up.

I began this article with an example of this campaign's success: the creator of Mallard Fillmore apparently believes that typical families pay twice as much in taxes as they in fact do. But the most striking example of what skillful marketing can accomplish is the campaign for repeal of the estate tax.

As demonstrated, the estate tax is a tax on the very, very well off. Yet advocates of repeal began portraying it as a terrible burden on the little guy. They renamed it the "death tax" and put out reports decrying its impact on struggling farmers and businessmen—reports that never provided real-world examples because actual cases of family farms or small businesses broken up to pay estate taxes are almost impossible to find. This campaign succeeded in creating a public perception that the estate tax falls broadly on the population. Earlier this year, a poll found that 49 percent of Americans believed that most families had to pay the estate tax, while only 33 percent gave the right answer that only a few families had to pay.

Still, while an insistent marketing campaign has convinced many Americans that they are overtaxed, it hasn't succeeded in making the issue a top priority with the public. Polls consistently show that voters regard safeguarding Social Security and Medicare as much more important than tax cuts.

Nonetheless, George W. Bush has pushed through tax cuts in each year of his presidency. Why did he push for these tax cuts, and how did he get them through?

You might think that you could turn to the administration's own pronouncements to learn why it has been so determined to cut taxes. But even if you try to take the administration at its word, there's a problem: the public rationale for tax cuts has shifted repeatedly over the past three years.

During the 2000 campaign and the initial selling of the 2001 tax cut, the Bush team insisted that the federal government was running an excessive budget surplus, which should be returned to taxpayers. By the summer of 2001, as it became clear that the projected budget surpluses would not materialize, the administration shifted to touting the tax cuts as a form of demand-side economic stimulus: by putting more money in consumers' pockets, the tax cuts would stimulate spending and help pull the economy out of recession. By 2003, the rationale had changed again: the administration argued that reducing taxes on dividend income, the core of its plan, would improve incentives and hence long-run growth—that is, it had turned to a supply-side argument.

These shifting rationales had one thing in common: none of them were credible. It was obvious to independent observers even in 2001 that the budget projections used to justify that year's tax cut exaggerated future revenues and understated future costs. It was similarly obvious that the 2001 tax cut was poorly designed as a demand stimulus. And we have already seen that the supply-side rationale for the 2003 tax cut was tested and found wanting by the Congressional Budget Office.

So what were the Bush tax cuts really about? The best answer seems to be that they were about securing a key part of the Republican base. Wealthy campaign contributors have a lot to gain from lower taxes, and since they aren't very likely to depend on Medicare, Social Security or Medicaid, they won't suffer if the beast gets starved. Equally important was the support of the party's intelligentsia, nurtured by policy centers like Heritage and professionally committed to the tax-cut crusade. The original Bush tax-cut proposal was devised in late 1999 not to win votes in the national election but to fend off a primary challenge from the supply-sider Steve Forbes, the presumptive favorite of that part of the base.

This brings us to the next question: how have these cuts been sold?

At this point, one must be blunt: the selling of the tax cuts has depended heavily on chicanery. The administration has used accounting trickery to hide the true budget impact of its proposals, and it has used misleading presentations to conceal the extent to which its tax cuts are tilted toward families with very high income.

The most important tool of accounting trickery, though not the only one, is the use of "sunset clauses" to understate the long-term budget impact of tax cuts. To keep the official 10-year cost of the 2001 tax cut down, the administration's Congressional allies wrote the law so that tax rates revert to their 2000 levels in 2011. But, of course, nobody expects the sunset to occur: when 2011 rolls around, Congress will be under immense pressure to extend the tax cuts.

The same strategy was used to hide the cost of the 2003 tax cut. Thanks to sunset clauses, its headline cost over the next decade was only $350 billion, but if the sunsets are canceled—as the president proposed in a speech early this month—the cost will be at least $800 billion.

Meanwhile, the administration has carried out a very successful campaign to portray these tax cuts as mainly aimed at middle-class families. This campaign is similar in spirit to the selling of estate-tax repeal as a populist measure, but considerably more sophisticated.

The reality is that the core measures of both the 2001 and 2003 tax cuts mainly benefit the very affluent. The centerpieces of the 2001 act were a reduction in the top income-tax rate and elimination of the estate tax—the first, by definition, benefiting only people with high incomes; the second benefiting only heirs to large estates. The core of the 2003 tax cut was a reduction in the tax rate on dividend income. This benefit, too, is concentrated on very high-income families.

According to estimates by the Tax Policy Center—a liberal-oriented institution, but one with a reputation for scrupulous accuracy—the 2001 tax cut, once fully phased in, will deliver 42 percent of its benefits to the top 1 percent of the income distribution. (Roughly speaking, that means families earning more than $330,000 per year.) The 2003 tax cut delivers a somewhat smaller share to the top 1 percent, 29.1 percent, but within that concentrates its benefits on the really, really rich. Families with incomes over $1 million a year—a mere 0.13 percent of the population—will receive 17.3 percent of this year's tax cut, more than the total received by the bottom 70 percent of American families. Indeed, the 2003 tax cut has already proved a major boon to some of America's wealthiest people: corporations in which executives or a single family hold a large fraction of stocks are suddenly paying much bigger dividends, which are now taxed at only 15 percent no matter how high the income of their recipient.

It might seem impossible to put a populist gloss on tax cuts this skewed toward the rich, but the administration has been remarkably successful in doing just that.

One technique involves exploiting the public's lack of statistical sophistication. In the selling of the 2003 tax cut, the catch phrase used by administration spokesmen was "92 million Americans will receive an average tax cut of $1,083." That sounded, and was intended to sound, as if every American family would get $1,083. Needless to say, that wasn't true.

Yet the catch phrase wasn't technically a lie: the Tax Policy Center estimates that 89 million people will receive tax cuts this year and that the total tax cut will be $99 billion, or about $1,100 for each of those 89 million people. But this calculation carefully leaves out the 50 million taxpayers who received no tax cut at all. And even among those who did get a tax cut, most got a lot less than $1,000, a number inflated by the very big tax cuts received by a few wealthy people. About half of American families received a tax cut of less than $100; the great majority, a tax cut of less than $500.

But the most original, you might say brilliant, aspect of the Bush administration's approach to tax cuts has involved the way the tax cuts themselves are structured.

David Stockman famously admitted that Reagan's middle-class tax cuts were a "Trojan horse" that allowed him to smuggle in what he really wanted, a cut in the top marginal rate. The Bush administration similarly follows a Trojan horse strategy, but an even cleverer one. The core measures in Bush's tax cuts benefit only the wealthy, but there are additional features that provide significant benefits to some—but only some—middle-class families. For example, the 2001 tax cut included a $400 child credit and also created a new 10 percent tax bracket, the so-called cutout. These measures had the effect of creating a "sweet spot" that could be exploited for political purposes. If a couple had multiple children, if the children were all still under 18 and if the couple's income was just high enough to allow it to take full advantage of the child credit, it could get a tax cut of as much as 4 percent of pretax income. Hence the couple with two children and an income of $40,000, receiving a tax cut of $1,600, who played such a large role in the administration's rhetoric. But while most couples have children, at any given time only a small minority of families contains two or more children under 18—and many of these families have income too low to take full advantage of the child tax credit. So that "typical" family wasn't typical at all. Last year, the actual tax break for families in the middle of the income distribution averaged $469, not $1,600.

So that's the story of the tax-cut offensive under the Bush administration: through a combination of hardball politics, deceptive budget arithmetic and systematic misrepresentation of who benefits, Bush's team has achieved a major reduction of taxes, especially for people with very high incomes.

But where does that leave the country?

6. A Planned Crisis

Right now, much of the public discussion of the Bush tax cuts focuses on their short-run impact. Critics say that the 2.7 million jobs lost since March 2001 prove that the administration's policies have failed, while the administration says that things would have been even worse without the tax cuts and that a solid recovery is just around the corner.

But this is the wrong debate. Even in the short run, the right question to ask isn't whether the tax cuts were better than nothing; they probably were. The right question is whether some other economic-stimulus plan could have achieved better results at a lower budget cost. And it is hard to deny that, on a jobs-per-dollar basis, the Bush tax cuts have been extremely ineffective. According to the Congressional Budget Office, half of this year's $400 billion budget deficit is due to Bush tax cuts. Now $200 billion is a lot of money; it is equivalent to the salaries of four million average workers. Even the administration doesn't claim its policies have created four million jobs. Surely some other policy—aid to state and local governments, tax breaks for the poor and middle class rather than the rich, maybe even W.P.A.-style public works—would have been more successful at getting the country back to work.

Meanwhile, the tax cuts are designed to remain in place even after the economy has recovered. Where will they leave us?

Here's the basic fact: partly, though not entirely, as a result of the tax cuts of the last three years, the government of the United States faces a fundamental fiscal shortfall. That is, the revenue it collects falls well short of the sums it needs to pay for existing programs. Even the U.S. government must, eventually, pay its bills, so something will have to give.

The numbers tell the tale. This year and next, the federal government will run budget deficits of more than $400 billion. Deficits may fall a bit, at least as a share of gross domestic product, when the economy recovers. But the relief will be modest and temporary. As Peter Fisher, under secretary of the treasury for domestic finance, puts it, the federal government is "a gigantic insurance company with a sideline business in defense and homeland security." And about a decade from now, this insurance company's policyholders will begin making a lot of claims. As the baby boomers retire, spending on Social Security benefits and Medicare will steadily rise, as will spending on Medicaid (because of rising medical costs). Eventually, unless there are sharp cuts in benefits, these three programs alone will consume a larger share of G.D.P. than the federal government currently collects in taxes.

Alan Auerbach, William Gale and Peter Orszag, fiscal experts at the Brookings Institution, have estimated the size of the "fiscal gap"—the increase in revenues or reduction in spending that would be needed to make the nation's finances sustainable in the long run. If you define the long run as 75 years, this gap turns out to be 4.5 percent of G.D.P. Or to put it another way, the gap is equal to 30 percent of what the federal government spends on all domestic programs. Of that gap, about 60 percent is the result of the Bush tax cuts. We would have faced a serious fiscal problem even if those tax cuts had never happened. But we face a much nastier problem now that they are in place. And more broadly, the tax-cut crusade will make it very hard for any future politicians to raise taxes.

So how will this gap be closed? The crucial point is that it cannot be closed without either fundamentally redefining the role of government or sharply raising taxes.

Politicians will, of course, promise to eliminate wasteful spending. But take out Social Security, Medicare, defense, Medicaid, government pensions, homeland security, interest on the public debt and veterans' benefits—none of them what people who complain about waste usually have in mind—and you are left with spending equal to about 3 percent of gross domestic product. And most of that goes for courts, highways, education and other useful things. Any savings from elimination of waste and fraud will amount to little more than a rounding-off error.

So let's put a few things back on the table. Let's assume that interest on the public debt will be paid, that spending on defense and homeland security will not be compromised and that the regular operations of government will continue to be financed. What we are left with, then, are the New Deal and Great Society programs: Social Security, Medicare, Medicaid and unemployment insurance. And to close the fiscal gap, spending on these programs would have to be cut by around 40 percent.

It's impossible to know how such spending cuts might unfold, but cuts of that magnitude would require drastic changes in the system. It goes almost without saying that the age at which Americans become eligible for retirement benefits would rise, that Social Security payments would fall sharply compared with average incomes, that Medicare patients would be forced to pay much more of their expenses out of pocket—or do without. And that would be only a start.

All this sounds politically impossible. In fact, politicians of both parties have been scrambling to expand, not reduce, Medicare benefits by adding prescription drug coverage. It's hard to imagine a situation under which the entitlement programs would be rolled back sufficiently to close the fiscal gap.

Yet closing the fiscal gap by raising taxes would mean rolling back all of the Bush tax cuts, and then some. And that also sounds politically impossible.

For the time being, there is a third alternative: borrow the difference between what we insist on spending and what we're willing to collect in taxes. That works as long as lenders believe that someday, somehow, we're going to get our fiscal act together. But this can't go on indefinitely. Eventually—I think within a decade, though not everyone agrees—the bond market will tell us that we have to make a choice.

In short, everything is going according to plan.

For the looming fiscal crisis doesn't represent a defeat for the leaders of the tax-cut crusade or a miscalculation on their part. Some supporters of President Bush may have really believed that his tax cuts were consistent with his promises to protect Social Security and expand Medicare; some people may still believe that the wondrous supply-side effects of tax cuts will make the budget deficit disappear. But for starve-the-beast tax-cutters, the coming crunch is exactly what they had in mind.

7. What Kind of Country?

The astonishing political success of the antitax crusade has, more or less deliberately, set the United States up for a fiscal crisis. How we respond to that crisis will determine what kind of country we become.

If Grover Norquist is right—and he has been right about a lot—the coming crisis will allow conservatives to move the nation a long way back toward the kind of limited government we had before Franklin Roosevelt. Lack of revenue, he says, will make it possible for conservative politicians—in the name of fiscal necessity—to dismantle immensely popular government programs that would otherwise have been untouchable.

In Norquist's vision, America a couple of decades from now will be a place in which elderly people make up a disproportionate share of the poor, as they did before Social Security. It will also be a country in which even middle-class elderly Americans are, in many cases, unable to afford expensive medical procedures or prescription drugs and in which poor Americans generally go without even basic health care. And it may well be a place in which only those who can afford expensive private schools can give their children a decent education.

But as Governor Riley of Alabama reminds us, that's a choice, not a necessity. The tax-cut crusade has created a situation in which something must give. But what gives—whether we decide that the New Deal and the Great Society must go or that taxes aren't such a bad thing after all—is up to us. The American people must decide what kind of a country we want to be.

PAUL KRUGMAN is a *Times* columnist and a professor at Princeton. His new book is *"The Great Unraveling: Losing Our Way in the New Century."*

The Realities of Immigration

LINDA CHAVEZ

What to do about immigration—both legal and illegal—has become one of the most controversial public-policy debates in recent memory. But why it has occurred at this particular moment is something of a mystery. The rate of immigration into the U.S., although high, is still below what it was even a few years ago, the peak having been reached in the late 1990s. President Bush first talked about comprehensive immigration reform almost immediately after assuming office, but he put the plan on hold after 9/11 and only reintroduced the idea in 2004. Why the current flap?

By far the biggest factor shaping the popular mood seems to have been the almost daily drumbeat on the issue from political talk-show hosts, most prominently CNN's Lou Dobbs and the Fox News Channel's Bill O'Reilly and Scan Hannity (both of whom also have popular radio shows), syndicated radio hosts Rush Limbaugh, Laura Ingraham, Michael Savage, and G. Gordon Liddy, and a plethora of local hosts reaching tens of millions of listeners each week. Stories about immigration have become a staple of cable news, with sensational footage of illegal crossings featured virtually every day.

Media saturation has led, in turn, to the emergence of immigration as a wedge issue in the still-nascent 2008 presidential campaign. Several aspiring Republican candidates—former House Speaker Newt Gingrich, Senate Majority Leader Bill Frist, and Senator George Allen—have worked to burnish their "get tough" credentials, while, on the other side of the issue, Senator John McCain has come forward as the lead sponsor of a bill to allow most illegal aliens to earn legal status. For their part, potential Democratic candidates have remained largely mum, unsure how the issue plays with their various constituencies.

And then there are the immigrants themselves, who have shown surprising political muscle, especially in response to legislation passed by the House that would turn the illegal aliens among them into felons. Millions of mostly Hispanic protesters have taken to the streets in our big cities in recent months, waving American flags and (more controversially) their own national flags while demanding recognition and better treatment. Though Hispanic leaders and pro-immigrant advocates point to the protests as evidence of a powerful new civil-rights movement, many other Americans see the demonstrators as proof of an alien invasion—and a looming threat to the country's prosperity and unity.

In short, it is hard to recall a time when there has been so much talk about immigration and immigration reform—or when so much of the talk has been misinformed, misleading, and ahistorical. Before policy-makers can decide what to do about immigration, the problem itself needs to be better defined, not just in terms of costs and benefits but in relation to America's deepest values.

Contrary to popular myth, immigrants have never been particularly welcome in the United States. Americans have always tended to romanticize the immigrants of their grandparents' generation while casting a skeptical eye on contemporary newcomers. In the first decades of the 20th century, descendants of Northern European immigrants resisted the arrival of Southern and Eastern Europeans, and today the descendants of those once unwanted Italians, Greeks, and Poles are deeply distrustful of current immigrants from Latin America. Congressman Tom Tancredo, a Republican from Colorado and an outspoken advocate of tighter restrictions, is fond of invoking the memory of his Italian immigrant grandfather to argue that he is not anti-immigrant, just anti-illegal immigration. He fails to mention that at the time his grandfather arrived, immigrants simply had to show up on American shores (or walk across the border) to gain legal entry.

With the exception of the infamous Alien and Sedition Acts of 1798, there were few laws regulating immigration for the first hundred years of the nation's history. Though nativist sentiment increased throughout the later decades of the 19th century, giving rise to the 1882 Chinese Exclusion Act, it was not until 1917 that Congress began methodically to limit all immigration, denying admission to most Asians and Pacific Islanders and, in 1924, imposing quotas on those deemed undesirable: Jews, Italians, and others from Southern and Eastern Europe. These restrictions remained largely in effect until 1952, when Congress lifted many of them, including the bar on Asians.

The modern immigration era commenced in 1965 with the passage of the Immigration and Nationality Act, which abolished all national-origin quotas, gave preference to close relatives of American citizens, refugees, and individuals with certain skills, and allowed for immigrants from the Western hemisphere on a first-come, first-served basis. The act's passage drew a huge wave, much of it from Latin America and Asia. From 1970 to 2000, the United States admitted more than 20 million persons as permanent residents.

By 2000, some 3 million of these new residents were formerly illegal aliens who had gained amnesty as part of the 1986 Immigration Reform and Control Act (IRCA). This, Congress's first serious attempt to stem the flow of illegal immigration, forced employers to determine the status of their workers and imposed heavy penalties on those hiring illegal entrants. But from the beginning, the law was fraught with problems. It created huge bureaucratic burdens, even for private individuals wanting to hire someone to cut their lawn or care for their children, and spawned a vast new document-fraud industry for immigrants eager to get hold of the necessary paperwork. The law has been a monumental failure. Today, some 11.5 million illegal aliens reside in the U.S.—quadruple the population of two decades ago, when IRCA was enacted—and the number is growing by an estimated 500,000 a year.

The status quo has thus become untenable, and particularly so since the attacks of 9/11, which prompted fears of future terrorists sneaking across our sieve-like borders as easily as would-be busboys, janitors, and construction workers. Though virtually all Americans agree that something must be done, finding a good solution has proven elusive. The Bush administration has significantly increased border enforcement, adding nearly 30-percent more border-patrol agents since 2001 and increasing funding by 66 percent. The border patrol now employs nearly as many agents as the FBI, over 12,000 by the end of this fiscal year (not counting the additional 6,000 proposed by the President in May). But with some 6,000 miles of land border to monitor, that figure represents only one agent per mile (assuming eight-hour, 'round-the-clock shifts). Still, there has been progress: illegal immigration has actually slowed a bit since its peak during the boom economy of the late 1990s—a fact rarely noted in the current debate—though it has begun climbing again.

The latest suggestion is to build a wall along the border with Mexico. Some sections of the border already have 10-foot-high steel fences in place, and bills recently passed by the House and Senate authorize the construction of hundreds of additional miles of fencing along the border in California, Arizona, New Mexico, and Texas. The President, too, has endorsed the idea of a more formidable barrier. The Minuteman Project, a group that fashions itself a citizens' patrol, has volunteered to build the fence on private property along the Arizona/Mexico border. But unless the United States is prepared to build fences on its southern and northern borders, illegal entry will continue, albeit in diminished numbers. (Some 200,000 illegal immigrants—the equivalent of 1.8 million in U.S. terms—now live in Canada; most are Asians, but they are increasingly being joined by Latin Americans who in many cases are hoping to make the United States their ultimate destination.) More problematic for advocates of a fence is that an estimated 45 percent of all illegal aliens enter lawfully and simply overstay the terms of their visas.

So what might alleviate the current situation? Restrictionists claim that better internal enforcement, with crackdowns on employers who hire illegal aliens, would deter more from coming. This might work if we were willing to adopt a national identification card for every person in the country and a sophisticated instant-check system to verify the employment eligibility of each of the nation's 150 million workers. But concern over immigration seems unlikely on its own to spark sufficient support for such a system. Even after 9/11, when some experts recommended national ID's as a necessary security measure, Americans were reluctant to endorse the idea, fearing its implications for privacy.

President Bush has now proposed a tamper-proof card that all foreign workers would be required to carry, though one can envision grave "profiling" difficulties with this, not least when native-born Hispanic and Asian workers are selectively asked to produce such identification. Moreover, an experimental version of a program to require instant checks of work eligibility—now included in both the House and the Senate immigration bills—produced a nearly 30-percent error rate for legal immigrants who were denied employment.

The real question is not whether the U.S. has the means to stop illegal immigration—no doubt, with sufficient resources, we could mostly do so—but whether we would be better off as a nation without these workers. Restrictionists claim that large-scale immigration—legal and illegal—has depressed wages, burdened government resources, and acted as a net drain on the economy. The Federation for American Immigration Reform (FAIR), the most prominent of the pressure groups on the issue, argues that, because of this influx, hourly earnings among American males have not increased appreciably in 30 years. As the restrictionists see it, if the U.S. got serious about defending its borders, there would be plenty of Americans willing to do the jobs now performed by workers from abroad.

Indeed, FAIR and other extremists on the issue wish not only to eliminate illegal immigration but drastically to reduce or halt legal immigration as well. Along with its public-policy arm, the Center for Immigration Studies (CIS), FAIR has long argued that the U.S. should aim for a population of just 150 million persons—that is, about half the current level. If such an agenda sounds suspiciously like views usually found on the Left, that is no accident.

One of the great ironies of the current immigration debate is the strange ideological bedfellows it has created. The founder of the modern anti-immigration movement, a Michigan physician named John Tanton, is the former national president of Zero Population Growth and a long-time activist with Planned Parenthood and several Left-leaning environmentalist groups. Tanton came to the issue of immigration primarily because of his fears about overpopulation and the destruction of natural resources. Through an umbrella organization, U.S. Inc., he has created or funded not only FAIR and CIS but such groups as NumbersUSA, Population-Environment Balance, Pro-English, and U.S. English.[1] The Social Contract Press, another of Tanton's outfits, is the English-language publisher of the apocalyptic—and frankly racist—1975 novel *Camp of the Saints,* written by the French right-wing author Jean Raspail. The book, which apparently had a considerable influence in shaping Tanton's own views, foretells the demise of Europe at the hands of hordes of East Indians who invade the continent, bringing with them disease, crime, and anarchy.

As for the more conventional claims advanced by restrictionists, they, too, are hard to credit. Despite the presence in our workforce of millions of illegal immigrants, the U.S. is currently creating slightly more than two million jobs a year and boasts an unemployment rate of 4.7 percent, which is lower than the average in each of the past four decades. More to the point perhaps, when the National Research Council (NRC) of the National Academy of Sciences evaluated the economic impact of immigration in its landmark 1997 study The New Americans: Economic, Demographic, and Fiscal Effects of Immigration, it found only a small negative impact on the earnings of Americans, and even then, only for workers at lower skill and education levels.

Moreover, the participation of immigrants in the labor force has had obvious positive effects. The NRC estimated that roughly 5 percent of household expenditures in the U.S. went to goods and services produced by immigrant labor—labor whose relative cheapness translated into lower prices for everything from chicken to new homes. These price advantages, the study found, were "spread quite uniformly across most types of domestic consumers," with a slightly greater benefit for higher-income households.

Many restrictionists argue that if Americans would simply cut their own lawns, clean their own houses, and care for their own children, there would be no need for immigrant labor. But even if this were true, the overall economy would hardly benefit from having fewer workers. If American women were unable to rely on immigrants to perform some household duties, more of them would be forced to stay home. A smaller labor force would also have devastating consequences when it comes to dealing with the national debt and government-funded entitlements like Social Security and Medicare, a point repeatedly made by former Federal Reserve Board Chairman Alan Greenspan. As he told a Senate committee in 2003, "short of a major increase in immigration, economic growth cannot be safely counted upon to eliminate deficits and the difficult choices that will be required to restore fiscal discipline." The following year, Greenspan noted that offsetting the fiscal effects of our own declining birthrate would require a level of immigration "much larger than almost all current projections assume."

The contributions that immigrants make to the economy must be weighed, of course, against the burdens they impose. FAIR and other restrictionist groups contend that immigrants are a huge drain on society because of the cost of providing public services to them—some $67 to $87 billion a year, according to one commonly cited study. Drawing on numbers from the NRC's 1997 report, FAIR argues that "the net fiscal drain on American taxpayers [from immigration] is between $166 and $226 a year per native household."

There is something to these assertions, though less than may at first appear. Much of the anxiety and resentment generated by immigrants is, indeed, a result of the very real costs they impose on state and local governments, especially in border states like California and Arizona. Providing education and health care to the children of immigrants is particularly expensive, and the federal government picks up only a fraction of the expense. But, again, there are countervailing factors. Illegal immigrants are hardly free-riders. An estimated three-quarters of them paid federal taxes in 2002, amounting to $7 billion in Social Security contributions and $1.5 billion in Medicare taxes, plus withholding for income taxes. They also pay state and local sales taxes and (as homeowners and renters) property taxes.

Moreover, FAIR and its ilk have a penchant for playing fast and loose with numbers. To support its assessment of immigration's overall fiscal burden, for instance, FAIR ignores the explicit cautions in a later NRC report about cross-sectional analyses that exclude the "concurrent descendants" of immigrants—that is, their adult children. These, overwhelmingly, are productive members of the workforce. As the NRC notes, when this more complete picture is taken into account, immigrants have "a positive federal impact of about $1,260 [per capita], exceeding their net cost [$680 per capita on average] at the state and local levels." Restrictionists also argue that fewer immigrants would mean more opportunities for low-skilled native workers. Of late, groups like the Minuteman Project have even taken to presenting themselves as champions of unemployed American blacks (a curious tactic, to say the least, considering the views on race and ethnicity of many in the anti-immigrant camp[2]).

But here, too, the factual evidence is mixed. Wages for American workers who have less than a high-school education have probably been adversely affected by large-scale immigration; the economist George Borjas estimates a reduction of 8 percent in hourly wages for native-born males in that category. But price competition is not the only reason that many employers favor immigrants over poorly educated natives. Human capital includes motivation, and there could hardly be two more disparately motivated groups than U.S.-born high-school dropouts and their foreign-born rivals in the labor market. Young American men usually leave high school because they become involved with drugs or crime, have difficulty with authority, cannot maintain regular hours, or struggle with learning. Immigrants, on the other hand, have demonstrated enormous initiative, reflecting, in the words of President Reagan, "a special kind of courage that enabled them to leave their own land, leave their friends and their countrymen, and come to this new and strange land."

Just as important, they possess a strong desire to work. Legal immigrants have an 86-percent rate of participation in the labor force; illegal immigrant males have a 94-percent rate. By contrast, among white males with less than a high-school education, the participation rate is 46 percent, while among blacks it is 40 percent. If all immigrants, or even only illegal aliens, disappeared from the American workforce, can anyone truly believe that poorly skilled whites and blacks would fill the gap? To the contrary, productivity would likely decline, and employers in many sectors would simply move their operations to countries like Mexico, China, and the Philippines, where many of our immigrants come from in the first place.

Of equal weight among foes of immigration are the cultural changes wrought by today's newcomers, especially those from Mexico. In his book *Who Are We? The Challenges to National Identity* (2004), the eminent political scientist Samuel P. Huntington warns that "Mexican immigration is leading toward the demographic reconquista of areas Americans took from Mexico by force in the 1830s and 1840s." Others have fretted about the aims of militant Mexican-American activists, pointing to "El Plan de Aztlan," a radical Hispanic manifesto hatched in 1969, which calls for "the control of our barrios, campos, pueblos, lands, our economy, our culture, and our political life," including "self-defense against the occupying forces of the oppressors"—that is, the U.S. government.

To be sure, the fantasy of a recaptured homeland exists mostly in the minds of a handful of already well-assimilated Mexican-American college professors and the students they manage to indoctrinate (self-described "victims" who often enjoy preferential admission to college and subsidized or free tuition). But such rhetoric understandably alarms many Americans, especially in light of the huge influx of Hispanic immigrants into the Southwest. Does it not seem likely that today's immigrants—because of their numbers, the constant flow of even more newcomers, and their proximity to their countries of origin—will be unable or unwilling to assimilate as previous ethnic groups have done?

There is no question that some public policies in the U.S. have actively discouraged assimilation. Bilingual education, the dominant method of instruction of Hispanic immigrant children for some 30 years, is the most obvious culprit, with its emphasis on retaining Spanish. But bilingual education is on the wane, having been challenged by statewide initiatives in California (1998), Arizona (2000), and Massachusetts (2004), and by policy shifts in several major cities and at the federal level. States that have moved to English-immersion instruction have seen test scores for Hispanic youngsters rise, in some cases substantially.

Evidence from the culture at large is also encouraging. On most measures of social and economic integration, Hispanic immigrants and their descendants have made steady strides up the ladder. English is the preferred language of virtually all U.S.-born Hispanics; indeed, according to a 2002 national survey by the Pew Hispanic Center and the Kaiser Family Foundation, 78 percent of third-generation Mexican-Americans cannot speak Spanish at all. In education, 86 percent of U.S.-born Hispanics complete high school, compared with 92 percent of non-Hispanic whites, and the drop-out rate among immigrant children who enroll in high school after they come here is no higher than for the native-born.

It remains true that attendance at four-year colleges is lower among Hispanics than for other groups, and Hispanics lag in attaining bachelor's degrees. But neither that nor their slightly lower rate of high-school attendance has kept Hispanic immigrants from pulling their economic weight. After controlling for education, English proficiency, age, and geographic location, Mexican-born males actually earn 2.4 percent more than comparable U.S.-born white males, according to a recent analysis of 2000 Census data by the National Research Council. Hispanic women, for their part, hold their own against U.S.-born white women with similar qualifications.

As for the effect of Hispanic immigrants on the country's social fabric, the NRC found that they are more likely than other Americans to live with their immediate relatives: 88.6 percent of Mexican immigrant households are made up of families, compared with 69.5 percent of non-Hispanic whites and 68.3 percent of blacks. These differences are partially attributable to the age structure of the Hispanic population, which is younger on average than the white or black population. But even after adjusting for age and immigrant generation, U.S. residents of Hispanic origin—and especially those from Mexico—are much more likely to live in family households. Despite increased out-of-wedlock births among Hispanics, about 67 percent of American children of Mexican origin live in two-parent families, as compared with 77 percent of white children but only 37 percent of black children.

Perhaps the strongest indicator of Hispanic integration into American life is the population's high rate of intermarriage. About a quarter of all Hispanics marry outside their ethnic group, almost exclusively to non-Hispanic white spouses, a rate that has remained virtually unchanged since 1980. And here a significant fact has been noted in a 2005 study by the Population Reference Bureau—namely, that "the majority of inter-Hispanic children are reported as Hispanic." Such intermarriages themselves, the study goes on, "may have been a factor in the phenomenal growth of the U.S. Hispanic population in recent years."

It has been widely predicted that, by mid-century, Hispanics will represent fully a quarter of the U.S. population. Such predictions fail to take into account that increasing numbers of these "Hispanics" will have only one grandparent or great-grandparentof Hispanic heritage. By that point, Hispanic ethnicity may well mean neither more nor less than German, Italian, or Irish ethnicity means today.

How, then, to proceed? Congress is under growing pressure to strengthen border control, but unless it also reaches some agreement on more comprehensive reforms, stauncher enforcement is unlikely to have much of an effect. With a growing economy and more jobs than our own population can readily absorb, the U.S. will continue to need immigrants. Illegal immigration already responds reasonably well to market forces. It has increased during boom times like the late 1990's and decreased again when jobs disappear, as in the latest recession. Trying to determine an ideal number makes no more sense than trying to predict how much steel or how many textiles we ought to import; government quotas can never match the efficiency of simple supply and demand. As President Bush has argued—and as the Senate has now agreed—a guest-worker program is the way to go.

Does this mean the U.S. should just open its borders to anyone who wants to come? Hardly. We still need an orderly process, one that includes background checks to insure that terrorists and criminals are not being admitted. It also makes sense to require that immigrants have at least a basic knowledge of English and to give preference to those who have advanced skills or needed talents.

Moreover, immigrants themselves have to take more responsibility for their status. Illegal aliens from Mexico now pay significant sums of money to "coyotes" who sneak them across the border. If they could come legally as guest workers, that same money might be put up as a surety bond to guarantee their return at the end of their employment contract, or perhaps to pay for health insurance. Nor is it good policy to allow immigrants to become welfare recipients or to benefit from affirmative action: restrictions on both sorts of programs have to be written into law and stringently applied.

A market-driven guest-worker program might be arranged in any number of ways. A proposal devised by the Vernon K. Krieble Foundation, a policy group based in Colorado, suggests that government-licensed, private-sector employment agencies be put in charge of administering the effort, setting up offices in other countries to process applicants and perform background checks. Workers would be issued tamper-proof identity cards only after signing agreements that would allow for deportation if they violated the terms of their contract or committed crimes in the U.S. Although the Krieble plan would offer no path to citizenship, workers who wanted to change their status could still apply for permanent residency and, ultimately, citizenship through the normal, lengthy process.

Do such schemes stand a chance politically? A poll commissioned by the Krieble Foundation found that most Americans (except those with less than a high-school education) consider an "efficient system for handling guest workers" to be more important than expanded law enforcement in strengthening the country's border. Similarly, a CNN tracking poll in May found that 81 percent of respondents favored legislation permitting illegal immigrants who have been in the U.S. more than five years to stay here and apply for citizenship, provided they had jobs and paid back taxes. True, other polls have contradicted these results, suggesting public ambivalence on the issue—and an openness to persuasion.

Regardless of what Congress does or does not do—the odds in favor of an agreement between the Senate and House on final legislation are still no better than 50–50—immigration is likely to continue at high levels for the foreseeable future. Barring a recession or another terrorist attack, the U.S. economy is likely to need some 1.5 to 2 million immigrants a year for some time to come. It would be far better for all concerned if those who wanted to work in the U.S. and had jobs waiting for them here could do so legally, in the light of day and with the full approval of the American people.

In 1918, at the height of the last great wave of immigrants and the hysteria that it prompted in some circles, Madison Grant, a Yale-educated eugenicist and leader of the immigration-restriction movement, made a prediction:

The result of unlimited immigration is showing plainly in the rapid decline in the birth rate of native Americans because the poorer classes of colonial stock, where they still exist, will not bring children into the world to compete in the labor market with the Slovak, the Italian, the Syrian, and the Jew. . . . The man of the old stock is being crowded out of many country districts by these foreigners, just as he is today being literally driven off the streets of New York City by the swarms of Polish Jews. These immigrants adopt the language of the native American, they wear his clothes, they steal his name, and they are beginning to take his women, but they seldom adopt his religion or understand his ideals, and while he is being elbowed out of his own home, the American looks calmly abroad and urges on others the suicidal ethics which are exterminating his own race.

Today, such alarmism reads as little more than a historical curiosity. Southern and Eastern European immigrants and their children did, in fact, assimilate, and in certain cases—most prominently that of the Jews—they exceeded the educational and economic attainments of Grant's "colonial stock."

Present-day restrictionists point to all sorts of special circumstances that supposedly made such acculturation possible in the past but render it impossible today. Then as now, however, the restrictionists are wrong, not least in their failure to understand the basic dynamic of American nationhood. There is no denying the challenge posed by assimilating today's newcomers, especially so many of them in so short a span of time. Nor is there any denying the cultural forces, mainly stemming from the Left, that have attenuated the sense of national identity among native-born American elites themselves and led to such misguided policies as bilingual education. But, provided that we commit ourselves to the goal, past experience and progress to date suggest the task is anything but impossible.

As jarring as many found the recent pictures of a million illegal aliens marching in our cities, the fact remains that many of the immigrants were carrying the American flag, and waving it proudly. They and their leaders understand what most restrictionists do not and what some Americans have forgotten or choose to deny: that the price of admission to America is, and must be, the willingness to become an American.

Notes

1. I was briefly president of U.S. English in the late 1980s but resigned when a previously undisclosed memo written by Tanton was published. In it, he warned of problems related to the "educability" of Hispanics and speculated that an influx of Catholics from south of the border might well lead the U.S. to "pitch out" the concept of church-state separation. Tanton was forced to resign as chairman of U.S. English and no longer has any affiliation with the group.

2. As the author and anti-immigration activist Peter Brimelow wrote in his 1995 book *Alien Nation,* "Americans have a legitimate interest in their country's racial balance . . . [and] a right to insist that their government stop shifting it." Himself an immigrant from England, Brimelow wants "more immigrants who look like me."

LINDA CHAVEZ, the author of *Out of the Barrio* (1991), among other books, is the chairman of the Center for Equal Opportunity in Washington, D.C. She is at work on a new book about immigration.

The Health of Nations

How Europe, Canada, and our own VA do health care better.

EZRA KLEIN

M edicine may be hard, but health insurance is simple. The rest of the world's industrialized nations have already figured it out, and done so without leaving 45 million of their countrymen uninsured and 16 million or so underinsured, and without letting costs spiral into the stratosphere and severely threaten their national economies.

Even better, these successes are not secret, and the mechanisms not unknown. Ask health researchers what should be done, and they will sigh and suggest something akin to what France or Germany does. Ask them what they think can be done, and their desperation to evade the opposition of the insurance industry and the pharmaceutical industry and conservatives and manufacturers and all the rest will leave them stammering out buzzwords and workarounds, regional purchasing alliances and health savings accounts. The subject's famed complexity is a function of the forces protecting the status quo, not the issue itself.

So let us, in these pages, shut out the political world for a moment, cease worrying about what Aetna, Pfizer, and Grover Norquist will say or do, and ask, simply: What should be done? To help answer that question, we will examine the best health-care systems in the world: those of Canada, France, Great Britain, Germany, and the U.S. Veterans Health Administration (VHA), whose inclusion I'll justify shortly.

Putting aside the VHA, America's annual per person health expenditures are about twice what anyone else spends. That actually understates the difference, as our 45 million uninsured citizens have radically restricted access to care, and so the spending on the median insured American is actually quite a bit higher. Canada, France, Great Britain, and Germany all cover their entire populations, and they do so for far less money than we spend. Indeed, Canada, whose system is the most costly of the group, spends only 52 percent per capita what we do.

While comparing outcomes is difficult because of various lifestyle and demographic differences in the populations served, none of the systems mentioned betray any detectable disadvantage in outcomes when compared with the United States, and a strong case can be made that they in fact perform better. Here, however, I largely restrict myself to comparisons of efficiency and equity. With that said, off we go.

Oh, Canada!

As described by the American press, Canada's health-care system takes the form of one long queue. The line begins on the westernmost edge of Vancouver, stretches all the way to Ottawa, and the overflow are encouraged to wait in Port Huron, Michigan, while sneering at the boorish habits of Americans. Nobody gets to sit.

Sadly for those invested in this odd knock against the Canadian system, the wait times are largely hype. A 2003 study found that the median wait time for elective surgeries in Canada was a little more than four weeks, while diagnostic tests took about three (with no wait times to speak of for emergency surgeries). By contrast, Organisation for Economic Co-operation and Development data from 2001 found that 32 percent of American patients waited more than a month for elective surgery, and 5 percent waited more than four months. That, of course, doesn't count the millions of Americans who never seek surgery, or even the basic care necessary for a diagnosis, because they lack health coverage. If you can't see a doctor in the first place, you never have to wait for treatment.

Canada's is a single-payer, rather than a socialized, system. That means the government is the primary purchaser of services, but the providers themselves are private. (In a socialized system, the physicians, nurses, and so forth are employed by the government.) The virtue of both the single-payer and the socialized systems, as compared with a largely private system, is that the government can wield its market share to bargain down prices—which, in all of our model systems, including the VHA, it does.

A particularly high-profile example of how this works is Canadian drug reimportation. The drugs being bought in Canada and smuggled over the border by hordes of lawbreaking American seniors are the very same pharmaceuticals, made in the very same factories, that we buy domestically. The Canadian provinces, however, bargain down the prices (Medicare is barred from doing the same) until we pay 60 percent more than they do.

Single-payer systems are also better at holding down administrative costs. A 2003 study in *The New Great Britain Journal of Medicine* found that the United States spends 345 percent more per capita on health administration than our neighbors up north. This is largely because the Canadian system doesn't have to employ insurance salespeople, or billing specialists in every doctor's office, or underwriters. Physicians don't have to negotiate different prices with dozens of insurance plans or fight with insurers for payment. Instead, they simply bill the government and are reimbursed.

The downside of a single-payer system in the Canadian style is that it constructs a system with a high floor and a low ceiling. If you don't like the government's care options, there's no real alternative. In this, Canada is rare. As we'll see with both France and Germany, other countries are able to preserve a largely nationalized system with universal access while allowing private options at the upper levels.

France

It's a common lament among health-policy wonks that the world's best health-care system resides in a country Americans are particularly loath to learn from. Yet France's system is hard to beat. Where Canada's system has a high floor and a low ceiling, France's has a high floor and no ceiling. The government provides basic insurance for all citizens, albeit with relatively robust co-pays, and then encourages the population to also purchase supplementary insurance—which 86 percent do, most of them through employers, with the poor being subsidized by the state. This allows for as high a level of care as an individual is willing to pay for, and may help explain why waiting lines are nearly unknown in France.

France's system is further prized for its high level of choice and responsiveness—attributes that led the World Health Organization to rank it the finest in the world (America's system came in at No. 37, between Costa Rica and Slovenia). The French can see any doctor or specialist they want, at any time they want, as many times as they want, no referrals or permissions needed. The French hospital system is similarly open. About 65 percent of the nation's hospital beds are public, but individuals can seek care at any hospital they want, public or private, and receive the same reimbursement rate no matter its status. Given all this, the French utilize more care than Americans do, averaging six physician visits a year to our 2.8, and they spend more time in the hospital as well. Yet they still manage to spend half per capita than we do, largely due to lower prices and a focus on preventive care.

That focus is abetted by the French system's innovative response to one of the trickier problems bedeviling health-policy experts: an economic concept called "moral hazard." Moral hazard describes people's tendency to overuse goods or services that offer more marginal benefit without a proportionate marginal cost. Translated into English, you eat more at a buffet because the refills are free, and you use more health care because insurers generally make you pay up front in premiums, rather than at the point of care. The obvious solution is to shift more of the cost away from premiums and into co-pays or deductibles, thus increasing the sensitivity of consumers to the real cost of each unit of care they purchase.

This has been the preferred solution of the right, which has argued for a move toward high-deductible care, in which individuals bear more financial risk and vulnerability. As the thinking goes, this increased exposure to the economic consequences of purchasing care will create savvier health-care consumers, and individuals will use less unnecessary care and demand better prices for what they do use.

Problem is, studies show that individuals are pretty bad at distinguishing necessary care from unnecessary care, and so they tend to cut down on mundane-but-important things like hypertension medicine, which leads to far costlier complications. Moreover, many health problems don't lend themselves to bargain shopping. It's a little tricky to try to negotiate prices from an ambulance gurney.

A wiser approach is to seek to separate cost-effective care from unproven treatments, and align the financial incentives to encourage the former and discourage the latter. The French have addressed this by creating what amounts to a tiered system for treatment reimbursement. As Jonathan Cohn explains in his new book, *Sick:*

> In order to prevent cost sharing from penalizing people with serious medical problems—the way Health Savings Accounts threaten to do—the [French] government limits every individual's out-of-pocket expenses. In addition, the government has identified thirty chronic conditions, such as diabetes and hypertension, for which there is usually no cost sharing, in order to make sure people don't skimp on preventive care that might head off future complications.

The French do the same for pharmaceuticals, which are grouped into one of three classes and reimbursed at 35 percent, 65 percent, or 100 percent of cost, depending on whether data show their use to be cost effective. It's a wise straddle of a tricky problem, and one that other nations would do well to emulate.

Great Britain

I include Great Britain not because its health system is very good but because its health system is very cheap. Per capita spending in Great Britain hovers around 40 percent what it is in the United States, and outcomes aren't noticeably worse. The absolute disparity between what we pay and what they get illuminates a troublesome finding in the health-care literature: Much of the health care we receive appears to do very little good, but we don't yet know how to separate the wheat from the chaff. Purchasing less of it, however, doesn't appear to do much damage.

What's interesting is that many of the trade-offs that our health-care system downplays, the English system emphasizes. Where our medical culture encourages near-infinite amounts of care, theirs subtly dissuades lavish health spending, preferring to direct finite funds to other priorities.

This sort of national prioritizing is made easier because Great Britain has a socialized system, wherein the government directly employs most of the providers. Great Britain contains costs in part by paying doctors through capitation, which gives doctors a flat monthly sum for every patient in their practice. Since most patients don't need care in a given month, the payments for the healthy subsidize the needs of the sick. Crucially, though, the fixed pool of monthly money means doctors make more for offering less treatment. With traditional fee-for-service arrangements, like ours, doctors gain by treating more. The British system, by contrast, lowers total costs by lowering the quantity of prescribed care. As University of San Francisco professors Thomas Bodenheimer and Kevin Grumbach write, "British physicians simply do less of nearly everything—perform fewer surgeries, prescribe fewer medications, and order fewer x-rays."

That may sound strange, but it also means that society pays for fewer of those surgeries, fewer of those medications, and fewer of those x-rays—and as far as we can tell, the English aren't suffering for it. Indeed, a 2006 study published in *The Journal of the American Medical Association* found that, on average, English people are much healthier than Americans are; they suffer from lower rates of diabetes, hypertension, heart disease, heart attack, stroke, lung disease, and cancer. According to the study's press release, the differences are vast enough that "those in the top education and income level in the U.S. had similar rates of diabetes and heart disease as those in the bottom education and income level in Great Britain."

Great Britain's example proves that it is possible to make economy a guiding virtue of a health system. We could do that on the supply side, through policies like capitation that would change the incentives for doctors, or on the demand side, by making patients pay more up front—or both, or neither. Americans may not want that system, in the same way that the owner of a Range Rover may not want a Corolla, but we should at least recognize that we have chosen to make health care a costly priority, and were we to decide to prioritize differently, we could.

Germany

The German system offers a possible model for those who want to retain the insurance industry but end its ability to profit by pricing out the sick and shifting financial risk onto individuals. The German system's insurers are 300 or so different "sickness funds" that act both as both payers and purchasers for their members' care. Originally, each fund covered only a particular region, profession, or company, but now each one has open enrollment. All, however, are heavily regulated, not for profit, and neither fully private nor publicly owned. The funds can't charge different prices based on age or health status, and they must continue covering members even when the members lose the job or status that got them into the fund in the first place. The equivalent would be if you could retain membership in your company's health-care plan after leaving the company.

The move toward open enrollment was an admission that interfund competition could have some positive effects. The fear, however, was that the funds would begin competing for the healthiest enrollees and maneuvering to avoid the sickest, creating the sort of adverse selection problems that bedevil American insurance. To avoid such a spiral, the government has instituted exactly the opposite sort of risk profiling that we have in the United States. Rather than identifying the unhealthy to charge them higher rates, as our insurers do, the government compels sickness funds with particularly healthy applicants to pay into a central fund; the government then redistributes those dollars to the funds with less-healthy enrollees. In other words, the government pays higher rates to sickness funds with unhealthy enrollees in order to level the playing field and make the funds compete on grounds of price and efficiency. In this way, the incentive to dump the sick and capture the well is completely erased. The burdens of bad luck and ill health are spread across the populace, rather than remaining confined to unlucky individuals.

The system works well enough that even though Germans are allowed to opt-out of the sickness funds, they largely don't.

Those with incomes of more than $60,000 a year are not required to join a sickness fund; about 10 percent of these citizens purchase private insurance and .02 percent choose to eschew coverage entirely. The retention of a private insurance option ensures that Germans have an escape hatch if the sickness funds cease providing responsive and comprehensive coverage; it also clears a channel for experimentation and the rapid introduction of new technologies. And the mix of private-public competition works to spur innovation: By 2005, Germany had spent $21.20 per capita wiring its system with health-information technology; America, meanwhile, had spent a mere 43 cents per capita, and most U.S. hospitals still have no systems to speak of.

What the German system has managed to achieve is competition without cruelty, deploying market forces without unleashing capitalism's natural capriciousness. They have not brought the provision of health care completely under the government's control, but neither have they allowed the private market, with its attendant and natural focus on profits, to have its way with their health system. It's a balance the United States has been unable to strike.

The Veterans Health Administration

The mistreatment and poor conditions at the Walter Reed Army Medical Center were a front-page story recently, and they were rather conclusive in showing the system's inadequacy. But don't be confused: Walter Reed is a military hospital, not a VHA hospital. Poor reporting inaccurately smeared the quietly remarkable reputation of the best medical system in America.

Over the last decade or two, the VHA system has become a worldwide leader in both the adoption and the invention of health-information technology, and it has leveraged its innovations into quantifiable gains in quality of care. As Harvard's Kennedy School noted when awarding the VHA its prestigious Innovations in American Government prize:

> [The] VHA's complete adoption of electronic health records and performance measures have resulted in high-quality, low-cost health care with high patient satisfaction. A recent RAND study found that VHA outperforms all other sectors of American health care across the spectrum of 294 measures of quality in disease prevention and treatment. For six straight years, VHA has led private-sector health care in the independent American Customer Satisfaction Index.

Indeed, the VHA's lead in care quality isn't disputed. *A New Great Britain Journal of Medicine* study from 2003 compared the VHA with fee-for-service Medicare on 11 measures of quality. The VHA came out "significantly better" on every single one. The *Annals of Internal Medicine* pitted the VHA against an array of managed-care systems to see which offered the best treatment for diabetics. The VHA triumphed in all seven of the tested metrics. The National Committee for Quality Assurance, meanwhile, ranks health plans on 17 different care metrics, from hypertension treatment to adherence to evidence-based treatments. As Phillip Longman, the author of *Best Care Anywhere,* a book chronicling the VHA's remarkable transformation, explains: "Winning

NCQA's seal of approval is the gold standard in the health-care industry. And who do you suppose is the highest ranking health care system? Johns Hopkins? Mayo Clinic? Massachusetts General? Nope. In every single category, the veterans health care system outperforms the highest-rated non-VHA hospitals."

What makes this such an explosive story is that the VHA is a truly socialized medical system. The unquestioned leader in American health care is a government agency that employs 198,000 federal workers from five different unions, and nonetheless maintains short wait times and high consumer satisfaction. Eighty-three percent of VHA hospital patients say they are satisfied with their care, 69 percent report being seen within 20 minutes of scheduled appointments, and 93 percent see a specialist within 30 days.

Critics will say that the VHA is not significantly cheaper than other American health care, but that's misleading. In fact, the VHA is also proving far better than the private sector at controlling costs. As Longman explains, "Veterans enrolled in [the VHA] are, as a group, older, sicker, poorer, and more prone to mental illness, homelessness, and substance abuse than the population as a whole. Half of all VHA enrollees are over age 65. More than a third smoke. One in five veterans has diabetes, compared with one in 14 U.S. residents in general." Yet the VHA's spending per patient in 2004 was $540 less than the national average, and the average American is healthier and younger (the nation includes children; the VHA doesn't).

The VHA's advantages come in part from its development of the health-information software VistA, which was created at taxpayer expense and is now distributed for free to any health systems that wish to use it. It's a remarkably adaptive program that helps in virtually every element of care delivery, greatly aiding efforts to analyze symptoms and patient reactions in order to improve diagnoses and treatments, reduce mistaken interventions, and eliminate all sorts of care redundancies.

The VHA also benefits from the relative freedoms of being a public, socialized system. It's a sad reality that in the American medical system, doctors make money treating the sick, not keeping patients well. Thus, we encourage intervention-based, rather than prevention-based, medicine. It's telling, for instance, that hospital emergency rooms, where we handle traumas, are legally required to treat the poor, but general practitioners, who can manage conditions and catch illnesses early and cheaply, can turn away the destitute.

Moreover, patients are transient, so early investments in their long-term health will offer financial rewards to other providers. And which HMO wants to be known as the one that's really good at treating diabetes? Signing up a bunch of diabetes patients is no way to turn a profit.

As Longman details, the VHA suffers from none of these problems. Its patients are patients for life, so investing early and often in their long-term health is cost-effective; the system was set up to deal with the sick, so the emphasis is on learning how to best manage diseases rather than avoid the diseased; and the doctors are salaried, so they have no incentives to either over- or undertreat patients. Moreover, the VHA is not only empowered to bargain down drug costs; it also uses formularies (lists of covered drugs), and so is actually empowered to walk away from a pharmaceutical company that won't meet its offer.

The results have been clear. "Between 1999 and 2003," writes Longman, "the number of patients enrolled in the VHA system increased by 70 percent, yet funding (not adjusted for inflation) increased by only 41 percent. So the VHA has not only become the health-care industry's best quality performer, it has done so while spending less and less on each patient." Pretty good for socialized medicine.

The goal of health care is to get everyone covered, at the lowest possible cost, with the highest possible quality. But in the United States, there is another element in the equation that mucks up the outcome: Our system seeks to get everyone covered, at the lowest possible cost, with the highest possible quality, while generating the maximum possible profits. Within that context, the trade-offs and outcomes all seem to benefit the last goal, and so we tolerate 45 million uninsured Americans, unbelievably high prices, and a fractured system that lacks the proper incentives to deliver high-quality care.

This makes it hard to move toward a preventive system, as Canada has, because preventive medicine pays less. It makes it hard to address moral-hazard issues wisely, as the French have, because it's unprofitable to insure diabetics, and less profitable still to make their care essentially free. It makes it hard to institute the cost savings that Great Britain has, because with less money flowing into the system, there would be far less profit to be made. It makes it hard to harness market forces while protecting against individual risk, as Germany has, because insurer business models are predicated on shifting risk to employers and individuals, and profits are made when insurers can keep that risk from being shifted back onto them. And it is impossible to implement the practices that have so improved the VHA, because doing so would require a single, coherent health system that stuck with its members through their life cycles rather than an endlessly fractured structure in which insurers pawn off their members as they grow old, ill, or unemployed.

That's not to say that there's no room for profit within the American health-care system, but that it's time the discussion stopped focusing on how to preserve the interests of moneyed stakeholders and started asking how to deliver the best care, for the lowest cost, at the highest quality—to every American. Such a system will probably still have private insurers (at least at the high end of care), pay enough to encourage pharmaceutical innovation, and allow for choice and competition and market pressures. But it will take as its guiding principle the health of the populace, rather than that of the providers. That, in the end, is what all the model health-care systems have in common. Except ours.

The *Real* Infrastructure Crisis

The nation's roads and bridges are in pretty good shape. It's the national will that is suspect.

BURT SOLOMON

It's a frighteningly familiar catastrophe to imagine. An earthquake in Northern California ruptures 30 levees along the converging Sacramento and San Joaquin rivers, and 300 billion gallons of saltwater rush inland from San Francisco Bay, flooding 16 islands and ruining the supply of fresh water across two-thirds of the nation's most populous state. Or picture this: In southern Kentucky, the 55-year-old Wolf Creek Dam (where water has seeped through the foundations for years) gives way. The breach lets loose the largest man-made reservoir east of the Mississippi River, flooding the communities along the Cumberland River and shorting out the electric guitars in Nashville.

These were the top two horror stories—"5 Disasters Coming Soon If We Don't Rebuild U.S. Infrastructure"—that *Popular Mechanics* conjured up for its readers last fall, after the collapse of a bridge in Minnesota killed 13 innocents on their way home from work. The stunning sight of an interstate highway plunging into the Mississippi River, just two weeks after a steam pipe exploded beneath Lexington Avenue in Midtown Manhattan—and less than two years after Hurricane Katrina brought New Orleans to its knees—dramatically brought the nation's fallible infrastructure to the public's attention. So, too, did the overwhelmed levees along the Midwestern rivers during the recent rains. And so did the garden-variety failures, such as the water main break on June 16 in Montgomery County, Md., bordering Washington that forced some of the capital's bigwigs to boil water before brushing their teeth.

In the mammoth but aging networks of roads, bridges, railroads, air traffic, sewers, pipelines, supplies of fresh water, and electricity grids that helped turn the United States into the world's economic superpower, other dangers lurk. All over the country, clean-water and wastewater facilities are wearing out. The combined sewers that 40 million people in 772 cities use could disgorge their raw contents into waterways when the next storm passes through. Every summer brings the possibility of blackouts.

Traffic gridlock has become a fact of life, jamming the highways and airways and creating bottlenecks of goods through the ports, especially around Los Angeles and New York City. The American Society of Civil Engineers has classified 3,500 of the nation's 79,000 dams as unsafe; in a 2005 report card

How Bad Is It?

- The total amount of money spent on infrastructure has **consistently been increasing,** mainly because of state and local investments.
- Even so, on a global scale, American infrastructure is **no longer on the cutting edge.**
- Both John McCain and Barack Obama have highlighted **infrastructure spending as an issue** in the presidential campaign.

on the nation's infrastructure, the society assigned grades that ranged from C+ (for the proper disposal of solid waste) down to D− (for the supply of drinking water and the treatment of wastewater).

Talk of the "crisis" in the nation's physical infrastructure has leapt beyond think-tank forums and earnest editorials. It has quickened legislators' interest, generated heartfelt lobbying on Capitol Hill—expected to climax next year when Congress must reauthorize the pork-laden highway program—and nosed its way into the presidential campaign.

Experts, however, consider "crisis" an overblown description of the perils that America's infrastructure poses. Federal investigators have tentatively concluded that the ill-fated Interstate-35W in Minnesota collapsed not because it was structurally deficient—although it was—but because of a design defect: The gusset plates connecting the steel beams were half as thick as they should have been. Nationwide, bridges are in better structural condition than they were 20 years ago, and the most critical of the nation's 4 million miles of roadways are in pretty good shape. In the transportation system, "the physical condition has not noticeably deteriorated . . . in the past two decades," said Katherine A. Siggerud, the managing director of physical infrastructure issues at the determinedly nonpolitical Government Accountability Office. "The condition of the most-traveled roads and bridges in the United States, the interstates and the national highways, [has] improved in quality."

The more serious problem is the lack of roads and the traffic congestion that this shortage creates, especially around major cities. In the nation's airways, too, congestion has become chronic, especially at airports in the Northeast. But Gerald Dillingham, the GAO's director of civil aviation issues, doesn't see a crisis in the near- or midterm, and he is hopeful that better technology and new ways of structuring the airways can stave off disaster for at least the next 15 years. The Transportation Department has calculated the overall economic cost of congestion at $200 billion a year, surely a drag on the nation's commerce, not to mention a vexation to anyone stuck in traffic. Still, in a $14 trillion economy, that amounts to 1.4 percent—a pittance.

Fixing the nation's infrastructure is "a matter of fine-tuning the economic production system," said Kenneth A. Small, an economist who specializes in transportation at the University of California (Irvine), "not a matter of moral outrage." Rudolph G. Penner, a senior fellow at the Urban Institute, said, "I'd call it a problem, not a crisis." Even the lobbyists who urge more spending on the nation's infrastructure acknowledge that the assertions of impending doom are an exaggeration. Janet F. Kavinoky, the director of transportation infrastructure at the U.S. Chamber of Commerce, is the executive director of Americans for Transportation Mobility, an alliance of construction companies and labor unions. "If you don't say it's a crisis," she explained, "nobody shows up at your press conference."

> **Even the lobbyists who urge more spending acknowledge that the assertions of impending doom are an exaggeration. "If you don't say it's a crisis, nobody shows up at your press conference."**
>
> —Janet F. Kavinoky, director of transportation infrastructure at the U.S. Chamber of Commerce

Nor is the country ignoring the issue. The nation's spending on infrastructure continues to rise; New Orleans is rebuilding the levees that Katrina breached. "The things that need to get done are getting done, by and large," said Timothy P. Lynch, the American Trucking Associations' senior vice president for federal relations and strategic planning.

This isn't to say, of course, that all is hunky-dory. The future of U.S. infrastructure could be grim indeed if too little is done. At the core, it's a question of cost. Bridges and roads are expensive—to build or to fix—and so are mass transit, airport runways, and almost everything else. The civil engineers issued a widely invoked price tag of $1.6 trillion over five years to do what needs to be done, but even champions of a strong infrastructure find such a number inflated—"a compilation of a wish list," the ATA's Lynch said.

Moreover, investment bankers say that plenty of capital is available for work that is critical to the nation's well-being. What may be missing, however, is the political will to spend this capital. Increasingly, legislators and local governments are trying to arrange infrastructure financing in ways that conceal the

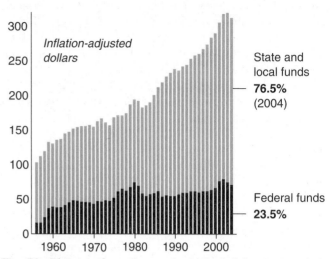

$350 billion

Inflation-adjusted dollars

State and local funds
76.5%
(2004)

Federal funds
23.5%

The Big Picture Spending on the nation's infrastructure has increased, but state and local governments are footing a larger share of the bill.

Total Public infrastructure Spending, 1956–2004.

Source: Congressional Budget Office.

true costs from taxpayers, who are reluctant to foot the bill, and that may transfer the financial burdens to future generations. If the measure of a society's responsibility is its willingness to invest for the long run, then the crisis in infrastructure is this: Do Americans possess the national will to pay for what their children and their children's children are going to need?

Ancient Rome Meets Reagan

Only occasionally has a civilization made its infrastructure an emblem of its ambition or greatness. Consider, notably, the marvels of ancient Rome—its roads, its aqueducts, its public baths and lavatories, its Colosseum and other sites of public entertainment. Conceived as a military necessity to assure the movement of troops through a far-flung empire, Rome's extravagant and enduring infrastructure took on other functions, too. As a public benefaction, it gave the state a way to justify its own existence, according to Garrett G. Fagan, a historian at Pennsylvania State University, and the many amenities that wealthy families financed served as "a kind of social compact between the upper classes and the poorer classes." The boldness and breadth of Roman infrastructure, Fagan said, "go a long way to explain why the empire lasted so long."

The United States has often shown a similar ambition. In 1808, after Thomas Jefferson's Louisiana Purchase added a vast wilderness that stretched as far as the future Montana, Treasury Secretary Albert Gallatin proposed a national transportation network of roads, rivers, and ports.

In the following decades, Henry Clay of Kentucky lent his legislative weight in the House, and then in the Senate, to the "internal improvements" of canals and railroads. Abraham Lincoln, even as he struggled to win the Civil War, pursued plans for a transcontinental railroad. Theodore Roosevelt, so fond of proclaiming the needs of "future generations," convened a conference of governors that resulted in water projects that irrigated the West and generated electricity cheaply; his list of ventures-still-undone gave TR's fifth cousin, Franklin D. Roosevelt, a starting point when he tried to spend the nation out of the Great Depression. Then, in the postwar boom of the 1950s, President Eisenhower pressed for a system of interstate highways that knitted the nation together and bolstered its economy. As late as the 1970s, after the Cuyahoga River in Cleveland caught fire in 1969, the federal government invested tens of billions of dollars in sewer systems and wastewater treatment plants.

Taxpayers' generosity toward the nation's infrastructure, however, took a dive during the 1980s. President Reagan's aversion to using taxes for domestic spending, exacerbated by Wall Street's obsession with quarterly earnings, encouraged a shortsightedness in assessing the public good. According to Sherle R. Schwenninger, the director of the New America Foundation's economic growth program, the money that government at all levels has devoted to infrastructure, as a proportion of the nation's total economic output, slipped from 3 percent during the 1950s and 1960s to only 2 percent in recent years.

"We've just not reinvested," former Council of Economic Advisers Chairman Martin N. Baily complained at a Brookings Institution forum last fall, "because nobody wanted to raise the taxes to do that." Even in Katrina-devastated Louisiana, when the Army Corps of Engineers announced in 2006 that its estimate for fixing the levees had ballooned from $3.5 billion to $9.5 billion, the state's politicians and editorial writers wailed.

Not to Worry

It wouldn't take many years, or so it is said, before the weeds poked up through a neglected interstate highway. Not to worry. Even as the nation's enthusiasm for long-term investments has flagged, the total amount of money spent on its infrastructure has continued to grow. As the federal share has shrunk (from 32 percent in 1982 to less than 24 percent in 2004, according to the Congressional Budget Office), state and local governments have picked up the slack. Counting all levels of government, public entities spent $312 billion on the nation's transportation and water infrastructure in 2004, three times as much—after taking inflation into account—as in 1956, when Eisenhower's heyday began. *(See chart.)*

Has the U.S. underfunded its infrastructure, on which its economy rests? "Compared to what we really need, I think so," said Penner, a former CBO director, "but relatively slightly."

Consider, for example, the state of the nation's bridges. Last summer's tragedy in Minnesota cast a spotlight on the Federal Highway Administration's alarming conclusion that, as of last December, 12 percent of the nation's bridges were structurally deficient. But less attention was paid to the fact that this proportion had shrunk from 13 percent in 2004 and nearly 19 percent in 1994. Nor was it widely noticed that the label of "structurally deficient" covered a range of poor conditions, from serious to far less so. Fewer than a tenth of the tens of thousands of bridges deemed deficient are anywhere close to falling down. (A Federal Highway Administration spokeswomen said the agency

does not have summary information about the location and size of the worst bridges.)

The surge of bridge inspections that followed the disaster in Minnesota turned up a second bridge with bowed gusset plates across the Mississippi in Minneapolis-St. Paul—it was immediately closed and slated for repairs—and another one in Duluth. The Minnesota Legislature found numerous shortcomings in the state inspectors' work on the I-35 bridge that had been tagged as structurally deficient for some cracking and fatigue. According to the National Transportation Safety Board's investigators, however, the inspectors were not the problem. Indeed, the investigators cited the effort to repair the bridge, which entailed piling construction supplies and equipment on its overburdened deck, and the thin gusset plates as the likely leading causes of the I-35 collapse. The more that they have learned about the disaster, the less it has served as a morality tale.

As for a fear of falling bridges, "I don't really think we're in a crisis," said economist Small. He also mentioned the "pretty strong" system of bridge inspections and placed the 13 deaths in Minnesota into the context of all U.S. traffic fatalities, which average 120 a day. "If you plot the statistics," he noted, "you might not notice the bump."

On the roads, too, drunk drivers or malfunctioning vehicles cause many more deaths than potholes or crumbling concrete. The roads are OK, but there aren't enough of them to hold the traffic, and building more will only increase demand. The gridlock is worst of all around Los Angeles, the San Francisco Bay area, Chicago, New York City, Atlanta, and Washington, but it has also spread into unlikelier venues. A third lane is being built along certain truck-clogged stretches of Interstate 80 in Iowa and Nebraska. The GAO's Siggerud pointed to "bottlenecks in every mode of transportation," which stand to get worse. The Federal Aviation Administration has predicted that air traffic may triple during the next two decades, and the American Road & Transportation Builders Association has forecast that the volume of cargo on U.S. roads will double. In Los Angeles, the freight volume is expected to triple as the population grows by 60 percent, producing strains that the U.S. chamber's Kavinoky warned "will paralyze the city."

Ian Grossman, the FHWA's associate administrator for public affairs, lamented the Little League games unattended and the volunteerism in decline because of congestion. "It shouldn't be a fact of life," he said.

The economic impact of the bottlenecks has been "woefully understudied," according to Robert Puentes, an expert in infrastructure at the Brookings Institution, who regards transportation policy as "a fact-free zone." But Clifford Winston, an economist at Brookings, has tried. His calculation of the annual economic cost of congestion is just a third of DOT's—$15 billion in air traffic and nearly $50 billion on the roads, counting the shipping delays, the higher inventories required, the wasted fuel, the value of gridlocked motorists' time, and other not-quite-tangible factors. The impediments are numerous, Winston said, but "none of them are big. That's why they persist."

The problem of congestion is, to a degree, self-limiting. It could injure the economy of a gridlocked metropolis, but by no more than 5 to 10 percent, according to Small, by driving business to the suburbs, exurbs, and smaller cities that stand to benefit from the big cities' pain.

Nor has congestion in the air been neglected. The air traffic system, in which 25 percent of last year's flights arrived late, has added runways in recent years in Atlanta, Boston, Cincinnati, Minneapolis, and St. Louis; starting this November it will add another runway at Chicago's O'Hare. The $13 billion that the FAA spends annually on infrastructure development for civil aviation falls a mere $1 billion short—pocket change, really—of what GAO analyst Dillingham believes it should spend. The next generation of air traffic control, based on a global positioning system instead of on radar, has been delayed—not because of the immense cost or the technology, Dillingham said, but because of the difficulty of integrating it into the existing system.

Scarier, perhaps, for the nation's economic future is the possibility that congestion or other strains on an elderly infrastructure will damage America's already shaky competitive position in global markets. The American business executives who leave South Korea's luxurious Incheon International Airport or Shanghai's modern, half-empty airport to arrive at New York's seedy JFK are bound to feel repulsed. Today, that is nothing more than inconvenience, but eventually, economists say, it could count.

"In a globalized economy," the New America Foundation's Schwenninger said, "there are only a few ways you can compete." Asian countries can claim lower wage rates and taxes, and Europe boasts governmental subsidies and an educated workforce. This leaves infrastructure, Schwenninger ventured, as American businesses' best hope for a competitive edge—more so than 20 to 30 years ago, and more important than education. Silicon Valley, he reported, has lost some of its silicon-wafer manufacturing to Texas and countries overseas because producers fear brownouts in California.

Yet the threat to U.S. competitiveness shouldn't be exaggerated, for other countries face similar problems with congestion. Gaining permission to build a new road or runway is even harder in cramped, environmentally conscious Europe. China and India are spending 9 percent and 5 percent, respectively, of their gross domestic product on infrastructure. The U.S., however, has an overwhelming advantage: Its elaborate infrastructure—4 million miles of roads, 600,000 bridges, 26,000 miles of commercially navigable waterways, 11,000 miles of transit lines, 500 train stations, 300 ports, 19,000 airports, 55,000 community drinking water systems, and 30,000 wastewater plants—is already built.

Ducking the Costs

Still, on matters of infrastructure, the United States is losing ground. "It would be an overstatement to say our system is in crisis," Brookings's Winston said. "At the same time, the annual costs of the inefficiencies [because of congestion] are large, growing, and unlikely to be addressed by the public sector."

No longer is American infrastructure on the cutting edge. "I think we are falling behind the rest of the world," Rep. Earl Blumenauer, an earnest veteran Democrat from Portland, Ore., said in an interview. He is pushing legislation to create a blue-ribbon commission that would frame a coherent national vision for dealing with the country's disparately owned and operated infrastructure, variously the responsibility of federal, state, or local governments or—for a majority of dams and many recent water systems—private owners. Besides the existing bottlenecks in the movement of goods, Blumenauer foresees "real problems with the backlog of projects"—for sewers, roads, water, bridges, etc.—within five to 10 years. And deferring maintenance, he noted, increases the costs, which is one reason he thinks that the astronomical price tags "tend to be understated, not overstated."

America was once on the cutting edge of infrastructure, but no more. "I think we are falling behind the rest of the world. . . . In the end, there's no substitute for making systematic investment."

—Rep. Earl Blumenauer, D-Ore., who wants to create a blue-ribbon commission on infrastructure

The GAO, among others, is more skeptical, not only of the civil engineers' $1.6 trillion, $300-billion-plus-a-year cost projection but also of a congressionally created panel's recommendations. The National Surface Transportation Policy and Revenue Study Commission announced in January that the nation must spend $225 billion annually—$140 billion more than at present—on its roads, waterways, and railroads. "Most of the needs assessments," the Urban Institute's Penner explained, "are very much influenced by special interests," using unrealistic assumptions and self-serving estimates.

How much the nation must spend, however, is certain to rise. For fresh water and wastewater alone, by the GAO's calculations, the infrastructure costs over the next 20 years will range between $400 billion and nearly $1.2 trillion to correct past underinvestment. The existing facilities, if not repaired or replaced, would probably take 10 to 20 years to deteriorate, an offical said, not two or three.

Given the presumed reluctance of American taxpayers to pay up front, such projections have quickened the search for politically palatable alternatives to financing infrastructure projects—artful ways of ducking the costs. Hence the rising popularity of public-private partnerships, "or as we called them, business deals," Everett M. Ehrlich, an expert on infrastructure financing, told the House Transportation and Infrastructure Committee in June. On May 19, Pennsylvania Gov. Ed Rendell had announced the winning $12.8 billion bid (submitted by a Spanish toll-road company and a division of Citigroup) for a 75-year lease of the Pennsylvania Turnpike. The idea wasn't original. The city of Chicago signed a $1.8 billion lease for the Chicago Skyway in 2005 and has received a half-dozen bids for privatizing Midway Airport. The Indiana Toll Road was leased in 2006 for $3.8 billion. A private company built and runs the Dulles Toll Road in Northern Virginia, and the Texas Legislature has imposed a two-year moratorium on a planned network of private toll roads out of concern that the deals were too lucrative for the operators.

A private operator, the thinking goes, can raise tolls with an abandon that would give politicians the willies, and investment banks are salivating at the prospect of jumping in. But the criticism has mounted. "Deferred maintenance will become a big part of creating profits for shareholders," Allen Zimmerman, a resident of South Whitehall Township, Pa., warned about leasing the turnpike, in a letter to *The Morning Call* of Allentown, Pa. Economists worry that a private operator might milk the drivers along the popular routes while ignoring the boondocks.

By the GAO's lights, the value of any given deal depends on the particulars, such as the quality of the management, the assurances of proper maintenance, and the uses to which a state will put the newfound revenues. Indiana is spending its bump in revenue on a 10-year transportation plan; Chicago, on the other hand, has pointedly refrained from any allocation. Pennsylvania officials have vowed to spend their windfall on transportation but have been "evasive," the ATA's Lynch said, about specifics.

At least so far, the greatest hindrance to an influx of private capital for the nation's infrastructure, according to Penner of the Urban Institute, is the paucity of investment opportunities. He also lacks faith in the other ideas being pitched on Capitol Hill that seek to lure capital while dodging the costs—notably, proposals to establish an infrastructure "bank" to leverage private investments and to institute a separate capital budget for the federal government. Nor does the direct approach—the possibility of federal appropriations—give him reason to hope. He fears that the entitlement programs (Social Security, Medicare, and Medicaid) will squeeze the budget, shrinking the discretionary spending on infrastructure projects.

Where, then, will the money come from? At Brookings, infrastructure expert Puentes thinks that relatively small, targeted investments can relieve the worst bottlenecks—those of national importance, such as the congestion at the port of Long Beach, Calif. In any event, simply relying on the construction of new highways and airport terminals won't suffice, in Small's view: "It's just too expensive."

Many economists favor another solution—congestion pricing. London, Stockholm, and Singapore now charge vehicles that drive into the central cities at busy times of the day. Michael Bloomberg, New York City's businessman-turned-mayor, pursued the idea until the state Legislature shot it down. Pure congestion pricing, a high-tech means of raising or lowering the toll depending on the traffic, is being tested on a highway north of San Diego, where the price of driving changes every few minutes. Such pricing would be one way for Americans to pay their way.

The Political Marketplace

On the night that Sen. Barack Obama of Illinois claimed the Democratic nomination for the presidency, he spoke to the nation about, among a litany of intentions, "investing in our crumbling infrastructure." Of course, he happened to be in Minnesota, less than 10 miles from where the I-35 bridge had collapsed. But

then he spoke of the problem again two days later while campaigning in Virginia and, later, at a roundtable with 16 Democratic governors. In trying to bolster his appeal to working-class voters in Flint, Mich., on June 16, Obama promised to use the money he would save from ending the war in Iraq on a National Infrastructure Reinvestment Bank that would spend $60 billion over 10 years. Stressing the issue helps Obama look sober and serious about the nation's long-term needs, which is useful for a candidate who is criticized for being inexperienced.

24% of infrastructure spending in 2004 was federally funded.

Sen. Hillary Rodham Clinton of New York, whom Obama bested for the nomination, demonstrated the versatility of infrastructure as a political issue. A week after the bridge fell in Minnesota, she delivered a speech in New Hampshire on infrastructure as "a silent crisis." She showed a thorough understanding of the issue ("Today nearly half the locks on our waterways are obsolete.") and offered a detailed plan of attack, including a $10 billion emergency repair fund, $1.5 billion for public transit, $1 billion for intercity passenger railways, and sundry other millions for additional projects. Nine months later, however, facing political death as Indiana Democrats readied to vote, she climbed onto the back of a pickup truck and appealed to voters beleaguered by the soaring price of fuel. Her idea? Suspend the federal gasoline tax, which pays for the upkeep on the nation's pivotal highways. Economists gagged at the thought, but Indiana Democrats rewarded her with a narrow victory.

The presumed Republican nominee, Sen. John McCain of Arizona, who agreed with Clinton on the gasoline tax, has also used infrastructure as a political football. It's a word he reveres. In campaign speeches, he has applied "infrastructure" to public health, alternative fuels, "the infrastructure of civil society," and "the Republican infrastructure." But in the conventional sense, he has linked it to one of his trademark issues. "The problem with roads and infrastructure and bridges and tunnels in America can be laid right at the doorstep of Congress," he said in May, four months after federal investigators blamed the Minnesota bridge collapse on a design flaw, "because the pork-barrel, earmark spending, such as the 'Bridge to Nowhere' in Alaska, has diverted people's hard-earned tax dollars that they pay at the gas pump." This charge drew a public rebuke from Tim Pawlenty, Minnesota's Republican governor, who is a national co-chairman of McCain's campaign and is often mentioned as a possible running mate. "I don't know what he's basing that on," Pawlenty said, "other than the general premise that projects got misprioritized throughout time."

One legislator's pork, of course, is another's infrastructure. Such criticism of "pork," as a result, has not dampened Congress's enthusiasm for spending money on highways and such. The 2005 highway legislation (known, improbably, as SAFETEA-LU) authorized $286 billion over six years, $32 billion more than the Bush administration wanted. But this amount was miserly compared with the House-approved $380 billion.

Members of Congress earmarked just one-tenth of the money for particular projects back home, and not all of those were considered boondoggles. An earmark, for instance, funded the newly built Woodrow Wilson Bridge along the Capital Beltway between Virginia and Maryland.

The lobbyists for the labor unions and the contractors that stand to benefit from road construction are already gearing up for next year's effort to reauthorize the highway bill. The pot will surely grow bigger—reportedly to $500 billion over six years—especially if a Democratic president works with a Democratic Congress. Spending on infrastructure has recently been touted by Rockefeller Foundation President Judith Rodin, among others, as a Keynesian response to an impending recession. And even if earmark-happy highway bills inevitably waste money, they may be worthy of praise for paying up front for whichever roads and bridges—to nowhere or to somewhere— the democratic system has deemed worthy. "In the end, there's no substitute for making systematic investment," Rep. Blume-nauer said.

As a political issue, infrastructure is the kind that democracies have a hard time with—a chronic, usually invisible problem that only occasionally becomes acute. For better or worse, however, politics has become inseparable from the battles over infrastruc-ture, sometimes to the point of amusement. When members of the House Transportation and Infrastructure Committee discussed the fateful gusset plates in Minnesota, the Republicans stressed the arbitrary nature of such a failure, which money would never have averted, while the Democrats kept mentioning the bridge's wear and tear, for which more money would have mattered. Par-tisan positions on gusset plates—who knew?

Still, the politics of infrastructure are far from straightfor-ward. Earmarks and pork find enthusiasts and critics within both political parties. Congestion pricing has produced odd bedfel-lows. Both Bush administration conservatives and environmen-tal activists approve of such a market mechanism that would save fuel and improve economic efficiency, while some Demo-crats worry about the effect of "Lexus lanes" on the poor.

The true political divide may lie between Americans who'll be willing and able to pay up front for the nation's needs— whether through taxes or tolls—and those who would rather skimp or burden their children. This sort of decision, between a world-class infrastructure and muddling through, will be made in the political marketplace. If Americans get disgusted enough, they'll do what it takes. Otherwise, they won't.

Speculators, Politicians, and Financial Disasters

JOHN STEELE GORDON

F ueled by easy credit, the real-estate market had been rising swiftly for some years. Members of Congress were determined to assure the continuation of that easy credit. Suddenly, the party came to a devastating halt. Defaults multiplied, banks began to fail. Soon the economic troubles spread beyond real estate. Depression stalked the land.

The year was 1836.

The nexus of excess speculation, political mischief, and financial disaster—the same tangle that led to our present economic crisis—has been long and deep. Its nature has changed over the years as Americans have endeavored, with varying success, to learn from the mistakes of the past. But it has always been there, and the commonalities from era to era are stark and stunning. Given the recurrence of these themes over the course of three centuries, there is every reason to believe that similar calamities will beset the system as long as human nature and human action play a role in the workings of markets.

L et us begin our account of the catastrophic effects of speculative bubbles and political gamesmanship with the collapse of 1836. Thanks to a growing population, prosperity, and the advancing frontier, poorly regulated state banks had been multiplying throughout the 1830's. In those days, chartered banks issued paper money, called banknotes, backed by their reserves. From 1828 to 1836, the amount in circulation had tripled, from $48 million to $149 million. Bank loans, meanwhile, had almost quadrupled to $525 million. Many of the loans went to finance speculation in real estate.

Much of this easy-credit-induced speculation had been caused, as it happens, by President Andrew Jackson. This was a terrific irony, since Jackson, who served as President from 1829 until 1837, hated speculation, paper money, and banks. His crusade to destroy the Second Bank of the United States, an obsession that led him to withdraw all federal funds from its coffers in 1833, removed the primary source of bank discipline in the United States. Jackson had transferred those federal funds to state banks, thereby enabling their outstanding loans to swell.

The real-estate component of the crisis began to take shape in 1832, when sales by the government of land on the frontier were running about $2.5 million a year. Some of the buyers were prospective settlers, but most were speculators hoping to turn a profit by borrowing most of the money needed and waiting for swiftly-rising values to put them in the black. By 1836, annual land sales totaled $25 million; in the summer of that year, they were running at the astonishing rate of $5 million a month.

While Jackson, who was not economically sophisticated, did not grasp how his own actions had fueled the speculation, he understood perfectly well what was happening. With characteristic if ill-advised decisiveness, he moved to stop it. Since members both of Congress and of his cabinet were personally involved in the speculation, he faced fierce opposition. But in July, as soon as Congress adjourned for the year, Jackson issued an executive order known as the "specie circular." This forbade the Land Office to accept anything but gold and silver (i.e., specie) in payment for land. Jackson hoped that the move would dampen the speculation, and it did. Unfortunately, it did far more: people began to exchange their banknotes for gold and silver. As the demand for specie soared, the banks called in loans in order to stay liquid.

The result was a credit crunch. Interest rates that had been at 7 percent a year rose to 2 and even 3 percent a month. Weaker, overextended banks began to fail. Bankruptcies spread. Even several state governments found they could not roll over their debts, forcing them into default. By April 1837, a month after Jackson left the presidency, the great New York diarist Philip Hone noted that "the immense fortunes which we heard so much about in the days of speculation have melted like the snows before an April sun."

The longest depression in American history had set in. Recovery would not begin until 1843. In Charles Dickens's *A Christmas Carol,* published that same year, Ebenezer Scrooge worries that a note payable to him in three days might be as worthless as "a mere United States security."

M odern standards preclude government officials and members of Congress from the sort of speculation that was rife in the 1830's. But today's affinities between Congressmen and lobbyists, affinities fueled by the largess of political-action committees, have produced many of the same consequences.

Consider the savings-and-loan (S&L) debacle of the 1980's. The crisis, which erupted only two decades ago but seems all but forgotten, was almost entirely the result of a failure of government to regulate effectively. And that was by design. Members of Congress put the protection of their political friends ahead of the interests of the financial system as a whole.

After the disaster of the Great Depression, three types of banks still survived—artifacts of the Democratic party's Jacksonian antipathy to powerful banks. Commercial banks offered depositors both checking and savings accounts, and made mostly commercial loans. Savings banks offered only savings accounts and specialized in commercial real-estate loans. Savings-and-loan associations ("thrifts") also offered only savings accounts; their loan portfolios were almost entirely in mortgages for single-family homes.

All this amounted, in effect, to a federally mandated cartel, coddling those already in the banking business and allowing very few new entrants. Between 1945 and 1965, the number of S&L's remained nearly constant at about 8,000, even as their assets grew more than tenfold from almost $9 billion to over $110 billion. This had something to do with the fact that the rate of interest paid on savings accounts was set by federal law at .25 percent higher than that paid by commercial banks, in order to compensate for the inability of savings banks and S&L's to offer checking accounts. Savings banks and S&L's were often called "3-6-3" institutions because they paid 3 percent on deposits, charged 6 percent on loans, and management hit the golf course at 3:00 P.M. on the dot.

These small banks were very well connected. As Democratic Senator David Pryor of Arkansas once explained:

> You got to remember that each community has a savings-and-loan; some have two; some have four, and each of them has seven or eight board members. They own the Chevy dealership and the shoe store. And when we saw these people, we said, gosh, these are the people who are building the homes for people, these are the people who represent a dream that has worked in this country.

They were also, of course, the sorts of people whose support politicians most wanted to have—people who donated campaign money and had significant political influence in their localities.

The banking situation remained stable in the two decades after World War II as the Federal Reserve was able to keep interest rates steady and inflation low. But when Lyndon Johnson tried to fund both guns (the Vietnam war) and butter (the Great Society), the cartel began to break down.

If the government's first priority had been the integrity of the banking system and the safety of deposits, the weakest banks would have been forced to merge with larger, sounder institutions. Most solvent savings banks and S&L's would then have been transmuted into commercial banks, which were required to have larger amounts of capital and reserves. And some did transmute themselves on their own. But by 1980 there were still well over 4,500 S&L's in operation, relics of an earlier time.

Why was the integrity of the banking system not the first priority? Part of the reason lay in the highly fragmented nature of the federal regulatory bureaucracy. A host of agencies—including the Comptroller of the Currency, the Federal Reserve, the FDIC and the FSLIC, state banking authorities, and the Federal Home Loan Bank Board (FHLBB)—oversaw the various forms of banks. Each of these agencies was more dedicated to protecting its own turf than to protecting the banking system as a whole.

Adding to the turmoil was the inflation that took off in the late 1960's. When the low interest rates that banks were permitted to pay failed to keep pace with inflation, depositors started to look elsewhere for a higher return. Many turned to money-market funds, which were regulated by the Securities and Exchange Commission rather than by the various banking authorities and were not restricted in the rate of interest they could pay. Money began to flow out of savings accounts and into these new funds, in a process known to banking specialists by the sonorous term "disintermediation."

By 1980, with inflation roaring above 12 percent—the highest in the country's peacetime history—the banks were bleeding deposits at a prodigious rate. The commercial banks could cope; their deposit base was mostly in checking accounts, which paid no interest, and their lending portfolios were largely made up of short-term loans whose average interest rates could be quickly adjusted, not long-term mortgages at fixed interest. But to the savings banks and S&L's, disintermediation was a mortal threat.

Rather than taking the political heat and forcing the consolidation of the banking industry into fewer, stronger, and more diversified banks, Washington rushed to the aid of the ailing S&L's with quick fixes that virtually guaranteed future disaster. First, Congress eliminated the interest-rate caps. Banks could now pay depositors whatever rates they chose. While it was at it, Congress also raised the amount of insurance on deposits, from $40,000 to $100,000 per depositor.

At the same time, the Federal Home Loan Bank Board changed the rules on brokered deposits. Since the 1960's, brokers had been making, on behalf of their customers, multiple deposits equal to the limit on insurance. This allowed wealthy customers to possess insured bank deposits of any cumulative size—an end-run around the limit that should never have been tolerated in the first place. Realizing that these deposits were "hot money," likely to chase the highest return, the Home Loan board forbade banks to have more than five percent of their deposit base in such instruments. But in 1980 it eliminated the restriction.

With no limits on interest rates that could be paid and no risk of loss to the customers, the regulators and Congress had created an economic oxymoron: a high-yield, no-risk security. As money flowed in to take advantage of the situation, the various S&L's competed among themselves to offer higher and higher interest rates. Meanwhile, however, their loan portfolios were still in long-term home mortgages, many yielding low interest.

As a result, they went broke. In 1980 the S&L's had a collective net worth slightly over $32 billion. By December 1982 that number had shrunk to less than $4 billion.

To remedy the disaster caused by the quick fixes of 1980, more quick fixes were instituted. The FHLBB lowered reserve requirements—the amount of money that banks must keep in highly liquid form, like Treasury notes, in order to meet any demand for withdrawals—from 5 to 3 percent of deposits. "With the proverbial stroke of the pen," the journalist L.J. Davis wrote, "sick thrifts were instantly returned to a state of ruddy health, while thrifts that only a moment before had been among the dead who walk were now reclassified as merely enfeebled."

For good measure, the Bank Board changed its accounting rules, allowing the thrifts to show handsome profits when they were, in fact, going bust. It was a case of regulators authorizing the banks they regulated to cook the books. Far worse, the rule that only locals could own an S&L was eliminated. Now anyone could buy a thrift. High-rollers began to move in, delighted to be able to assume the honorific title of "banker."

And Congress, ever anxious to help the Chevy dealers and shoe-store owners, lifted the limits on what the thrifts themselves could invest in. No longer were they limited to low-interest, long-term, single-family mortgages. Now they could lend up to 70 percent of their portfolios for commercial real-estate ventures and consumer needs. In short, Congress gave the S&L's permission to become full-service banks without requiring them to hold the capital and reserves of full-service banks.

Now came the turn of state-chartered thrifts, whose managers understandably wanted to enjoy the same freedoms enjoyed by federally-chartered S&L's. State governments from Albany to Sacramento were obliging. California, which had the largest number of state-chartered S&L's, allowed them to invest in anything from junk bonds to start-up software companies—in effect, to become venture-capital firms using government-guaranteed money. The consequence, as predictable as the next solar eclipse, was a collapse of the S&L's en masse. Between 1985 and 1995, over a thousand were shut down by the government or forced to merge. The cost to the public is estimated to have run $160 billion.

A s the sorry tale of the S&L crisis suggests, the road to financial hell is sometimes paved with good intentions. There was nothing malign in attempting to keep these institutions solvent and profitable; they were of long standing, and it seemed a noble exercise to preserve them. Perhaps even more noble, and with consequences that have already proved much more threatening, was the philosophy that would eventually lead the United States into its latest financial crisis—a crisis that begins, and ends, with mortgages.

A mortgage used to stay on the books of the issuing bank until it was paid off, often twenty or thirty years later. This greatly limited the number of mortgages a bank could initiate. In 1938, as part of the New Deal, the federal government established the Federal National Mortgage Association, nicknamed Fannie Mae, to help provide liquidity to the mortgage market.

Fannie Mae purchased mortgages from initiating banks and either held them in its own portfolio or packaged them as mortgage-backed securities to sell to investors. By taking these mortgages off the books of the issuing banks, Fannie Mae allowed the latter to issue new mortgages. Being a government entity and thus backed by the full faith and credit of the United States, it was able to borrow at substantially lower interest rates, earning the money to finance its operations on the difference between the money it borrowed and the interest earned on the mortgages it held.

Together with the GI Bill of 1944, which guaranteed the mortgages issued to veterans, Fannie Mae proved a great success. The number of Americans owning their own homes climbed steadily, from fewer than 15 percent of non-farm families in the 1930's to nearly 70 percent by the 1980's. Thus did Fannie Mae and the GI Bill prove to be powerful engines for increasing the size of the middle class.

I t can be argued that 70 percent is about as high a proportion as could, or should, be hoped for in home ownership. Many young people are not ready to buy a home; many old people prefer to rent. Some families move so frequently that home ownership makes no sense. Some people, like Congressman Charlie Rangel of New York, take advantage of local rent-control laws to obtain housing well below market rates, and therefore have no incentive to buy.

And some families simply lack the creditworthiness needed for a bank to be willing to lend them money, even on the security of real property. Perhaps their credit histories are too erratic; perhaps their incomes and net worth are lower than bank standards; or perhaps they lack the means to make a substantial down payment, which by reducing the amount of the mortgage can protect a bank from a downturn in the real-estate market.

But historically there was also a class, made up mostly of American blacks, for whom home ownership was out of reach. Although simple racial prejudice had long been a factor here, it was, ironically, the New Deal that institutionalized discrimination against blacks seeking mortgages. In 1935 the Federal Housing Administration (FHA), established in 1934 to insure home mortgages, asked the Home Owner's Loan Corporation—another New Deal agency, this one created to help prevent foreclosures—to draw up maps of residential areas according to the risk of lending in them. Affluent suburbs were outlined in blue, less desirable areas in yellow, and the least desirable in red.

The FHA used the maps to decide whether or not to insure a mortgage, which in turn caused banks to avoid the redlined neighborhoods. These tended to be in the inner city and to comprise largely black populations. As most blacks at this time were unable to buy in white neighborhoods, the effect of redlining was largely to exclude even affluent blacks from the mortgage market.

Even after the end of Jim Crow in the 1960's, the effect of redlining lingered, perhaps more out of habit than of racial prejudice. In 1977, responding to political pressure to abolish the practice, Congress finally passed the Community Reinvestment Act, requiring banks to offer credit throughout their marketing areas and rating them on their compliance. This effectively outlawed redlining.

Then, in 1995, regulations adopted by the Clinton administration took the Community Reinvestment Act to a new level. Instead of forbidding banks to discriminate against blacks and black neighborhoods, the new regulations positively forced banks to seek out such customers and areas. Without saying so, the revised law established quotas for loans to specific neighborhoods, specific income classes, and specific races. It also encouraged community groups to monitor compliance and allowed them to receive fees for marketing loans to target groups.

But the aggressive pursuit of an end to redlining also required the active participation of Fannie Mae, and thereby hangs a tale. Back in 1968, the Johnson administration had decided to "adjust" the federal books by taking Fannie Mae off the budget and establishing it as a "Government Sponsored Enterprise" (GSE). But while it was theoretically now an independent corporation, Fannie Mae did not have to adhere to the same rules regarding capitalization and oversight that bound most financial institutions. And in 1970 still another GSE was created, the Federal Home Loan Mortgage Corporation, or Freddie Mac, to expand further the secondary market in mortgage-backed securities.

This represented a huge moral hazard. The two institutions were supposedly independent of the government and owned by their stockholders. But it was widely assumed that there was an implicit government guarantee of both Fannie and Freddie's solvency and of the vast amounts of mortgage-based securities they issued. This assumption was by no means unreasonable. Fannie and Freddie were known to enjoy lower capitalization requirements than other financial institutions and to be held to a much less demanding regulatory regime. If the United States government had no worries about potential failure, why should the market?

Forward again to the Clinton changes in 1995. As part of them, Fannie and Freddie were now permitted to invest up to 40 times their capital in mortgages; banks, by contrast, were limited to only ten times their capital. Put briefly, in order to increase the number of mortgages Fannie and Freddie could underwrite, the federal government allowed them to become grossly undercapitalized—that is, grossly to reduce their one source of insurance against failure. The risk of a mammoth failure was then greatly augmented by the sheer number of mortgages given out in the country.

That was bad enough; then came politics to make it much worse. Fannie and Freddie quickly evolved into two of the largest financial institutions on the planet, with assets and liabilities in the trillions. But unlike other large, profit-seeking financial institutions, they were headquartered in Washington, D.C., and were political to their fingertips. Their management and boards tended to come from the political world, not the business world. And some were corrupt: the management of Fannie Mae manipulated the books in order to trigger executive bonuses worth tens of millions of dollars, and Freddie Mac was found in 2003 to have understated earnings by almost $5 billion.

Both companies, moreover, made generous political contributions, especially to those members of Congress who sat on oversight committees. Their charitable foundations could be counted on to kick in to causes that Congressmen and Senators deemed worthy. Many of the political contributions were illegal: in 2006, Freddie was fined $3.8 million—a record amount—for improper election activity.

By 2007, Fannie and Freddie owned about half of the $12 trillion in outstanding mortgages, an unprecedented concentration of debt—and of risk. Much of the debt was concentrated in the class of sub-prime mortgages that had proliferated after the 1995 regulations. These were mortgages given to people of questionable credit standing, in one of the attempts by the federal government to increase home ownership among the less well-to-do.

Since banks knew they could offload these subprime mortgages to Fannie and Freddie, they had no reason to be careful about issuing them. As for the firms that bought the mortgage-based securities issued by Fannie and Freddie, they thought they could rely on the government's implicit guarantee. AIG, the world's largest insurance firm, was happy to insure vast quantities of these securities against default; it must have seemed like insuring against the sun rising in the West.

Wall Street, politicians, and the press all acted as though one of the iron laws of economics, as unrepealable as Newton's law of universal gravity, had been set aside. That law, simply put, is that potential reward always equals potential risk. In the real world, unfortunately, a high-yield, no-risk investment cannot exist.

In 2006, after an astonishing and unsustainable climb in home values, the inevitable correction set in. By mid-2007, many sub-prime mortgages were backed by real estate that was now of lesser value than the amount of debt. As the market started to doubt the soundness of these mortgages, their value and even their salability began to deteriorate. So did the securities backed by them. Companies that had heavily invested in sub-prime mortgages saw their stock prices and their net worth erode sharply. This caused other companies to avoid lending them money. Credit markets began to tighten sharply as greed in the marketplace was replaced by fear.

A vicious downward spiral ensued. Bear Stearns, the smallest investment bank on Wall Street, was forced into a merger in March with JPMorgan Chase, with guarantees from the Federal Reserve. Fannie and Freddie were taken over by the government in early September; Merrill Lynch sold itself to Bank of America; AIG had to be bailed out by the government to the tune of $85 billion; Lehman Brothers filed for bankruptcy; Washington Mutual became the biggest bank failure in American history and was taken over by JPMorgan Chase; to avoid failure, Wachovia, the sixth largest bank in the country, was taken over by Wells Fargo. The most creditworthy institutions saw interest rates climb to unprecedented levels—even for overnight loans of bank reserves, which are the foundation of the high-functioning capitalist system of the West. Finally it became clear that only a systemic intervention by the government would stem the growing panic and allow credit markets to begin to function normally again.

Many people, especially liberal politicians, have blamed the disaster on the deregulation of the last 30 years. But they do so in order to avoid the blame's falling where it should—squarely on their own shoulders. For the same politicians now loudly proclaiming that deregulation caused the problem are the ones who fought tooth and nail to prevent increased regulation of Fannie and Freddie—the source of so much political money, their mother's milk.

To be sure, there is more than enough blame to go around. Forgetting the lessons of the past, Wall Street acted as though the only direction that markets and prices could move was up. Credit agencies like Moody's, Standard & Poor's, and Fitch gave high ratings to securities that, in retrospect, they clearly did not understand. The news media did not even try to investigate the often complex economics behind the housing market.

But remaining at the heart of the financial beast now abroad in the world are Fannie Mae and Freddie Mac and the mortgages they bought and turned into securities. Protected by their political patrons, they were allowed to pile up colossal debt on an inadequate capital base and to escape much of the regulatory oversight and rules to which other financial institutions are subject. Had they been treated as the potential risks to financial stability they were from the beginning, the housing bubble could not have grown so large and the pain that is now accompanying its end would not have hurt so much.

Herbert Hoover famously remarked that "the trouble with capitalism is capitalists. They're too greedy." That is true. But another and equal trouble with capitalism is politicians. Like the rest of us, they are made of all-too-human clay and can be easily blinded to reality by naked self-interest, at a cost we are only now beginning to fathom.

JOHN STEELE GORDON is the author of, among other books, *An Empire of Wealth: The Epic Story of American Economic Power* (2004). His "Look Who's Afraid of Free Trade" appeared in the February *Commentary*.

How Globalization Went Bad

From terrorism to global warming, the evils of globalization are more dangerous than ever before. What went wrong? The world became dependent on a single superpower. Only by correcting this imbalance can the world become a safer place.

S TEVEN W EBER ET AL.

T he world today is more dangerous and less orderly than it was supposed to be. Ten or 15 years ago, the naive expectations were that the "end of history" was near. The reality has been the opposite. The world has more international terrorism and more nuclear proliferation today than it did in 1990. International institutions are weaker. The threats of pandemic disease and climate change are stronger. Cleavages of religious and cultural ideology are more intense. The global financial system is more unbalanced and precarious.

It wasn't supposed to be like this. The end of the Cold War was supposed to make global politics and economics easier to manage, not harder. What went wrong? The bad news of the 21st century is that globalization has a significant dark side. The container ships that carry manufactured Chinese goods to and from the United States also carry drugs. The airplanes that fly passengers nonstop from New York to Singapore also transport infectious diseases. And the Internet has proved just as adept at spreading deadly, extremist ideologies as it has e-commerce.

The conventional belief is that the single greatest challenge of geopolitics today is managing this dark side of globalization, chipping away at the illegitimate co-travelers that exploit openness, mobility, and freedom, without putting too much sand in the gears. The current U.S. strategy is to push for more trade, more connectivity, more markets, and more openness. America does so for a good reason—it benefits from globalization more than any other country in the world. The United States acknowledges globalization's dark side but attributes it merely to exploitative behavior by criminals, religious extremists, and other anachronistic elements that can be eliminated. The dark side of globalization, America says, with very little subtlety, can be mitigated by the expansion of American power, sometimes unilaterally and sometimes through multilateral institutions, depending on how the United States likes it. In other words, America is aiming for a "flat," globalized world coordinated by a single superpower.

That's nice work if you can get it. But the United States almost certainly cannot. Not only because other countries won't let it, but, more profoundly, because that line of thinking is faulty. The predominance of American power has many benefits, but the management of globalization is not one of them. The mobility of ideas, capital, technology, and people is hardly new. But the rapid advance of globalization's evils is. Most of that advance has taken place since 1990. Why? Because what changed profoundly in the 1990s was the polarity of the international system. For the first time in modern history, globalization was superimposed onto a world with a single superpower. What we have discovered in the past 15 years is that it is a dangerous mixture. The negative effects of globalization since 1990 are not the result of globalization itself. They are the dark side of American predominance.

The world is paying a heavy price for the instability created by globalization and unipolarity, and the United States is bearing most of the burden.

The Dangers of Unipolarity

A straightforward piece of logic from market economics helps explain why unipolarity and globalization don't mix. Monopolies, regardless of who holds them, are almost always bad for both the market and the monopolist. We propose three simple axioms of "globalization under unipolarity" that reveal these dangers.

Axiom 1: Above a certain threshold of power, the rate at which new global problems are generated will exceed the rate at which old problems are fixed.

Power does two things in international politics: It enhances the capability of a state to do things, but it also increases the number of things that a state must worry about. At a certain point, the latter starts to overtake the former. It's the familiar law of diminishing returns. Because powerful states have large spheres of influence and their security and economic interests touch every region of the world, they are threatened by the risk of things going wrong—anywhere. That is particularly true for the United States, which leverages its ability to go anywhere and do anything through massive debt. No one knows exactly when the law of diminishing returns will kick in. But, historically, it starts to happen long before a single great power dominates the entire globe, which is why large empires from Byzantium to Rome have always reached a point of unsustainability.

That may already be happening to the United States today, on issues ranging from oil dependency and nuclear proliferation to pandemics and global warming. What Axiom 1 tells you is that more U.S. power is not the answer; it's actually part of the problem. A multipolar world would almost certainly manage the globe's pressing problems more effectively. The larger the number of great powers in the global system, the greater the chance that at least one of them would exercise some control over a given combination of space, other actors, and problems. Such reasoning doesn't rest on hopeful notions that the great powers will work together. They might do so. But even if they don't, the result is distributed governance, where some great power is interested in most every part of the world through productive competition.

Axiom 2: *In an increasingly networked world, places that fall between the networks are very dangerous places—and there will be more ungoverned zones when there is only one network to join.*

The second axiom acknowledges that highly connected networks can be efficient, robust, and resilient to shocks. But in a highly connected world, the pieces that fall between the networks are increasingly shut off from the benefits of connectivity. These problems fester in the form of failed states, mutate like pathogenic bacteria, and, in some cases, reconnect in subterranean networks such as al Qaeda. The truly dangerous places are the points where the subterranean networks touch the mainstream of global politics and economics. What made Afghanistan so dangerous under the Taliban was not that it was a failed state. It wasn't. It was a partially failed and partially connected state that worked the interstices of globalization through the drug trade, counterfeiting, and terrorism.

Can any single superpower monitor all the seams and back alleys of globalization? Hardly. In fact, a lone hegemon is unlikely to look closely at these problems, because more pressing issues are happening elsewhere, in places where trade and technology are growing. By contrast, a world of several great powers is a more interest-rich environment in which nations must look in less obvious places to find new sources of advantage. In such a system, it's harder for troublemakers to spring up, because the cracks and seams of globalization are held together by stronger ties.

Axiom 3: *Without a real chance to find useful allies to counter a superpower, opponents will try to neutralize power, by going underground, going nuclear, or going "bad."*

Axiom 3 is a story about the preferred strategies of the weak. It's a basic insight of international relations that states try to balance power. They protect themselves by joining groups that can hold a hegemonic threat at bay. But what if there is no viable group to join? In today's unipolar world, every nation from Venezuela to North Korea is looking for a way to constrain American power. But in the unipolar world, it's harder for states to join together to do that. So they turn to other means. They play a different game. Hamas, Iran, Somalia, North Korea, and Venezuela are not going to become allies anytime soon. Each is better off finding other ways to make life more difficult for Washington. Going nuclear is one way. Counterfeiting U.S. currency is another. Raising uncertainty about oil supplies is perhaps the most obvious method of all.

Here's the important downside of unipolar globalization. In a world with multiple great powers, many of these threats would be less troublesome. The relatively weak states would have a choice among potential partners with which to ally, enhancing their influence. Without that more attractive choice, facilitating the dark side of globalization becomes the most effective means of constraining American power.

Sharing Globalization's Burden

The world is paying a heavy price for the instability created by the combination of globalization and unipolarity, and the United States is bearing most of the burden. Consider the case of nuclear proliferation. There's effectively a market out there for proliferation, with its own supply (states willing to share nuclear technology) and demand (states that badly want a nuclear weapon). The overlap of unipolarity with globalization ratchets up both the supply and demand, to the detriment of U.S. national security.

It has become fashionable, in the wake of the Iraq war, to comment on the limits of conventional military force. But much of this analysis is overblown. The United States may not be able to stabilize and rebuild Iraq. But that doesn't matter much from the perspective of a government that thinks the Pentagon has it in its sights. In Tehran, Pyongyang, and many other capitals, including Beijing, the bottom line is simple: The U.S. military could, with conventional force, end those regimes tomorrow if it chose to do so. No country in the world can dream of challenging U.S. conventional military power. But they can certainly hope to deter America from using it. And the best deterrent yet invented is the threat of nuclear retaliation. Before 1989, states that felt threatened by the United States could turn to the Soviet Union's nuclear umbrella for protection. Now, they turn to people like A.Q. Khan. Having your own nuclear weapon used to be a luxury. Today, it is fast becoming a necessity.

North Korea is the clearest example. Few countries had it worse during the Cold War. North Korea was surrounded by feuding, nuclear-armed communist neighbors, it was officially at war with its southern neighbor, and it stared continuously at tens of thousands of U.S. troops on its border. But, for 40 years, North Korea didn't seek nuclear weapons. It didn't need to, because it had the Soviet nuclear umbrella. Within five years of the Soviet collapse, however, Pyongyang was pushing ahead full steam on plutonium reprocessing facilities. North Korea's founder, Kim Il Sung, barely flinched when former

U.S. President Bill Clinton's administration readied war plans to strike his nuclear installations preemptively. That brinkmanship paid off. Today North Korea is likely a nuclear power, and Kim's son rules the country with an iron fist. America's conventional military strength means a lot less to a nuclear North Korea. Saddam Hussein's great strategic blunder was that he took too long to get to the same place.

How would things be different in a multipolar world? For starters, great powers could split the job of policing proliferation, and even collaborate on some particularly hard cases. It's often forgotten now that, during the Cold War, the only state with a tougher nonproliferation policy than the United States was the Soviet Union. Not a single country that had a formal alliance with Moscow ever became a nuclear power. The Eastern bloc was full of countries with advanced technological capabilities in every area except one—nuclear weapons. Moscow simply wouldn't permit it. But today we see the uneven and inadequate level of effort that non-superpowers devote to stopping proliferation. The Europeans dangle carrots at Iran, but they are unwilling to consider serious sticks. The Chinese refuse to admit that there is a problem. And the Russians are aiding Iran's nuclear ambitions. When push comes to shove, nonproliferation today is almost entirely America's burden.

The same is true for global public health. Globalization is turning the world into an enormous petri dish for the incubation of infectious disease. Humans cannot outsmart disease, because it just evolves too quickly. Bacteria can reproduce a new generation in less than 30 minutes, while it takes us decades to come up with a new generation of antibiotics. Solutions are only possible when and where we get the upper hand. Poor countries where humans live in close proximity to farm animals are the best place to breed extremely dangerous zoonotic disease. These are often the same countries, perhaps not entirely coincidentally, that feel threatened by American power. Establishing an early warning system for these diseases—exactly what we lacked in the case of SARS a few years ago and exactly what we lack for avian flu today—will require a significant level of intervention into the very places that don't want it. That will be true as long as international intervention means American interference.

If there were rival great powers with different cultural and ideological leanings, globalization's darkest problem of all— terrorism—would look different.

The most likely sources of the next ebola or HIV-like pandemic are the countries that simply won't let U.S. or other Western agencies in, including the World Health Organization. Yet the threat is too arcane and not immediate enough for the West to force the issue. What's needed is another great power to take over a piece of the work, a power that has more immediate interests in the countries where diseases incubate and one that is seen as less of a threat. As long as the United States remains the world's lone superpower, we're not likely to get any help.

Even after HIV, SARS, and several years of mounting hysteria about avian flu, the world is still not ready for a viral pandemic in Southeast Asia or sub-Saharan Africa. America can't change that alone.

If there were rival great powers with different cultural and ideological leanings, globalization's darkest problem of all— terrorism—would also likely look quite different. The pundits are partly right: Today's international terrorism owes something to globalization. Al Qaeda uses the Internet to transmit messages, it uses credit cards and modern banking to move money, and it uses cell phones and laptops to plot attacks. But it's not globalization that turned Osama bin Laden from a small-time Saudi dissident into the symbolic head of a radical global movement. What created Osama bin Laden was the predominance of American power.

A terrorist organization needs a story to attract resources and recruits. Oftentimes, mere frustration over political, economic, or religious conditions is not enough. Al Qaeda understands that, and, for that reason, it weaves a narrative of global jihad against a "modernization," "Westernization," and a "Judeo-Christian" threat. There is really just one country that both spearheads and represents that threat: the United States. And so the most efficient way for a terrorist to gain a reputation is to attack the United States. The logic is the same for all monopolies. A few years ago, every computer hacker in the world wanted to bring down Microsoft, just as every aspiring terrorist wants to create a spectacle of destruction akin to the September 11 attacks inside the United States.

Al Qaeda cells have gone after alternate targets such as Britain, Egypt, and Spain. But these are not the acts that increase recruitment and fundraising, or mobilize the energy of otherwise disparate groups around the world. Nothing enhances the profile of a terrorist like killing an American, something Abu Musab al-Zarqawi understood well in Iraq. Even if al Qaeda's deepest aspirations lie with the demise of the Saudi regime, the predominance of U.S. power and its role supporting the house of Saud makes America the only enemy really worth fighting. A multipolar world would surely confuse this kind of clear framing that pits Islamism against the West. What would be al Qaeda's message if the Chinese were equally involved in propping up authoritarian regimes in the Islamic, oil-rich Gulf states? Does the al Qaeda story work if half its enemy is neither Western nor Christian?

Restoring the Balance

The consensus today in the U.S. foreign-policy community is that more American power is always better. Across the board. For both the United States and the rest of the globe. The National Security Strategy documents of 2002 and 2006 enshrine this consensus in phrases such as "a balance of power that favors freedom." The strategy explicitly defines the "balance" as a continued imbalance, as the United States continues "dissuading potential competitors . . . from challenging the United States, its allies, and its partners."

In no way is U.S. power inherently a bad thing. Nor is it true that no good comes from unipolarity. But there are significant downsides to the imbalance of power. That view is hardly revolutionary. It has a long pedigree in U.S. foreign-policy thought. It was the perspective, for instance, that George Kennan brought to the table in the late 1940s when he talked about the desirability of a European superpower to restrain the United States. Although the issues today are different than they were in Kennan's time, it's still the case that too much power may, as Kennan believed, lead to overreach. It may lead to arrogance. It may lead to insensitivity to the concerns of others. Though Kennan may have been prescient to voice these concerns, he couldn't have predicted the degree to which American unipolarity would lead to such an unstable overlap with modern-day globalization.

America has experienced this dangerous burden for 15 years, but it still refuses to see it for what it really is. Antiglobalization sentiment is coming today from both the right and the left. But by blaming globalization for what ails the world, the U.S. foreign-policy community is missing a very big part of what is undermining one of the most hopeful trends in modern history—the reconnection of societies, economies, and minds that political borders have kept apart for far too long.

America cannot indefinitely stave off the rise of another superpower. But, in today's networked and interdependent world, such an event is not entirely a cause for mourning. A shift in the global balance of power would, in fact, help the United States manage some of the most costly and dangerous consequences of globalization. As the international playing field levels, the scope of these problems and the threat they pose to America will only decrease. When that happens, the United States will find globalization is a far easier burden to bear.

Steven Weber is professor of political science and director of the Institute of International Studies at the University of California, Berkeley. **Naazneen Barma, Matthew Kroenig,** and **Ely Ratner** are PhD candidates at U.C., Berkeley, and research fellows at its New Era Foreign Policy Center.

Are Failed States a Threat to America?

The Bush administration's nation-building efforts are a big mistake.

JUSTIN LOGAN AND CHRISTOPHER PREBLE

Throughout the 1990s, conservatives castigated the Clinton administration for conducting foreign policy like social work, taking on vague, ill-defined missions in remote locales from Haiti to Bosnia. Although the editors of *The Weekly Standard* enthusiastically supported the Clinton administration's interventions in the Balkans, most on the right were encouraged when George W. Bush and his senior foreign policy adviser, Condoleezza Rice, came out strongly against such missions during the 2000 presidential campaign. In 2000 Rice famously declared that "we don't need to have the 82nd Airborne escorting kids to kindergarten." Bush was equally blunt. During one of his debates with Al Gore, he said: "I don't think our troops ought to be used for what's called nation building. . . . I mean, we're going to have some kind of nation-building corps from America? Absolutely not."

We agree. That's why we're alarmed that the Bush administration has created a nation-building corps from America: the State Department's new Office of the Coordinator for Reconstruction and Stabilization, which was established by Congress in July 2004. The office's mandate is to "help stabilize and reconstruct societies in transition from conflict or civil strife, so they can reach a sustainable path toward peace, democracy, and a market economy." Meanwhile, a November 2005 Defense Department directive makes stability operations a "core U.S. military mission." Such operations would involve on-the-ground assistance, not unlike the provisional reconstruction teams in Iraq; Secretary of State Condoleezza Rice says the office is presently looking at action in Haiti, Liberia, and Sudan. Beyond that, the details are unclear.

Bush and Rice's change of heart regarding nation building is usually attributed to 9/11. But while the terrorist attacks on the World Trade Center and the Pentagon certainly underscored the dangers that nontraditional threats can pose, they did not transform every poorly governed nation into a pressing national security concern. Nor did 9/11 change the dismal track record of past nation-building efforts. This debate has obvious relevance in Iraq, where the absence of a functioning state following the U.S. invasion is the most widely accepted argument against withdrawing American forces. But it has much wider implications for America's post-Cold War, post-9/11 foreign policy, pitting nation builders who want to protect the United States by fixing failed states against skeptics who believe such a strategy is unnecessary, impractical, and dangerous.

Depending on how you count, the U.S. is currently involved in as many as 10 nation-building missions—arguably more. Most of these—from Djibouti to Liberia to Kosovo—are far removed from America's national security interests, just as they were in the '90s. Taking on such missions in conflicted environments is even more worrisome today because it would threaten to embroil Americans in an array of foreign conflicts for indefinite periods of time with vague or ambiguous public mandates and little likelihood of success at a time when we should be focused on defeating Al Qaeda and other Islamic terrorist groups that intend to attack the United States. This approach to security policy squanders American power, American money, and American lives. Unless events in a failed state are genuinely likely to dramatically affect the lives of Americans, we should have normal diplomatic relations with their governments, assess potential threats discretely, and otherwise leave them alone.

Getting in on the Coming Anarchy

The idea that state failure is inherently threatening to the United States has been circulating for some time. In an influential 1994 article, *The Atlantic Monthly*'s Robert Kaplan sounded the alarm about "the coming anarchy," urging Western strategists to start worrying about "what is occurring . . . throughout West Africa and much of the underdeveloped world: the withering away of central governments, the rise of tribal and regional domains, the unchecked spread of disease, and the growing pervasiveness of war." He warned that "the coming upheaval, in which foreign embassies are shut down, states collapse, and contact with the outside world takes place through dangerous, disease-ridden coastal trading posts, will loom large in the century we are entering." He argued that insecurity and instability in remote regions should be high on the list of post-Cold War foreign policy concerns because the damage and depredations of the Third World would not always be contained, and would inevitably—though he doesn't really explain how—touch the lives of those in America and Western Europe. Although humanitarianism was the most frequently heard justification for the Clinton administration's attempts at nation building, the president's defenders in and out of government also offered a Kaplanesque rationale that fixing failed states would make the U.S. safer.

Despite his initial skepticism toward Clinton-era nation building, President Bush changed course dramatically after September 11, 2001. The United States National Security Strategy, released in September 2002, made "expand[ing] the circle of development by opening societies and building the infrastructure of democracy" a central plank of America's response to the 9/11 attacks. Part of the administration's new security policy would be to "help build police forces, court systems, and legal codes, local and provincial government institutions, and electoral systems." The overarching goal was to "make the world not just safer but better."

According to the administration's October 2005 National Intelligence Strategy, "the lack of freedom in one state endangers the peace and freedom of others, and . . . failed states are a refuge and breeding ground of extremism." The strategy therefore asks our overworked intelligence services not just to gather information on America's enemies but to "bolster the growth of democracy and sustain peaceful democratic states." The premise is, as the former Cato foreign policy analyst Gary Dempsey put it, that "if only we could populate the planet with 'good' states, we could eradicate international conflict and terrorism."

Many foreign policy pundits agree with the Bush administration's goal of making the world safe through democracy. Lawrence J. Korb and Robert O. Boorstin of the Center for American Progress, for example, warn in a 2005 report that "weak and failing states pose as great a danger to the American people and international stability as do potential conflicts among the great powers." A 2003 report from the Center for Strategic and International Studies agrees that "as a superpower with a global presence and global interests, the United States does have a stake in remedying failed states." In the course of commenting on a report from the Center for Global Development, Francis Fukuyama, a professor at the Johns Hopkins School of Advanced International Studies, argued that "it should be abundantly clear that state weakness and failure [are] the single most critical threat to U.S. national security."

Even foreign policy specialists known for their hard-nosed realism have succumbed to the idea that nation building is a matter of self-defense. A 2005 Council on Foreign Relations task force co-chaired by Brent Scowcroft, national security adviser in the first Bush administration and a critic of the current war in Iraq, produced a report that insists "action to stabilize and rebuild states marked by conflict is not 'foreign policy as social work,' a favorite quip of the 1990s. It is equally a humanitarian concern and a national security priority." The report says stability operations should be "a strategic priority for the armed forces" and the national security adviser should produce an "overarching policy associated with stabilization and reconstruction activities."

Those arguments suffer not so much from inaccuracy as from analytical sloppiness. It would be absurd to claim that the ongoing state failure in Haiti poses a national security threat of the same order as would state failure in Indonesia, with its population of 240 million, or in nuclear-armed Pakistan. In fact, the overwhelming majority of failed states have posed no security threat to the United States. Take, for example, the list of countries identified as failed or failing by *Foreign Policy* magazine and the Fund for Peace in 2005. Using 12 different indicators of state failure, the researchers derived state failure scores, and then listed 60 countries whose cumulative scores marked them as "critical," "in danger" or "borderline," ranked in order. If state failure is itself threatening, then we should get very concerned about the Democratic Republic of the Congo, Sierra Leone, Chad, Bangladesh, and on and on.

In short, state failure ranks rather low as an accurate metric for measuring threats. Likewise, while the lists of "failed states" and "security threats" will no doubt overlap, correlation does not equal causation. The obvious nonthreats that appear on all lists of failed states undermine the claim that there is something particular about failed states that is necessarily threatening.

The dangers that can arise from failed states are not the product of state failure itself. They are the result of other factors, such as the presence of terrorist cells or other malign actors. Afghanistan in the late 1990s met anyone's definition of a failed state, and the chaos in Afghanistan clearly contributed to Osama bin Laden's decision to relocate his operations there from Sudan in 1996. But the security threat to America arose from cooperation between Al Qaeda and the Taliban government, which tolerated the organization's training camps. Afghanistan under the Taliban was both a failed state and a threat, but in that respect it was a rarity. More common are failed states, from the Ivory Coast to Burma, that pose no threat to us at all.

It's true that Al Qaeda and other terrorist organizations can operate in failed states. But they also can (and do) operate in Germany, Canada, and other countries that are not failed states by any stretch of the imagination. Rather than making categorical statements about failed states, we should assess the extent to which any given state or nonstate actors within it intend and have the means to attack America. Afghanistan is a stark reminder that we must not overlook failed states, but it does not justify making them our top security concern.

That Fixer-Upper Isn't as Cheap as It Looks

If state failure does not in itself pose a threat to U.S. security, an ambitious program of nation building would, in turn, be a cure worse than the disease. One particularly troubling prospect is the erosion of internationally recognized sovereignty. As Winston Churchill said of democracy, sovereignty may be the worst system around, except for all the others. A system of sovereignty grants a kernel of legitimacy to regimes that rule barbarically; it values as equals countries that clearly are not; and it frequently enforces borders that were capriciously drawn by imperial powers. But it's far from clear that any available alternative is better.

Yet in his previous life as an academic, Stephen Krasner, the director of policy planning at the U.S. State Department, flatly declared that the "rules of conventional sovereignty no longer work." A stroll through the work of scholars who support nation building reveals such alternative concepts as "shared sovereignty," "trusteeships," even "postmodern imperialism." (The latter is supposed to mean an attempt to manipulate domestic politics in foreign countries without all that old-fashioned imperial messiness.)

If the United States proceeds on a course of nation building, based largely on the premise that sovereignty should be de-emphasized, where will that logic stop? Who gets to decide which states retain their sovereignty and which states forfeit it? Will other powers use our own rhetoric against us to justify expansionist foreign policies? It's not hard to envision potential flashpoints in eastern Europe and East Asia.

An American exceptionalist might reply that the United States gets to decide, because we're different. But such an argument is unlikely to prevent other countries from using our own logic against us. If we tug at the thread of sovereignty, the whole sweater may quickly unravel.

An aggressive nation-building strategy would also detract from the struggle against terrorism, by diverting attention and resources, puncturing the mystique of American power, and provoking anger through promiscuous foreign intervention. A prerequisite for nation building is establishing security in the target country, which requires the presence of foreign troops, something that often inspires terrorism. In a survey of suicide terrorism between 1980 and 2003, University of Chicago political scientist Robert A. Pape concluded that almost all suicide attacks "have in common . . . a specific secular and strategic goal: to compel modern democracies to withdraw military forces from territory that the terrorists consider to be their homeland."

Such risks might be justified if the chances of success were high. But history suggests they're not. In the most thorough survey of American nation-building missions, the RAND Corporation in 2003 evaluated seven cases: Japan and West Germany after World War II, Somalia in 1992–94, Haiti in 1994–96, Bosnia from 1995 to the present, Kosovo from 1999 to the present, and Afghanistan from 2001 to the present. Assessing the cases individually, the authors count Japan and West Germany as successes but all the others as failures to various degrees. They then try to determine what made the Japanese and West German operations succeed when all the nation-building efforts since have failed.

Their answer is complex and not entirely satisfying. To the extent that any clear conclusion can be drawn from this research, the report says, it is that "nation building . . . is a time- and resource-consuming effort." Indeed, "among controllable factors, the most important determinant is the level of effort— measured in time, manpower, and money."

In its 2004 Summer Study on Transition to and from Hostilities, the Defense Science Board, a panel that advises the Defense Department on strategy, reached a similar conclusion. Although "postconflict success often depends on significant political changes," it said, the "barriers to transformation of[an]

opponent's society [are] immense." And in the absence of a decisive outcome between warring parties (such as happened in World War II), there is always a danger that violence will continue.

Not surprisingly, successful nation building is highly contingent on security within the target country. The non-war-fighting roles a nation-building military has to play would be tremendously taxing for both the armed services and the U.S. treasury.

By the Defense Science Board's calculations, achieving "ambitious goals" in a failed state requires 20 foreign soldiers per 1,000 inhabitants. Applying this ratio to a few top-ranked failed states yields sobering results. Nation building in the Ivory Coast would require 345,000 foreign troops. Sudan would take 800,000. Iraq, where the U.S. and its allies currently have 153,000 troops, would need 520,000. And if history is any guide, effective execution would require deployments of 10 years or longer.

All this means that nation-building missions are extremely expensive, regardless of whether they succeed or fail. Zalmay Khalilzad, former U.S. ambassador to Afghanistan and current ambassador to Iraq, believes that in the case of Afghanistan, "it will take annual assistance [of $4.5 billion] or higher for five to seven years to achieve our goals." Operation Uphold Democracy in Haiti, which restored a government and installed 8,000 peacekeepers but left that country in its perpetual state of chaos, cost more than $2 billion. Operations Provide Relief and Restore Hope in Somalia, which provided tons of food as humanitarian relief (which were in turn looted by warlords) and eventually got dozens of Americans killed and injured, leading to a hasty and disastrous American retreat, ended up costing $2.2 billion. As of 2002 the United States had spent more than $23 billion intervening in the Balkans since the early '90s. In Iraq, we have already crested the $300 billion mark, having decided that the vagaries of Iraqi sectarian politics should decide our future mission in that country.

Even Francis Fukuyama, a staunch advocate of nation building, admits such efforts have "an extremely troubled record of success." As Fukuyama wrote in his 2005 book *State Building: Governance and World Order in the 21st Century,* "It is not simply that nation building hasn't worked; in cases like sub-Saharan Africa, many of these efforts have actually eroded institutional capacity over time." Put simply, there is no "model" for nation building. The few broad lessons we can draw indicate that success depends on a relentless determination to impose a nation's will, manifested in many years of occupation and billions of dollars in spending.

In this light, the position of the more extreme neo-imperialists is more realistic than that of nation builders who think we can fix failed states on the cheap. The Harvard historian Niall Ferguson argues that a proper approach to Iraq would put up to 1 million foreign troops on the ground there for up to 70 years. If resources were unlimited, or if the American people were prepared to shoulder such a burden, that might be a realistic suggestion. But the notion that such enterprises can be carried out quickly and inexpensively is badly mistaken.

A Really Distant Mirror

People who believe that failed states pose a threat to U.S. security and that nation building is the answer see the world as both simpler and more threatening than it is. Failed states generally do not represent security threats. At the same time, nation building in failed states is very difficult and usually unsuccessful.

There is certainly a point at which Robert Kaplan's "coming anarchy," if it were to materialize, would threaten American interests. Here's how Ferguson, in *Foreign Policy* magazine, describes a world in which America steps back from its role as a global policeman: "Waning empires. Religious revivals. Incipient anarchy. A coming retreat into fortified cities. These are the Dark Age experiences that a world without a hyperpower might quickly find itself reliving."

It's telling that to find a historical precedent on which to base his argument, Ferguson has to reach back to the ninth century. His prediction of a "Dark Age" hinges on a belief that America will collapse (because of excessive consumption, an inadequate army, and an imperial "attention deficit"), the European Union will collapse (because of an inflexible welfare state and shifting demographics), and China will collapse (because of a currency or banking crisis). There is little reason to believe that if America refuses to administer foreign countries, the world will go down this path. The fact that advocates of fixing failed states have to rely on such outlandish scenarios to build their case tells us a good deal about the merit of their arguments.

JUSTIN LOGAN (jlogan@cato.org) is a foreign policy analyst at the Cato Institute. **CHRISTOPHER PREBLE** (cpreble@cato.org) is director of foreign policy studies at the Cato Institute.

Bin Laden's Soft Support

How the next president can win over the world's most alienated Muslims.

KENNETH BALLEN

On a typically humid spring night in Jakarta in 2005, an Indonesian colleague and I were driven by some Islamist activists through the city's dense back alleyways to the dilapidated offices of a leading radical student publication. We were led up a narrow flight of stairs and into a small room, crammed with young university students. Standing at the center of the room was a thin, bearded man in a skull cap and flowing white robes. He was an imam, a mentor to the students and a popular leader of the PKS, the leading Islamist party in Indonesia—the world's largest Muslim nation.

After a few polite introductory remarks, the imam launched into a litany of complaints all too familiar to my colleague and me, who conduct public opinion research in Muslim countries. America, said the imam, is at war with Islam. America is killing Muslims by the millions. (This number was apparently calculated by holding the United States responsible for every Muslim conflict casualty over the past several decades.) Islamic fighters are striking back with violence, the only language America understands. This was followed by the standard harangue against Jews, the secret but controlling force behind American perfidy. His young followers reacted with fervent delight.

The imam's work done, he departed for the evening. But we decided to stay. There's an Indonesian custom called *jagongan* which holds that the most important conversations occur by talking through the night, and on that evening, we discovered the potency of *jagongan* firsthand.

Initially, the students took up their leader's refrain. Osama bin Laden, they told us, was a hero because he gave up his worldly possessions to defend Muslim freedom and stand up to America. But he was not responsible, they insisted, for the attacks of 9/11, which were clearly the work of the CIA and the Israeli intelligence service—how else to explain the fact that there were no Jews in the World Trade Center when it was destroyed?

Our discussions went on for hours, and though they were sometimes heated, there was an underlying friendliness to the students' manner that contrasted with their extreme rhetoric.

As the night wore on, the tone began to shift. The students were surprised to learn that I knew Jews who had been killed in the Twin Towers and their relatives who still struggle with their loss. My Indonesian colleague talked about Indonesian and other Muslims he knew in the United States and their daily lives and views. A tentative human bond developed between us and the students. Not long before dawn, as morning prayers approached, their insistent questioning took an unexpected turn: how could they obtain visas to study in the United States?

After that, whenever we had the chance to speak with young radicals in Indonesia, out of the hearing of their leaders and late at night, we'd always ask: How many of you want to study in America? Invariably, almost everyone said yes, and those who still disdained the Great Satan were eager to study in Canada, Australia, or France instead.

We were intrigued. What if supporters of al-Qaeda in countries like Pakistan or Saudi Arabia felt the same way as young Indonesians? Was their support for al-Qaeda—and their hatred of America—really as intense as it had first appeared?

Terror Free Tomorrow, our nonprofit polling organization, decided to pursue this question further. Over the past several years, we have conducted some thirty nationwide public opinion surveys in Indonesia, Bangladesh, India, Nigeria, Iran, Syria, Turkey, Pakistan, Saudi Arabia and elsewhere in the Muslim world. In the process, we've assembled the first comprehensive picture of how people who are sympathetic to al-Qaeda and Osama bin Laden feel about America—and what can be done to change their resentment.

Our findings will probably surprise you. Like most analysts, we had assumed that radical views in the Muslim world were the outgrowth of a deeply held ideology, unshakeable without profound shifts in American foreign policy. We were wrong. American actions may inflame Muslim opinion. But the solutions that can cool that hostility aren't always the ones you'd expect.

Since September 11, many Americans have been understandably alarmed by polls showing that a sizable minority of the world's Muslims express sympathy for al-Qaeda, Osama bin Laden, or the Taliban. Our own polls confirm this general pattern. In recent surveys, 15 percent of Saudis said they support bin Laden. Twenty four percent of Pakistanis said the same.

The first key fact to understand about such numbers is that people who say they support al-Qaeda or bin Laden aren't in any obvious or measurable way very distinguishable from their compatriots. Our surveys showed that those who express support for bin Laden and al-Qaeda mirror their countrymen in almost every respect, from gender to level of educational achievement. Al-Qaeda and bin Laden supporters are no more fervently Islamic in their practices or beliefs than other Muslims. Nor are they poorer or more disadvantaged— if anything, al-Qaeda and bin Laden sympathizers tend to earn more and to be better off than their fellow citizens.

More important, those who express sympathy for bin Laden turn out to have views that are remarkably similar to those who *don't* support bin Laden. Like their compatriots, people who favor al-Qaeda and bin Laden are principally motivated by their perception of Western hostility to Islam. In all our surveys, and those of others, the view of American antagonism is an almost universally held belief among Muslims everywhere. The U.S.-led war on terror, the wars in Iraq and Afghanistan, even our post-9/11 restrictions on visas (stories of upstanding Muslims denied entry to the United States for seemingly arbitrary reasons are a staple of the Muslim press) are seen as assaults on Islam in general and on Muslims in particular. At its core, Muslims feel that the United States does not respect their views, values, identity and the right to determine their own affairs.

None of this is necessarily surprising. More unexpected is this finding: both bin Laden supporters and non-bin Laden supporters hold remarkably similar political goals for their countries—goals that are often anathema to the ideology espoused by al-Qaeda. Three recent nationwide public opinion surveys of Pakistan and Saudi Arabia conducted by Terror Free Tomorrow at the end of 2007 and the beginning of 2008 illustrate our findings best.

Like other Pakistanis, bin Laden Supporters consider an independent judiciary, free elections and economic improvement the most important goals for their government.

Let's start with Pakistan, the second largest—and the only nuclear-armed—Muslim nation, now home base to bin Laden, al-Qaeda and the Taliban. In our latest survey this January, almost a quarter of the respondents said that they had a favorable opinion of bin Laden. But upon closer examination, this cohort was no more likely to have radical views than those Pakistanis who are not sympathetic to extremist groups. Like the rest of Pakistanis, bin Laden and al-Qaeda supporters consider an independent judiciary, free press, free elections and an improving economy the most important goals for their government. In fact, more than eight in ten bin Laden and al-Qaeda supporters chose these goals as their highest priority—significantly greater than the percentage that selected implementing strict Islamic Sharia law as their highest priority.

We found similar opinions in Saudi Arabia—home country of bin Laden and fifteen of the nineteen September 11th terrorists. In December 2007, our nationwide survey revealed that Saudis with a favorable opinion of bin Laden and al-Qaeda don't generally have implacable anti-American attitudes, or even support terrorist attacks. For the 15 percent of the Saudi population with a positive opinion of bin Laden, addressing the problem of terrorism is the most important priority they have for the Saudi government, chosen by more than 90 percent—about the same percentage as those who do not have a favorable view of bin Laden or al-Qaeda.

Why would so many Saudis and Pakistanis express sympathy for terrorist organizations and yet also favor democratic reforms and crackdowns on terrorist violence? One possibility is that these bin Laden supporters are not telling the truth to pollsters. Recent events in Pakistan, however, suggest that's not the case.

Before Pakistan held elections on February 18, 2008, we conducted a poll asking voters whether they would vote for al-Qaeda if it appeared on the ballot as a political party. Only 1 percent of Pakistanis said yes—a far smaller percentage than the 18 percent of Pakistanis who told us that they sympathize with al-Qaeda. The Taliban would have drawn just 3 percent of the vote. As it turned out, our survey almost exactly mirrored the actual election results. In areas near or in the home base of the Taliban and al-Qaeda, Islamist parties sympathetic to these groups suffered stinging defeats. In the North West Frontier Province, the Islamist parties lost fifty- seven of their sixty-eight seats in the provincial assembly. Evidently, professed support for al-Qaeda or the Taliban doesn't mean that Pakistanis actually want these groups to *rule* them.

So what makes some Pakistanis say they support al-Qaeda when they don't in the voting booth? The answer seems to be that they, like nearly all Pakistanis, are angry. They're angry at President Pervez Musharraf for his heavy-handed authoritarian rule, and angry at the United States for a host of real and perceived sins, including (until very recently) the Bush administration's strong backing of the Musharraf regime. Declaring solidarity with al-Qaeda or the Taliban is a way for Pakistanis to express this anger. If there is a difference between those who sympathize with bin Laden and those who do not, it is that bin Laden supporters feel their resentment more intensely.

Our polls show that the anger Muslims around the world feel towards the United States is not primarily directed at our people or values—even those who say they support bin Laden don't, for the most part, "hate us for our freedoms," as President Bush has claimed. Rather, what drives Islamic public opinion is a pervasive perception that the United States and the West are hostile towards Islam. This perception, right or wrong, is fed by a variety of American actions, from the wars in Iraq and Afghanistan to the overarching global war on terror. These actions are seen as profoundly disrespectful and humiliating because they amount to America forcing its will on the Muslim world.

A good illustration comes from our most recent survey of Saudi Arabia. It showed that among the highest priorities for Saudis are free elections and a free press. Yet it also showed that the least popular American policy is the U.S. push to spread democracy in the Middle East. The point is that Saudis want to determine their own affairs and not have the United States impose its values, even when they share those values.

Significantly, however, our polling indicates that there are steps that the United States can undertake that could dramatically reverse anti-American attitudes born of this sense of disrespect—if we ask first, rather than thinking we know what's best. Indeed, these steps are relatively easier to take than more fundamental changes, such as an immediate withdrawal from Iraq or Afghanistan.

For instance, six out of every ten Pakistanis who have a favorable view toward bin Laden and al-Qaeda said their opinion of America would significantly improve if the United States increased educational, medical and humanitarian aid to Pakistan, as well as the number of visas available to Pakistanis to work or study in the United States. In fact, *more* bin Laden and al-Qaeda supporters said their opinion of the United States would improve with such American policies than did non-bin Laden supporters. Not everyone would change their mind: One in ten bin Laden and al-Qaeda supporters said that their opinion of the United States would not change no matter what America does. This is al-Qaeda's real, far smaller core of fervent and intractable support.

The same trend holds in Saudi Arabia, which, of course, borders Iraq. While the leading step that would improve opinion of the United States would be an immediate withdrawal of American forces from Iraq, this was closely followed by a desire for the United States to increase visas and free trade. Like their fellow citizens, 88 percent of Saudis who have a favorable opinion of bin Laden cited U.S. withdrawal from Iraq as a policy change that would significantly elevate their view of the United States. Three-quarters cited increased visas to and free trade with the United States. And more than half of both supporters and non-supporters of bin Laden said that these actions would improve their opinion of the United States a great deal.

The prospect of the United States brokering a comprehensive peace between Israelis and Palestinians is distant, but if it became a reality, our surveys suggest that this would significantly change perceptions of America in the Muslim world, especially among Palestinians and Syrians. But right now in Saudi Arabia, less than a quarter of Saudis believe that a successful peace process would improve their opinion of the United States a great deal. By contrast, twice as many Saudis said that increased trade and visas would improve their disposition towards the United States a great deal. And Muslims who live further away from the Middle East place even less importance on the peace process. When Indonesians and Bangladeshis, for example, were given a menu of choices for future American policies, including increased educational scholarships, direct medical assistance, free trade, and stronger American support for resolving the Palestinian-Israeli conflict, the latter finished last or next to last.

This last finding shouldn't be surprising. While people everywhere may care strongly about the suffering of their coreligionists in foreign lands, they are naturally more focused on the problems they face at home. Consequently, it is often easier to win them over with actions that affect their lives and those of their countrymen directly. If the United States demonstrates that it respects people by helping to make tangible improvements in their daily lives, even the anti-American attitudes of those who have a positive opinion of al-Qaeda are likely to change dramatically as well.

As it happens, we have proof of just how effective such changes can be. After a massive tsunami struck Indonesia on December 26, 2004, the United States led an extraordinary international relief effort for the victims. Of course, America dispenses aid to many countries, but the money is normally funneled through governments, and ordinary citizens rarely see or experience the results. The Indonesian relief effort, by contrast, consisted of on-the-ground, people-to-people assistance, and was broadcast non-stop on Indonesian television. The assistance not only saved lives but demonstrated to Indonesians that America sincerely cared about their well-being.

Afterwards, public opinion among Indonesians dramatically swung in favor of the United States. This gain in America's reputation was accompanied by a corresponding decline in backing for the perceived symbols of the most radical anti-American views—bin Laden, al-Qaeda and their local Islamist allies.

To be sure, American aid wasn't the sole reason that the public turned against the radicals. The deaths caused by terrorist attacks and increased democratic participation inside Indonesia also contributed. But the U.S. humanitarian mission was one of the most important factors. Admiral Mike Mullen, Chairman of the Joint Chiefs of Staff, has said that this shift in Indonesian public opinion towards America is "one of the defining moments of this new century."

The Indonesian example is not the only one. After a devastating earthquake hit Pakistan in 2005, America stepped in with a similarly intensive relief effort. Afterwards, our surveys found that 79 percent of self-identified bin Laden supporters thought well of the United States because of the humanitarian mission. Among all Pakistanis, the U.S. government was more popular than al-Qaeda, the Taliban, or any Pakistani Islamist radical group—even among Pakistanis who thought favorably of these groups.

Of course, this doesn't mean that the United States can simply increase direct aid and visas without changing its overarching policies in the Muslim world. Again, America's relief efforts in Indonesia and Pakistan are instructive. Indonesia is ruled by a democratic government. And the United States has supported that government, in part with military training and assistance in its fight against domestic terror groups, rather than direct U.S. military action against those groups. Consequently, goodwill towards America among Indonesians has, for the most part, been sustained. Nearly three years after the tsunami, almost 60 percent of Indonesians said that American assistance had made them favorable towards the United States.

In Pakistan, on the other hand, America has unabashedly supported the unpopular and repressive rule of General Musharraf, and has also carried out military strikes inside Pakistan. Combined with the specter of the war on terror, these policies have dissolved the warm feelings generated by America's earthquake relief. In surveys we conducted in 2006, 2007 and 2008, we confirmed that the positive feelings that stemmed from the relief effort have almost entirely dissipated. Humanitarian policies provide an opening. Yet, absent other political and economic factors, they are unlikely to result in sustained, long-term improvements in public opinion.

Our polls provide three useful lessons for the next president. The first is this: don't be too alarmed by the apparent high level of support for bin Laden in the Muslim world. Such support is soft, and can be made softer still with the right policies.

To repair the dismal relationship between the U.S. and the Muslim world, a new president doesn't need to pull out of Iraq right away or solve the Israel-Palestine conflict overnight.

The second lesson is that in order to repair the dismal impression that many Muslims have of the United States, a new president doesn't need to pull all troops out of Iraq right away, or solve the Israel-Palestine conflict overnight. More modest—if still politically tricky—actions can have an immediate and dramatic impact. It is essential for the United States to adopt policies that reveal a different side of American power—one that demonstrates respect and compassion by

How We Can Help al-Qaeda Ruin Its Own Reputation

Terror Free Tomorrow's surveys reveal some good news: In many Muslim countries, public support for extremism is in decline. In Pakistan, for instance, popular regard for bin Laden and al-Qaeda has decreased by half in just six months. In the North West Frontier Province, near the Afghan border where al-Qaeda is based, that support has plunged from 70 percent last summer to single digits this year.

These changing attitudes are largely the result not of America's actions, but al-Qaeda's: citizens in Pakistan and other countries are becoming increasingly disgusted with the group's barbaric violence. This shift in mood is significant because history shows that success against terrorism almost always occurs when local residents turn on the terrorists themselves. Even more important, when al-Qaeda and the Taliban become unpopular, a democratically elected Pakistani government can aggressively isolate and pursue them without taking as many domestic political risks.

But the new Pakistani government's hand would be strengthened even further if the staunchly anti-American views of its citizens could be diminished. Don't forget, it is bin Laden's potency as an anti-American icon that drives much of his support. And as we saw in Indonesia, when opinion towards America improves, support for bin Laden and al-Qaeda declines as well. Put these two dynamics (declining sympathy for terrorists and rising regard for America) together, and you have a powerful tool against terrorists.

improving the lives of individual Muslims. Such policies include increasing student and work visas, direct humanitarian aid, and trade agreements. Since much of the Muslim anger towards the United States and the West is fueled by the widespread perception of a lack of respect, all of these people-based policies send a powerful, tangible message that we care about Muslims and regard them as equals.

The third lesson is that these practical, direct-to-the-public policy initiatives should be seen as an opening to a new American stance that, in both word and deed, manifests respectful relations between people. These initiatives need to be followed up with meaningful action on the major geostrategic issues that fuel Muslim resentment. We need to create more effective counterterrorism strategies, break the logjam on peace with Israel, and resolve the wars in Iraq and Afghanistan. Otherwise, whatever goodwill we create is likely to fade.

That goodwill is an invaluable asset to our national security. Negative public opinion towards the United States acts as a real political constraint on the leaders of Muslim countries, limiting their ability to work with America and its allies on everything from counterterrorism operations to negotiating peace agreements. When public opinion towards

America has improved and support for terror organizations has declined, governments—even with the overt help of the United States, as in Indonesia and the Philippines—have been able to isolate and target the terrorists.

In the wake of 9/11, America fell into a vicious cycle in which our major security policies, aimed at combating terrorism, actually made the threat of terrorism worse by inflaming popular sympathy for extremism. Turning that opinion around could be the first step towards finally getting our counterterrorism strategy right. And while first steps are often said to be the hardest, in this case, the opposite is true. Indeed, as we learned that night in Jakarta, the most important first step is the easiest. It is to listen.

KENNETH BALLEN is the president of Terror Free Tomorrow: The Center for Public Opinion, a nonpartisan, nonprofit organization which has conducted international polling in Pakistan, Iran, Syria, Indonesia, Saudi Arabia, India, Bangladesh, Nigeria, Turkey and elsewhere. The results of the surveys are at www.terrorfreetomorrow.org.

From *Washington Monthly,* May/June/July 2008, pp. 19–23. Copyright © 2008 by Washington Monthly. Reprinted by permission.

Test-Your-Knowledge Form

We encourage you to photocopy and use this page as a tool to assess how the articles in *Annual Editions* expand on the information in your textbook. By reflecting on the articles you will gain enhanced text information. You can also access this useful form on a product's book support Web site at *http://www.mhcls.com*.

NAME:

DATE:

TITLE AND NUMBER OF ARTICLE:

BRIEFLY STATE THE MAIN IDEA OF THIS ARTICLE:

LIST THREE IMPORTANT FACTS THAT THE AUTHOR USES TO SUPPORT THE MAIN IDEA:

WHAT INFORMATION OR IDEAS DISCUSSED IN THIS ARTICLE ARE ALSO DISCUSSED IN YOUR TEXTBOOK OR OTHER READINGS THAT YOU HAVE DONE? LIST THE TEXTBOOK CHAPTERS AND PAGE NUMBERS:

LIST ANY EXAMPLES OF BIAS OR FAULTY REASONING THAT YOU FOUND IN THE ARTICLE:

LIST ANY NEW TERMS/CONCEPTS THAT WERE DISCUSSED IN THE ARTICLE, AND WRITE A SHORT DEFINITION:

We Want Your Advice

ANNUAL EDITIONS revisions depend on two major opinion sources: one is our Advisory Board, listed in the front of this volume, which works with us in scanning the thousands of articles published in the public press each year; the other is you—the person actually using the book. Please help us and the users of the next edition by completing the prepaid article rating form on this page and returning it to us. Thank you for your help!

ANNUAL EDITIONS: American Government 09/10

ARTICLE RATING FORM

Here is an opportunity for you to have direct input into the next revision of this volume.
We would like you to rate each of the articles listed below, using the following scale:

1. **Excellent: should definitely be retained**
2. **Above average: should probably be retained**
3. **Below average: should probably be deleted**
4. **Poor: should definitely be deleted**

Your ratings will play a vital part in the next revision.
Please mail this prepaid form to us as soon as possible.
Thanks for your help!

RATING	ARTICLE	RATING	ARTICLE
	1. The Declaration of Independence		26. Court Approval
	2. The History of The Constitution of the United States		27. The Power Broker
	3. The Size and Variety of the Union as a Check on Faction: Federalist No. 10		28. Marking Time: Why Government Is Too Slow
			29. Worse than You Think
	4. Checks and Balances: Federalist No. 51		30. The Weakness of Our Political Parties
	5. America the Untethered		31. America the Liberal
	6. How Big Government Got Its Groove Back		32. America Observed
	7. The Changing Face of Poverty in America: Why Are So Many Women, Children, Racial and Cultural Minorities Still Poor?		33. Who Should Redistrict?
			34. Vote or Else
			35. The Presidential Nominating Process: The Beginnings of a New Era
	8. The Climate for Change		36. Shakedown on K Street
	9. Beyond Hillary: Strength in Numbers		37. Born Fighting
	10. It Is Time to Repair the Constitution's Flaws		38. Why They Lobby
	11. If Washington Blows Up		39. Starting Over
	12. Pursuit of Habeas		40. Sharp Pencils
	13. Is Judicial Review Obsolete?		41. Obama Buoyed by Coalition of the Ascendant
	14. Two Takes: Pulpit Politics Is Free Speech/ Campaigns Can Split Churches		42. The '08 Campaign: Sea Change for Politics as We Know It
	15. What Bush Got Right		43. Triumph of Temperament, Not Policy
	16. Small Ball after All?		44. The Other Winner
	17. A Liberal Shock Doctrine		45. Clicking and Choosing
	18. Living History		46. BHO: QED
	19. The Two Obamas		47. The Tax-Cut Con
	20. Veto This!		48. The Realities of Immigration
	21. When Congress Stops Wars: Partisan Politics and Presidential Power		49. The Health of Nations
			50. The *Real* Infrastructure Crisis
	22. The Case for Congress		51. Speculators, Politicians, and Financial Disasters
	23. This Is What a Speaker Looks Like		52. How Globalization Went Bad
	24. Life on Capitol Dunghill		53. Are Failed States a Threat to America?
	25. Remote Control		54. Bin Laden's Soft Support

||||

BUSINESS REPLY MAIL
FIRST CLASS MAIL PERMIT NO. 551 DUBUQUE IA

POSTAGE WILL BE PAID BY ADDRESSEE

McGraw-Hill Contemporary Learning Series
501 BELL STREET
DUBUQUE, IA 52001

ABOUT YOU

Name   Date
_____

Are you a teacher? ❏ A student? ❏
Your school's name
_____

Department
_____

Address   City   State   Zip
_____

School telephone #
_____

YOUR COMMENTS ARE IMPORTANT TO US!

Please fill in the following information:
For which course did you use this book?
_____

Did you use a text with this ANNUAL EDITION? ❏ yes ❏ no
What was the title of the text?
_____

What are your general reactions to the Annual Editions concept?
_____

Have you read any pertinent articles recently that you think should be included in the next edition? Explain.
_____

Are there any articles that you feel should be replaced in the next edition? Why?
_____

Are there any World Wide Web sites that you feel should be included in the next edition? Please annotate.
_____

May we contact you for editorial input? ❏ yes ❏ no
May we quote your comments? ❏ yes ❏ no